High-Performance Computing Series

Volume 1

Series Editor

Satoshi Matsuoka, RIKEN Center for Computational Science,
Kobe, Hyogo, Japan

The series publishes authored monographs, textbooks, and edited state-of-the-art collections covering the whole spectrum of technologies for supercomputers and high-performance computing, and computational science and engineering enabled by high-performance computing (HPC).

Areas of interest include, but are not limited to, relevant topics on HPC:

- Advanced algorithms for HPC
- Large-scale applications involving massive-scale HPC
- Innovative HPC processor and machine architectures
- High-performance/low-latency system interconnects
- HPC in the Cloud
- Data science/Big Data/visualization driven by HPC
- Convergence of machine learning/artificial intelligence with HPC
- Performance modeling, measurement, and tools for HPC
- Programing languages, compilers, and runtime systems for HPC
- Operating system and other system software for HPC
- HPC systems operations and management

More information about this series at http://www.springer.com/series/16381

Balazs Gerofi · Yutaka Ishikawa ·
Rolf Riesen · Robert W. Wisniewski
Editors

Operating Systems for Supercomputers and High Performance Computing

 Springer

Editors
Balazs Gerofi
RIKEN Center for Computational Science
Kobe, Japan

Yutaka Ishikawa
RIKEN Center for Computational Science
Kobe, Japan

Rolf Riesen
Intel Corporation
Hillsboro, OR, USA

Robert W. Wisniewski
Intel Corporation
New York, NY, USA

ISSN 2662-3420   ISSN 2662-3439 (electronic)
High-Performance Computing Series
ISBN 978-981-13-6626-0   ISBN 978-981-13-6624-6   (eBook)
https://doi.org/10.1007/978-981-13-6624-6

Library of Congress Control Number: 2019931539

Cover illustration: The picture is a part of Oakforest-PACS operated by University of Tsukuba and University of Tokyo

This Springer imprint is published by the registered company Springer Nature Singapore Pte Ltd.
The registered company address is: 152 Beach Road, #21-01/04 Gateway East, Singapore 189721, Singapore

*To my daughter, Lea, you'll always be
precious to me; may your dreams be realized.*
Robert Wisniewski

*I am most grateful for the three women who
helped me grow most as a person: Anni,
Anika, and Lee Ann.*
Rolf Riesen

*To my family, Masami, Ryo, and Yuko, for
understanding of my work.*
Yutaka Ishikawa

*To my parents, Lajos and Andrea, and my
wife, Mio, for all your love and support.*
Balazs Gerofi

Foreword

Few works are as timely and critical to the advancement of high-performance computing than is this new up-to-date treatise on leading-edge directions of operating systems. It is a firsthand product of many of the leaders in this rapidly evolving field and possibly the most comprehensive. While a mental image of a supercomputer may be that of a large room behind floor-to-ceiling glass with many rows of even more racks of computing hardware, it is the operating system and its user interface that projects the true identity and controlling paradigm of a high-performance computing system.

In essence, from the standpoint of programmers, users, administrators, and even system developers the operating system is the supercomputer. But as the physical platforms have evolved in scalability, heterogeneity, memory hierarchy, and application domain, so have the challenges and stress points of the intervening software stack presented and supported by the operating system.

The computer operating system extends back to the decade of the 1960s. Throughout this period, it has served the principal requirements of job control, memory management and protection, input/output drivers and queues, and real-time user interface. Yet while these needs have largely been sustained, their specific attributes and forms of implementation have been forced toward variations in response to the dramatically changing contexts of enabling technologies, architectures, and programming methods, models, and tools. For HPC, even more than other computing domains, advances to current and future operating systems are driven by the needs of efficiency and scalability of large single highly distributed jobs and myriad concurrent jobs comprising high-throughput workloads. With energy, size, cost, heterogeneity emerging as dominant attributes of future HPC systems, operating systems are experiencing innovation like never before.

One major factor that confronts almost all HPC operating systems is the traditional set of services expected by most applications, sometimes incorporated by the POSIX standards, but also additional functions have become common as systems have evolved. Because a large body of legacy codes, some of them mission critical, have come to employ this array of support, future operating systems for HPC are likely to require continuity of these capabilities. But at the same time, classical implementations have exhibited unfortunate characteristics when it comes to efficiencies such as OS noise and overheads related to scheduling impacting scalability.

This new and important book masterfully presents the major alternative concepts driving the future of operating system design for high-performance computing. In particular, it describes the major advances of monolithic operating system such as Linux and Unix that dominate the TOP500 list. It also presents the state of the art in lightweight kernels that exhibit high efficiency and scalability at the loss of generality. Finally, this work looks forward to possibly the most promising strategy of a hybrid structure combining full-service functionality with lightweight kernel operation. With this, it is likely that this new work will find its way on the shelves of almost everyone who is in any way engaged in the multidiscipline of high-performance computing.

Bloomington, USA   Thomas Sterling
August 2018   Indiana University

Contents

Acronyms

ABI	Application Binary Interface
AC	Application Core (in NIX OS)
ACK	Acknowledgment
ACPI	Advanced Configuration and Power Interface
ADB	Assignable Data Buffer (Earth Simulator)
ADFS	Advanced Distributed File Server (HI-UX/MPP)
AFB	Air Force Base
AI	Artificial Intelligence
AIX	Advanced Interactive eXecutive (IBM)
ALPS	Application Level Placement Scheduler (Cray)
AM	Active Messages
AMD	Advanced Micro Devices, Inc. (company)
AMG	Algebraic MultiGrid (benchmark)
AP	Arithmetic Processor (Earth Simulator)
API	Application Programming Interface
APIC	Advanced Programmable Interrupt Controller
APPC	APPlication Container specification
ARM	Advanced RISC Machines (company)
ARMCI	Aggregate Remote Memory Copy Interface
ASCI	Accelerated Strategic Computing Initiative (US Department of Energy)
ASCII	American Standard Code for Information Interchange
ASCR	Advanced Scientific Computing Research (US Department of Energy)
ASIC	Application-Specific Integrated Circuit
ASLR	Address Space Layout Randomization
ASTRON	Netherlands Institute for Radio Astronomy
AT&T	American Telephone & Telegraph
AVX	Advanced Vector Extension (Intel)
BBN	Bolt, Beranek and Newman (company)

BDEC	Big Data and Extreme-scale Computing (workshop)
BG	Blue Gene (IBM)
BGL	Blue Gene/L (IBM)
BGP	Blue Gene/P (IBM)
BGQ	Blue Gene/Q (IBM)
BIOS	Basic Input Output System (computer firmware)
BLAS	Basic Linear Algebra Subprograms
BLRTS	Blue Gene/L Run Time Supervisor (IBM)
BMBF	Bundesministerium für Bildung und Forschung (Federal Ministry of Education and Research, Germany)
BSAT	Butterfly Satellite (IMP packet switch)
BSD	Berkeley Software Distribution
BSP	Boot Strap Processor
BSP	Bulk Synchronous Programming
BSS	Block Started by Symbol (uninitialized data segment)
BT	Block Tri-diagonal solver (NAS benchmark)
CCS	Center for Computational Science (RIKEN)
CCS	Cluster Control Station (Earth Simulator)
CDC	Control Data Corp.
CFS	Completely Fair Scheduler (Linux)
CG	Conjugate Gradient (benchmark)
CIOD	Compute I/O user-space Daemon (Zepto OS)
CLANG	C LANGuages compiler front end for LLVM
CLE	Cray Linux Environment
CLUMP	CLUster of sMPs
CM	Connection Machine (Company)
CMCP	Core-Map Count based page replacement Policy (IHK/McKernel)
CMG	Core Memory Group (K Computer)
CMOS	Complementary Metal–Oxide–Semiconductor
CMU	Carnegie Mellon University
CN	Compute Node
CNIC	ASCI Option Red TFLOPS system network interface chip (Intel/Sandia National Laboratories)
CNK	Compute Node Kernel (IBM)
CNL	Compute Node Linux (Cray)
COFF	Common Object File Format
CORAL	Collaboration Oak Ridge Argonne Livermore (US DOE procurement activity)
COS	Cray Operating System
COSMO-SPECS	COnsortium for Small-scale MOdeling coupled with SPECtral bin cloud microphysicS (atmospheric model)
COTS	Commercial Off-The-Shelf
COW	Copy On Write
CPS	Columbia Physics System

CPU	Central Processing Unit
CQ	Completion Queue (Earth Simulator)
CSM	Cluster System Management (IBM)
CSP	Communicating Sequential Processes
CTSS	Cray Time-Sharing System
CUDA	Compute Unified Device Architecture (Nvidia)
DAC	Debug Address Compare (Blue Gene)
DARPA	Defense Advanced Research Projects Agency
DAXPY	Double precision scalar (Alpha) matrix (X) multiPlY and add
DC	DeCoupled (thread execution in L4)
DCMF	Deep Computing Messaging Framework (IBM)
DDR	Double Data Rate (memory)
DDT	Distributed Debugging Tool (Allinea)
DEC	Digital Equipment Corp.
DFG	Deutsche ForschungsGemeinschaft (Germany)
DGAS	Distributed Global Address Space
DI-MMAP	Data-Intensive Memory-MAP (Argo)
DIPC	Distributed IPC
DL	Deep Learning
DMA	Direct Memory Access
DMAATB	DMA address translation buffer (Earth Simulator)
DMI	Desktop Management Interface
DNA	DeoxyriboNucleic Acid (genetic code)
DOCK	Molecular Docking
DOD	Department of Defense
DOE	Department of Energy
DRAM	Dynamic Random-Access Memory
DTK	Data Transfer Kit (University of Wisconsin)
DVS	Data Virtualization Service (Cray)
EDRAM	Embedded Dynamic Random-Access Memory (IBM)
ELF	Executable and Linkable Format
EP	Embarrassingly Parallel (NAS benchmark)
EPCC	Edinburgh Parallel Computing Centre
EPT	Extended Page Table
ES	Earth Simulator
ESF	Europäischer SozialFond (Germany)
ESRDC	Earth Simulator Research Center
EXS	Exception Status (Earth Simulator)
FC	Fiber Channel
FDR	Fourteen Data Rate (Infiniband)
FEFS	Reliable File System (K Computer)
FFMK	Fast Fault-tolerant MicroKernel
FFT	Fast Fourier Transform (benchmark)
FIFO	First In, First Out
FM	Fast Messages

FMA	Fused Multiply Add
FOS	Factored OS
FPR	Floating Point Registers
FPU	Floating Point Unit
FS	File System (PEC FS in FusedOS)
FTQ	Fixed Time Quantum (benchmark)
FUSE	File system in USErspace
FUTEX	Fast Userspace muTEX
FWK	Full Weight Kernel
FWQ	Fixed Work Quantum (benchmark)
GA	General Availability
GB	Giga Bytes (one billion bytes)
GCC	GNU C Compiler
GDB	GNU debugger
GDDR	Graphics Double Data Rate (memory)
GIB	Global Information Bus (Argo)
GMD	Grand Molecular Dynamics
GMT	Greenwich Mean Time
GNATB	Global Node Address Translation Buffer (Earth Simulator)
GNU	GNU is Not Unix
GPFS	General Parallel File System (IBM)
GPL	General Public License (GNU)
GPR	General-Purpose Register
GPU	Graphics Processing Unit
GRM	Global Resource Manager (Argo)
GSATB	Global Storage Address Translation Buffer (Earth Simulator)
GTC	Gyrokinetic Toroidal Code
HAL	Hardware Abstraction Layer
HCA	Host Channel Adapter (InfiniBand)
HDB	Hobbes Data Base (Hobbes)
HI	Hitachi (company)
HPC	High-Performance Computing
HPCCG	High-Performance Computing Conjugate Gradients (Mantevo benchmark, Sandia National Laboratories)
HPCG	High-Performance Conjugate Gradient (benchmark)
HPF	High-Performance Fortran
HPL	High-Performance Linpack (benchmark)
HPMMAP	High-Performance Memory Mapping and Allocation Platform (Brian Kocoloski, John Lange)
HPX	High-Performance ParalleX
HSFS	Hitachi Striping File System (HI-UX/MPP)
HSS	Hardware Supervisory System (Cray)
HWT	HardWare Thread
HXB	Hyper Crossbar Network (HI-UX/MPP)
IB	InfiniBand (network)

IBM	International Business Machines
ICC	Intel Connect Controller (K Computer)
ICC	Inter-Core Call (NIX)
ID	IDentifier
IEEE	Institute of Electrical and Electronics Engineers
IHK	Interface for Heterogeneous Kernels (IHK/McKernel)
IKC	Inter-Kernel Communication (IHK/McKernel)
IMB	Intel MPI Benchmarks
IMP	Interface Message Processor
INA	Inter-Node Access (Earth Simulator)
INRIA	Institut National de Recherche en Informatique et en Automatique (France)
IO	Input/Output (I/O)
IOCS	Input Output Control Station (Earth Simulator)
IOU	I/O Units (HI-UX/MPP)
IP	Internet Protocol
IPC	Inter-Processor Communication
IPDPS	IEEE International Parallel Distributed Processing Symposium
IPI	Inter-Processor Interrupt
IPL	Initial Program Load
IRIX	Unix-like OS for Iris line of computers by SGI
IRQ	Interrupt ReQuest
IRS	Implicit Radiation Solver (benchmark)
IS	Integer Sort (NAS benchmark)
ISA	Instruction Set Architecture
ISO	International Organization for Standardization
ISUG	Intel Supercomputer User's Group
ISV	Independent Software Vendor
IXS	Internode Crossbar Switch (Earth Simulator)
JCAHPC	Joint Center for Advanced High-Performance Computing
JID	CPU job InDentifier (Earth Simulator)
JS	Job Scheduler (Earth Simulator)
JTAG	Joint Test Action Group (IEEE standard)
JVM	Java Virtual Machine
KB	Kilo Bytes (one thousand bytes)
KEK	High-Energy Accelerator Research Organization (Japan)
KKT	Kernel-to-Kernel Transfer (HI-UX/MPP)
KNC	Knights Corner (Intel)
KNEM	Kernel Nemesis (intra-node messaging)
KNL	Knights Landing (Intel)
KSR	Kendall Square Research (company)
KVM	Kernel Virtual Machine (Linux)
LAMMPS	Large-scale Atomic/Molecular Massively Parallel Simulator (Sandia National Laboratories)
LANL	Los Alamos National Laboratory

LHM	Load Host Memory (Earth Simulator instruction)
LID	Local Identifier (Earth Simulator)
LiMIC	Linux Kernel Module for MPI Intra-Node Communication (Ohio State)
LINPACK	LINear equations software PACKage
LL	Load Leveler
LLC	Last Level Cache
LLC	Limited Liability Corp.
LLNL	Lawrence Livermore National Laboratory
LOFAR	LOw Frequency ARray (radio telescope)
LRIOT	Livermore Random I/O Toolkit (benchmark)
LRU	Least Recently Used (cache policy)
LSI	Large-Scale Integration
LU	Lower Upper (benchmark, algorithm)
LULESH	Livermore Unstructured Lagrangian Explicit Shock Hydrodynamics (benchmark)
LWK	Lightweight Kernel
MB	Mega Bytes (one million bytes)
MCDRAM	Multi-Channel DRAM
MESI	Modified Exclusive Shared Invalid (cache protocol)
MEXT	Ministry of Education, Culture, Sports, Science and Technology (Japan)
MGDC	Quantum Molecular Dynamics Code
MILC	MIMD Lattice Computation (benchmark)
MIMD	Multiple Instruction Multiple Data (Flynn taxonomy)
MIPS	Million Instructions Per Second
MIPS	MIPS Computer Systems, Inc. (Company)
MIT	Massachusetts Institute of Technology
ML	Machine Learning
MMAP	Memory Map
MMIO	Memory-Mapped I/O
MMU	Main Memory Unit (Earth Simulator)
MMU	Memory Management Unit (more common)
MN	Minnesota
MONC	Timer interrupt and the MONitor Call (Earth Simulator instruction)
MOSIX	Multicomputer Operating System for unIX
MPCRL	Massively Parallel Computing Research Laboratory (Sandia National Laboratory)
MPI	Message Passing Interface
MPICH	Message Passing Interface Chameleon
MPP	Massively Parallel Processor
MPPG	Message Passing Process Group (Earth Simulator)
MR	Memory Region (Earth Simulator)
MSI	Message Signaled Interrupts

MTA	Multi-Threaded Architecture (Tera/Cray)
MTBF	Mean Time Between Failures
MTC	Many-Task Computing (ZeptoOS)
MTRR	Memory Type Range Register
MTTL	Multi-Threaded Template Library
MTTR	Memory Type Range Register
MUDM	Message Unit Data Mover (IBM)
MUTEX	MUTual EXclusion (algorithm)
NACK	Not ACKnowledged (Networking)
NAS	NASA Advanced Supercomputing division (benchmarks)
NASA	National Aeronautics and Space Administration
NCAR	National Center for Atmospheric Research
NCSA	National Center for Supercomputing Applications
NEC	Nippon Electric Company, Ltd
NERSC	National Energy Research Scientific Computing Center
NFS	Network File System
NIC	Network Interface Controller
NLTSS	New Livermore Time-Sharing System
NOW	Network of Workstations
NPB	NAS Parallel Benchmarks
NPTL	Native POSIX Thread Library
NRL	Naval Research Laboratory
NRM	Node Resource Manager (Argo)
NSA	National Security Agency (US government)
NT	New Technology (Windows-NT)
NTP	Network Time Protocol
NUMA	Non-Uniform Memory Access (architecture)
NVL	Node Virtualization Layer (Hobbes)
NVRAM	Non-Volatile Random-Access Memory
NY	New York
NYU	New York University
OFED	Open Fabrics Enterprise Distribution (OpenFabrics Alliance)
OFP	Oakforest-PACS (Japan)
OpenMP	Open Multi-Processing (API)
OR	Oregon
ORNL	Oak Ridge National Laboratory
OS	Operating System
OSF	Open Software Foundation
OSF/1 AD	Open Software Foundation Advanced Development (OS)
OSI	Open Systems Interconnection (ISO networking model)
OSS	Open-Source Software
OST	Object Storage Target
PACS	Parallel Advanced System for Computational Sciences (Japan)
PAMI	Parallel Active Messaging Interface (IBM)

PA-RISC	Precision Architecture Reduced Instruction Set Computer (Hewlett-Packard)
PC	Personal Computer
PCB	Process Control Block (data structure)
PCI	Peripheral Component Interconnect (computer interface)
PCT	Process Control Thread (Sandia National Laboratories)
PDP	Programmed Data Processor (DEC)
PE	Parallel Environment (HI-UX/MPP)
PEC	Power-Efficient Core (FusedOS)
PGAS	Partitioned Global Address Space
PGD	Page Global Directory (Linux)
PID	Process IDentifier
PLB	Picture-Level Benchmark
PMA	Process Management Agent (HI-UX/MPP)
PMD	Page Middle Directory (Linux)
PMM	Process Management Manager (HI-UX/MPP)
PN	Processor Nodes (Earth Simulator)
PNU	Processor Network Unit (Earth Simulator)
POP	Parallel Ocean Program
POSIX	Portable Operating System Interface for Unix
POWER	Performance Optimization With Enhanced RISC (IBM)
PowerPC	POWER—Performance Computing (IBM)
PROSE	Parallel Real-Time OS for Secure Environments (Sandia National Laboratories)
PS	Process Status
PSNAP	Performance and architecture laboratory System Noise Activity Program (benchmark)
PSPT	Partially Separated Page Tables (IHK/McKernel)
PT	Page Table (memory)
PTE	Page Table Entry
PU	Processing Unit (HI-UX/MPP)
PVFS	Parallel Virtual File System
PVM	Parallel Virtual Machine
PVP	Pseudo Vector Processing (HI-UX/MPP)
QCD	Quantum Chromodynamics
QCDSP	QCD on Digital Signal Processors (Columbia University)
QEMU	Quick EMUlator (hypervisor)
QK	Quintessential Kernel (Sandia National Laboratories)
QP	Queue Pair (communication)
RAID	Redundant Array of Independent Disks
RAM	Random-Access Memory
RAPL	Running Average Power Limit (Intel)
RAS	Reliability, Availability, and Servicability
RCA	Resiliency Communication Agent (Cray)
RCU	Read-Copy-Update

RCU	Remote access Control Unit (Earth Simulator)
RD	Reliable Datagram (Earth Simulator)
RDMA	Remote Direct Memory Access
RHEL	Red Hat Enterprise Linux
RIKEN	Institute of Physical and Chemical Research (Japan)
RISC	Reduced Instruction Set Computer
ROSS	Runtime and Operating Systems for Supercomputers (workshop)
RPC	Remote Procedure Call
RQ	Receive Queue (Earth Simulator)
RSCC	RIKEN Super Combined Cluster
RWCP	Real World Computing Partnership (Japan)
RWTH	Rheinisch-Westfälische Technische Hochschule (University)
SAN	Storage Area Network
SC	Super Computing
SCALAPACK	Scalable Linear Algebra PACKage (Netlib)
SCC	Single-Chip Cloud Computer (Intel)
SCCS	Super Cluster Control Station (Earth Simulator)
SCSI	Small Computer System Interface
SDSC	San Diego Supercomputer Center
SE	Speculative Execution
SFF	Striping File Feature (HI-UX/MPP)
SFS	Supercomputing File System (Earth Simulator)
SGI	Silicon Graphics, Inc.
SHM	Store Host Memory (Earth Simulator)
SIMD	Single Instruction, Multiple Data (Flynn taxonomy)
SIOU	Supervisory I/O Unit (HI-UX/MPP)
SLURM	Simple Linux Utility for Resource Management
SMP	Symmetric Multi-Processor
SMT	Simultaneous Multi-Threading
SNC	Sub-NUMA Cluster (Intel)
SNL	Sandia National Laboratories
SOC	System On a Chip
SPARC	Scalable Processor Architecture (Sun Microsystems)
SPMD	Single Program, Multiple Data (Flynn taxonomy)
SPU	Scalar Processing Unit (Earth Simulator)
SQ	Send Queue (Earth Simulator)
SRAM	Static Random-Access Memory
SRQ	Shared Receive Queues (SCore)
SSD	Solid-State Drive
SSE	Streaming SIMD Extensions (Intel)
SSI	Single System Image
STOC	Single-Thread-Optimized Cores (FusedOS)
SUNMOS	Sandia/University of New Mexico Operating System
SUSE	Software- und System-Entwicklung (Linux distribution)

SVE	Scalable Vector Extension
TB	Terabyte (one trillion bytes)
TC	Time-sharing Core (NIX)
TCP	Transmission Control Protocol
TEPS	Traversed Edges Per Second (Graph 500)
TFLOPS	Tera Flops (one trillion floating point operations per second)
THP	Transparent Huge Page (Linux)
TLB	Translation Lookaside Buffer
TM	Transactional Memory
TMC	Thinking Machines Corp.
TSS	Time-Sharing System
TTY	Teletypewriter (terminal)
TU	Technical University
TUN	Network TUNnel
UC	University of California
UD	Unreliable Datagram (Earth Simulator)
UDP	User Datagram Protocol
UK	United Kingdom
ULT	User-Level Thread (SCore)
UMA	Uniform Memory Access (architecture)
UMT	Unstructured Mesh Transport (benchmark)
UNICOS	UNIx Cray Operating System (Cray)
UNM	The University of New Mexico
UPC	Unified Parallel C (Berkeley)
USA	United States of America
VAX	Virtual Address Extension (DEC)
VDA	Visualization and Data Analysis
VE	Vector Engine (Earth Simulator)
VEOS	Vector Engine Operating System (Earth Simulator)
VESHM	Vector Engine Shared Memory (Earth Simulator)
VFS	Virtual File System
VH	Vector Host (Earth Simulator)
VHDL	Very High-level Design Language
VM	Virtual Machine
VMA	Virtual Memory Area (Linux)
VMM	Virtual Machine Monitor
VMS	Virtual Memory System (DEC)
VOP	Virtual file system OPeration
VPU	Vector Processing Unit (Earth Simulator)
VT	Virtualization Technology (Intel)
WWW	World Wide Web
XML	eXtensible Markup Language
XPMEM	Cross Partition MEMory

XPPSL	Intel Xeon Phi Processor Software
XPRESS	eXascale PRogramming Environment and System Software
ZCB	ZeptoOS Compute Binaries
ZIH	Center for Information Services and High Performance Computing (TU Dresden)
ZOID	ZeptoOS I/O Daemon

List of Figures

List of Tables

Part I
Introduction

Chapter 1
Introduction to HPC Operating Systems

Balazs Gerofi, Yutaka Ishikawa, Rolf Riesen and Robert W. Wisniewski

1.1 HPC and HPC Operating Systems

The fastest computers in the world over the last three decades have been vector machines and then massively parallel, distributed memory systems. These machines have helped scientists in fields such as astronomy, biology, chemistry, mathematics, medicine, engineering, and physics, reach a deeper understanding of natural phenomena through numerical analysis and ever more detailed simulations from atoms to galaxies.

Over the years, these machines have evolved from pure scientific simulation instruments into areas like cloud computing, big data analytics, and machine learning. The Operating Systems (OSs) which control and manage the resources of these extremely complex and large systems needed to evolve as well. The sixteen chapters in this book describe how High-Performance Computing (HPC) OSs have adapted to the changing requirements placed on high-end parallel computing systems. Each chapter was written by leading experts in the field, and in most cases by the OS creators themselves. We limited the scope of OSs considered to those that target capability class, ultra-scale machines, and whose main focus is scalability with the highest performance possible.

B. Gerofi (✉) · Y. Ishikawa
RIKEN Center for Computational Science, Kobe, Japan
e-mail: bgerofi@riken.jp

Y. Ishikawa
e-mail: yutaka.ishikawa@riken.jp

R. Riesen
Intel Corporation, Hillsboro, OR, USA
e-mail: rolf.riesen@intel.com

R. W. Wisniewski
Intel Corporation, New York, NY, USA
e-mail: robert.w.wisniewski@intel.com

© Springer Nature Singapore Pte Ltd. 2019
B. Gerofi et al. (eds.), *Operating Systems for Supercomputers
and High Performance Computing*, High-Performance Computing Series,
https://doi.org/10.1007/978-981-13-6624-6_1

The primary motivation of the book is to explain the design principles used, to show the insights that went into the creation of the OS, and to extract what was learned in the process. In designing any system or piece of system software, there are trade-offs that must be made; e.g., introduce a layer of abstraction for better separation, but incur a performance penalty. In software for HPC machines, trade-offs have historically been made to achieve higher performance sometimes sacrificing ease of use and productivity.

This book assumes the reader has some understanding of what an OS is and does. Most of the chapters in this book concentrate on the OS kernel; i.e., the part of the OS that runs in privileged mode and acts as an interface between user-level applications and the underlying hardware. With a couple of exceptions, each chapter discusses the OSs used on the *compute nodes* of a system. A complete system includes other nodes that perform specific services such as I/O, machine-wide management, or serve as login and compile nodes.

The main portion of the book is divided into three parts. Part II has three chapters on lightweight kernels (LWKs). These small and efficient kernels have been used on systems in the 1990s and the beginning of this century. From these three chapters, we learn why these LWKs were needed, and also why they have fallen out of favor.

The scientific community has used Unix-based OSs for a long time. It is only natural that these users wanted to see something similar on their supercomputers. The six projects in Part III are descriptions of how Unix and Linux were made to work on supercomputers. Linux, in particular, is currently the dominant OS for these systems and the authors in Part III explain what they did to turn general purpose Linux into an HPC OS able to run a capability-class supercomputer.

Part IV describes current research in the field: Multi-kernels that combine Linux compatibility with the scalability and performance of an LWK. Seven chapters provide an insight into the thinking behind these projects and show why this is an active area of research. There are similarities in the goals and general approaches of these new systems, but the details of implementation and the compromises each system has to make, differ significantly.

Over the last 30 years, HPC machines have undergone significant changes, but one thing has remained constant: the drive toward using the latest technology to deliver the maximum performance in a given generation. This has led to aggressive designs of machines utilizing the latest, and pushing the envelope of current and coming, technology. HPC machines saw active use of vectors, then parallelism, including node, core, and symmetric multithreading. Oftentimes, technologies are employed in HPC systems before they become mainstream, and sometimes help drive a technology to become more generally used.

Historically, an important aspect of HPC computation has been dense matrix operations. The High-Performance Linpack (HPL) yardstick was created to track the progress and power consumption of supercomputers. The TOP500 list, www.top500.org, has been used since June 1993, to track HPL performance of the 500 most powerful machines in the world. The speed of the supercomputers on the list has increased by a factor of 2 million from 60 GFlops (FLoating Point Operations per Second) in 1993 to 122 PFlops in June 2018.

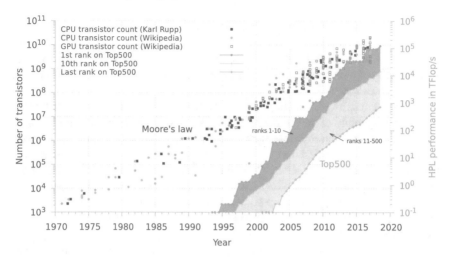

Fig. 1.1 Moore's law and Top 500 growth comparison

In about the same amount of time, Moore's law has yielded a factor of 6,200: from the Intel Pentium with 3.1 million transistors in 1993 to the 19.2 billion Advanced Micro Devices (AMD) Epyc in 2017. The difference in growth indicates that supercomputer performance improvements are not due solely to the effects of Moore's law.

Figure 1.1 shows this relationship. The blue and black data points are individual CPUs and Graphics Processing Unit (GPUs). The left y-axis is the number of transistors in each of these integrated circuits plotted against the year they first appeared.[1] The line-connected points associated with the right y-axis track the top-ranked, the 10th-ranked, and the bottom-ranked systems on the TOP500 list over time.[2,3]

Because it is well structured and dense, HPL achieves a higher Flops rate than most applications. This, in combination with a series of trends in computer hardware (compute capability has improved more rapidly than memory and I/O latency and bandwidth) led to the introduction of two new metrics and corresponding lists that track them: The Green500 (www.top500.org/green500) and the High-Performance Conjugate Gradient (HPCG) (www.hpcg-benchmark.org) benchmark. While these lists do not comprehensively define HPC, they have played an important role as vendors use them as key metrics when designing machines, and customers use them in evaluating and purchasing machines.

---

[1] Karl Rupp transistor count data from https://www.karlrupp.net/2015/06/40-years-of-microprocessor-trend-data/. Wikipedia transistor count data from https://en.wikipedia.org/wiki/Transistor_count.

[2] TOP500 data from www.top500.org.

[3] TOP500 is a registered trademark of PROMETEUS Professor Meuer Technologieberatung und -Services GmbH.

Big data, analytics, and machine learning are driving new usage models for HPC systems. In time, a set of benchmarks and lists tracking the results will emerge. And, undoubtedly, discussions and panels will be held on whether these new metrics represent the true performance of a machine. Just like when HPL first started to be used as a yardstick.

HPC system software, and in particular the OS, has been driven to ensure that the maximum capability of the hardware is delivered through to the application. OSs for other domains have faced issues such as interactions with a wide range of devices, supporting a highly varied user base, or complex scheduling trade-offs between a myriad of applications. For HPC OSs, many of those issues have historically not been an issue. Instead the HPC OS, where it can, provides hardware access directly to users. A common scenario is to allocate and establish protection at resource initialization or first request from the user, and then grant direct access to that resource until the user is finished.

One observation that will become apparent when reading the book is that earlier HPC OSs trended toward special-purpose and simplification. Particularly, the collection of chapters on LWKs shows a deliberate emphasis on providing the minimum capability needed to support an often smaller—compared to general purpose computing—set of applications.

The OSs in Part III of the book bring Unix/Linux functionality to HPC, but even these OSs eschew non-HPC features from the kernel in order to achieve high performance and scalability. Much of the OS work in HPC has been on providing high-performance mechanisms while still providing the requisite protection, and on determining how to walk the line between just enough and too much functionality.

1.2 Approaches

Over time, there have been three primary approaches that developers have taken in order to provide OSs for HPC machines. As shown in Fig. 1.2, large HPC machines have different types of nodes. There are those dedicated to managing the system, nodes for user application development, nodes for I/O, and compute nodes where applications run and perform computations. While all the nodes need to have OSs, this book describes the issues and challenges involved when designing and implementing OSs for the compute nodes.

The first approach, employed by some early machines, is to use an LWK. As the name implies, an LWK provides the bare minimum of functionality needed. These LWKs were written from scratch and specific to the node architecture they ran on. Examples include the Sandia/University of New Mexico Operating System (SUN-MOS) (Maccabe et al. 1994), Puma (Wheat et al. 1994), Catamount (Kelly and Brightwell 2005), and CNK (Giampapa et al. 2010).

Early LWKs had minimal functionality and did not focus on providing Portable Operating System Interface for Unix (POSIX) or Linux compatibility. As Linux gained momentum across all markets including HPC, later LWKs, such as the last

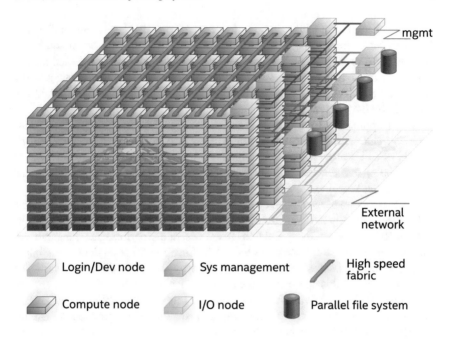

Fig. 1.2 Depiction of major, common subsystem partitioning in large HPC machines

Compute Node Kernel (CNK) on Blue Gene/Q, spent more effort on providing as much Linux compatibility as possible. However, none provided the full feature set of Linux. Therefore, there were applications that could not run on a given LWK.

In the early days of HPC the set of applications, runtimes, and libraries that were desired was small, so this was less of an issue. As HPC progressed, limited functionality became a bigger problem. Even though LWKs became richer overtime, the burgeoning use of HPC called for a greater reliance on standard functionality provided by full-weight kernels (FWKs), and there are only a few machines on the Top 500 list today that run an LWK. Nevertheless, the lessons learned from LWKs and how they achieved top performance remains valuable as researchers and implementers work on future HPC OSs.

The second approach is to use an FWK on the compute nodes. While running Linux or another FWK may seem to avoid the compatibility issues, that is not always the case. In order to achieve high performance, and especially scalability, FWKs need to be judiciously patched to reduce the number of extraneous daemons and other noise causing agents. Note, in this context, *noise* refers to computation that is neither the application code, nor system code called as a direct result of an application request. Additionally, FWKs are modified to reduce the amount of memory needed. In some cases, Linux mechanisms; e.g., memory management, are altered to infuse HPC capabilities.

These changes can cause the OSs to deviate from standard functionality, and therefore not be fully compatible with the original FWK. In the past, vendors provided variants of Unix as the FWK. However, in the Top 500 list published in June 2018, 95% of the machines ran some variant of Linux. Some of these machines run the kernels provided by Linux distributions, while others have been modified and enhanced by the vendor.

A third approach is to run an LWK and an FWK on the compute node at the same time. This *multi-kernel* approach is a more recent direction enabled by the increasing number of CPU cores on each chip. From a high level, the goal is to use an LWK to service the system requests that are performance critical and affect scalability, and to use a Linux kernel to provide compatibility.

System calls are triaged based on the services they request and on the set of system calls implemented by the LWK. A multi-kernel LWK usually only handles those calls that directly manage memory and CPU resources, or are performance sensitive. All other system calls are forwarded to the FWK. Each multi-kernel does this slightly differently and the set of system calls handled by the LWK differs as well. The primary benefit of this approach is the ability to achieve high performance and the scalability of LWKs while providing the compatibility of FWKs. While multi-kernels show promise, none are currently running as the default OS on production systems, but IHK/McKernel is available in the production environment on Oakforest-PACS.

The other benefit of this approach is simplification of the LWK. When an LWK is run as the sole OS kernel, it must boot the node, provide device drivers, and provide other capabilities not directly related to running an HPC application at maximum performance. This functionality which, from an architectural purity perspective, should not be part of the LWK, can be handled by the FWK.

The results to date indicate multi-kernel LWKs allow for better performance, but the approach is not necessarily a panacea for providing full compatibility. Some compatibility is eschewed by design. There are inherent traits in POSIX (Gerofi et al. 2016) and demand-paged OSs that prevent extreme scaling and best possible parallel performance. Nevertheless, multi-kernels strive to provide as much up-to-date Linux functionality as possible. To that end, they must track Linux kernel developments. As the Linux kernel code advances, the multi-kernel must be updated to work with the new Linux kernel version. How this is done, and how much work it involves, is a key distinguishing feature of multi-kernels.

1.3   Important Milestones

In order to help the reader navigate this book and put things into a historical perspective, we provide a timeline in table form of major events that had an impact on HPC OS research. This includes the deployment of important systems and other associated events that had impact; e.g., the progression of the Message-Passing Interface (MPI) standard and Linux kernel availability (Table 1.1).

Table 1.1 A timeline of events related to HPC OS research

Year	Month	Event	Chapters
1976		Cray-1	7
1985		Cray-2 achieves over 1 GFlops	7
1991	Jan	Start of SUNMOS project at Sandia National Laboratories and UNM (Maccabe and Wheat 1993)	3
	Aug	Linus Torvalds publicly announces Linux availability (Torvalds 2001)	
1992	Jul	Start of the Real World Computing Project (RWCP) which developed SCore	8
	Nov	MPI Forum meetings start	
1993	Jan	Preliminary implementation of Puma on a 1,024-node nCube 2 (Wheat et al. 1994)	3
	Jul	First Slackware distribution (Hicks et al. 2005)	
	Nov	Fujitsu Numerical Wind Tunnel ranked 1st with 124 GFlops	
	Nov	Paragon (XP/S35) with 512 nodes running SUNMOS ranked 9th with 15.2 GFlops	3
1994	Jun	Intel Paragon XP/S140 with 3,680 processors (1,840 nodes) reaches 143.4 GFlops (rank 1 using a machine advertised as having 140 GFlops peak)	3
	Jun	Hitachi announces the SR2001	4
	Jun	Version 1.0 of MPI standard released	
		L4 family tree of microkernels originates	19
		Linux 1.0	
		Beowulf clusters introduced	
1995	Apr	MPI-2 meetings start	
	Jun	Version 1.1 of MPI released	
	Jul	Hitachi announces the SR2201 (Fujii et al. 1997)	4
1996		Linux 2.0 with SMP support	
1997	Jul	MPI-2.0 standard released	
	May	Eric S. Raymond publishes *"The Cathedral and the Bazaar"* (Raymond 2001)	
	Jun	Intel ASCI Red with 7,264 processors (3,632 nodes) reaches 1,068 GFlops (rank 1)	
1998	May	Hitachi develops the SR8000 (Tamaki et al. 1999)	4
1999	Dec	Portals 3.0 SAND report (Brightwell et al. 1999)	3
2002	Mar	NEC Earth Simulator begins operation	
2003	May	Hitachi announces the SR11000 (Tamaki et al. 1999)	4
2004	Nov	IBM Blue Gene/L debuts on TOP500 list with 70.72 TFlops	5
		ZeptoOS project starts	10

(continued)

Table 1.1 (continued)

Year	Month	Event	Chapters
2005	Jun	Red Storm running Catamount, Cray XT3 5,000 processors debuts with 15,250 GFlops (rank 10)	3
		Development of K Computer begins	11
2007	Jun	IBM unveils Blue Gene/P	5
		Cray introduces Compute Node Linux (CNL) to replace Catamount on XT-3 (Wallace 2007)	
2008	May	IBM Road Runner reaches 1.026 PFlops running Red Hat Enterprise Linux	
2009	Nov	Jaguar Cray XT5 takes #1 spot on TOP500 running CLE/CNL at 1.7 PFlops	
2010	Nov	Tianhe-1A achieves 2.6 PFlops	
2011	Apr	NIX project starts	16
	Jun	Fujitsu K Computer secures the #1 spot on the TOP500 list	11
	Nov	IBM announces Blue Gene/P	5
		Linux 3.0	
		FusedOS project starts	14
2012		IBM Blue Gene/Q	5
		IHK/McKernel project starts	17
	Sep	MPI 3.0	
	Nov	Titan Cray XK7 takes #1 spot on the TOP500 list running CLE/CNL at 17.6 PFlops	
2013		Argo project starts	12
		Hobbes project starts	15
2014	Jan	Start of *mOS* project (Wisniewski et al. 2014)	18
2015	Jun	MPI 3.1	
		Linux 4.0	
2016		Sunway TaihuLight	
2017	Jun	Piz Daint Cray XC50 takes #3 spot on the TOP500 list running CLE/CNL at 19.6 PFlops—fastest machine in Europe	
2018	Jun	Summit, an IBM Power System debutes as the highest ranked system on the TOP500 list	

A high-level observation from the timeline below is that in the late 1980s and early 1990s, vector machines dominated the high end of computing systems. As time progressed, distributed memory, highly parallel systems began to climb the Top-500 list and replace the vector processors. We list some of these systems in the table to highlight the market growth of Massively Parallel Processors (MPPs) in the list. Also listed are significant HPC OS achievements.

Below, we describe some milestones in more detail.

1976: Early on supercomputers ran proprietary and home-grown OSs. They were highly tailored to the machine they ran on and not portable to other machines. Though the software environment was not too extensive in this era, it also implied that the user-level software layer that ran on the OS was fairly tied to the machine.

1985: The Cray 2 introduced a more general-purpose OS. Although not general purpose like Linux is viewed today, this showed the value for future supercomputers to use OSs based on standards. See Chap. 7.

1991: Sandia National Laboratories made a conscious shift from vector machines to massively parallel systems. The Massively Parallel Computing Research Laboratory (MPCRL) was founded and the SUNMOS project, in collaboration with the University of New Mexico began. This led to a series of influential LWKs and research into HPC system software continues to this day. See Chap. 3.

In the same year, Linus Torvalds publicly announced Linux availability. Although its rise was quick, it took another decade before it began to be adopted in high-end HPC systems. Today, Linux dominates that, and many other, computing markets.

1992: The MPI Forum began to meet. Up to this point in time, each vendor had their own message-passing system. Applications and libraries needed to be ported every time when a new system was acquired or a new machine generation arrived.

Also in 1992, the Real-World Computing Project (RWCP) began in Japan. The RWCP was a 10-year, government-funded project from 1992 to 2001. The project was not focused on any one specific goal, but pursued the development of a massively parallel machine, creation of a parallel OS, a programming environment, and investigated "soft" information technologies (similar to artificial intelligence today). As part of this project, SCore, a cluster OS, was developed. See Chap. 8.

1994: Beowulf led the way to supercomputers being more accessible to commodity users. This was true both from a hardware point of view; a Beowulf cluster was built out of parts (CPUs and networks) any organization could purchase. It also used standard Unix-based and eventually Linux OSs. Due to the comparative ease of access, and broad accessibility, this methodology opened the door to Linux becoming the dominant OS in supercomputers. See Chap. 6.

An LWK-based system running SUNMOS became the fastest computer on the Top 500 list.

1997: The "magical" teraflops barrier was broken with the Accelerated Strategic Computing Initiative (ASCI) Option Red system running Cougar, a descendant of SUNMOS and Puma. See Chap. 3.

2004: With the introduction of massive node parallelism, OS noise came to the foreground of supercomputing. Blue Gene/L's CNK followed the LWK approach. Although an LWK, over its three generations, it would introduce greater and greater Linux compatibility. It provided Linux compatibility with ultra scalability, and demonstrated unprecedented levels of scalability that were achievable due to its low noise and high reliability. See Chap. 5.

2008: Another significant performance barrier was broken: The IBM Road Runner system at Los Alamos National Laboratory reached 1 petaflops running Red Hat Enterprise Linux.

2010: Tianhe-1A was the first Chinese system to reach the number one spot on the Top 500 list. It beat its nearest competitor, Jaguar at Oak Ridge National Laboratory, by a factor of almost 1.5. It ran a Linux variant and further cemented the foothold Linux had taken even at the very top of the Top 500 list.

2011: The K Computer with 88,000 nodes and 705,024 cores, further demonstrated that a Linux-based OS could scale to capability-class machines. See Chap. 11.

2012: This generation of CNK for Blue.

Gene/Q saw a significant step toward greater Linux compatibility including a limited form of priority scheduling, and greater than one software thread per hardware thread. A separate core, the 17th core, was introduced for OS use, allowing more sophisticated OS functionality while still isolating the application from noise. See Chap. 5.

2016: The Sunway TaihuLight system in China almost reached the 100 petaflops barrier. It ran RaiseOS 2.0.5, a significantly modified Linux version. Four cores per compute node were dedicated for system purposes.

2018: The Unites States regained the number one spot on the Top 500 list with the IBM Power System named Summit at Oak Ridge National Laboratories. It ran Red Hat Enterprise Linux (RHEL) version 7.4.

The shift overtime from custom OSs to a vendor provided Unix, and then Linux, is evident in the above timeline. The predominance of Linux on the current Top 500 list (running on 95% of the machines) is a clear indicator that while many machines use specifically configured unmodified or patched Linux kernels for vendor differentiation, Linux is the current OS of choice. What the future will bring remains to be determined, but with the increasing complexity of the software stack and the volume of Linux-based system software that needs to be present to run the supercomputer, HPC OS designers today need to ensure their OS is Linux compatible.

1.4   Current Trends

As we noted above, the majority of this book is on OSs for classical HPC, and the lessons learned from those experiences. There are four important trends in HPC to which those lessons will need to be applied. While the book does not delve into them, we briefly describe them here so the reader can have them in mind when reading the book.

Containers: Containers are being used for two reasons in HPC. The first is to provide a convenient packaging mechanism that is semi-resilient to changes in the version of the OS, runtimes, and libraries available on the machine. Such packaging does not remove the challenges of running at scale or performance on HPC machines but allows developers to concentrate on those aspects rather than on building the application.

The second reason to use containers is for isolation. Increasingly, HPC machines are being used for simultaneously running multiple executables, such as a simulation application concurrently with an analytics application. While some of the new applications do not exhibit the same deleterious effect due to noise as many simulation applications do, to perform well, the simulation application still needs a low-noise environment. Containers can help provide that.

AI, ML, and DL: Artificial Intelligence (AI), Machine Learning (ML), and Deep Learning (DL) are having sharp and profound effects across many areas of computer science and HPC is no exception. Like in other areas, HPC researchers and practitioners have, with alacrity, adopted AI and ML into their workflows. ML techniques have allowed new insights to be gleaned from the vast amounts of data and also have allowed features or characteristics to be more readily identified for more in-depth simulation. These technologies provide a challenge because they rely on a large amount of system software, runtimes, and libraries that is not usually found on HPC systems and is sometimes difficult to integrate with the existing system software code base, without impacting machine performance and scalability.

A second aspect that not only affects the system software stack, but the OS as well, is that these applications tend to be more dynamic both in terms of their scheduling requirements and their use of memory. In a similar vein, their workflows are often more dynamic and less suitable to a batch scheduling paradigm that has been the de facto standard in HPC. The importance of providing tighter coupling for data movement between the HPC portion and AI portion of the workflow opens up opportunities and challenges across the system software stack including the OS.

Big Data and Analytics: The recognition of the confluence of HPC and big data and analytics has perhaps existed longer than the melding of AI and HPC as witnessed by efforts such as the Big Data and Extreme-scale Computing (BDEC) workshops (BDEC Committee 2017). Further, some simulation applications have used massive amounts of data for a long time. The introduction of concurrently running analytics that, like AI, use a different set of runtimes and libraries is a more recent development. The addition of these runtimes and libraries introduces similar challenges and opportunities to those described above for AI. The combination of simulation, AI, and analytics is sometimes referred to as the three pillars of HPC and likely represents an important trend that system software including OSs will need to support.

Cloud: For a while, there has been discussion around the convergence of Cloud and HPC and debate around exactly what that would mean. The likely form that may take, based on current trends, is for cloud providers to offer nodes that have HPC services and varying degrees of coupling between the nodes. What remains to be seen is how valuable a tighter coupling in the cloud will be for parties interested in HPC cloud services. The need for virtualization and elasticity drives a set of additional requirements the OS must support.

1.5 Organization of this Book

There are several themes throughout the book the reader may value. First, we have provided OS experiences from major trends including the introduction of high-speed networks, introduction of massive parallelism, introduction of accelerators, etc., as well as OSs from major milestones throughout HPC. This thread allows the reader to understand both a historical perspective as well as a flow of how OSs have adapted to new technologies and new changes.

Second, we have grouped the OS efforts in three primary categories so the reader can compare and contrast different efforts within a given area. Those three parts are LWK, Unix and Linux, and multi-kernels. Most chapters, where appropriate, provide a timeline of the OSs discussed, which machines they have run on, an overview of the architecture and design, and a lessons-learned section.

Each part of the book, the LWK, Unix- and Linux-based systems, and multi-kernels, is divided into an introduction describing the relevance of the collection of work and then a set of chapters representing that work. For the most part, chapters are self-contained and can be read in any order. Each has a reference section at the end. In addition, we provide a book-wide index and bibliography that lists the references encountered in all chapters.

References

BDEC Committee. (2017). The BDEC "Pathways to convergence" report. http://www.exascale.org/bdec/.

Boku, T., Itakura, K., Nakamura, H., & Nakazawa, K. (1997). CP-PACS: A massively parallel processor for large scale scientific calculations. In *Proceedings of ACM 11th International Conference on Supercomputing, Vienna, Austria* (pp. 108–115).

Brightwell, R., Hudson, T., Riesen, R., & Maccabe, A. B. (1999). The Portals 3.0 message passing interface. Technical report SAND99-2959, Sandia National Laboratories.

Fujii, H., Yasuda, Y., Akashi, H., Inagami, Y., Koga, M., Ishihara, O., et al. (1997). Architecture and performance of the Hitachi SR2201 massively parallel processor system. In *Proceedings of IEEE 11th International Symposium on Parallel Processing (IPPS97)* (pp. 233–241).

Gerofi, B., Takagi, M., Hori, A., Nakamura, G., Shirasawa, T., & Ishikawa, Y. (2016). On the scalability, performance isolation and device driver transparency of the IHK/McKernel hybrid lightweight kernel. *2016 IEEE International Parallel and Distributed Processing Symposium (IPDPS)* (pp. 1041–1050)

Giampapa, M., Gooding, T., Inglett, T., & Wisniewski, R. (2010). Experiences with a lightweight supercomputer kernel: Lessons learned from Blue Gene's CNK. In *2010 International Conference for High Performance Computing, Networking, Storage and Analysis (SC)*.

Hicks, A., Lumens, C., Cantrell, D., & Johnson, L. (2005). *Slackware Linux essentials*. Brentwood, CA: Slackware Linux Inc.

Kelly, S. M., & Brightwell, R. (2005). Software architecture of the light weight kernel, Catamount. In *47th Cray User Group Conference, CUG, Albuquerque, NM*.

Maccabe, A. B. & Wheat, S. R. (1993). Message passing in PUMA. Technical report SAND93-0935, Sandia National Laboratories.

Maccabe, A. B., McCurley, K. S., Riesen, R., & Wheat, S. R. (1994). SUNMOS for the Intel Paragon: A brief user's guide. In *Proceedings of the Intel Supercomputer Users' Group. 1994 Annual North America Users' Conference* (pp. 245–251).

Raymond, E. S. (2001). *The Cathedral & the Bazaar: Musings on Linux and Open Source by an Accidental Revolutionary*. O'Reilly Media.

Tamaki, Y., Sukegawa, N., Ito, M., Tanaka, Y., Fukagawa, M., Sumimoto, T., et al. (1999). Node architecture and performance evaluation of the Hitachi Super Technical Server SR8000. In *Proceedings of 12th International Conference on Parallel and Distributed Computing Systems* (pp. 487–493).

Torvalds, L. (2001). *Just for fun: The story of an accidental revolutionary*. New York, NY: Harper Business.

Wallace, D. (2007). Compute Node Linux: Overview, progress to date & roadmap. In *Proceedings of the Cray User Group (CUG)*.

Wheat, S. R., Maccabe, A. B., Riesen, R., van Dresser, D. W., & Stallcup, T. M. (1994). PUMA: An operating system for massively parallel systems. *Scientific Programming, 3*, 275–288.

Wisniewski, R. W., Inglett, T., Keppel, P., Murty, R., and Riesen, R. (2014). mOS: An architecture for extreme-scale operating systems. In *Proceedings of the 4th International Workshop on Runtime and Operating Systems for Supercomputers, ROSS '14* (pp. 2:1–2:8). New York, NY, USA: ACM.

Part II
Lightweight Kernels

Chapter 2
Overview: The Birth of Lightweight Kernels

Rolf Riesen, Balazs Gerofi, Yutaka Ishikawa and Robert W. Wisniewski

Lightweight operating system kernels (LWKs), as we define them today (Riesen et al. 2015) for high-end high-performance computing (HPC) systems, started to appear in the late 1980s and early 1990s. Supercomputers, and the applications that made use of them, had specific requirements and challenges that made multi-user workstation operating systems (OSs) unsuitable for these machines.

We list the challenges that led to the creation of LWKs and include three chapters of example LWK projects: Sandia National Laboratories' line of LWKs (Riesen et al. 2009) in Chap. 3, Hitachi's HI-UX/MPP series of OSs (Kitai et al. 1993) in Chap. 4, and IBM's line of LWKs for its Blue Gene systems (Giampapa et al. 2010) in Chap. 5.

The arrival of large-scale, distributed memory systems prompted the rethinking of OSs for scientific computers. These systems had regular, well-defined network topologies with high-speed interfaces whose speed exceeded memory bandwidth. Hypercube and mesh topologies of various degrees, i.e., number of adjacent nodes, were common. The compute node kernel needed only to compute simple routes to reach all other nodes in the system.

The early network interfaces were primitive by today's standard; often just a First-In, First-Out (FIFO) and a couple of Direct Memory Access (DMA) engines that needed to be kept busy by the OS kernel. The lack of sophistication in

R. Riesen (✉)
Intel Corporation, Hillsboro, OR, USA
e-mail: rolf.riesen@intel.com

B. Gerofi · Y. Ishikawa
RIKEN Center for Computational Science, Kobe, Japan
e-mail: bgerofi@riken.jp

Y. Ishikawa
e-mail: yutaka.ishikawa@riken.jp

R. W. Wisniewski
Intel Corporation, New York, NY, USA
e-mail: robert.w.wisniewski@intel.com

© Springer Nature Singapore Pte Ltd. 2019
B. Gerofi et al. (eds.), *Operating Systems for Supercomputers and High Performance Computing*, High-Performance Computing Series,
https://doi.org/10.1007/978-981-13-6624-6_2

the network interface had to be compensated for by kernel drivers and user-level message-passing libraries. The Message-Passing Interface (MPI) had not been created yet and each vendor supplied their own message-passing interface, e.g., Vertex on the nCube (Palmer 1988) and NX (Pierce 1988; Nugent 1988) on Intel's iPSC series of multi-computers. A special issue of the Parallel Computing journal from 1994 provides an excellent overview of the state of the art around that time. An overview article in that issue provides a nice summary (McBryan 1994).

During that era, compute nodes were homogeneous and had small amounts of physical memory, and usually no local disk storage. That meant that the OS needed to have a very small memory footprint. On the other hand, the introduction of Massively Parallel Processors (MPP) meant that each of these machines had numerous compute nodes which made space sharing feasible.

In order to support applications written for different supercomputers, a common, efficient Application Programming Interface (API) was needed to map the various vendor message passing APIs onto the LWK of a given machine. Because each machine was different, and pre-MPI applications often had their own message-passing libraries, an efficient layer between them and the hardware underneath was required.

In that era, message passing was built into the LWK. As the MPI standard changed and matured, the LWKs had to adapt and were used as test vehicles for MPI Forum proposals. When these new features were incorporated into the MPI standard, the LWKs needed to change again.

At Sandia National Laboratories, this lead to the creation of Portals (Maccabe and Wheat 1993; Brightwell et al. 2003) which were at the time, together with the necessary hardware drivers, built into the LWK for performance and efficiency. Related efforts included the Aggregate Remote Memory Copy Interface (ARMCI) (Nieplocha and Carpenter 1999), Active Messages (AM) (v. Eicken et al. 1992; Riesen et al. 1994) which originated on the Connection Machine (CM-5), Parallel Virtual Machine (PVM) (Sunderam 1990), and later, Parallel Active Messaging Interface (PAMI) (Kumar et al. 2012) on the Blue Gene family of systems.

The rapid changes in programming models, system architecture, and usage introduced challenges that required new approaches to OSs on these machines. Because they were programmed using Bulk Synchronous Programming (BSP) paradigms, deterministic behavior became important and the reduction of OS noise became an important design requirement.

All of this was in contrast to the network of workstations (Anderson et al. 1995) approach. Through most of the 1990s, the traditional approach of porting versions of Unix no longer worked for MPPs, although it was attempted (Saini and Simon 1994). LWKs were more scalable and had better performance on MPPs. The three chapters in this part of the book describe major efforts of that era to design and implement LWKs. Enjoy!

References

Anderson, T. E., Culler, D. E., & Patterson, D. A. (1995). The berkeley networks of workstations (NOW) project. In *Proceedings of the 40th IEEE Computer Society International Conference, COMPCON '95* (p. 322). Washington, DC, USA: IEEE Computer Society.

Brightwell, R., Maccabe, A. B., & Riesen, R. (2003). Design, implementation, and performance of MPI on Portals 3.0. *The International Journal of High Performance Computing Applications, 17*(1), 7–20.

Giampapa, M., Gooding, T., Inglett, T., & Wisniewski, R. (2010). Experiences with a lightweight supercomputer kernel: Lessons learned from Blue Gene's CNK. In *2010 International Conference for High Performance Computing, Networking, Storage and Analysis (SC)*.

Kitai, K., Isobe, T., Tanaka, Y., Tamaki, Y., Fukagawa, M., Tanaka, T., et al. (1993). Parallel processing architecture for the Hitachi S-3800 shared-memory vector multiprocessor. In *ICS'93 Proceedings of the 7th International Conference on Supercomputing*.

Kumar, S., Mamidala, A., Faraj, D., Smith, B., Blocksome, M., Cernohous, B., et al. (2012). PAMI: A parallel active message interface for the Blue Gene/Q supercomputer. In *2012 IEEE 26th International Parallel Distributed Processing Symposium (IPDPS)* (pp. 763–773).

Maccabe, A. B., & Wheat, S. R. (1993). Message passing in PUMA. Technical report SAND93-0935, Sandia National Laboratories.

McBryan, O. A. (1994). An overview of message passing environments. *Parallel Computing, 20*(4), 417–444. Message Passing Interfaces.

Nieplocha, J., & Carpenter, B. (1999). ARMCI: A portable remote memory copy library for distributed array libraries and compiler run-time systems. In *International Parallel Processing Symposium (IPPS)* (pp. 533–546). Berlin, Heidelberg: Springer.

Nugent, S. F. (1988). The iPSC/2 direct-connect communications technology. In *Proceedings of the Third Conference on Hypercube Concurrent Computers and Applications: Architecture, Software, Computer Systems, and General Issues - Volume 1, C3P* (pp. 51–60). New York, NY, USA: ACM.

Palmer, J. F. (1988). The NCUBE family of high-performance parallel computer systems. In *Proceedings of the Third Conference on Hypercube Concurrent Computers and Applications: Architecture, Software, Computer Systems, and General Issues - Volume 1, C3P* (pp. 847–851). New York, NY, USA: ACM.

Pierce, P. (1988). The NX/2 operating system. In *Proceedings of the Third Conference on Hypercube Concurrent Computers and Applications: Architecture, Software, Computer Systems, and General Issues - Volume 1, C3P* (pp. 384–390). New York, NY, USA: ACM.

Riesen, R., Maccabe, A. B., & Wheat, S. R. (1994). Active messages versus explicit message passing under SUNMOS. In *Proceedings of the Intel Supercomputer Users' Group. 1994 Annual North America Users' Conference* (pp. 297–303).

Riesen, R., Brightwell, R., Bridges, P. G., Hudson, T., Maccabe, A. B., Widener, P. M., et al. (2009). Designing and implementing lightweight kernels for capability computing. *Concurrency and Computation: Practice and Experience, 21*(6), 793–817.

Riesen, R., Maccabe, A. B., Gerofi, B., Lombard, D. N., Lange, J. J., Pedretti, K., et al. (2015). What is a lightweight kernel? In *Proceedings of the 5th International Workshop on Runtime and Operating Systems for Supercomputers, ROSS '15*. New York, NY, USA: ACM.

Saini, S., & Simon, H. (1994). Applications performance under OSF/1 AD and SUNMOS on Intel Paragon XP/S-15. In *Supercomputing '94, Proceedings* (pp. 580–589).

Sunderam, V. S. (1990). PVM: A framework for parallel distributed computing. *Concurrency: Practice and Experience, 2*(4), 315–339.

v. Eicken, T., Culler, D. E., Goldstein, S. C., & Schauser, K. E. (1992). Active messages: A mechanism for integrated communication and computation. In *Proceedings the 19th Annual International Symposium on Computer Architecture* (pp. 256–266).

Chapter 3
Sandia Line of LWKs

Ron Brightwell, Kurt Ferreira, Arthur B. Maccabe, Kevin Pedretti
and Rolf Riesen

Abstract Sandia National Laboratories has been engaged in operating systems research for high-performance computing for more than two decades. The focus has always been extremely parallel systems and the most efficient systems software possible to complete the scientific work demanded by the laboratories' mission. This chapter provides a chronological overview of the operating systems developed at Sandia and the University of New Mexico. Along the way we highlight why certain design decisions were made, what we have learned from our failures, and what has worked well. We summarize these lessons at the end of the chapter, but hope that the more detailed explanations in the text may be useful to future HPC OS designers.

This contribution has been authored by Sandia National Laboratories, a multimission laboratory managed and operated by National Technology and Engineering Solutions of Sandia, LLC, a wholly owned subsidiary of Honeywell International Inc., for the U.S. Department of Energy's National Nuclear Security Administration under contract DE-NA0003525, by UT-Battelle, LLC under Contract No. DE-AC05-00OR22725 with the U.S. Department of Energy, and by Oak Ridge National Laboratory under Contract No. DE-AC05-00OR22275 with the U.S. Department of Energy, Office of Science. The United States Government retains and the publisher, by accepting the contribution for publication, acknowledges that the United States Government retains a non-exclusive, paid-up, irrevocable, worldwide license to publish or reproduce the published form of this manuscript, or allow others to do so, for United States Government purposes.

R. Brightwell (✉) · K. Ferreira · K. Pedretti
Sandia National laboratories, Center for Computing Research, Albuquerque, NM, USA
e-mail: rbbrigh@sandia.gov

K. Ferreira
e-mail: kbferre@sandia.gov

K. Pedretti
e-mail: ktpedre@sandia.gov

A. B. Maccabe
Oak Ridge National Laboratory, Computer Science and Mathematics Division,
Oak Ridge, TN, USA
e-mail: maccabeab@ornl.gov

R. Riesen
Intel Corporation, Hillsboro, OR, USA
e-mail: rolf.riesen@intel.com

© Springer Nature Singapore Pte Ltd. 2019
B. Gerofi et al. (eds.), *Operating Systems for Supercomputers
and High Performance Computing*, High-Performance Computing Series,
https://doi.org/10.1007/978-981-13-6624-6_3

3.1 Introduction

Several of the Operating Systems (OSs) described in this chapter have been used in production systems: The Sandia/University of New Mexico Operating System (SUN-MOS) on the Intel Paragon, Puma on the Intel Accelerated Strategic Computing Initiative (ASCI) option Red, and Catamount on Cray Red Storm . However, these systems are best understood in the context of the research programs they have enabled. SUNMOS, for example, was developed to enable experimentation with different styles of message passing prior to the wide adoption of the Message Passing Interface (MPI). The eventual deployment of SUNMOS on the Paragon was the result of a risk mitigation strategy when it became apparent that the vendor-supplied OS, Open Software Foundation Advanced Development (OSF/1 AD), could not scale to the size of the Paragon system being deployed at Sandia (over 1,800 compute nodes).

The systems covered in this chapter were developed in a collaboration between staff at Sandia National Laboratories and faculty and students at the University of New Mexico (UNM) starting in January of 1991. While groups at many other institutions have contributed to these systems (including Northwestern, Georgia Tech, MIT, University of Pittsburgh, Oak Ridge National Laboratory, and several vendors), the partnership between the University of New Mexico and Sandia remains at the core of this ongoing activity.

Where possible, we have emphasized the development of mechanisms that can be used to implement multiple policies. While there is a clear conceptual difference between mechanism and policy, the practical difference is frequently much less clear. For example, synchronous, two-sided communication may seem like the description of a mechanism. However, synchronous, two-sided communication can easily be implemented using asynchronous, one-sided communication primitives, but the converse is not true, leading us to conclude that the former embeds more policy than the latter. In this sense, the overarching philosophy underlying these systems is best summarized by this quote: *"Perfection is achieved, not when there is nothing more to add, but when there is nothing left to remove."*[1]

Our insistence on minimal features meant that we could more easily understand the impact that adding a new feature would have in terms of scalability and performance. Because we were focused on understanding performance and scalability and not on supporting a product, we engaged application developers as peers rather than customers, resulting in a co-design experience. Co-design is most apparent when something fails, e.g., when an application fails due to limitations in a critical resource-like communication end points. Production systems must adopt a philosophy in which "the customer is always right," avoiding failure whenever possible even when this results in an extremely inefficient use of resources. In environments where direct interaction with peers is possible and common, failures lead to conversations and opportunities to learn. In most instances, our goal was to expose these limitations as early as possible ("fail early; fail often").

---

[1] Antoine de Saint Exupéry, Wind, Sand, and Stars.

The following factors have influenced our approach to the design and development of Lightweight Kernels (LWKs):

Node Architecture: One of the key goals of any OS is to provide access to the computational, storage, and communication resources. In the early days, compute nodes were relatively simple, consisting of one or two processing cores, a simple memory system (including 1 or 2 levels of cache), and a network interface connected to a high-performance interconnect. Needless to say, this has changed significantly over the years, and these changes have affected our kernels.

Shared Services: Shared services, like a shared file system, present two challenges: authentication needed to enable access control, and a way to find the services. While the required authentication is most properly associated with the shared service, many OSs and shared servers blur this boundary (e.g., in Unix-based systems the concept of file and access control are fundamentally integrated into the OS). Our systems' architectures have included location services needed to find shared servers and other mechanisms needed to ensure that the needed authentication can be trusted.

Usage Model: High-Performance Computing (HPC) systems have, for the most part, adopted a simple resource management strategy based on a batch job queue with space-shared allocation of compute nodes. In this usage model, all of the resources on a compute node are allocated to a single application and, as such, there is no inherent competition for these resources. While this model has dominated HPC system for many years, there are indications that HPC systems may need to embrace other usage models and we have considered mechanisms to enable additional usage models.

Applications (Programming Models): OSs tend to provide support for a specific programming model. In essence, the programming model provides the context for how the resources of a compute node are presented to the application programmer. When we started the SUNMOS project, the essential programming model was based on distributed memory with explicit message passing between the processes in an application. As the two-sided communication primitives of MPI became the dominant message-passing library, our systems evolved to emphasize support for MPI, but were always based on one-sided, asynchronous primitives and we have continued to experiment with evolving programming models including MPI+X and MPI-everywhere. More recently, we have considered application coupling, in which independently developed applications are coupled together to address a bigger problem, as a metaprogramming model. Chapter 15 in this book explores this approach in greater depth.

History: The final factor that has driven our thinking is a bit more elusive than the factors we have considered to this point. Beyond the programming model, application developers frequently rely on a collection of tools and methods that are implicitly supported by the OS. In scientific computing, this has traditionally meant the need to support a Unix-like environment. Early efforts that used other environments, e.g., Windows-NT (New Technology), were not successful. Given the recent emphasis on data-driven science, we can expect that this will expand to include workflow systems.

The remainder of this chapter presents the series of OSs that we have developed in the past 25+ years, mostly in chronological order. As with any activity that spans multiple decades, there have been several digressions along the way. We have chosen to highlight the systems that we believe have had the most impact and have helped us understand the fundamental aspects of scalability.

3.2   SUNMOS

In the late 1980s, Sandia National Laboratories created the Massively Parallel Computing Research Laboratory (MPCRL), directed by Ed Barsis, to explore how massively parallel, distributed memory computing systems could be applied to critical problems in national security. Among the systems to support this research, the MPCRL had acquired an nCube 2 system with 1,024 processing nodes connected in a hypercube configuration. The nCube 2 system was hosted by a Sun workstation: users logged into the Sun workstation and launched jobs on the nCube using an application called "xnc" (eXecute on nCube) which monitored the application and provided standard I/O capabilities. The compute nodes on the nCube ran a minimal OS, called Vertex, that interacted with the Sun workstation and supported message passing between the compute nodes.

Several application developers in the MPCRL were experimenting with different message-passing semantics to improve application performance. This experimentation required changes to Vertex. Vertex was proprietary and written in assembly language, leading to relatively long turnaround times for the changes that were needed to complete this research. In January of 1991, a small team consisting of staff from Sandia and faculty and students from UNM set out to develop SUNMOS, a clone of Vertex, written in C, that could be used to facilitate the needed research. The first version of SUNMOS was completed by the summer of 1991 and we began to explore, in collaboration with the application developers, several enhancements to the message-passing library.

In retrospect, two of the message-passing features that we explored in SUNMOS on the nCube system stand out as worthy of discussion: multiplexed transmission for large messages and zero-copy transmission for pre-posted receives. The hypercube interconnection of the nCube meant that there were multiple, nonintersecting paths between any two nodes in the system. The individual links in the hypercube provided data transfer rates of 2.2 MB/s. By exploiting multiple paths, we were able to achieve bandwidths approaching 10 MB/s for large messages.

The nCube 2 had uncommon hardware features for systems at the time. There were 13 Direct Memory Access (DMA) engines that each could feed up to 16 kB of data into one of the hypercube links. Writing a device driver in a full-weight kernel to take advantage of this hardware would have been time-consuming and required multiplexing kernel expertise. In SUNMOS the task was relatively easy and accomplished by a graduate student unfamiliar with the inner workings of Unix, in a few months. Figures 3.1 and 3.2 show some early work we did in SUNMOS to accelerate disk I/O.

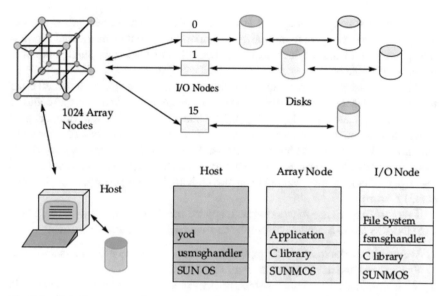

Fig. 3.1 nCube 2 system configuration using Sun/OS on the host and SUNMOS on the compute and I/O nodes

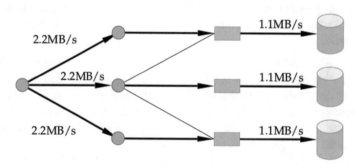

Fig. 3.2 Multiple channel usage on nCube 2

While the multiplexed transfer demonstrated our ability to experiment with message-passing implementations, the zero-copy message transmission had a much more significant impact on our thinking. Like most early message-passing systems, Vertex allocated a portion of system memory for incoming messages and copied the message body into application space when the matching receive was complete. In SUNMOS, applications could specify the buffer in application space where the message body would be deposited when it arrived; alternatively, SUNMOS could return a pointer to the location of the message body in system space. The first alternative avoided a memory copy when messages arrived after the matching receive was posted, and the second avoided a memory copy when the message arrived before the matching receive was posted. Avoiding memory copies had two advantages. First, this approach reduced the time (and improved the bandwidth) for message transfers by avoiding the copy from system space to application space. Second, it allowed the application developers to minimize the amount of system memory used for message passing, allowing the developer more control in managing the small amount of memory available on each node.

Working closely with application developers, we experimented with several other features in SUNMOS. An interesting one was a mechanism, diskmalloc, that could be used by an application developer to explicitly manage transfers to and from backing store, when their application was too large to fit into the memory available on a compute node. While we could have implemented a traditional, demand paged, virtual memory system, these enhancements would not have given application developers the degree of control they wanted to ensure high application performance (Womble et al. 1993a, b).

This early experience in working with application developers in the development of SUNMOS led to a design philosophy that we have maintained over time:

1. We would work closely with application/library developers to understand what they needed and develop mechanisms that they could use.
2. We maintained an absolute insistence on measurable performance. If a feature did not have demonstrated performance benefits on applications, it was not included in SUNMOS.
3. Whenever possible, we would leave the management of resources to the application/library developer, minimizing the policy decisions that had to be made in SUNMOS.

In January of 1992, the Sandia/UNM team started on the design of Puma, a next-generation OS that would build upon our experience of working with application/library developers in SUNMOS, adding important features (e.g., multitasking) that were missing in SUNMOS. Here, it should be noted that Puma was originally an acronym that encapsulated much of our design philosophy: Performance-oriented, user-managed, messaging architecture. While designing Puma, we continued to support SUNMOS for application development and in 1993; when Sandia needed to mitigate a risk related to the system software for the Intel Paragon, we chose SUNMOS over Puma because SUNMOS had been used in a more production-like environment.

In 1993, Sandia purchased a large Intel Paragon system with over 1,800 compute nodes. Like most large systems, the Intel Paragon was assembled in increments. Early in the assembly of this system, it became apparent that the vendor-supplied OS, OSF/1 AD, a Mach-based micro-kernel from the Open Software Foundation, would not easily scale to the size of the system being built at Sandia. The Intel developers only had access to a small system (16 nodes), and many of the mechanisms that worked flawlessly on small systems created serious problems on larger systems. For example, OSF/1 AD, launched an application by simply sending the page table for the application to all of the compute nodes; on the start of execution, each compute node would encounter an immediate page fault for the first page of the application executable. On a small system, this works fine; however, on a large system, the I/O system becomes saturated with individual (apparently unrelated) requests for the same collection of pages. In SUNMOS and Puma, we pushed the entire image to the compute nodes, using a fan-out collective operation, taking advantage of the fact that all compute nodes used by the same application had an image that was mostly identical.[2] Moreover, at 16 MB per compute node, memory was a scarce resource: SUNMOS required less than 256 kB, while OSF/1 AD consumed approximately 10 MB, leaving only 6 MB for the application.

On the nCube 2, the SUNMOS job launcher yod[3] ran on a front-end system. The Intel Paragon did not have a front-end system with user access. It was the first system where we partitioned nodes. The job launcher yod now ran in the service/login partition, while parallel applications ran in the compute partition.

SUNMOS on the Intel Paragon was a tremendous success (Bolen et al. 1995). Beyond Sandia, SUNMOS was used on over a dozen Intel Paragon systems worldwide. The basic communication mechanisms provided by SUNMOS proved to be very versatile. Libraries supported high-performance implementations of many other message-passing systems, including NX (Pierce 1994) (the native message-passing layer supported by Intel on the Paragon and the earlier iPSC/860; Cilk (the work stealing system developed at Massachusetts Institute of Technology (MIT)), Active Messages, and an early implementation of MPI.

While SUNMOS was largely successful, it had many limitations, some that we were working to address in Puma and others that we did not know how to address while ensuring scalability. An example of the latter was the inability to support dynamic libraries. SUNMOS did not include any mechanisms to support dynamic linking and including all of the libraries that might be used by an application would have exceeded the amount of memory available. Traditional, single-node systems address this difficulty by using dynamic linking; external libraries are only linked into the executable image when they are referenced during execution. While there was some demand to provide support for additional features, we did not have the resources needed to add these features and the potential list was very large. Ultimately, we viewed this as a case of diminishing returns: each additional feature required more effort to support and enabled a smaller number of applications. While we were not able to address the challenges associated with arbitrary programming systems in SUNMOS or Puma, we eventually settled on an approach based on virtualization that we would explore in the Kitten/Palacios systems.

Perhaps, the single most critical challenge that we faced in developing SUNMOS was the lack of drivers for specific hardware devices. Support from Intel was critical in getting SUNMOS to work effectively on the Paragon. Intel provided extensive documentation on their hardware and in several cases adapted hardware drivers so that it could be used in SUNMOS. One of the most impressive aspects of Linux and Microsoft Windows is their inclusion of drivers to support such a wide range of

---

[2]The developers of OSF/1 AD eventually developed the notion of "paging trees" where an intermediate compute node could supply a page that it already had, rather than forwarding the request to an I/O node. This had nearly the same performance of SUNMOS, but came long after SUNMOS was working effectively on the large system. From our perspective, it seemed unnecessary to require that the compute nodes to discover something that was known, for the sake of relying on a mechanism (demand paging) that was not clearly of benefit in this system.

[3]The name yod is a one-letter shift from xnc, the job launcher on the nCube 2.

hardware. As the dominant system at the time, Microsoft was able to define interfaces and demand that hardware vendors provide drivers for their hardware. Linux has addressed this challenge by a combination of voluntary support from vendors and an enormous community of developers who are willing to invest the time and effort needed to build the required software.

3.3   Puma

The successor to SUNMOS was Puma. This was a from-scratch design incorporating the lessons learned from SUNMOS. Figure 3.3 shows an architectural overview of Puma. It consists of the Quintessential Kernel (QK), the Process Control Thread (PCT), and the required libraries to run applications on Puma.

Most of the code in the QK and libraries implemented the Portals message-passing Application Programming Interface (API). Portals are described in Sect. 3.4. In this section, we concentrate on the remaining parts of Puma.

3.3.1   From SUNMOS to Puma

While SUNMOS had great performance and scalability, only very few applications ran on it. Due to the success of SUNMOS, there was interest in running other types of applications on its successor: "Database engines, video servers, and other applications, such as simulations of economic models, should run well under Puma." Due to the small memory footprint and deterministic performance, it was also desirable to explore the viability of supporting secure, real-time systems (Riesen et al. 1998, p. 15).

Expanding the application space was important, but the main design goal remained scalability on massively parallel machines. The QK had to be minimal to achieve the

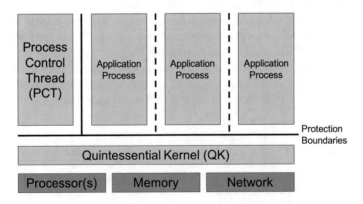

Fig. 3.3 Puma architecture diagram

performance goals of simplicity, low memory footprint, and high message-passing performance. The network interfaces at that time were primitive and required constant attention from the kernel to operate at peak.

SUNMOS was a monolithic code base that was difficult to adapt to new use cases, e.g., Split-C and Active Messages (Riesen et al. 1994). We did manage to port Split-C and Cilk (Blumofe et al. 1995) to SUNMOS, but each was a big effort, made the SUNMOS code more complicated, and made future porting efforts even more difficult. Therefore, the Puma design separates policy, mechanism, and message passing into clearly defined subsystems. The principle of separating mechanism and policy dates back to Hydra (Wulf et al. 1974) and Per Brinch Hansen's nucleus (Hansen 1970).

Another reason for the QK was to have a cleaner separation between the OS kernel and the message passing and device driver code. Moreover, MPI was evolving and we needed to be able to change the message-passing code without rewriting the OS kernel portion or the network driver every time the fledgling MPI standard changed.

3.3.2   Puma Architecture

By design, a QK does not support many of the features needed by the application types Puma was supposed to support. Therefore, we created the PCT. It set the policies for the compute node, and the QK implemented the mechanisms to enforce these policies. Our goal was to move as much functionality out of privileged kernel space into user space as possible.

The PCT was responsible for memory management and process control. It ran in user space, but had more privileges, in the form of QK services, than a regular application. Whenever we implemented a new service, we separated out the policy part, and only implemented the mechanisms needed to enforce these policies in the QK. During the design phase of Puma we anticipated many different PCTs, each written for a specific application domain and usage. The PCT was meant to make Puma flexible and adaptable. In the end, only one PCT was ever written.

Similar to SUNMOS before, the nodes of an Massively Parallel Processor (MPP) system running Puma were grouped into service, I/O, and compute partitions, see Fig. 3.4. The nodes in the service partition ran a full-featured host OS to enable users to log into the system, perform administrative tasks, and start parallel applications. In the case of the Intel Paragon, the Paragon OS, a variant of OSF/1 AD, authenticated users and provided fully distributed Unix services.

Nodes that had I/O devices such as disks attached to them were logically in the I/O partition. They were controlled by the host OS or Puma. The compute partition consisted of nodes dedicated to run parallel applications. A copy of the Puma QK and PCT ran on each node in the compute partition.

At the lowest level, Puma provided a send operation to transmit data to other nodes in the system, and Portals to receive messages. Portals let a user-level application

Fig. 3.4 Partitioning of a
system running Puma

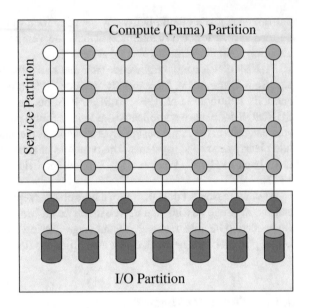

or library define the location, size, and structure of the memory used to receive
messages. Portals could specify matching criteria and the operation (read or write)
applied to the user memory. We discuss Portals in more detail in the next section.

3.3.3 Designing an OS for Massively Parallel Systems

At the time we started designing Puma, distributed (computing) systems had been
investigated for nearly two decades. Several research groups had been working on
distributed OSs that looked to its users like an ordinary centralized OS, but ran on
multiple, independent CPU cores (Tanenbaum and van Renesse 1985).

With the advent of MPP systems, it seemed straightforward to use the technology
developed for distributed systems and apply it to the latest generation of supercomputers. After all, the individual nodes of an MPP system are similar to workstations
lacking only an attached keyboard, monitor, and usually disk. Furthermore, many
MPP and large distributed systems were used to compute similar problems.

Attempts to treat an MPP system as if it were the same as a distributed system have
produced disappointing results. Performance had often not been as high as expected
and had been well below the limits imposed by the hardware.

There are fundamental differences in the structure, usage, and performance of
MPP and distributed systems. An OS for MPP machines has to take advantage of
these differences and provides a different set of services to the applications than an
OS designed for a distributed environment.

During the design of Puma, we spent considerable time and effort exploring and
defining these differences (Riesen et al. 1998). Looking back, the distributed systems
of the past have evolved into cloud computing, while high-end HPC systems, in our

opinion, still require a different type of OS to achieve the highest level of performance and scalability.

A distributed system has resources that become available at various times, while an MPP system is built to solve specific problems. Its size and configuration is a known quantity. Furthermore, MPP systems usually solve problems that are larger in problem size and parallelism, and use fine-grained parallelism.

While parallelism is higher, resource sharing is lower. Space sharing instead of time sharing is the norm in MPP systems. The network, including its bisection bandwidth and topology, is a crucial component and affects the performance of the system as much as processor and memory speeds.

3.3.4   Influence on the Design of Puma

The differences between distributed and MPP systems influenced the design of Puma.

Puma could multi-task applications on a node, but we anticipated that few high-performance applications would make use of this feature. A change in the PCT was needed to allow multitasking.

Puma provided much more Unix functionality than SUNMOS, but was not completely Unix compatible. (This was before Linux!) Some features were left out because they do not scale to thousands of nodes. Other features did not seem to be required by high-performance MPP applications. Many of the features left out for performance reasons are those dealing with direct user interactions or user management. User logins, password management, screen control, and keyboard or serial line protocols are examples of features left out of Puma.

Practically, all the services a Puma application could request were routed by the library and the QK into the service partition. The Puma libraries and PCTs were aware of what services were available and which nodes in the service partition provided them. This allowed us to streamline service requests. Arguments are marshaled up and the requests were sent into the service partition. There were no provisions in the kernel or the PCT to try to find the services locally. The reason we were able to simplify Puma's design in this manner was that message passing was fast and the compute nodes did not have any devices attached to them.

Puma did not provide demand paged virtual memory. Most MPP systems did not have a disk attached to each node. Therefore, paging would have been prohibitively expensive and would interfere with the activities of other nodes using the same network paths and disks. Well-designed applications can better determine which memory pages are not needed anymore. These pages can be filled with more data from disk. Taking advantage of high-performance I/O and network access is much more efficient than a general memory page replacement strategy implemented in the OS (Womble et al. 1993a, b).

Under Puma, an application could send messages to any other node in the system. The receiving kernel checked whether the destination portal existed and whether the sending process had the right to send to or receive from that portal. This improved send performance and required no state information on the sending node. For example, there was no complicated protocol to ensure that the receiving process will accept the message or that the receiving process even exists. Performing the few checks that are necessary to ensure integrity of the system could be done faster on the receive side because information about the sender (from the message header) and information about the receiver (from the process' control structures) was available to the kernel at the time it needed to make the decision where to put the message or whether to discard it. Eliminating message authentication is only possible if the network can be trusted.

Puma built on the assumption that the nodes were homogeneous. There were no provisions in the QK to handle byte swapping or to convert to other protocols. This lead to a very shallow protocol stack and allowed us to streamline message-passing operations. A homogeneous environment also allowed Puma to access unique resources, such as the additional CPU cores on each Intel Paragon node, efficiently. For dual-socket single-core per-socket nodes on the Paragon, it was possible under Puma to use the additional core either as a message co-processor or as a second compute processor. In the first case, the two cores exchanged information through a shared memory region. One of the cores was always in the kernel and handled the message passing. The other core remained at the user level and ran the application. In the second mode, both cores were at the user level running individual threads of the application. One of the cores trapped into the kernel to send and receive messages on behalf of both threads (Maccabe et al. 1996).

For each application, Puma built a node map that gave the application exact information about the location and distances of each node it was running on. This information is very important for applications that need to optimize their communication patterns. Puma was able to provide this information easily because the environment was static.

MPI was still being invented. We had a port of MPI over Portals, but supported several other message-passing APIs as well that were important for compatibility with other systems in operation at that time. However, it was not uncommon for application writers to have their own message-passing libraries specific to their application, and port them to the best available message-passing API available on a given machine. In the case of Puma, that was the Portals API.

3.4 Portals

Network performance is a critical aspect of any massively parallel distributed memory machine. Minimizing the cost of communication directly impacts the ability of an application to scale to the full size of the system. Much of the focus of Sandia/UNM LWKs has been on developing a scalable, high-performance, and flexible network communication programming interface called Portals (Brightwell et al. 2002). In this section, we describe the characteristics of the hardware environment and the LWK design that influenced the design and evolution of Portals.

3.4.1   MPP Network Hardware Influences

In early Sandia MPP systems, the Network Interface Controller (NIC) was directly attached to the memory bus in an effort to minimize the latency of inter-node data transfers. The OS was able to direct the flow of data into and out of the network in much the same way as it would manipulate processor registers. Unlike the systems that followed where the NIC was a separate piece of hardware attached via a relatively slow I/O bus, such as Peripheral Component Interconnect (PCI) or HyperTransport, having the NIC attached to the memory bus allowed for much more sophisticated methods of handling network transfers.

The NICs in these MPP systems were little more than Direct Memory Access (DMA) engines. The DMA engines were interrupt driven and asynchronous. An arriving header packet from the network would generate an interrupt that was serviced by the LWK. In the interrupt handler, the LWK would inspect the message header and determine where in memory to deposit the data. The LWK would then program the network registers appropriately, exit the interrupt handler, and continue running the interrupted application. An interrupt was also generated when the transfer of the incoming message had been completed. The LWK would run again and perform any operations associated with message completion. Sending a message involved a trap into the LWK, which would validate the destination information and the address of the memory to be sent, build a trusted message header, and then program the NIC. Sending a message was also asynchronous. The trap could return before the message was completely sent. An interrupt handler would increment a counter in the send descriptor to indicate completion of the send operation.

Unlike kernel-level network protocol stacks, where the OS manages a set of buffers that the NIC uses to move packets or messages to and from the network, which are then copied between user space and kernel space via system calls, user-level networks move data directly between user space and the network with no intermediate copies by the kernel. In early Sandia MPP systems, the bandwidth between main memory and the processor(s) was nearly identical to the bandwidth between nodes in the network. Any memory-to-memory copies would essentially cut the achievable network bandwidth in half.

An important characteristic of the network hardware in early Sandia MPP systems was that the network was circuit-switched using wormhole routing, which uses source routing rather than logical routing. When sending data from one node to another, the entire message was sent in one complete transfer. The initial header part of the message contained the route to the destination, and each network switch would inspect the incoming message to establish the path to the next switch or to the destination. The data would then flow as a single transfer from the source node through the switches to the destination node. The end of the message would essentially tear down the path through the network that the header had established. More modern networks are packet-switched, where individual messages are decomposed into packets that are then routed individually through the network. Modern network switches also use logical routing, where each individual switch examines the destination of an incoming packet and determines the path the packet should take, typically via a lookup table.

The network architecture of these early Sandia MPP systems influenced many of the design decisions of Sandia LWKs and the Portals network programming interface. For example, because the network hardware employed wormhole routing, if an incoming message arrived at a destination node, but the incoming message was not entirely consumed or drained from the network, then the tail of the message would not be able to tear down the path through the network that the header had established, potentially blocking a path through the network. Once a path through the network became blocked, it was likely that other messages trying to traverse a blocked path would also become blocked, leading to a completely blocked network. The only way to clear these blocked messages and reset the network was to reboot the entire machine. Since the OS was responsible for draining the network, a kernel panic on one node would likely cause the entire machine to go down. One advantage of the LWK architecture and implementation was that the QK could be made small and reliable. Limiting the amount of functionality in the OS and reducing the amount of code in LWK significantly increased the reliability of the system. An essential capability of the QK was to drain messages from the network to keep the network paths from being blocked. Even if the destination process had faulted or been killed, the network would still continue to function properly.

Since the network in the Sandia MPP systems used source routing, each node needed to contain, or be able to calculate, the route to every other node in the system. In order to send a message to a destination node, the only required information was the ID of the destination node and the ID of the destination process. As such, there was no fundamental need to perform address resolution or explicitly establish a connection with another process in order to communicate. And since all of the programming models that were targeted were fully connected (e.g., MPI_COMM_WORLD() allows implicitly for communication between any two MPI ranks), a connectionless model of communication was chosen.

3.4.2   LWK Design Influences

Several aspects of the design of the Sandia LWK are reflected in the design decisions and functionality of Portals.

Portals needed to be able to support multiple upper level protocols within an application. In addition to the need for communication between processes in the parallel application using MPI or NX, system calls and I/O were also implemented over the network. A remote procedure call (RPC) interface was used to implement a subset of Portable Operating System Interface for Unix (POSIX) system calls. An application system call was translated into an RPC to the yod process running on the service node. Yod would perform the actual system call and ship the results back to the application process as part of the RPC protocol. A similar approach was used for any file I/O. The application process would communicate with I/O servers in the I/O partition, and those servers would move data to or from the compute node over the network. Unlike Unix-based OSs that have native support for kernel-based protocols like Transmission Control Protocol/Internet Protocol (TCP/IP) and User Datagram Protocol/Internet Protocol (UDP/IP), the low-level network programming layer in the LWK needed to be able to support a myriad of network protocols.

Since it was necessary for an application process to communicate with I/O servers and yod, the network programming layer also needed to be able to support communication between arbitrary processes. It was not possible to restrict communication to only those processes launched as part of a parallel job, so the network programming interface needed to have an addressing and a trust model that would support sending to and receiving messages from any system or user process. Applications and services could explicitly choose the processes from which they could receive messages through the use of access control lists that could restrict incoming messages based on the source group or rank.

3.4.3 Portals Evolution

The Portals networking layer has evolved over several generations of programming interfaces, hardware, and systems. The first three versions (0–2) of the programming interface were designed for MPP systems running a Sandia LWK. Version 3.0 was the first interface that was aimed at systems composed of commodity computing and networking hardware running a general-purpose OS like Linux. The overarching goals and approaches of Portals are discussed below, followed by specific details on factors influencing successive versions of the implementations and interfaces.

The Portals network programming interface was designed to serve as protocol building blocks that could be used to build upper level protocols. One of the main concepts of Portals was to be able to assemble the fundamental building blocks to implement a variety of communication protocols. Over time, these building blocks have evolved based on the needs of the upper level protocols and the capabilities of the underlying network hardware.

Communication in Portals is one-sided, but unlike other one-sided interfaces where the origin process determines the memory to be accessed at the target process, Portals is receiver-based. For example, when writing to a remote process, the origin does not write to a specific virtual address or descriptor at the target. Instead, the origin provides information in the message that allows the target to determine where to place the incoming data. This approach allows for implementing both two-sided message-passing protocols as well as one-sided protocols using the same building blocks. The target can allow the origin to control the placement of data, but this option has to be explicitly enabled by the target. Other interfaces, such as the Verbs interface for InfiniBand, require two separate mechanisms, one each for two-sided (send/receive) and one-sided (Remote Direct Memory Access (RDMA) read/write) operations.

One of the most important capabilities for Portals was to provide scalable buffering for two-sided message-passing protocols. Portals building blocks were designed with functionality that did not require the amount of memory used for buffering unexpected messages to scale linearly with the number of communicating endpoints, nodes, or processes. Because early Sandia MPPs had a limited amount of memory, it was desirable to be able to use as little memory as possible to buffer incoming network messages. Portals building blocks were designed to allow for flexible buffering based on the communication requirements of the application.

Network progress is one of the fundamental issues that Portals has been used to explore. Portals was designed to provide a progress guarantee for upper level protocols, including MPI. For MPI point-to-point messages, if a matching receive has been pre-posted for an incoming message, the message will complete at both the sender and the receiver without any further calls into the MPI or Portals library. Very few high-performance networks have provided this capability. For most networks, it is necessary to make further library calls, enable a network progress thread, or dedicate host processor resources to continually check the network to make sure that operations complete. In effect, Portals assumes the existences of hardware on the NIC, or inside an interrupt handler, that can be used to ensure progress.

Closely associated with progress, Portals was designed to be able to maximize the overlap of computation and communication as well as the overlap of communication and communication. Providing a fully asynchronous model of communication with a strong progress guarantee provides the ability for an application to initiate a communication operation and perform computation while the communication progresses. Despite the fact that some systems are limited by memory bandwidth such that the computation and communication cannot be fully overlapped, it is nevertheless a highly desirable feature for many applications.

Another differentiating characteristic of Portals is that its primary role is not to serve as a network portability abstraction layer. While it can serve as such, it is primarily intended to be a vehicle for software/hardware co-design. Portals is intended to encapsulate the functionality that an HPC network should provide. Portals is not intended to be a software interface layered on top of multiple underlying networks, exposing a common set of capabilities. Rather, it is intended to help network hardware designers provide the semantics necessary to meet the demands of HPC applications and extreme-scale parallel computing systems.

3.5 Rise of Clusters

In the late 1980s and early 1990s, there were several vendors building and deploying distributed memory MPP systems. Most of the systems were composed of custom hardware—specialized processors optimized for floating-point performance or high-speed networks designed specifically for parallel processing. By the mid-1990s, the performance of commodity microprocessors began to approach that of more specialized processors used in HPC systems, and several MPP vendors began to transition to more mass-market chips. Intel used the Pentium Pro in ASCI Red as a follow-on to their i860-based Paragon system. Even Cray Research, which established the super-computing market with custom vector processors, opted for the Digital Equipment Corp. (DEC) Alpha processor in their initial MPP product, the T3D. As MPP systems based on commodity microprocessors began to increase in popularity, cluster sys-tems using commodity workstations or Personal Computers (PCs) began to emerge. The majority of these cluster systems also used commodity Ethernet hardware, but alternative gigabit network technologies, like Myrinet (Boden et al. 1995), began to be available as well.

By the late 1990s, it became difficult to distinguish between integrated MPP sys-tems and cluster systems based on Commodity Off-The-Shelf (COTS) hardware. One clear distinction between these systems was the software environment. Similar to early MPP systems, COTS clusters initially ran Unix-based workstation OSs with additional software that allowed the individual machines to work together. Eventu-ally, open-source Linux became the OS of choice for COTS clusters. By the end of the decade, the number of custom MPP systems was quickly dwindling, giving way to a plethora of new vendors offering integrated COTS cluster systems.

The evolution away from MPP systems to COTS clusters also impacted the evolu-tion of Sandia LWKs. Following the success of Puma/Cougar on ASCI Red, Sandia embarked on the Cplant (Brightwell et al. 2000) project in 1997, which was a COTS cluster based on DEC Alpha processors and Myrinet. The initial plan for the software environment was to port the Puma LWK and the rest of the system software developed for ASCI Red to this new system. Unfortunately, the COTS hardware environment turned out to be significantly more complex than that of custom MPP systems. For example, MPP systems were designed to network boot and had a minimal amount of hardware that needed to be initialized. In order to boot the nodes in the first Cplant cluster, each Basic Input Output System (BIOS) had to be reconfigured for network boot, each node board had to be rewired to always be on (otherwise the machine only came on when the power button was physically pushed), and the node would not function until the PCI bus infrastructure was enabled and necessary components on the bus were discovered and configured. The increased complexity made it signifi-cantly more difficult for a small team to port an LWK to COTS hardware. Instead, we decided to modify Linux to reflect as many of the important aspects of our LWKs as possible.

The Cplant project lasted through several generations of systems based on Alpha processors and Myrinet. Despite the fact that the compute nodes were running Linux, the software environment of Cplant machines resembled previous LWK environ-ments, providing the user community at Sandia a familiar environment in which to port and develop applications. Unlike previous MPP systems where the focus was largely on the compute node OS, Cplant required a significant amount of effort in more aspects of the system, including system administration, networking, and the parallel file system. Cplant was also being developed at a time when the pace of Linux development was relatively fast. It was increasingly difficult for a group of less than a dozen full-time researchers to develop, test, deploy, and support a custom cluster software environment, even when leveraging open-source software and a broadening cluster computing community. The last Cplant system was deployed in 2002.

3.6 LWK Interlude

In 2002, Sandia entered into a partnership with Cray, Inc., to develop Red Storm, which was an MPP composed of more than ten thousand Advanced Micro Devices, Inc. (AMD) Opteron processors connected by a custom high-performance network/router chip, called the SeaStar. Red Storm was similar in many ways to previous MPP systems from Intel. The requirements for the compute node OS for Red Storm were too stringent to be met by Linux, so Cray contracted Sandia to help with the port of the Cougar LWK to this new system. The majority of work in porting Cougar to the Opteron processor was enhancing the OS for 64-bit addressing. The SeaStar network was one of the first high-speed networks to take advantage of AMD'sHyperTransport interface. Cray also chose to adopt Sandia's Portals network programming layer for Red Storm, leveraging the much of the network software that had been developed for Cplant. The enhanced 64-bit LWK was dubbed Catamount. Since Cougar was highly tuned and very reliable production LWK for ASCI Red , there was a strong desire to minimize the amount of changes needed for Catamount. However, there was a significant amount of code cleanup, and several features of Cougar were stripped out of Catamount, including the ability to support the different modes for utilizing multiple processors. At the time Catamount was being developed, Cray did not foresee the need to support more than one processor per node. This decision proved problematic when dual-core Opteron processors became available within 2 years of the initial release of single-core processors, and quad-core processors followed the dual-core version in a similar time frame. Sandia eventually added support for multi-core processors to Catamount, including a novel memory-mapping technique that allowed processes on separate cores to easily read and write each other's memory (Brightwell et al. 2008).

Red Storm was the initial prototype for what became the Cray XT3 platform, which was released in 2004. The Cray XT4 followed in 2006, and both of these platforms continued to run Catamount as the vendor-supported compute node OS. In 2007, Cray released the XT5 system, which replaced Catamount with Cray's Compute Node Linux (CNL), which was a carefully tuned, limited functionality Linux kernel. Catamount on the Cray XT4 was the last Sandia LWK to run as a vendor-supported OS on large-scale production systems.

Cray's decision to move to Linux was motivated by several factors. Extensive performance comparisons between Catamount and CNL were inconclusive. While some applications were shown to perform and scale better using Catamount, other applications ran significantly faster with CNL (Hammond et al. 2010). With no clear performance advantage for an LWK—especially one that did not originate at Cray— the move to Linux was inevitable. Relatively little effort was expended to understand the application performance issues that arose between Catamount and CNL, but, with the dominance of Linux clusters in the community, many applications had been developed and tuned in a Linux environment.

As Linux was becoming ubiquitous in HPC, the demand for more system services and more Linux-like capabilities on large-scale parallel computing systems became overwhelming. Despite performance and scalability problems associated with running more full-featured general-purpose OSs, namely OS noise (Petrini et al. 2003), applications and application developers became willing to forego ultimate performance and scalability in favor of a more standard software environment across a variety of machines, from laptops to clusters to leadership-class systems. The Configurable OS project (Tournier et al. 2006) was a response to this demand. The main idea of this project was to modularize the system software environment so that the OS would contain only the features that the application desired. The project was able to provide the basic infrastructure to enable this capability by deconstructing Catamount, but it became apparent that the majority of applications either expected a full-featured OS environment or LWK environment. Very few applications existed in the intervening spectrum of functionality.

3.7 Kitten

After Cray and Sandia had partnered to develop Catamount for the Red Storm supercomputer and subsequent line of Cray XT systems, a number of challenges emerged. These included the following:

1. Catamount was not well-designed for multi- and many-core processors, which were the future path of the computing industry.
2. New multi-threaded programming models were rapidly emerging and research was needed to understand how to support these in a highly scalable LWK OS environment.
3. Users were expecting more functionality than could be reasonably provided by an LWK.
4. The code base was proprietary, closed-source, and had export control restrictions.

To address these challenges, a Sandia laboratory-directed R&D project was initiated in 2008 with the charter to (1) design and implement a next-generation LWK architected for multi-core processors from the ground up, and (2) explore ways to leverage commodity hardware support for virtualization, a hot industry trend, to address the functionality limitations of prior LWK designs. A key idea of the effort was to provide a streamlined LWK environment as the baseline case and to augment it with a lightweight hypervisor capability, enabling full-featured guest OSs to be loaded when required. This gave users' additional flexibility and the choice of runtime environment—highly scalable yet limited functionality LWK versus full-featured but less-efficient general-purpose OS supported by the hypervisor. The project eventually led to the development of the Kitten LWK and its integration with the Palacios hypervisor (Lange et al. 2010).

Figure 3.5 provides an overview of Kitten's architecture and its main capabilities. The two main components of Kitten—the kernel and `init` task—are shaded in gray in the figure and roughly correspond to the QK/PCT architecture described earlier in this chapter. The kernel presents a set of Application Programming Interface (APIs) to user space, including a set of Kitten-specific APIs that the `init` task uses to manage physical resources and set up new user space execution contexts, generically called tasks. These tasks can be native LWK processes and threads or guest virtual machine instances managed by Palacios. Palacios supports unmodified guest OSs and has been demonstrated to support tightly coupled HPC applications running at scale with near-native performance on Red Storm (Lange et al. 2011).

In order to accelerate development of Kitten, Linux source code was leveraged for nonperformance critical functionality such as bootstrap initialization, Nonuniform Memory Access (NUMA) topology detection, Advanced Configuration and Power Interface (ACPI), and PCI support. Performance critical components including physical memory management, virtual address space management, and task management were rewritten from scratch for Kitten. Importantly, these subsystems were designed to be NUMA aware and support large numbers of processor cores and memories, addressing a limitation of prior LWK designs. The largest system to date that Kitten has booted on is an Intel Knights Landing processor with 272 OS-visible processors and two NUMA memory domains.

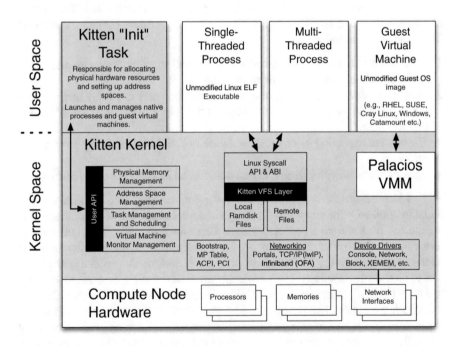

Fig. 3.5 High-level architecture of the Kitten LWK

Utilizing Linux code had the additional benefit that it becomes straightforward to adopt the Linux system call API and user space Application Binary Interface (ABI) for Kitten's native LWK environment. This enabled LWK executables to be built using standard Linux tool chains and, in particular, eliminated the need to develop custom LWK ports of compiler tool chains and system libraries such as libc, as was necessary for prior LWKs. This also meant that multi-threaded programming models such as POSIX Threads (Pthreads), Open Multi-Processing (OpenMP), High-Performance ParalleX (HPX), and other emerging runtime systems designed for Linux also ran on Kitten with little or no modification.

Kitten is open-source software distributed according to the General Public License (GPLv2) license and has been utilized by several research projects. Each of the challenges listed at the beginning of this section has been addressed by Kitten and it is now a modern stand-alone LWK implementation suitable for use on next-generation supercomputers. Chapter 15 describes how Kitten has been adapted by the Hobbes project into a multi-kernel architecture.

3.8 Lessons Learned

We have provided background information and our experiences over the last two and a half decades throughout this chapter. Here, we collect our insights in a more succinct manner.

- Minimality of system software is not an end goal for production systems, but there are times when minimality of system software is very important.

  - The reduced complexity of a minimal OS can be critical to conducting research on the structure of system software.
  - A minimal OS can provide a valuable baseline for more full-featured OSs to know what level of performance is achievable and help determine the source(s) of the gap.
  - When computing systems that have been undergoing rapid change begin to stabilize, system software developers have a better sense of how additional functions can be added (or not removed) with limited impact on overall system performance.

- Risk mitigation is important. Vendor software for leading-edge systems does not always work as planned out of the box.
- The OS plays a crucial role in message passing. Initially as the driver to move data efficiently, and, as NICs got smarter, by getting out of the way and reducing the amount of noise in the system.
- Co-design with application and runtime developers is essential.

  - The ability to understand *what* they wanted and needed to do, versus being handed requirements on *how* to they wanted to do it, improved the APIs, set expectations, and produced better OSs and applications/runtimes.

- In HPC, focusing on the P, i.e., performance, is essential to success.

  - A feature that does not demonstrably improve application performance needs to be left out.
  - Even features that may not negatively impact performance now may prove to be a hindrance in the future when adding other features or debugging performance issues.

- If at all possible, provide the ability for applications to manage resources directly. The application and library developers usually have insight into what resource management strategies will work best.

  - The increasing complexity of applications and systems has made this approach much more difficult. Applications are further removed from the kernel, and hardware is not only more complicated, but some components now have built-in adaptive management strategies that cannot be modified directly by software.

- There was only one device driver—for the NIC—in early systems, and it was simple.

  - Supporting additional and more complex drivers for modern devices and usage is very difficult.

- Willingness to start over, from scratch, opens the new design not only to lessons learned in the previous effort, but also frees the design team to incorporate new ideas.
- An MPP used for scientific simulations and numerical analysis is not the same as a distributed system.

  - The OS and system software need to be designed and written specifically for an MPP in order to get the highest possible performance.

- External, disruptive events, such as the advent of clusters and Linux, require flexibility.

  - Although we switched to Linux for our Cplant clusters, we tried as much as possible to incorporate our Puma and Portals design principles into the new software stack.
  - While not entirely successful, it taught us what parts were important and how to bring them forward to modern architectures.

- Learnings and experiences from the past are valuable but not always easy to apply to new trends.

  - Vocabulary changes as the decades pass by, the new generation of designers is no longer familiar with the struggles of the past and dismisses older work because it seems to no longer apply.
  - It is important for the "old guard" to translate old concepts and language and demonstrate their usefulness on modern architectures.

- Modularity is a nice concept, but it is rarely used.

  - Unless the OS team provides the necessary modules from the start, few application or runtime designers will write their own.
  - This is worse today as users have come to expect that "everything" is available on Linux.

- Large-scale testbed platforms are invaluable for system software research and development.

  - Much of the success of the Sandia OSs can be attributed to having access to extreme-scale platforms with the ability to easily change between OS environments.

Acknowledgements Stephen R. Wheat (Sandia) and Arthur B. Maccabe (UNM) founded the project in 1991. Soon, a host of others, often students, joined and began working on SUNMOS, designing Puma, and their successors over the years.

Some of the early key contributors in no particular order were Clint Kaul (the original implementer of SUNMOS), David van Dresser, T. Mack Stallcup (Intel), Lance Shuler, Ron Brightwell, Rolf Riesen, Kevin McCurley, Chu Jong, Gabi Istrail, Lee Ann Fisk, Trammel Hudson. (All Sandia, except where noted.)

In later years, Kevin Pedretti, Keith Underwood, Brian Barett, and Kurt Ferreira made significant contributions to Portals and later versions of our LWKs.

We also wish to acknowledge the help and ideas from the following people: Miguel Alvarez, Antoni Ferrara, Al Audete, Bob Benner, Steve Chapin, Kenneth Ingham, Betsy Matthews, J. Lance Mumma, Lisa Kennicott, Michael Levenhagen, Francisco Reverbel, Heather Richards, Brian Sanchez, Doug Sanchez, Judy Sturtevant, Bob van Sant, Jeff VanDyke.

Many of the people mentioned above started at UNM and subsequently went on to hold positions at Sandia.

References

Blumofe, R. D., Joerg, C. F., Kuszmaul, B. C., Leiserson, C. E., Randall, K. H., & Zhou, Y. (1995). Cilk: An efficient multithreaded runtime system. In *Proceedings of the Fifth ACM SIGPLAN Symposium on Principles and Practice of Parallel Programming, PPOPP '95* (pp. 207–216). New York, NY, USA: ACM.

Boden, N. J., Cohen, D., Felderman, R. E., Kulawik, A. E., Seitz, C. L., Seizovic, J. N., et al. (1995). Myrinet: A gigabit-per-second local area network. *IEEE Micro, 15*(1), 29–36.

Bolen, J., Davis, A., Dazey, B., Gupta, S., Henry, G., Robboy, D., et al. (1995). Massively parallel distributed computing. In *Proceedings of the Intel Supercomputer Users' Group. 1995 Annual North America Users' Conference.*

Brightwell, R., Fisk, L. A., Greenberg, D. S., Hudson, T., Levenhagen, M., Maccabe, A. B., et al. (2000). Massively parallel computing using commodity components. *Parallel Computing, 26*(2–3), 243–266.

Brightwell, R., Hudson, T., & Pedretti, K. (2008). SMARTMAP: Operating system support for efficient data sharing among processes on a multi-core processor. In *Proceedings of the International Conference for High Performance Computing, Networking, Storage, and Analysis (SC'08).*

Brightwell, R., Maccabe, A. B., & Riesen, R. (2002). Design and implementation of MPI on Portals 3.0. In D. Kranzlmüller, P. Kacsuk, J. Dongarra, & J. Volkert (Eds.), *Recent Advances in Parallel Virtual Machine and Message Passing Interface: 9th European PVM/MPI Users' Group Meeting, Linz, Austria, September 29–October 2, 2002. Proceedings* (Vol. 2474, pp. 331–340). Lecture Notes in Computer Science. Berlin: Springer.

Hammond, S., Mudalige, G., Smith, J. A., Davis, J. A., Jarvis, S., Holt, J., et al. (2010). To upgrade or not to upgrade? Catamount versus Cray Linux Environment. In *2010 IEEE International Symposium on Parallel Distributed Processing, Workshops and Phd Forum (IPDPSW)*.

Hansen, P. B. (1970). The nucleus of a multiprogramming system. *Communications of the ACM, 13*(4), 238–250.

Lange, J., Pedretti, K., Hudson, T., Dinda, P., Cui, Z., Xia, L., et al. (2010). Palacios and Kitten: New high performance operating systems for scalable virtualized and native supercomputing. In *Proceedings of the 2010 IEEE International Symposium on Parallel Distributed Processing (IPDPS)*.

Lange, J. R., Pedretti, K., Dinda, P., Bridges, P. G., Bae, C., Soltero, P., et al. (2011). Minimal-overhead virtualization of a large scale supercomputer. In *Proceedings of the 7th ACM SIG-PLAN/SIGOPS International Conference on Virtual Execution Environments (VEE)*.

Maccabe, A. B., Riesen, R., & van Dresser, D. W. (1996). Dynamic processor modes in Puma. *Bulletin of the Technical Committee on Operating Systems and Application Environments (TCOS), 8*(2), 4–12.

Petrini, F., Kerbyson, D. J., & Pakin, S. (2003). The case of the missing supercomputer performance: Achieving optimal performance on the 8,192 processors of ASCI Q. In *Proceedings of the 2003 ACM/IEEE conference on Supercomputing, SC '03*. New York, NY. USA: ACM.

Pierce, P. (1994). The NX message passing interface. *Parallel Computing, 20*(4), 463–480. Message Passing Interfaces.

Riesen, R., Brightwell, R., & Maccabe, A. B. (1998). Differences between distributed and parallel systems. Technical report SAND98-2221, Sandia National Laboratories.

Riesen, R., Maccabe, A. B., and Wheat, S. R. (1994). Active messages versus explicit message passing under SUNMOS. In *Proceedings of the Intel Supercomputer Users' Group. 1994 Annual North America Users' Conference* (pp. 297–303).

Tanenbaum, A. S., & van Renesse, R. (1985). Distributed operating systems. *ACM Computing Surveys, 17*(4), 419–470.

Tournier, J.-C., Bridges, P. G., Maccabe, A. B., Widener, P. M., Abudayyeh, Z., Brightwell, R., et al. (2006). Towards a framework for dedicated operating systems development in high-end computing. *Operating Systems Review: Special Issue on System Software for High-End Computing Systems, 40*(2), 16–21.

Womble, D., Greenberg, D., Wheat, S., & Riesen, R. (1993a). Beyond core: Making parallel computer I/O practical. In *DAGS'93 Proceedings*. (pp. 56–63).

Womble, D. E., Greenberg, D. S., Riesen, R. E., & Wheat, S. R. (1993b). Out of core, out of mind: Practical parallel I/O. In *Proceedings of the Scalable Libraries Conference* (pp. 10–16). Mississippi State University.

Wulf, W., Cohen, E., Corwin, W., Jones, A., Levin, R., Pierson, C., et al. (1974). HYDRA: The kernel of a multiprocessor operating system. *Communications of the ACM, 17*(6), 337–345.

Chapter 4
Hitachi HI-UX/MPP Series

Masaaki Shimizu

Abstract This chapter discusses the HI-UX/MPP Series architecture, developed by Hitachi for massively parallel supercomputers, including an implementation overview, improvements, positive and negative results, and lessons learned. HI-UX/MPP is composed of a Mach 3.0 microkernel (Mach) with the minimal functionality required to run applications, and an OSF/1 Unix server, which provides Unix functionality. HI-UX/MPP 02-00 for the SR2201 used a pure microkernel architecture, with compute nodes running only Mach due to small memory and processor resources. HI-UX/MPP 02-00 achieved operation of a 2,048-node computer as a single system, using a kernel with low OS noise and able to utilize computing resources efficiently. HI-UX/MPP 03-00 for the SR8000 improved Unix performance by placing Mach and an OSF/1 Unix server in the same address space and caching Unix functionality on compute nodes. It also reduced OS noise by using a dedicated OS processor. For the SR11000, AIX from IBM was used as the main OS, but a Hybrid OS was configured, with Mach implemented over AIX and running the HSFS distributed parallel files system from OSF/1 Unix. This showed that a specialized OS could be run over a general OS at low cost.

4.1 Introduction

When Hitachi transitioned from the S-3800 (Kitai et al. 1993) shared memory vector supercomputer to RISC processor-based supercomputers in the 1990s, it used a massively parallel distributed memory hardware configuration to build a system with several thousands of compute nodes. For the OS, a microkernel architecture was adopted and a minimal kernel for running applications was used on compute nodes, and a server providing Unix functionality was used on I/O nodes. For the SR2201, Unix functionality did not run on compute nodes, reducing OS noise, and for the SR8000, a dedicated OS processor was provided to reduce any effect of the OS on

M. Shimizu (✉)
Research & Development Group, Hitachi, Ltd., Tokyo, Japan
e-mail: shmz@acm.org

© Springer Nature Singapore Pte Ltd. 2019   47
B. Gerofi et al. (eds.), *Operating Systems for Supercomputers
and High Performance Computing*, High-Performance Computing Series,
https://doi.org/10.1007/978-981-13-6624-6_4

Table 4.1 OS structure for each generation of HI-UX/MPP

Machine generation	Year	OS generation	Processing nodes (Compute nodes)	I/O and SIOU nodes
SR2201 (CP-PACS)	1994	HI-UX/MPP 02-00	Mach 3.0	OSF/1 Unix Server
SR8000	1998	HI-UX/MPP 03-00	Mach 3.0 + OSF/1 Client Using dedicated OS Processor	OSF/1 Unix Server
SR11000	2003	AIX (or Linux) + HI-UX/MPP	AIX (or Linux) + Mach 3.0 emulation + OSF/1 File Server	AIX (or Linux) + Mach 3.0 emulation + OSF/1 File Server

application programs. For the SR11000 and later, due to increasing development costs, issues with distributed OS performance, increasing performance of general-purpose OSs, and increasing performance of memory, processors and other hardware, a hybrid OS with a lightweight kernel running on top of a general-purpose OS was used. An overview of OS structure for each generation of HI-UX/MPP is given in Table 4.1. HI-UX/MPP for the SR2201 is discussed in Sect. 4.2, HI-UX/MPP 03-00 for the SR8000 in Sect. 4.3, and the Hybrid OS for the SR11000 in Sect. 4.4. Finally, Sect. 4.5 discusses knowledge gained in the development of HI-UX/MPP and the effects it has on current OSs.

4.2   HI-UX/MPP 02-00 for SR2201(CP-PACS)

In June 1994, Hitachi announced the SR2001 (Fujii et al. 1997), RISC-based distributed memory massively parallel computer. This was followed by the SR2201 in July 1995. SR2201 was a commercialized version of CP-PACS (Boku et al. 1997), which was jointly developed by Tsukuba University and Hitachi. In the TOP500 rankings of supercomputers, the University of Tokyo's 1,024-node SR2201 ranked first in June 1996, and Tsukuba University's 2,048-node CP-PACS ranked first in November 1996. The Hitachi Massively Parallel Processor Operating System (HI-UX/MPP) was developed for these massively parallel computers. HI-UX/MPP is a parallel operating system based on the Open Software Foundation Microkernel—Advanced Development (OSF/1 AD)Release 1 microkernel architecture (The Open Group Consortium 2019; Rogado 1992; Zajcew et al. 1993). A feature of HI-UX/MPP is that functionality can be managed by a single OS, even on massively parallel configurations with many nodes using the microkernel. HI-UX/MPP 01-00 was developed first for the SR2001, and then enhanced to create HI-UX/MPP 02-00 for the SR2201. The rest of this section discusses mainly HI-UX/MPP 02-00 for the SR2201.

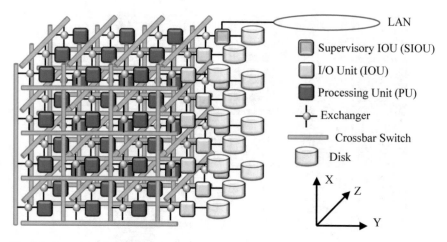

Fig. 4.1 Overview of SR2201 hardware

4.2.1   Hardware Background of SR2201

An overview of the SR2201 hardware configuration is shown in Fig. 4.1. It has Processing Units (PU) which are compute nodes, I/O Units (IOU) which are I/O nodes, and Supervisory I/O Units (SIOU) which have both system management and I/O functionality. These nodes are arranged in a three-dimensional mesh, each connected with a crossbar switch. The network is called the Hyper-Crossbar-Network(HXB). PU nodes consist of a 32-bit PA-RISC architecture *HARP-1E* Processor developed by Hitachi, a main memory control unit, a memory controller, DRAM, and an internode network interface. IOU and SIOU nodes have external interfaces such as SCSI, Ethernet, and RS232C in addition to the PU node components. The HARP-1E processor has a Pseudo-vector Processing (PVP) function that uses many registers as a sliding window to achieve main memory access performance comparable with vector processors. A system with 2,048 nodes using 150 MHz 300-MFlops processors had total system performance of 614.4 GFlops.

4.2.2   HI-UX/MPP 02-00

As mentioned earlier, HI-UX/MPP uses a microkernel architecture. It consists of a Mach 3.0 microkernel (Accetta et al. 1986) with the minimal functionality needed to run application programs, and an OSF/1 server providing Unix functionality. Mach runs on all nodes, and the OSF/1 server runs only on IOU and SIOU nodes. Mach abstracts the hardware resources on each node, and by having Mach handle communication on each node, resources on all nodes of the massively parallel computer can be accessed transparently. The OSF/1 server operates as a single Unix system,

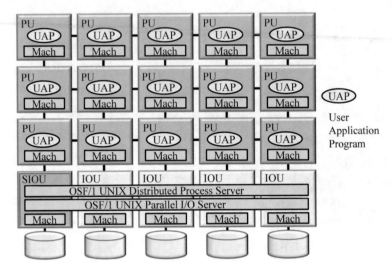

Fig. 4.2 HI-UX/MPP 02-00 architecture

even on the 2,048-node configuration, by using this Mach functionality. The device files on all nodes can be seen from any node, and processes on all 2,048 nodes are managed together. Distributed I/O using multiple I/O nodes is also integrated into the parallel-distributed file system, enabling shared access from any node. Rather than having OS configuration files and executable files on each node, there is just one set for the system. This greatly simplifies system installation, configuration changes, and operation. HI-UX/MPP also supports parallel program runtime environments, MPI, and batch job management systems as a standard feature. The structure of HI-UX/MPP 02-00 is shown in Fig. 4.2. Figure 4.3 illustrates execution of a process on a PU node from a login node (SIOU). The important elements of HI-UX/MPP 02-00 are discussed below, including the Mach microkernel, Mach IPC, and the OSF/1 Unix server.

4.2.2.1   Mach 3.0 Microkernel

The architecture of the Unix system based on Mach 3.0 is shown in Fig. 4.4. The Mach microkernel abstracts the hardware of compute nodes and provides lower level OS functions to higher level server software and applications. Specifically, it includes real memory management functions, device drivers, Mach message control functions, and mechanisms for task management and thread scheduling. In an ordinary Unix operating system, tasks are conceptualized as having a one-to-one correspondence with processes and are the basis for resource allocation. A task's resources include threads, virtual memory space, message ports, and exception vectors. The Mach microkernel interface employs a message interface called the Mach message (Mach

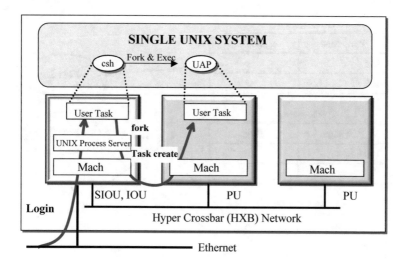

Fig. 4.3 Running a process on a PU from a login node

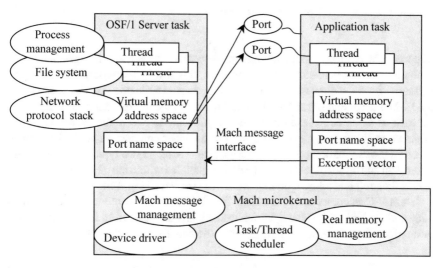

Fig. 4.4 Unix system architecture based on the Mach microkernel

IPC) interface. The abovementioned objects, including threads and memory, are manipulated by sending Mach messages specifying the port allocated to the object.

4.2.2.2 Mach IPC

Mach Inter-process Communication (IPC) provides a mechanism for sending messages inside a node and between different nodes. Messaging involves the concepts

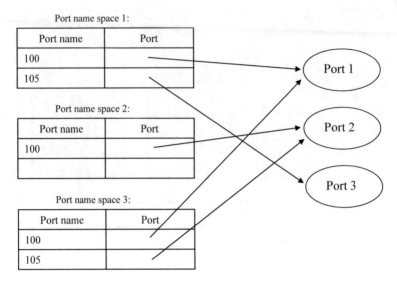

Fig. 4.5 Relationship between port names and ports

of ports, which are communication paths between objects and messages, which are sent and received between ports. In practice, this involves inserting and removing messages from the queue of a port inside the kernel. Port names are the names specified when accessing ports, and these are managed using different port namespaces for each Mach task. An example of the relationship between port names and ports is shown in Fig. 4.5. A message consists of a header and data payload. The header specifies the destination port and message size. There are two types of data payload: inline data and out-of-line data. Inline data is included within the payload. Out-of-line data is data referenced by a pointer within the message (Fig. 4.6).

Mach IPC is composed of a mechanism that provides communication within a node and the Norma IPC layer, which extends this mechanism so that it can be used in distributed environments. Norma IPC abstracts the ports and messages used in

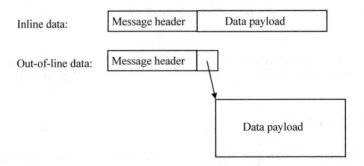

Fig. 4.6 Inline data and out-of-line data

Mach IPC to extend it to internode communication, while maintaining the semantics of intra-node Mach IPC Specifically, ports and Mach messages, which are only distinguishable within a node, are transformed into a network format that is unique throughout the system. Mach messages that have been converted into the network format are actually transmitted by KKT (Kernel-to-Kernel Transfer), which provides communication paths between the Mach kernels of different nodes.

4.2.2.3   OSF/1 Server

All Unix system calls issued by application programs are transferred to the OSF/1 Server for execution. The OSF/1 server creates and executes processes in the same way as an ordinary Unix, but is implemented using Mach microkernel interfaces such as task creation, memory allocation, and thread execution. Features of the HI-UX/MPP system OSF/1 server, designed for scientific computers, include a distributed process server and a distributed parallel file system.

Distributed Process Server

The OSF/1 server unifies management of processes on the entire system. In the initial version HI-UX/MPP 01-00 for the SR2001, the process server only ran on the SIOU nodes. With SR2201, the load of managing processes on several thousand nodes as well as the terminals of many logged in users became an issue, so from the beginning the system was divided into multiple subsystems to reduce the load. By dividing it into subsystems, each subsystem can have its own SIOU. This made management of operation little difficult, so later the process server was also distributed, making both SIOU nodes and the multiple IOU nodes distributed. Specifically, the mechanism decides the host IOU for each user that logs in.

Distributed Process Server

HI-UX/MPP uses Advanced Distributed File Server (ADFS) for the remote file system, making it possible to handle the distributed memory computer as a single system. Specifically, by overlaying a file system that integrates management of namespaces on the file systems of all shared nodes, ADFS creates a common, single-tree file system shared by all nodes. Parallel I/O functions are also supported by a file striping function, called Striping File Feature (SFF), which enables high-speed parallel I/O performance. An advantage of SFF is that it supports both block striping and file striping (Fig. 4.7).

   SFF block striping is a scheme where files are arranged in stripes on multiple disks in blocks of a specific size. This is effective for increasing I/O performance for large individual files. However, when applied to simultaneous I/O of large numbers of files, the data transfer requires random disk access and a large amount of communication between nodes, because each file is striped onto many different disks. This makes it difficult to achieve the best disk device performance or exploit the full benefits of multiple disk devices. For the simultaneous I/O of large numbers of files, it is more

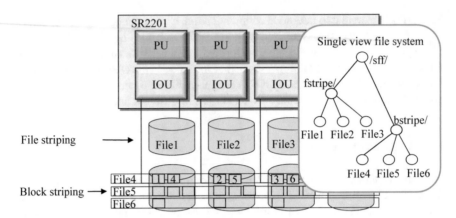

Fig. 4.7 Overview of the striping file feature

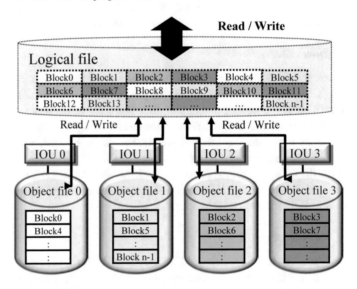

Fig. 4.8 Overview of SFF block striping

effective to use a file striping scheme where individual files are stored on the same disk. The striping scheme must be decided when the file system is configured, so it is important to consider operational design when setting up the file system.

The SFF striping function employs an object file system scheme for file striping. Specifically, the group of real files distributed on the disks at each node of the distributed file system is used as object files, and the user sees the set of object files as a single logical file. In block striping, a single logical file is striped across the object files of multiple nodes (Fig. 4.8), and in file striping, a single logical file corresponds to an object file at a particular node.

When seen from each node managing the object file system, the fact that each object file is a single real file inside the node produces better performance in an SFF file system with an object file system structure. The file I/O performance within a node can easily be optimized by employing measures such as disk block allocation and read-ahead/batch write functions. Also, scalability can be increased by making the performance of each node less dependent on the other nodes, so that each node can perform I/O operations independently. By optimizing the object file system structure and the file I/O performance at each node, we achieved both high single-disk performance and high-performance scalability for disks and nodes. Also, with the block striping and file striping functions, we achieved a combination of large individual file I/O performance and simultaneous I/O performance for large numbers of files.

4.2.3   Lessons Learned from HI-UX/MPP 02-00

Compared to today's standards (2018), the SR2201 processor performance was low and the main memory size of 256 MB was small. As such, a microkernel OS with the minimal functionality was used for compute nodes. This was also after the S-3800 single-node system, so we were pursuing the ideal of managing a massively parallel computer using a single OS. We review the past and state the advantages, disadvantages and lessons learned with respect to HI-UX/MPP 02-00.

Advantages

As mentioned earlier, advantages for a massively parallel computer include the small OS footprint on each compute node and the small amount of OS noise from daemons and other unneeded OS components. In terms of operability, being able to control all processes, files, and OS configuration settings from a single administration node was a great advantage. Also, having a single set of OS, command binary files and setting files for the system were a big advantage for installation and operation.

Disadvantages

The approach of distributing OS functionality over multiple nodes seems elegant from the perspective of OS design, but it had many issues with respect to performance and reliability.

Regarding performance, OS functionality was separated, and the use of Mach IPC for communication between objects within and between nodes introduced a large amount of overhead. Unix system calls also are usually completed with a single-system call in shared memory, but in HI-UX/MPP, several IPC calls to the Unix server on an external node were required, so latency was up to ten times that of Unix. For this reason, many techniques such as read-ahead and batch write were introduced to reduce latency for I/O and other system calls, and to increase throughput. When forking processes, Mach uses a copy-on-write mechanism, so initially only the address space is generated. When a page is touched later, a page fault occurs and the data is actually transferred. However, when parallel processes are forked on several thousand nodes simultaneously, there is a rush of page requests from the nodes, resulting in degradation of performance. This issue was resolved by introducing a mechanism that sent page contents to each node in a pipeline when starting the processes.

Regarding reliability, the entire system of thousands of nodes was run as a single OS, so a fault in a single node could bring down the whole system. Much study was devoted to isolating fault nodes, but it was extremely difficult to release resources from a fault node while it still had OS-internal locks and tokens.

Summary

HI-UX/MPP 02-00 for the SR2201 was a distributed OS with a simple structure, pursuing an ideal, but it had many issues in terms of performance and reliability. HI-UX/MPP 03-00 for the SR8000, discussed in the next section, implemented many improvements, particularly in terms of performance.

4.3   HI-UX/MPP 03-00 for SR8000

Hitachi developed the SR8000 (Tamaki et al. 1999) supercomputer, which integrated the systems of the S3800 vector computer series and the SR2201 massively parallel computer series, and it was announced in May 1998. The University of Tokyo's SR8000/128 ranked fourth in the TOP500 rankings of supercomputer performance in June 1999, and in June 2000, the SR8000-F1/112 at Leibniz Rechenzentrum in Germany ranked first in Europe, and the SR8000-F1/100 at the High Energy Accelerator Research Organization (KEK) ranked first in Japan. The SR8000/MPP at Tokyo University also ranked first in Japan in June 2001. It was used from March 2001 to March 2006 by the Japan Meteorological Agency for numerical weather prediction. HI-UX/MPP 03-00 was the OS used on the SR8000. It was developed based on OSF/1 AD release 2, and included improvements over HI-UX/MPP 02-00, which was used on the SR2201. Specific improvements to address performance issues relative to 02-00, which had a pure microkernel architecture, included placing Mach and the Unix server in the same address space to improve inter-OS communication performance, and caching Unix functionality on compute nodes to reduce the frequency of inter-OS communication. These performance measures could also increase OS noise, so a dedicated processor was added for the OS.

4.3.1   Hardware Background of SR8000

The SR8000 incorporated major changes relative to the SR2201. It adopted Simultaneous Multiprocessor (SMP) to increase compute node performance. Nodes incorporated eight compute processors and a single OS processor. The processor architecture was also changed from PA-RISC to PowerPC. This processor was developed

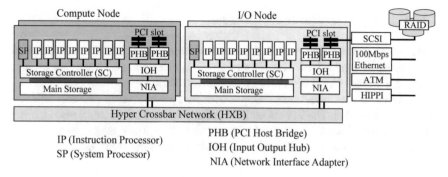

Fig. 4.9 Overview of SR8000 hardware

Table 4.2 Comparison of SR2201 and SR8000/MPP architecture

	SR2201	SR8000/MPP
Node configuration	Single Processor/node	8 IP (Compute Processor), 1 SP (OS Processor)
Processor performance	0.3 GFlops	1.8 GFlops
Node performance	0.3 GFlops	14.4 GFlops
Memory/node	0.25 GB (256 MB)	16 GB
Total number of processors	1,024	1,152
Total number of nodes	1,024	144
Internode network	Hyper-crossbar (3D)	Hyper-crossbar (3D)
Internode performance	0.3 GB/s (one-way)×2	1.6 GB/s (one-way)×2
Total system performance	307.2 GFlops	2,073.6 GFlop

at Hitachi and code-named *Griffin*. A 64-bit rather than 32-bit architecture was also used to support larger amounts of memory. The hyper-crossbar network was highly rated, so it was adopted with some improvements as the internode network interface. As with SR2201, compute nodes had no I/O other than the internode network, and only I/O nodes were connected to storage, external networks, and consoles. Figure 4.9 shows an overview of the SR8000 hardware architecture. A comparison of the architectures of the SR2201 and SR8000/MPP supplied to the University of Tokyo is also shown in Table 4.2.

4.3.2   HI-UX/MPP 03-00

With HI-UX/MPP 03-00, the base OS changed from OSF/1 AD release 1 to release 2 (AD2) (Roy et al. 1993), and changes were made to handle hardware changes and to increase performance. These changes are discussed below.

4.3.2.1 Support for Hardware Changes

The number of processors increased from one to nine, so many structures such as OS resource locks were added. Handling of physical memory and virtual storage also changed with the change of processor architecture from PA-RISC to PowerPC. OS-internal data structures had to be changed because PowerPC is big-endian, while PA-RISC is little-endian. The sizes of address variable types and structures also changed with the change from a 32-bit to a 64-bit address space. Thus, major changes in the hardware architecture necessitated review and testing of the entire OS.

4.3.2.2 Running a Unix Server in Mach Kernel Space

With SR2201, the OSF/1 Unix server ran as a single process in user space, just like user programs. Thus, communication between the Unix server and Mach kernel required page mapping and data copying to cross between the different memory spaces. With HI-UX/MPP 03-00 on the SR8000, the OSF/1 Unix server ran in kernel space, the same as the Mach kernel. This significantly reduced the overhead of calls between the Unix server and Mach.

4.3.2.3 Running a Unix Client (AD2 Client) on Compute Nodes

On SR2201, the OSF/1 Unix server ran only on I/O nodes and not on compute nodes. When an application on a compute node made a Unix system call, delegation software called *emulator* in the same application space forward the system call to the applicable Unix server node. In this way, system calls resulted in communication between nodes. With HI-UX/MPP 03-00 on the SR8000, the OSF/1 Unix process management function was divided into two layers: a Process Management Manager (PMM), which unified management of processes in the entire system, and Process Management Agents (PMA), which managed information specific to processes on a node. A PMA running on a compute node then cached system calls and minimized system call communication external to the node.

4.3.2.4 Distributed Caching

Similar to how OSF/1 server ran a PMA on compute nodes, the Advanced Distributed File Server (ADFS) file system also partitioned functionality into an ADFS server and ADFS clients, and operated with ADFS clients on compute nodes. The ADFS client could perform local caching of file data. The architecture of HI-UX/MPP 03-00 with the changes described above is shown in Fig. 4.10.

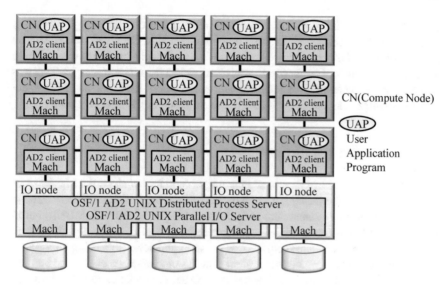

Fig. 4.10 HI-UX/MPP 03-00 architecture

4.3.2.5 Running SIMD-SMP

The SR8000 achieved compute performance increases through parallelization using multiple processors, and not incorporating a vector processor. To increase processor utilization, it introduced a gang scheduling function. With SIMD-SMP, for example, a program originally with a loop from 1 to 200 would be divided into 8 threads, each executing 25 loops, and each of these threads would be run simultaneously in parallel on 8 processors in the node, as shown in Fig. 4.11. Programs are partitioned and threaded automatically by a parallelizing compiler. For cases when multiple jobs can be executed simultaneously, changes were made to the OS scheduler to enable

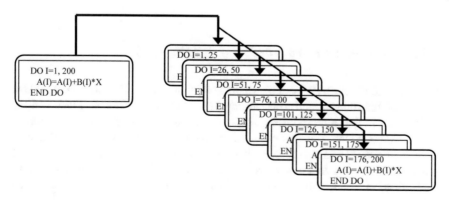

Fig. 4.11 SIMD-SMP parallel execution

such sets of programs to be run at the same time. This was called gang scheduling. Since some Unix server functions run on compute nodes, OS noise could occur on any of the processors performing SIMD-SMP. As such, while programs were running in SIMD-SMP mode, OS execution was restricted to the ninth processor. This was implemented by changing the interrupt vector on each of the processors. When not in SIMD-SMP mode, the OS was able to interrupt any of the nine processors.

4.3.2.6   Extended Storage (ES)

The SR2201 did not have an extended storage function, but since the SR8000 was also a successor to the S-3800, it implemented ES. In the S-3800, DRAM extended memory was used to complement main memory implemented with SRAM, but in the SR8000, ES was implemented as high-speed secondary storage. Specifically, at system startup, part of main memory was set apart and accessible using an S-3800-compatible API, like a simple file system. The ES on each node could also be used as a single, large, integrated, and shared ES. I/O between application programs and node ES were capable of 10 Gbyte/s transfers by having all processors participate in data copy operations. Disk equipment at the time of the SR8000 used the ultrawide SCSI standard, yielding 40 Mbyte/s per disk, so ES was very fast in comparison. ES was not cleared even through system restarts, so it was also used as temporary file storage and to pass data between jobs.

4.3.2.7   Other Improvements

Performance improvements were made to Norma IPC, which was used to implement distributed Mach IPC, to create Distributed IPC (DIPC). The Striping File Feature (SFF) was modified to support the ADFS client and increase performance, creating the Hitachi Striping File System (HSFS). Support for MPI-I/O was also added.

4.3.3   Lessons Learned from HI-UX/MPP 03-00

In contrast to the SR2201 ideal distributed OS architecture, HI-UX/MPP 03-00 for the SR8000 introduced performance improvements such as placing Mach and the Unix server in the same address space, and caching Unix functionality in compute nodes. However, some single-system functionality from the SR2201 era remained. New functionality was also tried, such as the ninth, OS-dedicated processor, and the processor scheduling function supporting the SIMD-SMP execution model. Advantages, disadvantages, and lessons learned with HI-UX/MPP 03-00 are discussed below.

Advantages

Inheriting from the SR2201, this system emphasized reducing OS noise and providing a single system. To reduce OS noise, a mechanism to isolate one processor for the OS was introduced, so that other parallel processors would not delay at synchronization in SMP configurations. The single-system functionality was also inherited from the SR2201. Specifically, only one set of OS configuration files, executable files, and user configuration files was used for the system, and individual nodes did not need to have their own copies. Processes on all nodes were also visible using commands such as PS, facilitating operation from a single administration node. Performance improvements over SR2201 were achieved by caching OS functionality in compute nodes and placing Mach and Unix in the same address space.

Disadvantages

Toward the end of the SR8000 era, PC clusters composed of workstations had begun to appear, and issues with TSS (Time Sharing System) performance, cost, and reliability remained. Even with HI-UX/MPP 03-00 for the SR8000, system calls that could not be handled locally in the node had latency up to ten times that of a single-node OS, due to the microkernel architecture. As such, it was weak when used like a workstation, with a general user logging into a terminal. Specifically, tasks generating many small I/O operations, such as compiling or file access, or that generated a ps command for the whole system, were slow.

    The cost of continually developing entire OSs for supercomputers that shipped only in limited numbers was also an issue. From a business perspective, supporting the latest OS technologies, processors, file system functions, and devices in the roughly 1,000K lines of source code was a major burden. Compared to a PC cluster with loosely coupled, independent workstations, a single system with several hundred tightly coupled nodes still had reliability issues in that all nodes could sometimes be brought down by a single faulty node.

Summary

Although HI-UX/MPP 03-00 for the SR8000 implemented many performance measures relative to the SR2201, considering PC cluster methods and the low development cost of PC clusters, it fell out of sync with developments in the industry.

4.4   Hybrid Kernel for SR11000

As a successor to the SR8000, Hitachi announced the SR11000 in May 2003. A 5.35-Tflops SR11000/J1 was delivered to the University of Tokyo in March 2005, and a 21.5 Tflops SR11000/K1 was delivered to the Japan Meteorological Agency in March 2006. The main OS for these was IBM AIX (International Business Machines Corporation), with a Hybrid kernel running some of the HI-UX/MPP functions on top of AIX Reasons that HI-UX/MMPP was not used overall included that the spread of PC clusters was increasing the need for interactive performance and the high OS processing latency of HI-UX/MPP was becoming an issue, and the increasing cost of maintaining a dedicated OS.

4.4.1 Hardware Background of SR11000

The SR11000 series used POWER4+, POWER5, and POWER5+ 64-bit PowerPC processors developed jointly with IBM. Instead of the pseudo-vector functionality in the SR8000, it incorporates an inter-processor high-speed barrier synchronization function proposed by Hitachi. The node architecture of the SR11000 was also a Hitachi design, and the system boards were manufactured by Hitachi. Within a node, 16 SMP processors were used, and a multistage crossbar network from IBM was used between nodes. As with the SR8000, it had both compute nodes and I/O nodes. An overview of the hardware architecture of the SR11000 is shown in Fig. 4.12.

4.4.2 SR11000 Operating System

Much discussion and evaluation in areas of development cost, performance, and reliability was involved in deciding the OS for the SR11000. HI-UX/MPP was actually ported to the POWER processor, and OS performance was evaluated. This yielded performance improvements of up to 1/5 in system call latency on a POWER proces-

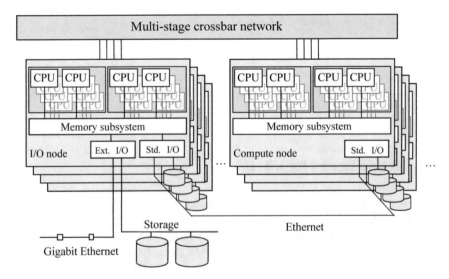

Fig. 4.12 Overview of SR11000 hardware

sor clocked similarly to the SR8000. This may have been due to the effectiveness of the POWER processor L2 cache on the relatively long HI-UX/MPP OS code. Ultimately, for reasons of development cost and time, IBM AIX was used. AIX ran independently on each node, so a cluster management middleware was used to manage multiple nodes. Several cluster management middleware packages, including CSM, LL, and PE, were used. Simple descriptions of each follow.

The Cluster System Management (CSM) software performs centralized management of multiple SR11000 nodes. This software executes remote management commands in parallel on each node. The Load Leveler (LL) is job management software. It manages the loads on all nodes and controls the assignment of jobs. It also provides functions for parallel computing, including functions for gang scheduling across nodes and checkpoint restart functions. The Parallel Environment (PE) provides an MPI library and an environment for compilation and execution of parallel programs.

To achieve high I/O performance within nodes and high overall I/O performance in a file system shared among nodes, HSFS (Shimizu et al. 2005, 2006) from the SR8000 was ported to the SR11000. However, since HSFS was highly dependent on Mach IPC, Mach was first ported to run on AIX to provide a base for running HSFS, which was the shared file service function of HI-UX/MPP. This is described in detail in the next section.

4.4.2.1 HI-UX/MPP on AIX

Even after deciding on AIX as the base OS for the SR11000, we studied whether a lightweight, low-cost port of HI-UX/MPP could be created to run on AIX or Linux. This was because we were considering the usefulness of the HI-UX/MPP single system, which was able to manage users and OS settings centrally. Specifically, it would involve implementing Mach kernel and OSF/1 Unix server functionality using AIX or Linux functions and resources. We concluded that a lightweight implementation would be possible since Mach IPC uses a general-purpose AIX/Linux Sockets, Mach task control could be mapped to AIX/Linux processes, and Mach device drivers could call AIX/Linux device drivers. By implementing Mach functionality on the cluster, OSF/1 Unix server functionality dependent on Mach could be implemented with almost no modifications. The AIX-based system architecture studied is shown in Fig. 4.13.

4.4.2.2 HSFS on AIX

Finally, only the HSFS distributed shared file system functionality was ported to AIX. Development cost, generality, and reliability were emphasized in this port. Regarding cost, the size of the HSFS source code, 162 K lines, was an issue. HSFS assumes the distributed OS functionality provided by Mach, so revising it for a cluster system would require redesign, reimplementation, and testing, which would be expensive.

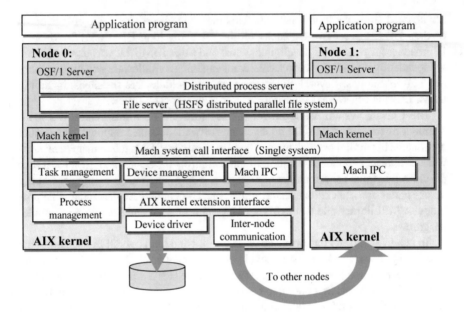

Fig. 4.13 Distributed OS functions on AIX cluster system

As such, we decided to implement the Mach kernel, upon which HSFS depends, and have HSFS use that Mach functionality, as indicated in Sect. 4.2.2.1. In this way, the HSFS part was completed with almost no changes. The Mach implementation was streamlined by calling the device drivers of the hosting AIX rather than having its own device drivers. As a result, the 706 K line Mach kernel was implemented over AIX with only 20 K lines. Regarding generality, HSFS was separated into a host OS- and processor-dependent part, and a nondependent part for this implementation. The dependent part was implemented as a wrapper layer, so that it could be used with multiple platforms beyond AIX, such as Linux or other business servers. Kernel extensions and kernel module functionality were used for the implementations over AIX and Linux. The implementation architecture is shown in Fig. 4.14. Implementation of the main functionality is described below.

Adding A Wrapper to OS-Dependent Components

We provided a layer to transform system calls and functions into an HI-UX/MPP interface incorporating the AIX-dependent include files. Components not dependent on the host OS were compiled using the original HI-UX/MPP including files. We also implemented endian conversion in this layer when this function was ported to x86 Linux.

Mach Memory Management

In Mach itself and in services that use Mach functions, memory is allocated and released by calling Mach memory management functions such as `kmem_alloc()` and

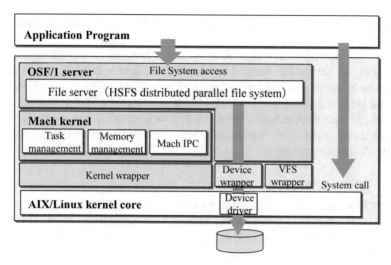

Fig. 4.14 Mach and HSFS on AIX

vm_alloc(). To ensure the API and memory management behavior are compatible with the Mach kernel, they are implemented by pre-allocating memory from the AIX heap and performing memory management independently.

Mach task management and thread management

Services that use Mach functions must be managed as Mach tasks. The HSFS service (described below) is also managed as a Mach task. Task resources are the Mach thread and port namespace. The Mach thread can be executed by establishing a one-to-one correspondence with AIX threads.

Mach IPC

As mentioned regarding HI-UX/MPP for SR2201 and SR8000, Mach IPC is divided into a mechanism that provides communication inside nodes, and a DIPC (Distributed IPC) layer that extends it for use in distributed environments. Mach messages are transmitted via DIPC between real nodes by KKT (kernel-to-kernel transfer), which provides a communication path between the Mach kernel of one node and the Mach kernel of another node. In the SR11000, the KKT layer must be implemented on AIX. The KKT interface to DIPC is used to ensure compatibility, while in our implementation we used sockets for communication with lower layers. In the multistage crossbar network of the SR11000, there are dedicated APIs besides sockets. Although these were advantageous in terms of performance, we chose a generic socket interface after considering the porting of distributed OS functions and HSFS to a Linux-based general-purpose PC cluster. In a PC cluster, it is possible to use sockets for a range of different network interfaces such as InfiniBand, 10 Gbit Ethernet and Myrinet. To reduce the overhead of TCP/IP and sockets, we used multiple socket streams to speed up the transmissions. Specifically, in out-of-line transmission, we opted for parallel transmission by providing a socket with 1 to 8 threads.

The implementation described above made it possible to use Mach functions that are highly compatible with HI-UX/MPP 03-00 for the SR8000 in AIX cluster system environments. We used these functions to implement HSFS. As with the Mach function components, we divided HSFS into components that are dependent on the host OS and components that are not dependent on the host OS, and we implemented the dependent components as wrapper layers. These include the VFS wrapper layer and the device wrapper layer.

VFS Wrapper Layer

The HSFS file system is registered in the OS via the VFS interface so that it can be made available to users. AIX is interfaced with VFS and HSFS by the VFS wrapper layer. Calls from AIX to VFS/VOP entry points are converted into calls to VFS/VOP entry points in the HSFS server core.

Device Wrapper Layer

This is the interface layer between the AIX device drivers and HSFS. I/O requests in the HSFS server core are converted into calls to AIX device driver routines. Also, I/O completion notifications from AIX device drivers are transformed into I/O completion processing in the HSFS server core via the I/O completion thread of the device wrapper layer.

HSFS Server Core

This is a ported version of the main file server code of HI-UX/MPP 03-00 and contains no platform-dependent code.

The above implementation made it possible to port the system to multiple platforms, including AIX, while minimizing modifications to the HSFS server core, which constitutes the bulk of the source code. The only modifications to the HSFS server core consisted of changing the source code to call each wrapper layer. After AIX, the file system was also ported to x86 Linux. The porting of HSFS was accomplished by providing a VFS wrapper and device wrappers.

As PC cluster supercomputers became more common, the need to address performance issues increased, and performance improvements to file creation, file deletion, and I/O for small units of data were made. Specifically, the ADFS, which is the remote file system, and SFF, which is the local file system, was causing many communication calls. It was therefore eliminated and communication between nodes was done directly using SFF. This implementation increased file creation performance by a factor of 10–1,000 instances per second.

Measures were also taken to ensure reliability on cluster systems, and usability on business servers, specifically, processes to switch metadata servers when an I/O node failed, and to close a file system client when a compute node failed, and I/O fencing functionality were implemented or improved.

4.4.2.3 HSFS on Linux

When implementing HSFS on AIX, the OS-dependent parts and OS-independent parts were implemented separately, which made porting to Linux easier. This port was made into a product and shipped in the Hitachi HA8000-tc/RS425, which is actually a PC cluster product. If high I/O performance is required, the SR11000 (HSFS server on AIX) can be used as the I/O server, and the HA8000 (HSFS client on Linux) can be used for compute nodes.

4.4.3 Lessons Learned from Hybrid Kernel for SR11000

For the SR11000, we moved to an AIX cluster system to reduce development costs. However, to utilize our HI-UX/MPP assets, we tried implementing the Mach kernel and HI-UX/MPP file system on AIX. We also made improvements to I/O performance for small units of data and to reliability, to meet PC cluster performance requirements. Advantages, disadvantages, and lessons learned with the Hybrid Kernel for SR11000 are discussed below.

Advantages

We were able to implement the HSFS distributed parallel file system at low cost on AIX clusters and PC clusters. To meet the needs of PC clusters, we improved performance for I/O in small units and for metadata, and implemented fault resistance to prevent loss of PC cluster benefits. As of 2018, the SR16000 or SR24000 also uses HSFS. In addition, HSFS is also being used with business servers in banks, Japanese government ministry, and television broadcasting companies.

Disadvantages

Because one OS was implemented on top of another OS, we had some difficulties with the behavior of AIX, which was the underlying OS. One specific issue we had with the HSFS functionality, which we wanted to execute with asynchronous multithreading, was that the AIX scheduler would not execute the threads immediately. We also did not implement all HI-UX/MPP functionality on a general-purpose OS due to development costs. Also, regarding HSFS, the Lustre (Cluster File Systems Incorporated 2002) OS-distributed parallel file system is used by many sites and has developed with the support of the community, so as a single company, developing and providing a proprietary file system has limitations.

Summary

By building a dedicated OS on top of a general OS, we were able to achieve both a low-cost dedicated OS and the innovation of the general OS. We also found that OSs should be used more proactively in the file system, such as using HSFS on Lustre.

4.5 Conclusion

We have discussed the architecture of the HI-UX/MPP series of operating systems used on the massively parallel computer systems built by Hitachi in the 1990s: the SR2001, SR2201, and SR8000; along with an overview of the implementations, improvements made with each generation, advantages, disadvantages, and lessons learned.

With HI-UX/MPP 02-00 for the SR2201, the performance of processors was low and the main memory of nodes was only 256 MB at the time. For this reason, a lightweight kernel (Mach microkernel) with minimal functionality was used as the compute node OS. It was also a successor to the S-3800 single-node system, so it provided single-system functionality, with a single OS managing a massively parallel computer. This had advantages in that the compute node OS consumed little memory and generated little OS noise, and only one set of OS binary, command, and configuration files were needed, making operation easier. Disadvantages included high latency for system calls to the Unix server, which was on a separate node, and issues with reliability due to running a single-system OS, because a fault on one node could bring down all nodes.

HI-UX/MPP 03-00 for the SR8000 introduced OS performance measures, including placing Mach and the Unix server in the same address space and caching Unix functionality on the compute nodes. Advantages retained from the SR2201 included low OS noise and providing a single system. To reduce OS noise, we implemented functionality to eliminate synchronization delays when processing OS interrupts while running parallel programs with SMP. Specifically, a ninth processor for the OS was added to the eight compute processors, and interrupts were handled by this ninth processor during parallel execution. This feature for maintaining synchronization of parallel programs is increasingly important in 2018, with the prevalence of multi-core and many-core processors. For example, an OS assistant core was used in the PRIMEHPC FX100 (Next Generation Technical Computing Unit Fujitsu Limited 2014) announced by Fujitsu in 2014. Disadvantages included system call latency, which was increasingly becoming an issue as PC clusters became common. In addition to batch performance, TSS performance became more important, as users logged in to use the system. The cost of continuing to develop dedicated OSs for products with low production rates was also becoming a burden.

For the SR11000 and later systems, we implemented Mach and the HSFS distributed parallel file system over general-purpose OSs, including AIX and Linux, calling functionality of those OSs. Advantages of adopting this dedicated OS over general OS structure included having dedicated OS functionality at low cost, while also gaining the innovation of the general OS.

The HI-UX/MPP project has had various influences on later operating systems. We developed a heterogeneity-aware cluster OS (Shimizu et al. 2008; Shimizu and Yonezawa 2010) as part of a national project in preparation to build the K computer (RIKEN Advanced Institute for Computational Science 2018). This work was based on distributed OS experience gained from SR2001 through SR11000.

The heterogeneity-aware cluster OS was also a forerunner of Mckernel (Shimosawa et al. 2014; Gerofi et al. 2016), which uses a multi-kernel scheme with x86 Linux on host nodes and a lightweight kernel on compute nodes that have different processors than the host. It was also a forerunner of SX-Aurora TSUBASA (NEC Corporation 2017) announced by NEC in 2017. Processors will likely continue to diversify according to application in the future, with GPUs, fat-core processors, and many-core processors. Rather than running the same OS on all of these processors, we expect the necessary OS functions will be run on the required processors, which is the essence of the distributed OS approach.

Acknowledgements The author would like to thank our Hitachi colleagues who provided the document, specifically Naonobu Sukegawa, Yoshiko Nagasaka, Toshiyuki Ukai, Masamichi Okajima, Kazumasa Tobe, Fujio Fujita, Tsuneo Iida, Masaaki Iwasaki, Yoshiko Yasuda, Hiroaki Fujii, Katsuyoshi Kitai, Yasushi Inagami, Kenichi Kasai.

References

Accetta, M. J., Baron, R. V., Bolosky, W. J., Golub, D. B., Rashid, R. F., Tevanian, A., et al. (1986). Mach: A new kernel foundation for UNIX development. In *Proceedings of the USENIX Summer Conference*.

Boku, T., Itakura, K., Nakamura, H., & Nakazawa, K. (1997). CP-PACS: A massively parallel processor for large scale scientific calculations. In *Proceedings of ACM 11th international conference on Supercomputing* (pp. 108–115). Vienna, Austria.

Cluster File Systems Incorporated (2002). Lustre: A scalable, high-performance file system. Technical report.

Fujii, H., Yasuda, Y., Akashi, H., Inagami, Y., Koga, M., Ishihara, O., et al. (1997). Architecture and performance of the Hitachi SR2201 massively parallel processor system. In *Proceedings of IEEE 11th International Symposium on Parallel Processing (IPPS97)* (pp. 233–241).

Gerofi, B., Takagi, M., Hori, A., Nakamura, G., Shirasawa, T., & Ishikawa, Y. (2016). On the scalability, performance isolation and device driver transparency of the IHK/McKernel hybrid lightweight kernel. In *2016 IEEE International Parallel and Distributed Processing Symposium (IPDPS)* (pp. 1041–1050).

International Business Machines Corporation. IBM power systems software - AIX: Overview. https://www.ibm.com/power/operating-systems/aix.

Kitai, K., Isobe, T., Tanaka, Y., Tamaki, Y., Fukagawa, M., Tanaka, T., et al. (1993). Parallel processing architecture for the Hitachi S-3800 shared-memory vector multiprocessor. In *ICS '93 Proceedings of the 7th International Conference on Supercomputing*.

NEC Corporation (2017). SX-Aurora TSUBASA. http://jpn.nec.com/hpc/sxauroratsubasa/index.html.

Next Generation Technical Computing Unit, Fujitsu Limited (2014). White paper, FUJITSU Supercomputer PRIMEHPC FX100 evolution to the next generation, 2014. https://www.fujitsu.com/global/Images/primehpc-fx100-hard-en.pdfl.

RIKEN Advanced Institute for Computational Science (2018). K Computer. http://www.aics.riken.jp/en/k-computer/about/.

Rogado, J. (1992). *A strawman proposal for the cluster project*. OSF Research Institute: Technical report.

Roy, P., Noveck, D., & Netterwala, D. (1993). *The file system architecture of OSF/1 AD Version 2*. OSF Research Institute, Cambridge, MA: Technical report.

Shimizu, M., & Yonezawa, A. (2010). Remote process execution and remote file I/O for hetero-geneous processors in cluster systems. In *Proceedings of 2010 10th IEEE/ACM International Conference on Cluster, Cloud and Grid Computing (CCGrid)* (pp. 145–154). Melbourne: VIC.

Shimizu, M., Ukai, T., Sanpei, H., Iida, T., & Fujita, F. (2005). HSFS: Hitachi striping file system for super technical server SR11000 (in Japanese). In *Forum on Information Technology (FIT2005) Letters*.

Shimizu, M., Tobe, K., Hitomi, Y., Ukai, T., Sanpei, H., Iida, T., et al. (2006). An implementation of single system functionality in the cluster environment (in Japanese). In *Proceedings of the 4th IPSJ Symposium on Advanced Computing Systems and Infrastructures (SACSIS 2006)* (Vol. 2006, No. 5, pp. 289–296).

Shimizu, M., Ogasawara, K., Funyu, M., & Yonezawa, A. (2008). Remote process management for the heterogeneous system (in Japanese). *Transactions of ACS, 49*(No. SIG2 (ACS21)):10–19.

Shimosawa, T., Gerofi, B., Takagi, M., Nakamura, G., Shirasawa, T., Saeki, Y., et al. (2014). Interface for Heterogeneous Kernels: A framework to enable hybrid OS designs targeting high performance computing on manycore architectures. In *21th International Conference on High Performance Computing* HiPC.

Tamaki, Y., Sukegawa, N., Ito, M., Tanaka, Y., Fukagawa, M., Sumimoto, T., et al. (1999). Node architecture and performance evaluation of the hitachi super technical server SR8000. In *Proceedings of 12th International Conference on Parallel and Distributed Computing Systems* (pp. 487–493).

The Open Group Consortium. Open software foundation. http://www.opengroup.org/.

Zajcew, R., Roy, P., Black, D., Peak, C., Guedes, P., Kemp, B., et al. (1993). An OSF/1 Unix for massively parallel multicomputers. In *Proceedings of the Winter 1993 USENIX Conference* (pp. 449–468).

Chapter 5
Blue Gene Line of LWKs

**Thomas Gooding, Bryan Rosenburg, Mark Giampapa,
Todd Inglett and Robert W. Wisniewski**

Abstract The following chapter covers the design and implementation of the lightweight kernels in the Blue Gene family of supercomputers. This lightweight kernel, known as Compute Node Kernel (CNK), provides a high-degree Linux compatibility and supports many Linux-like system calls and a familiar application environment. File and socket I/O is provided by function shipping those system calls to a process running on a Linux-based I/O node.

5.1 Introduction

The primary goal of the Blue Gene family of supercomputers was to achieve high aggregate performance utilizing many low-power purpose-built processors to achieve. The largest production deployment was at Lawrence Livermore National Labs (LLNL) in 2012 and contained 98,304 Blue Gene/Q compute nodes with 1,671,168 processor cores. Each processor core was 4-way SMT capable, for up to 6,684,672 hardware threads. It was the number one computer on the TOP500 list in June 2012.

T. Gooding (✉)
IBM, Rochester, MN, USA
e-mail: tgooding@us.ibm.com

B. Rosenburg
IBM, Yorktown Heights, Yorktown Heights, NY, USA
e-mail: rosnbrg@us.ibm.com

M. Giampapa · R. W. Wisniewski
Worked on while at IBM, New York, USA
e-mail: giampapa@us.ibm.com

R. W. Wisniewski
e-mail: bobww123@gmail.com

T. Inglett
Worked on while at IBM, Rochester, MN, USA
e-mail: tinglett@gmail.com

© Springer Nature Singapore Pte Ltd. 2019
B. Gerofi et al. (eds.), *Operating Systems for Supercomputers
and High Performance Computing*, High-Performance Computing Series,
https://doi.org/10.1007/978-981-13-6624-6_5

Table 5.1 Overview of Blue Gene family

Name	Year	CPU	Bits	Nodes	Cores	HWT	Tasks/Node	Tflops
BG/L	2004	PowerPC 440	32-bit	106,496	2	1	2	596.0
BG/S	2005	PowerPC 440	32-bit	128	2	1	2	0.7
BG/P	2007	PowerPC 450	32-bit	40,960	4	1	4	557.0
BG/Q	2011	POWER/A2	64-bit	122,880	17	4	64	20,132.0

As discussed below, this scale presented several challenges regarding scaling, reliability, and failure reporting. The compute node hardware also contained several specialized units designed for high-performance computing applications, e.g., specialized cache prefetch controls, transactional memory, speculative execution, and user-mode low-latency access to the network.

There were two approaches to get software to scale well to large supercomputers. It is possible to start with an existing software base, analyze its scalability bottlenecks, fix them, and iterate. Alternatively, a new code base can be designed from the beginning to scale to large numbers of nodes. This was the approach for the original kernel on Blue Gene/L. The compute node kernels in Blue Gene/P and, ultimately, Blue Gene/Q, provided more functionality (python, threading) while maintaining the scaling philosophy and requirements. Blue Gene/Q's Compute Node Kernel (CNK) dispelled the notion that a lightweight kernel must be lightweight on functionality.

In June 2007 Blue Gene/P became available. The CNK running on BG/P, is consistent in design philosophy with BG/L's kernel. It is lightweight, very low noise, designed to scale to hundreds of thousands of nodes, and continues to provide performance reproducibility. In June 2012, Blue Gene/Q was introduced and continued the design pattern using CNK on the compute nodes and off-loading I/O to I/O nodes. For both BG/P, and BG/Q, we leveraged open source software to provide a large range of POSIX semantics and a familiar Linux programming environment. In addition to leveraging open source software, much of the software stack is itself open source, see Fig. 5.1.

At the start of the Blue Gene program, there were concerns expressed about the Lightweight Kernel (LWK) approach centered on the (lack of) completeness of a Linux environment. We found different reasons why a Linux environment was viewed positively. Ordered by decreasing requirements these include:

1. Desire to run standard applications out-of-the-box;
2. Ability to work in an open source environment and leverage the pool of people familiar with the Linux model;
3. Desire for a familiar runtime environment: pthreads, libc, etc.;
4. Ability to make standard POSIX system calls.

We will denote providing a standard Linux code base running on a compute node with all functionality allowing applications to run out-of-the-box, as a Full-Weight Kernel (FWK) approach. A common distinguishing characteristic of LWKs is that

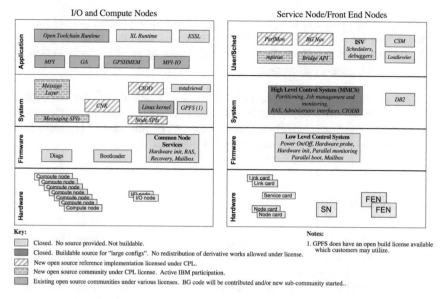

Fig. 5.1 Blue Gene/P open source software stack

they set up resources that are then passed to the application to use directly, while FWKs tend to maintain ownership. Although Linux provides advantages, from a research perspective it does not allow as much flexibility or ease of exploration. Thus, for researchers wanting to explore the effects of different kernel policies on HPC applications, CNK provides a more easily modifiable base. Further, the Linux community has not eagerly embraced HPC patches, while they fit well into CNK. The downside of exploring HPC innovations in an LWK is that all applications may not run out-of-the-box, and thus it may be more difficult understanding the benefits of an idea on a particular application of interest. In addition to the research advantages of being unencumbered by the Linux model and weight, an LWK approach offers other advantages:

- High performance: the focus of an LWK is on performance. System design involves trade-offs. LWKs tend to choose the high-performance path, while FWKs tend to focus on generality.
- Low noise and performance stability: an LWK approach provides a low-noise environment with stable application performance facilitating optimization.
- Ability to work with partial or broken hardware: bringing up a new chip is challenging. For supercomputer vendors who innovate with hardware, a simple small kernel to bring up a new chip offers a more controllable environment, allows quick work-arounds to hardware bugs, and facilitates testing.
- Reproducibility: related to the previous item, CNK provides a cycle-by-cycle reproducible environment critical to debugging within a chip and diagnosing problems across 100,000s of nodes.

- Ability to customize to unique hardware features and system software requirements: An LWK is nimble, allowing it to be easily modified to leverage unique hardware for HPC applications, and to provide customized features for the system software to increase performance.

We chose to continue the LWK approach on each generation of Blue Gene supercomputers. We do, however, recognize the value of having a Linux-like environment. By leveraging open source software components, CNK provides a Linux-like environment while maintaining the above LWK advantages.

5.2 CNK Design

As described in the introduction, keeping CNK small and lightweight offers advantages. However, a trend in HPC applications over the last decade has been toward more complex applications requiring more functionality from the operating system environment. As Linux has gained broader acceptance in the HPC space, more applications are written assuming a Linux environment. To combine the objectives of a lightweight kernel, more functionality, and a Linux environment, we leveraged components from the open source community such as libc, pthreads, etc., and layered them on top of CNK. Although work was needed to provide this integration, it was not significantly more than providing our own proprietary limited-functionality libraries, threading, etc. Once we provided the base layer of support for Linux packages in CNK, additional Linux functionality was also available. A downside of leveraging Linux is that when it changes, the code leveraging it needs to be modified as well. A tight intertwining could lead to substantial work. For CNK, we took libc and above and not the kernel code and below. The one advantage of drawing the line between libc and the kernel is that that interface tends to be more stable, while internal kernel interfaces tend to be more fluid. In this section, we describe the three key areas of support, namely, file I/O, runtime environment, including threading and dynamic linking, and memory management that are part of CNK's base layer of support (Fig. 5.2).

5.2.1 CNK Interactions with the I/O Node

In previous work (Giampapa et al. 2010), we described how we achieved I/O scalability on Blue Gene/L. At a high level, this I/O node structure exists on all Blue Gene systems. Essentially, by off-loading I/O, we perform aggregation allowing a manageable number of file system clients and reduce the noise on the compute nodes.

On BG/P, on the I/O nodes, we shifted to creating a dedicated I/O proxy process for each MPI process, and each thread within the MPI process has a dedicated thread within the I/O proxy process. This allowed CNK's file system to be stateless, with file system state (e.g., current working directory, file offsets) kept on the I/O node

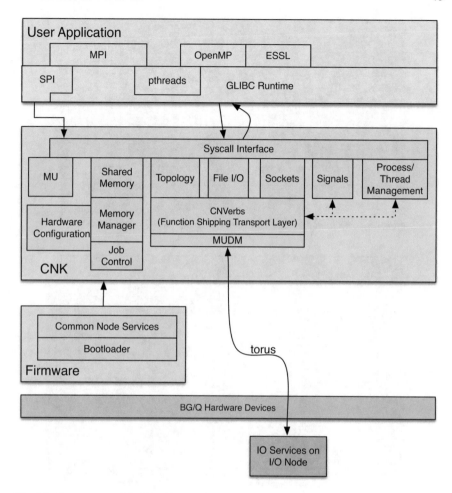

Fig. 5.2 Components of the Blue Gene/Q CNK kernel

side. This design was not particularly well-suited for Blue Gene/Q, which could have 64 hardware threads, 5 software threads per hardware thread, 4 MiB buffers, and a supported compute-to-ionode ratio of up to 256:1. The ionode would have needed 320 GiB of memory for the interface alone.

Instead, Blue Gene/Q merged the concepts between BG/L and BG/P. There was one sysiod process per compute node which handled file I/O operations. itself trackedCNK file system state and translated file descriptors into the handles returned by sysiod (Fig. 5.3).

When an application makes a system call that performs I/O, CNK marshals the parameters into a message and functionships that request to the sysiod process running on an I/O node. For example, a write system call sends a message containing the file descriptor number, length of the buffer, and the buffer data. The sysiod

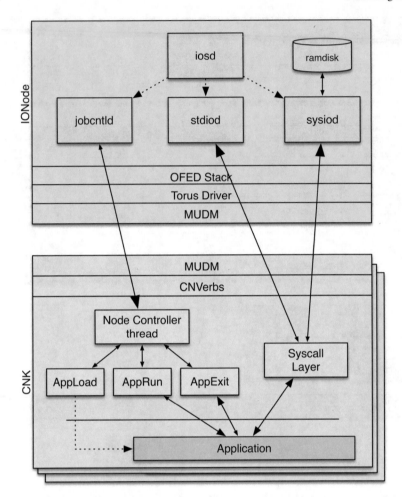

Fig. 5.3 Components of the Blue Gene/Q CNK kernel

process receives and decodes the message, de-marshals the arguments, and performs the system call that was requested by the compute node process. When the system call completes, the results are marshaled and sent back to the compute node that originated the request.

For file I/O operations that require state, such as the open and stat system calls, CNK sends the current working directory and sysiod uses *openat* or statat system calls instead. This way, the sysiod process does not need to change directories or track the current directory for each call.

Another challenge on Blue Gene/Q was the torus messaging hardware featured RDMA (Remote Direct Memory Access) send and receives to the I/O node, which was not available on earlier Blue Gene hardware for the I/O node. To utilize this, we created a Linux device driver and a Message Unit Data Moved library (MUDM).

MUDM was shared between Linux and CNK and provided a common transport layer. On the Linux side, the device driver connected MUDM with the OFED software stack. The `sysiod` process would register memory and perform OFED verbs. CNK implemented only a subset of the verbs necessary to establish connections and send/receive RDMA packets. File I/O on CNK was able to perform read/write operations directly from user memory as the torus hardware did not have page alignment restrictions.

From the Linux kernel perspective, the ioproxies perform standard I/O operations, e.g., a file system operation from CNK behaves as if it was performed from Linux (although the blocking of data is different due to the collective network and Compute I/O Daemon (CIOD) protocol). The calls produce the same result codes, network file system nuances, etc. Additionally, file systems that are installed on the I/O nodes (such as NFS, Spectrum Scale, PVFS, Lustre) are available to CNK processes via the ioproxy. Thus, in a lightweight and low-noise manner, CNK can provide the full suite of I/O system calls available to Linux.

Our experiences with the I/O offload strategy, and in particular the 1-to-1 mapping of ioproxies to Compute Node (CN) processes have been positive. The amount of code required in CNK to implement the offload is minimal, and running Linux allows us to easily inherit the POSIX semantics.

5.2.2 CNK Runtime Support

BG/L had a customized version of libc toolchain to accommodate system call limitations. Although libc was mostly unmodified, it proved to be difficult to manage and support. In reviewing the value, we assessed that the customization only saved a little complexity in the CNK system calls. Therefore, on BG/P and BG/Q we made it a design objective to keep libc unmodified. The goal was to unify the toolchains between a standard Linux software stack and the CNK software stack, resulting in less maintenance and better testing coverage.

5.2.3 Threading Support

We examined what it would take to use the NPTL (Native POSIX Thread Library) threading package in libc on CNK. An investigation showed it required only a small number of system calls beyond our current set. A subset of both *clone* and set tid address were needed for thread creation (e.g., pthread create). For atomic operations, such as pthread mutex, a full implementation of FUTEX was needed. For thread signaling and cancelation, we needed to implement sigaction. Although we probably could have had a basic custom threading package implemented sooner, by leveraging NPTL, CNK provides a full-featured pthread package that is well understood by application developers.

This path was not without concerns. One was that Linux uses *clone* support for both thread and process creation. We analyzed the libc code and determined that libc uses the *clone* system call with a static set of flags. The flags to *clone* are validated against the expected flags, but we did not need to reference the flags elsewhere in the kernel. Other parameters to *clone* included the child's stack and thread local storage pointers, as well as the child–parent thread IDs. The libc library performs a *uname* system call to determine the kernel capabilities so we set CNK's version field in *uname* to 2.6.19.2 to indicate to libc that we have the proper support. For stack creation, libc uses standard `malloc()` calls to allocate the storage. Many stack allocations exceed 1 MB, invoking the *mmap* system call as opposed to *brk*. However, CNK supports both *brk* and *mmap*, so this is not an issue.

One of the simplifications we made to the threading support was in the thread scheduler. Unlike Linux and other full-featured kernels, CNK provides a simple non-preemptive scheduler, with a small fixed number of threads per core.

5.2.4 Dynamic Linking Support

Starting with BG/P, CNK added support for Python. Although Python is an interpreted language, it can be extended via libraries. Traditionally, those libraries are demand-loaded through dynamic libraries. One option to provide dynamic linking was to merge the application's dynamic libraries outside of the compute nodes as an additional step in job launch. This would have been simple, but may not have been practical because `dlopen()`-type functionality would be needed. Another option was to support the ld.so dynamic linker from libc or implement a dynamic linker similar to it. Similar to our analysis of NPTL, we determined that ld.so did not need many system calls in order to achieve functionality, and again by going this path we provided a more standard and well-understood solution. Concretely, ld.so needed to statically load at a fixed virtual address that was not equal to the initial virtual addresses of the application, and ld.so needed MAP COPY support from the *mmap* system call.

One of the simplifications we made was that a mapped file would always load the full library into memory, rather than page-faulting many small pages across the network. We also decided not to honor page permission settings, i.e., read, write, or execute, on the dynamic library's text/read-only data. For example, applications could therefore unintentionally modify their text or read-only data. This was a conscious design decision consistent with the lightweight philosophy. Providing this permission support would have required dynamic page misses and faulting pages from across networked storage. This would have significantly increased complexity of the kernel and introduced noise. By loading the entire library into memory at load time, this OS noise is contained in application startup or use of dlopen and can be coordinated between nodes by the application.

5.2.5 Memory Management

Most operating systems maintain logical page tables and allow for translation misses to fill in the hardware page tables as necessary. This general solution allows for page faults, a fine granularity of permission control, and sharing of data. There are, however, costs to this approach. For example, there is a performance penalty associated with the translation miss. Further, translation misses do not necessarily occur at the same time on all nodes, and become another contributor of OS noise. Another complication arises from the power-efficient network hardware that does not implement sophisticated page translation facilities.

To meet performance and simplicity goals, CNK implements a memory translation mapping that is static for the duration of the process. A process can query the static map during initialization and reference it during runtime without having to coordinate with CNK. In order to keep the mapping simple, CNK implements the following four address ranges that are contiguous in physical memory: (1) text (and read-only data) (.text, .rodata), (2) data (globals) (.bss, .data), (3) heap and stack, and (4) shared memory (Fig. 5.4).

When an application is loaded, the ELF (Executable and Linkable Format) section information of the application indicates the location and size of the text and data segments. The numbers of processes per node and size of the shared memory region are specified by the user. This information is passed into a partitioning algorithm, which tiles the virtual and physical memory and generates a static mapping that makes effective use of the different hardware page sizes (1, 16 MB, and 1 GB) and that respects hardware alignment constraints. Blue Gene/Q also had a feature of the translation lookaside buffers (TLB) to exclude bytes at the beginning of the TLB.

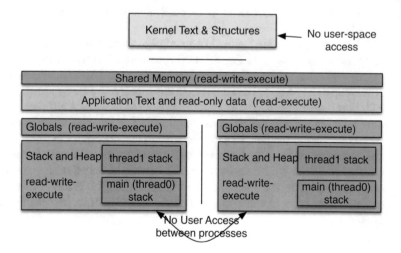

Fig. 5.4 CNK memory layout

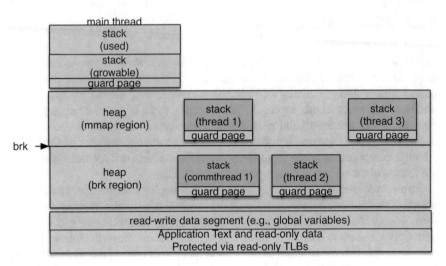

Fig. 5.5 Memory protection

This proved extremely useful in creating a static TLB mapping with limited page sizes without illegal range overlaps.

During application execution, memory may be allocated via the standard *brk* and *mmap* system calls. The *mmap* system call tracks which memory ranges have been allocated. It also coalesces memory when buffers are freed, or permissions on those buffers change. However, since CNK statically maps memory, the *mmap* system call does not need to perform any adjustments, or handle page faults. It merely provides free addresses to the application. With this strategy, libc could be enhanced to perform all of the memory management in user space, but that would have led to a customized version of libc.

A useful memory protection feature is a guard page to prevent stack storage from descending into heap storage, see Fig. 5.5. CNK provides this functionality by using the Blue Gene/Q Debug Address Compare (DAC) registers and Blue Gene/Q used the memory wakeup unit to detect. The guard range is determined by the application. The libc NPTL library performs a *mprotect* system call prior to the *clone*. CNK remembers the last mprotect range and makes an assumption during the *clone* syscall that the last mprotect applies to the new thread. The guard page covering the main thread is special. It resides on the heap boundary and a memory allocation performed by another thread could move the heap boundary. That newly allocated storage could be legitimately referenced by the main thread. So when the heap boundary is extended, CNK issues an inter-processor interrupt to the main thread in order to reposition the guard area.

5.2.6 17th Core on Blue Gene/Q

The Blue Gene/Q node has 17 A2 cores. As most HPC applications partition by a power-of-2, CNK offloaded all of its job, network, RAS (Reliability, Availability, and Serviceability) functionality onto that 17th core. Cores 0–15 were dedicated to the application, and core 16 was assigned to CNK. Within core 16, CNK further divided roles on hardware thread number. Hardware threads 0 and 1 were assigned to application agents. Hardware thread 2 was dedicated to job management. Hardware thread 3 was dedicated to the RDMA network driver (MUDM). An application agent was a very small executable that was implicitly loaded with the application. We only defined one application agent in the Blue Gene program, which was an agent to manage torus congestion at scale.

5.3 Emerging Technologies

5.3.1 Transactional Memory and Speculative Execution Support

The Blue Gene/Q chip was the first shipping processor with transactional memorysupport. Transactional memory allows the application to perform work on shared data structures in memory without a classic FUTEX lock. It accomplishes this with a special feature of the BG/Q L2 controller which keeps track of the memory version currently operating on each of the hardware threads. Once the thread has exited the section of code, it attempts to commit its memory version to a nonspeculative state. If there are conflicts, the application must retry the memory updates. Speculative execution takes a similar approach but for OpenMP-style applications. The important difference with speculative execution is that the program execution order must be strictly maintained.

When a segmentation violation occurs during execution, the CNK signal handlers would check speculation state. If in speculation mode, it would rollback the transaction and notify the Transaction Memory(TM) or Speculative Execution (SE) runtime via signal handler.

There were several scenarios that required special decision logic that determined which conflicting thread (if any) would retain its speculative state. As a design decision, we did not want to create additional complexity by creating a speculative stack frame for signal handlers to runtime. Fortunately, there was enough L2 register information and runtime expectations that we were able to place the decision logic in the kernel. The kernel would only signal to the user application after it revoked speculative thread state.

5.3.2   Resiliency

The Blue Gene/Q hardware was developed with very robust error reporting. A common source of errors is external to the SoC, such as the memory, although hardware machine-check processor errors were reported through a mechanism external to the kernel. Most error conditions needed to be reported by the processor itself by posting RAS events to a small boot EDRAM (Embedded DRAM) "mailbox" location that was accessible through JTAG (IEEE 2013) by the control system.

5.3.3   Stateless Threads

Blue Gene/P introduced the notion of a commThread, which is a very lightweight stateless thread. When the thread entered this state, it would issue a stateless non-portable *sched_yield* system call. This would skip the saving of general-purpose, floating-point, and vector registers to thread state. When the thread became runnable, it would also be able to skip the restoration of the register states. Normally, the thread would be waiting for an event from the hardware.

5.3.4   Persistent Memory

Data management is becoming increasingly important to HPC applications as the relative cost of storage bandwidth to flops increases. A standard HPC data model is for an application to start with a clean memory slate, load the data from disk, perform computation, and store the data to disk. For consecutive applications accessing the same data, this can add unnecessary overhead. To address this challenge, on BG/P, we developed a feature that allows an application to tag memory as persistent. When the next job is started, memory tagged as persistent is preserved, assuming the correct privileges. The application specifies the persistent memory by name, in a manner similar to the standard shm *open*/*mmap* methods. One important feature for persistent memory is that the virtual addresses used by the first application are preserved during the run of the second application. Thus, the persistent memory region can contain linked-list-style pointer structures. The persistent memory could also be used by an application in a manner similar to ramfs offered by Linux.

5.4   Using CNK for SOC Chip Design and Bringup

The development of microprocessors typically requires many test cases that can run in thousands of cycles. Accurate software simulators of an Verilog/VHDL design operate around 7 orders of magnitude slower than native hardware.

The Blue Gene family of supercomputers utilizes System-On-a-Chip (SOC) technology. SOC has reliability advantages and enables performance, cost, and packaging optimizations, but comes with some challenges. We found it valuable to employ a lightweight kernel approach so that CNK could participate actively in the Blue Gene chip architecture, design and analysis process, and the logic verification and debug process. To be engaged in these early stages, CNK was designed to be functional without requiring the entire chip logic to be working. The startup and runtime configuration of CNK contains independent control flags and configuration parameters that support it running even when many features of the hardware did not exist (during design) or were broken (during chip bringup). Computational kernels of important applications were extracted and executed in simulation, enabling performance measurements on a wide range of configurations even before major units of the chip were in place. As an example, the BG/P memory system contains L2 Cache configuration parameters that control the mapping of physical memory to cache controllers and to memory banks within the cache. CNK enabled application kernels to be run with varied mappings of code and data memory traffic to the L2 cache banks, allowing measurement of cache effects, and optimizing the memory system hierarchy to minimize conflicts. Sensitivities of applications to cache sizes and prefetching algorithms were measured. Using these controls also enabled verification of the logic, and measurement of performance, in the presence of artificially created conflicts.

A key feature of CNK is the ability to provide perfect, cycle-by-cycle, reproducibility on hardware of test cases and application codes. Reproducibility enables debugging the hardware via logic scans, which are destructive to the chip state. This technique requires performing logic scans on successive runs, each scan taken one cycle later than on the previous run. The scans are assembled into a logic waveform display that spans hundreds or thousands of cycles, enabling logic designers to see events leading up to the problem under investigation.

CNK support for reproducibility requires that the kernel be able to tolerate a chip reset at any point, and be able to restart identically from that state each time. The only persistent state that exists in a BG/P chip is located in DRAM during Self-Refresh. CNK prepares for full reset by performing a barrier over all cores, rendezvousing all cores in the Boot SRAM, flushing all levels of cache to DDR, placing the DDR in self-refresh, and finally toggling reset to all functional units, which causes the chip to boot. Upon boot, CNK checks if it has been restarted in reproducible mode, and if so, rather than interacting with the service node, initializes all functional units on the chip and takes the DDR out of self-refresh. Following those steps, CNK runs through its initial startup sequence to reinitialize all critical memory contents. The number of cycles that CNK can run in reproducible mode is bounded only by the point at which external I/O becomes necessarily.

BG/P and BG/Q provided Clock Stop hardware that assists the kernel in stopping on specific cycles. A challenge with this hardware is that it only supports a single chip, and thus debugging a communication bug that spans multiple chips is difficult. To overcome this problem, the CNK reboot process was modified to use the BG/P Global Barrier network to coordinate reboots across multiple chips. Across these reboots intended to be multi-chip reproducible, the barrier network was set to remain active and configured, but special code ensured a consistent state in all arbiters and state machines involved in the barrier network hardware. This allowed one chip to initiate a packet transfer on exactly the same cycle relative to the other chip that was used to capture logic scans.

There are many bugs encountered when bringing up a new chip. As an example, we describe a bug where the above capabilities proved immensely helpful. In one area of the chip, there was a borderline timing bug whose manifestation was dependent both on manufacturing variability and on local temperature variations or electrical noise during execution. The bug thus did not occur on every chip, nor did it occur on every run on a chip that had the potential to exhibit the problem. Consistent re-creation of the problem therefore proved elusive, and its nature prevented recreating it in simulation. One piece of evidence that lead to the bug being tracked down was waveforms (hardware traces) gathered on reproducible runs across multiple chips, and using those to determine characteristics of a chip at the point it diverged from the expected cycle-reproducible run.

Another important aspect of a lightweight approach manifests itself during chip design. During chip design, the VHDL cycle-accurate simulator runs at 10 Hz. In such an environment, CNK boots in a couple of hours, while Linux takes weeks. Even stripped down, Linux takes days to boot, making it difficult to run verification tests. The examples in this section illustrate the advantages we garnered with CNK's reproducibility; these would be more difficult to achieve with non-lightweight approaches.

5.5 Properties of CNK

In this section, we provide the performance results of our CNK design. In particular, we present results demonstrating that CNK yields very low noise, describes a set of applications that run on CNK unmodified demonstrating Linux compatibility|, and describes the high performance achieved through CNK's design by the messaging layers, and we finish by showing the performance stability of CNK on sample applications. Throughout the section, we describe the features of CNK that would be more challenging on an FWK.

5.5.1 Low Noise

OS jitter or noise in a large parallel system is magnified when an application synchronizes across a large number of nodes. Delays incurred by the application at random times each cause a delay in an operation, and at large scale many nodes compound the delay causing a noticeable performance impact (Petrini et al. 2003). There has been a lot of work on understanding noise, and more recent characterizations (Ferreira et al. 2008) have described the salient characteristics of noise that affect applications performance. Potential techniques to address this problem are (1) coordinate the delays so they are not compounded by scale, or (2) eliminate the delays. There are limits to how effective the former is, and its effectiveness is also application dependent. CNK takes the latter approach.

One way to measure the noise of a kernel is performed by the FWQ (Fixed Work Quanta) benchmark (Lawrence Livermore National Laboratory 2019). This is a single-node benchmark, i.e., no network communication, that measures a fixed loop of work that, without noise, should take the same time to execute for each iteration. The configuration we used for CNK included 12,000 timed samples of a DAXPY (double precision ax + y linear algebra routine) on a 256 element vector that fits in L1 cache. The DAXPY operation was repeated 256 times to provide work that consumes approximately 0.0008 s (658 k cycles) for each sample on a BG/P core. This is performed in parallel by a thread on each of the four cores of a Blue Gene/P node. Ideally, all iterations would take the same number of cycles at the minimum value of 658,958. The node was running Linux based on SUSE kernel version 2.6.16. Efforts were made to reduce noise on Linux; all processes were suspended except for `init`, a single shell, the FWQ benchmark, and various kernel daemons that cannot be suspended. The minimum time on any core for any iteration was 658,958 processor cycles. This value was achieved both on Linux and on CNK. We were able to demonstrate the low noise achievable with an LWK strategy. The maximum variation is less than 0.006. For Linux, the maximum cycle time varied by 38,076 cycles on core 0, 10,194 cycles on core 1,42,000 cycles on core 2 and 36,470 cycles on core 3. This is variation is greater than 5% on cores 0, 2, and 3.

The impact of noise reduction on application performance is not necessarily a linear mapping. Small amount of noise may not affect behavior, while moderate amounts may have an additive impact. Other work (Ferreira et al. 2008) has done a good job characterizing the impact of noise on application performance.

5.5.2 *Functionality*

One indication of CNK functionality is the applications it supports. OpenMP-based benchmarks such as AMG (Henson and Yang 2002), IRS (Lawrence Livermore National Laboratory 2003a), and SPhot (Lawrence Livermore National Laboratory 2001) run threaded on CNK without modification. The UMT (Lawrence Livermore National Lab 2017) benchmark also runs without modification, and it is driven by a Python script, which uses dynamic linking. UMT also uses OpenMP threads. Flash (Rosner et al. 2000), MILC (NERSC 2013), CPS, LAMMPS (Plimpton 1995), Chroma, NEK, GTC, DOCK5/6, QBOX, MGDC, RXFF, GMD, DNS3D, HYPO4D, PLB, and CACTUS (Goodale et al. 2003) are known to scale on CNK to more than 130,000 cores. Additional functionality for unique hardware features was demonstrated in an earlier version of CNK to support the 2007 Gordon Bell Prize for Kelvin–Helmholtz instability in molten metals (Glosli et al. 2007). CNK was able to handle L1 parity errors by signaling the application with the error to allow the application to perform recovery without need for heavy I/O-bound checkpoint/restart cycles.

5.5.3 Achieving High-Performance System Software

Another important metric is how well and with how much effort other system software can achieve high performance. A key performance area for HPC software is messaging performance. Some applications are latency sensitive due to a reliance on many short messages, while others' performance depends on achieving high bandwidth. The Blue Gene DCMF (Deep Computing Messaging Framework) relies on CNK's ability to allow the messaging hardware to be used from user space, the ability to know the virtual to physical mapping from user space, and the ability to have large physically contiguous chunks of memory available in user space. Data taken from previous work (Kumar et al. 2008) is shown in Table 5.1 that illustrates low latency obtained through the use of user space accessibility. DCMF achieves maximum bandwidth by utilizing large physically contiguous memory. These came effectively for free with CNK's design and implementation, but modifying a vanilla Linux, especially to provide large physically contiguous memory, would be difficult.

5.5.4 Performance Stability

To demonstrate performance stability, we ran 36 runs of Linpack on Blue Gene/P racks. Each rack produced 11.94 Tflops. The execution time varied from 16,080.89 to 16,083.00 s, for a maximum variation of 2.11 s (.01%) over a 4 h and 28 min run and a standard deviation of less than 1.14 s. Another example of repeatability is demonstrated by repeated execution of a benchmark under CNK compared to the same benchmark under Linux. This experiment measured the performance of the mpiBench `MPI_Allreduce()` test, which is a test in the Phloem benchmark suite (Lawrence Livermore National Laboratory 2003b). The test measured the time to perform a double-sum allreduce on 16 Blue Gene/P nodes over one million iterations. Over this time the test produced a standard deviation of 0.0007 microseconds (effectively 0, likely a floating-point precision error). A similar test was performed with Linux on Blue Gene/P I/O nodes interconnected by 10 Gbps Ethernet. Background daemons were suspended as allowed, but NFS was required to capture results between tests. This test was the same double-sum allreduce, but executing on only 4 Blue Gene/P I/O nodes over 100,000 iterations. The Linux test was executed twenty times and produced a standard deviation of 8.9 microseconds. Whether or not this level of variance has a significant application impact would need more study, but application groups (Alam et al. 2008) have found that BG/P's performance stability allowed them to more easily and more effectively tune their applications.

5.6 What is Not CNK

CNK is designed to be simple. We have consciously limited the functionality of CNK to stay consistent with our scalability design philosophy. This philosophy makes kernel implementation feasible for a small team and improves its reliability.

Simplification is performed across the major components of the kernel. However, there are applications for which the functionality is not sufficient and need a more complete set of Linux functionality. In this section, we describe what is not in CNK and in the next section describe the pros and cons of the boundaries we have drawn and describe how easy or difficult it is to achieve a given functionality in Linux and CNK.

5.6.1   I/O Subsystem

The I/O subsystems in CNK are virtually nonexistent. This is accomplished by function shipping the requests to a dedicated I/O node. Correct semantics are difficult to achieve in POSIX I/O and would take considerable time to stabilize if they were implemented in CNK. This is true for both network file systems and standard networking protocols such as TCP/IP. Delegating the file system to a separate Linux node means that complex problems such as file system caching, readahead, writebehind, client consistency, and scalability need not be implemented in CNK. CNK also does not need to provide a virtual file system layer or module loading layer to support such file systems, nor do file systems need to be ported to CNK. Linux provides this functionality and leverages a large user and development community for finding and fixing problems. Also, a driver layer for the Blue Gene specialized network hardware is unnecessary because this hardware is fixed on Blue Gene. Although this does keep CNK simple, there are some consequences. For example, to *mmap* a file, CNK copies in the data and only allows read-only access.

5.6.2   Memory Management

Much of CNK's memory management architecture is driven by the goal of providing static TLB mapping for an application's address space. CNK does not implement demand paging, or copy-on-write, and as a file system is not implemented by CNK there is no need to implement a unified page cache between the virtual memory manager and file system. Further, CNK has simplified its own use of memory by placing strict limits on sizes of kernel data structures, allocating all of its structures statically. CNK does not maintain a heap of intermingled data structures throughout physical memory. This simple strategy for memory management makes debugging memory corruption problems easier and makes protection of DMA directly programmed by application code straightforward.

5.6.3   Scheduler

Thread scheduling under BG/Q's CNK runs under first-in, first-out policy without preemption. Applications can use *sched_setaffinity* to move/place software threads on specific hardware threads. The scheduler has a simple decision limited to threads sharing a core when a thread specifically blocks on a FUTEX or explicitly yields. Sharing a core is rare in HPC applications, so generally a thread enters the kernel only to wait until a FUTEX may be granted by another core rather than yield to a thread on the same core. I/O function shipping is made trivial by not yielding the core to another thread during an I/O system call. This has the side effect of never switching kernel context during execution of a system call on a kernel stack. Instead, the scheduler only has to consider the case of context switching user state.

5.7 HPC Applications

The design point we chose for CNK has its advantages and disadvantages. In this section, we describe the pros and cons we have had from our experiences with CNK and then how easy or difficult it is to achieve a given functionality in Linux and CNK.

5.7.1 Pros for HPC Applications

Many of the design simplifications in CNK enhance the performance of HPC applications without requiring application effort. CNK provides strict processor affinity for processes and threads. This avoids unnecessary context switch overhead and improves L1 cache use. As this is common in HPC application, this limitation rarely has a negative impact and instead relieves the application of affinity responsibility. Similarly, CNK pins memory with huge TLB entries to avoid TLB misses. Using huge TLB pages in Linux is often a nontrivial enhancement to an application, especially if the huge pages are used to back the application code or stack or are requested on-the-fly, for example, for messaging. CNK requires no application modification to take advantage of the large pages. Linux has become easier over time, but still requires tuning and is not automatic. Another advantage of the memory layout provided by CNK is that nearly the full 4 GB 32-bit address space of a task can be mapped on a 32-bit processor. Linux typically limits a task to 3 GB of the address space due to 32-bit limitations. While this was on issue on BG/P, on next-generation Blue Gene hardware, with 64-bit processors, it is not an issue.

Simple memory mappings allow CNK applications to directly drive the DMA torus hardware without concern of corrupting the kernel. This results in simplified hardware and improved DMA latency because a special I/O memory management unit and the related system call overhead for setting up communication windows are unnecessary. Function shipping of the I/O system calls provides up to two orders of magnitude reduction in file system clients. Finally, the simplicity of CNK allows it to initialize quickly and makes it easier to provide cycle-reproducible debugging.

5.7.2   Cons for HPC applications

There are downsides to the simplification of CNK. The strict affinity enforced by the scheduler does not allow applications to use threads in creative ways. For example, it is not possible to run low-priority background threads while a primary thread performs compute work. CNK also does not allow a node to be divided nonuniformly. MPI cannot spawn dynamic tasks because CNK does not allow *fork*/exec operations. Some applications overcommit threads to cores for load-balancing purposes, and the CNK threading model does not allow that, though Charm++ accomplishes this with a user-mode threading library.

In order to provide static mapping with a limited number of TLB entries, the memory subsystem may waste physical memory as large pages are tiled together. The dynamic linker does not protect read-only and text sections of dynamic libraries loaded after the application starts. The lack of a unified page cache means that pages of code and read-only data cannot be discarded when memory pressure is high. The lack of a page cache also means that dynamic objects are not shared between tasks that physically share a node. Other disadvantages include that CNK divides memory on a node evenly among the tasks on the node. If one task's memory grows more than another, the application could run out of memory before all the memory of a node was consumed. Also, CNK requires the user to define the size of the shared memory allocation up-front as the application is launched. Finally, the application cannot take advantage of the scripting environment offered by a full-featured operating system; an application cannot be structured as a shell script that forks off related executables.

5.7.3   Ease of Functionality for CNK Versus Linux

In this section, we combine and summarize the previous sections on design and experience. Table 5.2 lists a series of mechanisms, capabilities, and requirements

Table 5.2   Ease of using different capabilities in CNK and Linux

Description	CNK	Linux
Large page use	easy	medium
Using multiple large page sizes	easy	medium
Large physically contiguous memory	easy	easy-hard
No TLB misses	easy	not available
Full memory protection	easy	easy
Efficient dynamic linking	hard	medium
Full *mmap* support	not available	easy
Predictable scheduling	easy	not available
Over commit of threads	medium	medium
Cycle-reproducible execution	medium	not available

Table 5.3 Ease of implementing different capabilities in CNK and Linux

Description	CNK	Linux
Large physically contiguous memory	easy	hard
No TLB misses	medium	not possible
Full memory protection	medium	exists
Efficient dynamic linking	medium	medium
BG/Q Transactional Memory	hard	extremely hard
Cycle-reproducible execution	medium	hard

that HPC applications may be interested in using. Columns two and three indicate how difficult it is to use that feature in each of the systems: easy, medium, or hard.

For the features that are listed as not-avail in Tables 5.2, 5.3 indicates the difficulty of implementing them in that OS. The Linux that was evaluated was from the 2.6.30 generation, and CNK is BG/P's CNK.

References

Alam, S., Barrett, R., Fahey, B. M., Kuehn, M. R., McCurdy, J., Rogers, C., et al. (2008). In *Proceedings of the 2008 ACM/IEEE Conference on Supercomputing, SC 2008. Early evaluation of IBM BlueGene/P* (pp. 23:1–23:12). USA: IEEE Press.

Ferreira, K . B., Bridges, P., & Brightwell, R. (2008). Characterizing application sensitivity to OS interference using kernel-level noise injection. In *International Conference for High Performance Computing, Networking, Storage and Analysis, 2008. SC 2008.*

Giampapa, M., Gooding, T., Inglett, T., & Wisniewski, R. (2010). Experiences with a lightweight supercomputer kernel: Lessons learned from Blue Gene's CNK. In *2010 International Conference for High Performance Computing, Networking, Storage and Analysis (SC).*

Glosli, J. N., Richards, D. F., Caspersen, K. J., Rudd, R. E., Gunnels, J. A., & Streitz, F. H. (2007). Extending stability beyond CPU millennium: A micron-scale atomistic simulation of Kelvin-Helmholtz instability. In *Proceedings of the 2007 ACM/IEEE Conference on Supercomputing, SC 2007* (pp. 58:1–58:11). USA: ACM.

Goodale, T., Allen, G., Lanfermann, G., Massó, J., Radke, T., Seidel, E., et al. (2003). The Cactus framework and toolkit: Design and applications. In *5th International Conference on Vector and Parallel Processing – VECPAR'2002.*, Lecture Notes in Computer Science Berlin: Springer.

Henson, V. E., & Yang, U. M. (2002). BoomerAMG: A parallel algebraic multigrid solver and preconditioner. https://codesign.llnl.gov/amg2013.php.

IEEE. (2013). IEEE Standard test access port and boundary-scan architecture. *IEEE Std., 1149,* 1.

Kumar, S., Dozsa, G., Almasi, G., Heidelberger, P., Chen, D., Giampapa, M. E., et al. (2008). The Deep Computing Messaging Framework: Generalized scalable message passing on the Blue Gene/P supercomputer. In *22nd Annual International Conference on Supercomputing, ICS* (pp. 94–103).

Lawrence Livermore National Lab (2017). UMT: Unstructured Mesh Transport. https://asc.llnl.gov/CORAL-benchmarks/Summaries/UMT2013_Summary_v1.2.pdf.

Lawrence Livermore National Laboratory. The FTQ/FWQ Benchmark.

Lawrence Livermore National Laboratory (2001). SPhot: Single Physics Photon Transport. https://asc.llnl.gov/sequoia/benchmarks/SPhot_summary_v1.0.pdf.

Lawrence Livermore National Laboratory (2003a). IRS: Implicit Radiation Solver. https://asc.llnl.gov/sequoia/benchmarks/IRS_summary_v1.0.pdf.

Lawrence Livermore National Laboratory (2003b). The Phloem benchmark. https://asc.llnl.gov/sequoia/benchmarks/PhloemMPIBenchmarks_summary_v1.0.pdf.

NERSC (2013). MIMD Lattice Computation (MILC). http://www.nersc.gov/users/computational-systems/cori/nersc-8-procurement/trinity-nersc-8-rfp/nersc-8-trinity-benchmarks/milc.

Petrini, F., Kerbyson, D. J., & Pakin, S. (2003). The case of the missing supercomputer performance: Achieving optimal performance on the 8,192 processors of ASCI Q. In *Proceedings of the 2003 ACM/IEEE conference on Supercomputing, SC 2003*. USA: ACM.

Plimpton, S. (1995). Fast parallel algorithms for short-range molecular dynamics. *Journal of Computational Physics, 117*(1), 1–19.

Rosner, R., Calder, A., Dursi, J., Fryxell, B., Lamb, D. Q., Niemeyer, J. C., et al. (2000). Flash code: studying astrophysical thermonuclear flashes. *Computing in Science Engineering, 2*(2), 33–41.

Part III
Unix/Linux Based Systems

Chapter 6
Overview: The Rise of Linux

Rolf Riesen, Balazs Gerofi, Yutaka Ishikawa and Robert W. Wisniewski

The transition from vector computers to Massively Parallel Processors (MPPs) in the late 1980s and the early 1990s produced a plethora of system manufacturers, for example, Alliant, BBN Butterfly, Convex, Intel, Kendall Square Research (KSR), MasPar, Meiko, nCube, Parsytec, Sequent, Silicon Graphics Inc. (SGI), Supertek, SUPRENUM Supercomputer GmbH, Tera Computer Corp., and Thinking Machines Corp. (TMC). An article based on TOP500 results up to that time summarizes the market trends very clearly (Strohmaier et al. 2019). By the end of the decade all but a few had disappeared. They went bankrupt, got bought, merged, or just stopped making supercomputers.

Each of these machines had a different Operating System (OS) and its own way to send and receive messages. Initially, specialized Lightweight Kernels (LWKs) were used on some of these systems, but there was a strong demand for standardization, more features, and Portable Operating System Interface for Unix (POSIX) compatibility.

In the 1990s, it was not yet clear what message-passing interface would eventually succeed, but by the end of the decade the second version of the Message-Passing Interface (MPI) (Snir et al. 1998; Gropp et al. 1998) standard had been released, and vendor-specific message-passing Application Programming Interfaces (APIs)

R. Riesen (✉)
Intel Corporation, Oregon, USA
e-mail: rolf.riesen@intel.com

B. Gerofi · Y. Ishikawa
RIKEN Center for Computational Science, Kobe, Japan
e-mail: bgerofi@riken.jp

Y. Ishikawa
e-mail: yutaka.ishikawa@riken.jp

R. W. Wisniewski
Intel Corporation, New York, USA
e-mail: robert.w.wisniewski@intel.com

© Springer Nature Singapore Pte Ltd. 2019
B. Gerofi et al. (eds.), *Operating Systems for Supercomputers
and High Performance Computing*, High-Performance Computing Series,
https://doi.org/10.1007/978-981-13-6624-6_6

95

had mostly disappeared. However, the premier MPI workshop was still called Euro PVM/MPI since Parallel Virtual Machine (PVM) (Geist et al. 1994), which was created several years before the MPI forum began to meet, was still in regular use.

The evolution of message-passing mechanisms and MPI had a profound impact on the transition from LWKs to Linux. Early LWKs contained mechanisms to send messages with low latency and high bandwidth. Each major application had its own communication layer so it could be easily ported to a new OS or machine. Performance portability was important, and there was reluctance to move to MPI. It was also not clear how these highly tuned mechanisms would get implemented in Linux.

The limited variety of supercomputer choices in the mid-1990s encouraged research laboratories to pursue their own cluster-building efforts. Thomas Sterling and Don Becker built Beowulf at the National Aeronautics and Space Administration (NASA) (Sterling et al. 1995), and Sandia National Laboratories had the Computational Plant (Cplant) (Riesen et al. 1999; Brightwell et al. 2000) with the idea that computes cycles should be delivered like electricity, and the plant should grow and get pruned to adapt to the demand for compute cycles. A Cplant consisted of computational units that could be added or removed, depending on demand. When new hardware was added, older generation hardware would be pruned.[1]

There were many other similar efforts in the mid-1990s to use Commercial off-the-Shelf (COTS) components to augment the capabilities of the disappearing supercomputers. Oak Ridge National Laboratory created the Stone Soup Computer (Hargrove et al. 2001), Hyglac was built at the California Institute of Technology and the Jet Propulsion Laboratory, and Loki was constructed at Los Alamos National Laboratory (Warren et al. 1997a, b).

Soon, new and established companies began building clusters based on the Beowulf principle. For example, the Los Lobos cluster at the University of New Mexico in 2000 was the first-ever Linux-based production parallel computer built by IBM. It used a Myrinet network (Boden et al. 1995).

While the advent of the killer micros (Brooks 1990; Markoff 1991) enabled this revolution using commodity components, the second ingredient was Linux. It was a young OS that by the mid-90s did not have Ethernet drivers or support for Symmetric Multi-processing (SMP). However, with the help of the open-source community, it grew quickly and by 1999 it started to get used in production High-Performance Computing (HPC) systems. In the 1999 TOP500 list, the top-most system running Linux was at rank 51, but the situation began to change quickly. Today, Linux is well established in the top ten and dominates the entire list.

Thanks to a free operating system (OS) and commodity hardware, lower cost supercomputing had arrived. This posed a dilemma for the HPC OS community. Linux compatibility was now expected, and the old LWKs could not provide that. At the same time, Linux was still struggling to perform and scale well on large-scale systems (Hammond et al. 2010). This led to two camps: Those who attempted to build more Linux functionality into LWKs, and those who tried to strip Linux to make it behave more like an LWK. Neither of these two approaches fully succeeded, which led to the multi-kernels that make up Part III of this book.

---

[1]This appears similar to the goals of cloud computing.

In this part of the book, we present five Unix/Linux-based OS approaches for HPC that exemplify the efforts to bring Unix-like features to supercomputing, while adding message passing and finding ways to improve Linux performance on these systems. We start with Cray's Compute Node Linux in Chap. 7, then move to SCore (Hori 2001) in Chap. 8, the Earth Simulator (Yanagawa and Suehiro 2004) and SUPER-UX in Chap. 9, ZeptoOS (Yoshii et al. 2009) in Chap. 10, and K Computer (Ajima et al. 2012) in Chap. 11. A sixth Chap. 12 discusses Argo (Perarnau et al. 2017). It stands apart from the other projects in this part of the book, since its aim is to devise a system-wide OS, while most other chapters in this book describe compute node OSs.

Although the focus of this part of the book is on Unix-like OSs for HPC, note Sect. 7.8 in the Cray chapter. In the long lineup of OSs for Cray supercomputers, we find an LWK that is based on work done at Sandia National Laboratories and described in Chap. 3 in the first part of the book.

References

Ajima, Y., Inoue, T., Hiramoto, S., Takagi, Y., & Shimizu, T. (2012). The Tofu interconnect. *IEEE Micro*, *32*(1), 21–31.

Boden, N. J., Cohen, D., Felderman, R. E., Kulawik, A. E., Seitz, C. L., Seizovic, J. N., et al. (1995). Myrinet: A gigabit-per-second local area network. *IEEE Micro*, *15*(1), 29–36.

Brightwell, R., Fisk, L. A., Greenberg, D. S., Hudson, T., Levenhagen, M., Maccabe, A. B., et al. (2000). Massively parallel computing using commodity components. *Parallel Computing*, *26*(2–3), 243–266.

Brooks, E. (1990). Attack of the killer micros. *Talk at Supercomputing 1991*.

Geist, A., Beguelin, A., Dongarra, J., Jiang, W., Manchek, R., & Sunderam, V. (1994). *PVM: Parallel Virtual Machine: A Users' Guide and Tutorial for Networked Parallel Computing*. USA: MIT Press.

Gropp, W., Huss-Lederman, S., Lumsdaine, A., Lusk, E., Nitzberg, B., Saphir, W., et al. (1998). *MPI - The Complete Reference: Volume 2, The MPI-2 Extensions*. USA: MIT Press.

Hammond, S., Mudalige, G., Smith, J. A., Davis, J. A., Jarvis, S., Holt, J., et al. (2010). To upgrade or not to upgrade? Catamount versus cray linux environment. In *2010 IEEE International Symposium on Parallel Distributed Processing, Workshops and Phd Forum (IPDPSW)*.

Hargrove, W. W., Hoffman, F. M., & Sterling, T. (2001). *The Do-it-yourself Supercomputer.*, *265*(2), 72–79.

Hori, A. (2001). SCore: An integrated cluster system software package for high performance cluster computing. In *IEEE International Conference on Cluster Computing (CLUSTER)* 8–11 October 2001. USA: Newport Beach.

Markoff, J. (1991). The attack of the 'killer micros'. *The New York Times*.

Perarnau, S., Zounmevo, J. A., Dreher, M., Essen, B. C. V., Gioiosa, R., Iskra, K., et al. (2017). Argo NodeOS: Toward unified resource management for exascale. In *IEEE International Parallel and Distributed Processing Symposium (IPDPS)*.

Riesen, R., Brightwell, R., Fisk, L. A., Hudson, T., Otto, J., & Maccabe, A. B. (1999). Cplant. In *Proceedings of the Second Extreme Linux workshop at the. (1999) USENIX Annual Technical Conference*. California.

Snir, M., Otto, S., Huss-Lederman, S., Walker, D., & Dongarra, J. (1998). *MPI-The Complete Reference, Volume 1: The MPI Core* (2nd ed.) (revised). USA: MIT Press.

Sterling, T. L., Savarese, D., Becker, D. J., Dorband, J. E., Ranawake, U. A., & Packer, C. V. (1995). Beowulf: A parallel workstation for scientific computation. In P. Banerjee (Ed.), *Proceedings of the 1995 International Conference on Parallel Processing* (pp. 11–14). USA: CRC Press.

Strohmaier, E., Dongarra, J. J., Meuer, H. W., and Simon, H. D. The marketplace for high-performance computers. *Parallel Computing*, 25(13–14):1517–1544.

Warren, M. S., Becker, D. J., Goda, M. P., Salmon, J. K., & Sterling, T. (1997a). Parallel supercomputing with commodity components. In *International Conference on Parallel and Distributed Processing Techniques and Applications*.

Warren, M. S., Salmon, J. K., Becker, D. J., Goda, M. P., Sterling, T., & Winckelmans, W. (1997b). Pentium Pro inside: I. a treecode at 430 Gigaflops on ASCI Red, II. price/performance of $50/Mflop on Loki and Hyglac. In *Supercomputing, ACM/IEEE 1997 Conference* (p. 61)

Yanagawa, T., & Suehiro, K. (2004). Software system of the earth simulator. *Parallel Computing*, 30(12), 1315–1327. The Earth Simulator.

Yoshii, K., Iskra, K., Naik, H., Beckman, P., & Broekema, P. (2009). Characterizing the performance of "Big Memory" on Blue Gene Linux. In *2nd International Workshop on Parallel Programming Models and Systems Software for High-End Computing, P2S2* (pp. 65–72).

Chapter 7
Cray Compute Node Linux

Larry Kaplan and Jim Harrell

Abstract Unix, and now Linux, have become prevalent in high-performance computing (HPC) systems, including systems at the very high end. These operating systems were not originally intended for scalable HPC usage, but have been adapted to fulfill that role, while preserving their ability to support a wide range of applications and use cases. While Cray Research and some related commercial efforts had started with proprietary operating systems, Unix or Linux was eventually chosen to provide this wider applicability. This chapter describes the evolution of the use of Unix and Linux at Cray, along with similar activities at two other companies that followed similar paths, BBN Advanced Computers Inc. and Tera Computer Company (later merged with Cray to form Cray Inc.).

7.1 Milestones

This section describes a number of hardware and software systems produced over the years. Table 7.1 places the systems in order of delivery and provides the year the first system was available.

7.2 Background—HPC Before Unix

The scientific systems of the 1970s and early 1980s were dominated by proprietary processors and systems from a small group of vendors. Each vendor had their own operating system (OS). There was a Fortran standard, but most computer companies provided extra features for Fortran and programs that used these were difficult to port. This extended to a lack of portability even between product lines from the same

L. Kaplan (✉) · J. Harrell
Cray Inc., Seattle, WA, USA
e-mail: lkaplan@cray.com

J. Harrell
e-mail: ejh@cray.com

© Springer Nature Singapore Pte Ltd. 2019 99
B. Gerofi et al. (eds.), *Operating Systems for Supercomputers
and High Performance Computing*, High-Performance Computing Series,
https://doi.org/10.1007/978-981-13-6624-6_7

Table 7.1 Cray software and hardware systems produced over time

Year	System	Comments
1976	Cray-1	First Cray delivery - No Unix Operating System (OS)
1984	UNICOS	Initial deliveries of UNICOS (Unix) OS
1984	Butterfly	No Unix OS
1988	GP1000 Unix	BSD/Mach on Butterfly Hardware
1990	TC2000 nX	Second-Generation Butterfly (removed Mach)
1991	UNICOS Max	UNICOS and Mach on distributed massively parallel processor (MPP)
1994	UNICOS/mk	Single system image (SSI) on an MPP
1997	MTK	BSD with custom Microkernel for MTA
2004	UNICOS lc	Distributed system with Linux and Catamount Microkernel
2006	CNL/CLE	Compute Node Linux and Cray Linux Environment
2008	XMT	MTK on single-chip MTA processors, integrated with CLE

vendor. Control Data (CDC) and International Business Machines (IBM) supported multiple OSs on their different products (Various 1989; Morton 2015). Some of this was caused by technology changes from one system to the next, but the result was that migration from a previous system to a new one required a substantive porting effort. The OSs were usually monolithic—all the services provided within one or a small set of related modules.

The large scientific systems were carefully managed resources that were often difficult to access and debug. Most of the operational use was in a "batch job" mode, where jobs were submitted, executed in sequence, and output printed for the user. These systems, and the time on the systems, were expensive, required substantial infrastructure, and also a support team. Because the machine time was so valuable scheduling it efficiently was considered important even if it impinged on usability. The batch job process sometimes took a day or more from job submission to job completion depending on the operational schedule of the system.

The first systems to use Unix as an OS were part of an alternative to the big science systems, and were called "minicomputers". Minicomputers had been around in the industry for some years and other OSs like Digital Equipment Corporation's (DEC) virtual memory system (VMS) were quite popular as well. Minicomputer systems were much smaller physically and did not require the infrastructure that the bigger systems demanded. These systems emphasized productivity and were more available to users than the systems in basement computer complexes. HPC users ported and developed applications on minicomputers because these systems were so much easier to use and debug than the larger centralized systems. There was also a distinct drive to decentralize. The larger systems were often considered to be controlled by a bureaucracy, where a minicomputer could be controlled by a department. As the number of these systems would grow within a site, a new interest also blossomed, networking.

The first Cray systems were first delivered in the late 1970s without an OS. For Cray, software beyond the Fortran compiler was not initially a customer requirement. This was not unusual in technical computing. Rather, the customers enjoyed the opportunity to experiment and felt they were part of the development of these systems. The Department of Defense, DoD, developed a lightweight OS called Folklore (Unknown 1996). The system had interesting capabilities described glowingly by the people who used it. Because of security issues, Folklore was not offered to the Cray community. The Department of Energy, DoE, labs at Los Alamos and Livermore labs developed several related systems, Cray Time-Sharing System (CTSS) (Laboratory 1982), and later NLTSS (Brugger and Streletz 2001). The systems were designed to run Fortran jobs on Cray-1 systems. Interestingly, these systems were written in a variant of Fortran. This was unusual because at this time most system software was written in assembly language for performance reasons. These systems were not the only place these features were incorporated, but it showed a clear interest in interactive use and in recovering application state after a failure.

The first Cray Research OS was called Cray Operating System (COS). COS was developed with and at the National Center for Atmospheric Research, NCAR, during the acceptance of the first Cray Research delivery that required software in 1975–76. Written entirely in assembler, the OS was based on Control Data Corporation (CDC) style OSs. The system was familiar to CDC users. The system architecture depended on a customer provided "front-end" for services such as input and output. The Cray system was a "back-end" that ran jobs submitted on the front-end system. COS had a rudimentary network protocol to transfer jobs and files. The OS and scratch storage were focused on running applications with minimal interference from system software and services. There were a lot of efforts to keep Cray systems as remote batch access only. These efforts came both from customers, who saw the systems as too important to have users working on them from terminals, and also from Cray analysts who felt the system would not work well as a minicomputer. As an example of the issues, the context switch of a process required saving the state of all registers, including vector registers. Some effort had been made to speed this process, but it was still time consuming to save all the registers and restore them. In order to make this faster when a system call was being processed, the OS would only save one vector register for use by the OS, and only save the rest of the vector registers if the scheduler was going to switch to a different process on return from OS processing.

7.2.1 BBN Chrysalis and the Original Butterfly Machine

The original Butterfly line of computers from Bolt, Beranek, and Newman (BBN) was developed in early 1980s under Defense Advanced Research Projects Agency (DARPA) funding as part of their Packet Speech Project. It was a Motorola 68K based non-uniform memory architecture (NUMA) multiple instruction, multiple data (MIMD) parallel computer with a proprietary multistage packet-switched network in a folded butterfly topology that scaled up to 256 nodes. It provided a shared memory environment across the machine and used the proprietary Chrysalis OS, which implemented some Unix-like capabilities but was master/slave, using a DEC Virtual Address Extension (VAX) or Sun workstation as the front end (Crowther et al. 1985). The Butterfly Multiprocessor was originally used for special purposed devices such as the "Voice Funnel" packet voice multiplexer (Rettberg et al. 1979), as the Butterfly Satellite (BSAT) interface message processor (IMP) packet switch for the DARPA Wideband Satellite Network (Edmond et al. 1986), and as the Butterfly Internet Gateway providing internetwork connectivity in the early Internet (Partridge and Blumenthal 2006; Sheltzer et al. 1983). It was also used for simulation tasks such as finite element analysis, electronic circuit design, and battlefield management (LeBlanc et al. 1988).

7.3   Cray Research and Unix

By the early 1980s, there were growing pressures on the proprietary OSs. The costs of developing and supporting software were rising. At Cray Research, new employees from universities, many who had learned Unix in their classes, had to be retrained, and employees who transferred from other companies had to "convert" to the COS environment in order to begin learning how to use Cray systems. Software, for some, had become an almost religious issue. The customers who developed their own OSs were becoming less interested in the constant demands of supporting existing systems and the work to migrate complicated system-level code to newer systems. There was always something new in the next system such as addressing changes, multiple processors, input/output channel, and devices changing. In order to support these customers, Cray built large "support" centers in both Maryland and California. These centers took on parts of the support and development of the customer OS.

The Cray customers were also continuing to look at new OSs. Forest Baskett and a team at Los Alamos National Laboratory (LANL) worked on the development of a Unix-like OS on a Cray-1 system called Demos (Baskett et al. 1977). This was interesting because it was the first attempt to port Unix to a Cray and likely one of the first to use a Unix-like OS on an HPC system. Unfortunately, the development project was a failure. The system was never put into production and development on the project was stopped. The precise reason for the failure of the program is lost, but as with many failures, the blame affected anything and anyone involved. Many blamed Unix, making the assertion that Unix could never be an HPC OS.

In this same period, i.e., the early 1980s, Seymour Cray started the Cray-2 program. The Cray-2 was a complete departure from the Cray-1. The architecture, instruction set , memory and addressing, and I/O architecture were new. The question that Cray Research faced was how to develop an OS for the Cray-2. How does a small company develop and support a second OS? And what happens when there is a Cray-3? Converting COS to run on both Cray-1 and Cray-2 would be a huge undertaking. Reprogramming a hundred thousand lines of assembly language would be a daunting task. There were alternatives. The DoD and DoE both vied to have their software become the basis of the Cray-2 software. The choice was hotly debated. Cray groups supported customer OSs that were written in a higher level language, but because it was a variant of Fortran it was not in wide use and having a large number of people who could write and fix code in that variant was lost.

Unix was not considered to be ready for use in HPC systems. The Unix environment was dependent on the C language. C was not yet supported by Cray. There was no multiprocessor support. Unix was known for poor I/O performance. The file system was targeted at small block size devices and had none of the features, such as striping, to improve device performance. Unix was most often delivered on DEC Programmed Data Processor (PDP) systems. These were used in small group environments. This was not a full-featured OS with a substantive programming environment. But Unix was being used a lot of places. The system had its own text processing support and was quite useful for writing documents and technical reports.

In 1982, the head of software for the Cray-2 group announced that System V Unix from American Telephone and Telegraph (AT & T) would be the base for the Cray-2. The goal was simple—be the fastest system on the planet. Unix was not the goal. Unix was simply a vehicle for providing a portable environment for the Cray-2 and future systems. The system was planned to be mostly batch with some networking in the future. The Cray software groups embarked on developing a C compiler and Unix expertise.

The decision surprised many in the industry. Cray's partnerships with IBM were strained when Cray began using DEC systems for front-ends to Cray-2 Unix internally. Cray was a heavy user of IBM systems both internally and at customer sites. IBM felt Cray should wait until IBM made a Unix that was more "usable". There was a slowing of COS development projects. The plan was to move COS to a *Guest OS* under Unix, and eventually discontinue it. Both the decision to move to Unix and discontinue COS were unpopular especially with DoD, DoE, and NCAR.

At the same time, a small group was given the task of porting Unix to a Cray-1. The main goal was to focus on Cray-1 performance. Initial applications were quite close to COS performance, but this was only as long as system calls and especially any I/O were avoided. The former Demos team members were reaching out to Cray developers warning them that there were no solutions to these problems. I/O was a problem and development of interim and long-term solutions to Unix I/O and file system problems were a large part of the effort taken on by a growing team. The Cray-1 group added a Berkeley Software Distribution (BSD) implementation of Transmission Control Protocol/Internet Protocol (TCP/IP) and a number of BSD features into the Cray-1 version of the OS starting an internal struggle over SysV versus BSD. This struggle was a mirror of the larger Unix market place. There were two different Cray Unix systems for several years. Interactive use of a Cray was part of the same debate, made even hotter as the capability to use vi, a character mode text editor first introduced in BSD Unix, across a network became available. The issue was each character across the network became a context switch on the Cray-1, which was an expensive operation. As a compromise, Cray networking development worked very hard to make a line mode telnet part of the standard. But the capability of running programs like vi was left as a customer choice to enable or disable.

The development of Unix on Cray-2 and Cray-1 took several years to get to a first release. Unix development at Cray was widely known in the industry, watched by customers and also Unix aficionados. Cray lab customers and commercial customers were not impressed with Cray Unix. The demo systems had performance issues and there were lots of bugs. But Unix did create opportunities. In 1984, Apple and Bell Labs at Murray Hill ordered Cray-1 systems. Apple was using the system to do mechanical design. Bell Labs had been an early Cray customer using the system to do computer memory design, but this new system was purchased by the Unix group at Murray Hill. These were the first systems delivered with Unix. These were quickly followed by orders from other Unix enclaves such as University of California (UC) Berkeley. The new Unix-based OS was given the name UNICOS (UNI 1995). Cray began working with Sun and using Sun systems for internal development. The idea of networked Unix systems, tuned for computation, user access, and storage becomes an important direction for UNICOS development.

The development of Unix functionality was overshadowed by the HPC/COS feature development. Over a period of 2–4 years, Cray added COS style features such as symmetric multiprocessor support, a multithreaded kernel eventually for up to 32 processor systems (T90), checkpoint/restart, a new high-performance file system, and substantive modifications to the system for security and performance.

The support of Symmetric Multiprocessors and kernel multithreading were important and invasive undertakings. Initially, the Unix community was divided on whether processors should be symmetric or asymmetric. In a symmetric configuration, all processors process user and kernel tasks. An asymmetric processor configuration assigns one processor to kernel and user tasks, and the remainder executes only user processes. This was because the kernel had no locks to allow multiple processors to overlap without potentially corrupting a system call in progress. Initial two processor DEC systems were configured as asymmetric systems. Cray was certain that the cost of its processors would drive its customers toward the symmetric use model. But without a comprehensive locking infrastructure, Unix system call processing could take most of a system due to processors waiting for access to kernel structures. By the time there were four and eight processor systems, this became a serious issue and a long development project.

The kernel was a half million lines of code by the late 1980s. This was a huge increase from the original twenty thousand line kernel. Every developer wanted to be an OS developer and vied to get code into the kernel. However, no single person can "know" a half million lines. Subtle bugs were problematic to find and fix. Context switch times were still high, so the concept of making kernel services run as user-level services was no closer than before Unix. One attempt at a user-level daemon was an early implementation of Berkeley sockets by BBN. While the performance was close to the BSD kernel version of sockets, the demon consumed 100% of the processor making it unusable in practice. UNICOS/mk was proposed as a solution to the problems of kernel size and complexity in UNICOS. UNICOS/mk is described in a later section.

7.4   BBN/nX

The BBN Butterfly computer with its proprietary OS, described earlier, had some success. But around 1987 the designers and users of the Butterfly clamored for a full-featured OS with more tools and capabilities. Given that the platform supported up to 256 nodes and processors in a single system image (and OS instance), something that considered the issue of scalability was desired. Thus, a survey of Unix-based OSs was performed. Standard System V Unix at the time did not support parallelism, and BSD only had experimental support (potentially up to four nodes). However, Carnegie Mellon University (CMU) had been researching Mach and had restructured BSD on top of what appeared to be a more scalable Mach microkernel.

7.4.1   BBN GP1000

The Mach/BSD OS was selected and named Mach 1000. When this was brought to the Butterfly platform, the product was renamed the GP1000 (Howe 1988). Various features were added to the OS to help with the operation of the machine. The idea of processor *clusters* within the machine was one of these. Clusters were groups of processors that could be assigned to individual users. User applications could then be scheduled within individual clusters. A default public-shared cluster-supported interactive and program-development work. Interfaces were also provided to *bind* both processes (when forking) and memory (when allocated) to specific nodes in the system. This worked well up to around eight nodes, but then ran into scaling issues.

The main issue was the use of a global lock to handle virtual memory activities including page faults (Black et al. 1991). In addition, copy-on-write (COW) faults were handled in a non-scalable way in the original Mach Virtual Memory (VM) system, through the use of shadow objects. For processes that were distant descendants of init, this resulted in long chains of shadow objects that needed to be traversed in order to find the original pre-COW pages. The Mach VM system was completely replaced with finer grained locking and *herd* objects for COW pages, eliminating the use of long chains of shadow objects (Barach et al. 1990).

One of the other significant tasks in making the BSD layer more parallel friendly was the introduction of spinlocks associated with each traditional Unix sleep channel. Unix sleep/wakeup mechanisms were stateless, in that only processes actually on the sleep channel at the time of the wakeup call would actually be woken up. Subsequent callers of sleep on that channel would not get woken up until the next wakeup call. This differs from stateful signaling mechanisms such as condition variables, which once signaled, no longer block on wait. With the stateless sleep channel, a race exists where a process could observe it needs to sleep and be about to put itself on the sleep channel, when another process on a different node satisfies the reason for the sleep and issues the wakeup, before the first process has finished adding itself. This would result in the first process missing the wakeup and potentially never getting woken up.

The solution is to wrap the test for needing to sleep and actually getting on the sleep channel inside a spin lock, and to drop that lock just before context switching away from the sleeping process. The wakeup can then take the lock and guarantee that any sleeper has fully registered on the channel. This is similar to the interrupt race that is solved using interrupt masking, but since this happens in a multiprocessor parallel context, a spinlock is needed for protection.

7.4.2   TC2000

Around 1989, BBN started looking at the next generation of the Butterfly line and selected the Motorola 88K processor. The network was also improved and changed to a circuit-switched network with the same basic topology (Beeler 1990; Brooks et al. 1991). The Mach/BSD OS was renamed nX and ported to the system (LeBlanc et al. 1988). Many of the Mach components were removed or replaced by this time. Support for NFS and MIT X windows was also added at this time.

One of the significant new features in the TC2000 was support for a hardware-provided distributed global memory region with automated interleaving. The previous GP1000 system could automatically process native processor loads and stores (and some atomic operations) to remote memories, but the hardware presented those memories as separate contiguous physical regions local to each node. The new interleaving hardware provided the ability to distribute the physical address space of a region across all of the nodes in the system. This Distributed Global Address Space (DGAS), rather than the traditional Partitioned Global Address Space (PGAS), was then managed as a separate allocation pool. The interleaver was designed specifically to avoid stride access conflicts (Kaplan 1991).

7.4.3   BBN Lessons Learned

The Butterfly line provided a successful parallel implementation of Unix using the BSD/Mach base, though a lot of work was needed to replace and/or enhance the parts of the OS that were not scalable. Ultimately, the largest system deployed in production was a 128 node TC2000 at LLNL.

Using Mach, a research-oriented OS, ultimately did not prove practical for production, though it did provide a good conceptual starting point for some of the required functionality. The idea of a serverized OS was not necessary for the goals of these systems. And though parallelism was addressed in Mach, unfortunately some of the design choices were not scalable enough. Ultimately applying these concepts to standard BSD resulted in a production-worthy OS and some of the lessons learned were successfully carried forward to future work on the Tera MTA (described in Sect. 7.7) and other systems. This was especially true of the work on sleep/wakeup.

7.5   UNICOS-Max

The first Cray Massively Parallel Processor, MPP, was the T3D. The system returned to the front-end/back-end architecture. A Cray C90 was used as the front-end and an attached MPP, based on DEC Alpha processors and a Cray interconnect, was the back-end. The UNICOS-MAX system software consisted of UNICOS, used on the C90, and a Mach- based microkernel, used on the Alpha processors. The C90 moved data to the MPP and started application routines that executed on the Alpha processors. The system allowed Cray to make the first foray into MPPs without a substantive investment. Mach provided a simple base that could be made performant by limiting the scope of the OS functions it provided to a minimum necessary to execute a process. The UNICOS system provided a user interface simplifying the work on the MPP. This model of MPP as a back-end was the norm in the late 1980s and early 1990s.

7.6   UNICOS/mk

In 1992, a second MPP development project was started, called the T3E. Cray decided to drop Mach and the front-end/back-end architecture. The T3E would have a fully-featured UNICOS—including interactive access. But UNICOS could not be run across hundreds of processors and it was not possible to coordinate across nodes in the same way as a symmetric multiprocessor (SMP). Cray had been looking at Mach and other microkernels at the time as a way of solving the reliability problems of larger kernels (more lines of code) on Cray-1 systems by making OS services semi-independent of a base microkernel. The serverized UNICOS on a single SMP would run all the services in the same address space.

The microkernel that was chosen as a base was from a French company, Chorus Microsystems. The company was staffed by an international group of systems designers, including several people from the UltraComputer Project at NYU. The Chorus Architecture fit the serverization goals of Cray, and the memory design did not require virtual memory. Some of the Cray systems that would be using microkernels did not support virtual memory. Virtual Memory had been a sticking point with Mach, which required virtual memory support. Further, as the Open Software Foundation Advanced Development (OSF/1 AD) system showed, the performance advantages of Mach supporting a BSD kernel depended on user library access to kernel memory. This security hole may have been one of the factors that eventually scuttled OSF/1 AD and Mach. Mach had been an important part of the DARPA's MPP program. And the leadership within the MPP program at DARPA expressed their displeasure that Cray had chosen a French company to work with on its MPP software.

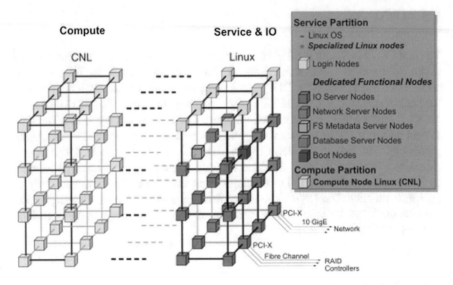

Fig. 7.1 Specialized nodes

The name chosen for the new system was UNICOS/mk. UNICOS was both the base software providing the services and user interfaces. The underlying microkernel was represented with the/mk.

The T3E would use the same overall serverized OS architecture but use the many nodes of the MPP to scale system services. The configuration would specialize nodes to perform specific services—application support or system service support. Compute nodes would only execute user processes and the most basic of system services. Services that could be performed locally on a compute node for an application were processed there. As a system scaled up the number of compute nodes, the expectation of more service requests could be met by independently scaling services on service nodes. But the overall system—up to the 512 processor maximum—was a single system image.

Specializing nodes, as shown in Fig. 7.1, made the system more flexible and scalable. Controlling the services run on nodes had the side effect of making them more reliable. By running a specific and limited set of activities, the nodes became less likely to be perturbed by unusual system activity. Further, confining users to nodes that only performed specific services made the system more secure.

This scalability depended on the interconnect being fast and reliable. The T3E hardware interconnect was not designed with supporting the load of system calls as a first priority. The application usage was the primary focus of the design of the network. But the network was sufficiently capable to allow interactive, X windows application debugging, and other services not thought possible on an HPC system.

One of the issues with MPP performance was noise, where noise is defined as operations not contributing to the process' progress. Because many HPC programs ran in bulk synchronous mode, anything that interfered with the forward progress of a process on one node affected the entire application across all nodes. Applications needed processes to run in lockstep. If an OS on one node was interrupted for a service request it affected the processes on all the other nodes. Reducing what ran on a compute node to the minimum, a microkernel, and a process manager, ensured the application would not be interfered with—finally something Seymour Cray could like in software—while more complicated system calls could be processed on nodes dedicated to just system call management.

Service nodes were an additional "cost". Internally and with customers, the expense of service nodes to support an application was viewed with suspicion. Cray hardware engineers made this a bit easier by adding nodes to the T3E blades—for resiliency. Each system had an extra node per blade, so the resiliency nodes scaled with the system size. A 512-processor system was actually a 544-processor system. The service nodes were using the resilient nodes meant to replace failed hardware. The customer was given 512 *compute* nodes which fit their application needs. For most systems the resiliency nodes were more than sufficient to run the OS services for that scale of system.

There were technical difficulties with UNICOS/mk. Unix process management and file system management were deeply intertwined. There was no clean way to separate these functions entirely as servers. There were always some interactions that required some boundary crossing. Some of the servers, like the network server, were never completed. The T3E depended on a single external network gateway through the life of the product. Multiple gateways were possible, but never implemented. And the grand goal of using serverized UNICOS across the MPP and SMP product lines was never accomplished. The context switch times of the T90 were too high and the benefits were insufficient for the effort. The level of effort to develop the T3E software was very high—a large part of Cray software development was involved in UNICOS/mk for several years. In the end, 88 T3E systems were sold. Cray Inc. sold and serviced T3E systems into the late 2000s.

7.7   Tera/Cray MTA

In 1988 the Tera Computer Company was founded to produce a new type of high-performance computer based on an aggressively multithreaded processor architecture called the Multithreaded Architecture (MTA) (Alverson et al. 1990, 1995). This processor was unique in several ways, which presented some challenges for OS implementations. Each of the potential 256 processors supported 128 completely independent hardware threads (in order to provide latency tolerance). The system presented primarily a uniform memory architecture (UMA) across all processors and threads, except for program code segments. All data was treated as having no locality due to the latency hiding attributes of the processor. However, each individual hardware thread could only issue an instruction at most once every 21 clock cycles on a given processor. This resulted in fairly slow serial performance. The processor was non-von Neumann. The code/program access paths were independent of the data paths and used separate address spaces. The data address space was segmented (with variable sized segments) and not paged. Finally, the processors did not support interrupts. Asynchronous events were handled by polling due to the large number of available hardware threads. Traps were always handled at the privileged level in which they were raised (no privilege escalation on traps). Gateway instructions were used to increase privilege. The system interconnect was a sparsely populated three-dimensional torus.

7.7.1   Tera MTK

In the early 1990s, as with other projects around the same time frame, Tera wanted a fully functional OS that had familiar interfaces and tools available for it. Unix/Linux scalability had improved since BBN considered it. BSD now had reasonable support for parallelism, though there remained scaling issues to address. But Linux did not scale, as at the time the Big Kernel Lock had not been introduced (appeared in version 2.0 in 1996). This led to Tera to select BSD as the basis for the OS. However, due to the significant differences in the MTA processor architecture from standard processors, it was decided to use a custom microkernel to handle the low-level chores of process, memory, and hardware management. The resulting OS was called MTK.

The MTA processor had three usable privilege levels (plus one for initialization). So it was decided to put the microkernel at *kernel* level and the BSD code at the *supervisor* level, leaving the normal user level and a special "Initial Program Load (IPL)" level also available. This was deemed useful since the microkernel was smaller and completely understood by the implementers, whereas the BSD layer was quite large and not necessarily fully understood. The microkernel was written primarily in C++ along with some amount of assembler code as needed. Calls from the BSD layer that were involved in memory or process management were implemented through a set of kernel "library" calls to access the microkernel functionality.

The microkernel was designed with scalability in mind from the start. The BSD layer needed more work to scale properly, including the work previously described (on BBN nX) for handling sleep/wakeup. Management of the Unix process table was also improved. Within the microkernel condition-style variables were often used instead, leveraging the MTA's two-phased locking protocols.

With the large amount of parallelism and large number of fine-grained locks introduced into the system, lock-based deadlock became more and more of an issue. MTK had support for managing a lock hierarchy so that strict lock ordering could be used to address the issue. The lock hierarchy system had both a dynamic and a static mode of operation. In the dynamic mode, the lock orders and levels were computed dynamically. This worked well at first, but soon became overwhelmed by the number of locks and the different ways they were acquired. So a static lock hierarchy and ordering was eventually used, though the initial static hierarchy was set up based on information from earlier dynamic runs.

The lack of hardware interrupts required innovative solutions to implement basic OS services. The microkernel dedicated one of the 128 streams, or hardware threads, per processor as *the listener* thread. The listener would poll an Inter-Processor Communication (IPC) queue for requests, check timeouts, and perform other housekeeping chores. The listener would create a new thread to handle each chunk of discovered work and continue checking.

Process scheduling on the MTA was handled a bit differently due to the desire to co-schedule all of the components of a process on the different processors. This is a bit different than other MPPs of the day that could only support one process running on a node at a time and time-shared the rest. While there were 128 hardware threads per processor on the MTA, shareable dynamically in hardware across multiple separate address spaces or process contexts, there were 16 sets of contexts available in each processor, one of which was reserved for OS use. So, 15 teams could be simultaneously running on any given processor, space sharing the machine. A hierarchy of structures was created underneath the process structure, most notably including a *Team* level that consisted of all of the threads on a given processor. The scheduler in the microkernel could then ensure that all of the Teams of a process were scheduled simultaneously on their respective processors. This was handled using two types of schedulers, one for large jobs consisting of multiple teams operating across the system, and one for small jobs that had only one team (even if that team had multiple threads) which operated on each individual node (Alverson et al. 1995). Typically, up to 2 or 3 large jobs were scheduled across the system along with up to another 12 small jobs scheduled locally on each processor, depending on the demand. By scheduling multiple jobs simultaneously on each node, the multithreaded processor could be kept busy, leveraging its latency tolerance capabilities and providing overall greater throughput.

The MTA provided reserve_stream and create_stream instructions, which allowed a user runtime library to allocate/destroy hardware threads on processors that the process had a team without OS intervention. The user runtime only needed to request OS intervention when the number of additional hardware resources required exceeded those available to existing teams and additional teams were needed. This division of fine-grain thread scheduling at the user level and coarse-grain team scheduling in the OS reduced the cost of adding hardware resources, allowing more parallelism to be realized.

Given that one of the original MTA's major features was the presentation of a primarily UMA, hardware support was required to provide the appropriate distribution of memory references across the machine, while also avoiding the issue of parallel stride access conflicts, similar to what was done in the BBN TC2000 described earlier. For the MTA, this was accomplished using an address scrambler based on a Galois Field matrix of two elements (GF2). The resulting physical address space was then managed using a global memory manager. This was the only "data" memory available on the MTA. Program memory was managed locally to each node.

The largest original MTA produced was only nine processors due to issues with the GaAs manufacturing process being used and the resulting low circuit densities. The MTA design was ported to CMOS and renamed the MTA-2 in 2000. A 40-node

MTA-2 system was deployed at the Naval Research Lab (NRL). With 40 processors each with potentially 128 separate hardware threads in the kernel, this represented a very high level of concurrency support (up to over 5,000 simultaneous threads in the kernel).

7.7.2 Cray XMT

In the mid-2000s, it was decided to bring the Tera MTA architecture over to the Cray XT product line (described in Sect. 7.9). XMT was the follow on to the MTA and was deployed using the Cray XT infrastructure. By designing an MTA processor variant called Threadstorm to be pin compatible with the Advanced Micro Devices (AMD) Opteron of the time, Cray was able to simply remove the Opteron from a Cray compute blade and insert a Threadstorm processor. The SeaStar network interface controller (NIC) was enhanced to support the load/store interface required for Threadstorm. The original XMT was designed to scale to 512 nodes and later to 2,048 nodes.

The speeds and feeds of XMT differed from MTA, and the convenience of a completely uniform memory architecture began to fade. As such, NUMA effects were now considered, especially in terms of processor stack allocations and certain kernel data structures that had affinity. These changes mostly affected the MTK microkernel but did have some effect on the BSD layer. The main change was the introduction of local "data" memory managers for each node, in addition to the global memory manager that already existed. The BSD layer was also updated to a more modern version at this time.

Given that the Threadstorm (and original MTA) processors did not have good single thread performance, a more appropriate front-end was desired. XT service nodes provided this front-end and ran the Cray Linux Environment (CLE, as described in Sect. 7.9). MTK became more of a back-end OS, and users no longer "logged in" to MTK (only to CLE) nor did they run interactively on the Threadstorm nodes.

XMT systems were designed to scale further than the original MTA and MTA-2. And since they relied primarily on the platform manufacturing capabilities of the popular XT line, the systems were far more stable than the originals. This resulted in the need to address additional scalability issues within MTK. One significant example came in the handling of remote segment table address space management. Remote procedure call (RPC) was used to propagate any memory mapping or unmapping requests to all processors in the system since the address translation hardware could only be accessed locally on each processor. This did result in issues, especially in the face of non-trivial numbers of memory allocation calls. This was addressed, as many such issues were, by changing from strict mutual exclusion locking to reader/writer locks. Much time was spent understanding and designing the correct type of reader/writer priority.

The largest XMT system ever delivered was 512 nodes and ultimately demonstrated good scalability even with the resulting amount of concurrency (potentially 65,536 simultaneous threads in one OS instance).

7.7.3 MTA Lessons Learned

Probably, the most important lesson learned with the MTA architecture is that scaling is hard. The amount of parallelism on a node, subsequently magnified via moderate node counts, really puts a lot of scaling stress on a single instance OS. Having a manageable lock hierarchy was an important part of addressing this issue, along with using proper complex locks (such as reader/writer rather than simple mutual exclusion).

Much of the rest of the work described in this section was more about the specific peculiarities of the MTA processor and so are not as relevant for the future on commodity processors. However, some of it may one day be relevant for some of the accelerator technologies being considered for the future.

7.8 UNICOS/lc

One of the first large projects after the formation of the new Cray Inc. in 2000 was the Redstorm project with Sandia National Laboratories. This called for a new, more commodity-based MPP with an HPC interconnect. The system was built using AMD Opteron processors connected to a proprietary Cray SeaStar network. The OS for Redstorm, UNICOS/lc, was modeled on node specialization—service nodes and compute nodes. The service nodes were, by now, Linux based, and the compute nodes ran a specialized kernel called Catamount developed by Sandia and Cray. This was not a single system image. It had lightweight—low noise—compute nodes with a small OS that did not require a large development group to support. The system was initially deployed with a total of 512 service nodes and over ten thousand single-core compute nodes, though the service nodes were split evenly between classified and unclassified uses. It was later upgraded to nearly 13,000 dual-core compute nodes. Much of this system architecture was inherited from the previous ASCI Red, though the service node OS on that previous system was not Linux (and the compute nodes used a predecessor to Catamount called Cougar).

The choice of Linux on the service nodes was readily accepted by customers. At this point, most proprietary Unix OSs were being dropped. Cray Research's UNICOS was not a viable alternative given the ×86 processor and the long-term support costs. Linux had reached a point where as a server OS it could support both the features and functionality needed. Linux also was a complete Unix-like implementation. Linux was not just functionally equivalent to Unix, applications like awk (a program for processing and analyzing text files in Unix and Linux) had exactly the same behaviors as they did in Unix, which is unusual given that the implementation of kernel, libraries, and awk had to be done without benefit of using Unix code in order to be free from AT & T license issues.

Redstorm was aimed at high scalability for MPI applications. The network was optimized for MPI message processing, and the compute node kernels were similarly organized to support a small set of local system calls and forward other system calls to servers running on service nodes that processed the system calls through Linux system requests. The server concept worked because of the low system call needs of Catamount applications and the better context switch times of $\times 86$ processors and Linux.

7.9   Rise of Linux on HPC Systems

While Redstorm with Catamount was successful, there were limits to the breadth of applications that were effectively supported and there was a strong desire to make XT systems usable by a broader HPC community. Some of the issues that were encountered included nonstandard (non-Unix/Linux) behaviors and issues with the age and maintainability of the Catamount code base. Some of these issues, especially the latter, were addressed by later microkernel work such as the Catamount follow-on called Kitten, but ultimately Cray decided that it wanted to put Linux on all of the compute nodes. The main driver for Cray was the desire to support a wide range of applications, including independent software vendor (ISV) applications, which was not practical without a standard Linux OS base.

This did cause consternation among some Cray customers, though most did agree that this was the right direction, even though a number doubted it could be accomplished. How could a lightweight—low noise—kernel that would support a broader set of Unix (now Linux) applications be developed for XT? Other HPC companies were using their own lightweight kernels and claiming that this was the only path to scale and performance. However, Beowulf cluster style systems were claiming high scale and performance using full Linux systems on all nodes—in some cases just turning off some demons on application nodes.

Cray modified the Linux kernel removing substantial amounts of functionality and "deadening out" other unnecessary functions to create a lightweight compute node OS, called Compute Node Linux (CNL). Removing Catamount and replacing the services with Linux service, sometimes directly on the compute nodes, allowed the system to look more like a single system and to process file and network requests in a more single system manner. Rather than doing library-based I/O system call offload, with all of its behavioral quirks, normal VFS- based I/O calls were supported through the Linux kernel.

Listing all of the kernel configuration changes made to accomplish this would take too much space, but some of the main areas that were configured for lower activity or completely shut off included: the read-copy-update (RCU) subsystem, some of the kernel memory allocators and related support, many scheduling features,

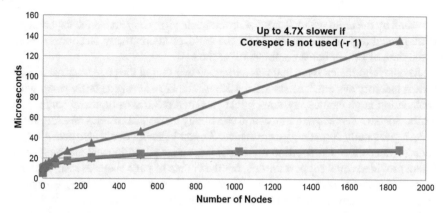

Fig. 7.2 8-Byte `MPI_Allreduce()` with/without core specialization (XC40 KNL   68 ranks/node)

many unneeded network features and protocols, many file system types and features, support for many devices not present in Cray systems, and some debugging support.

Later on, further improvements were made to CNL to support HPC applications. With the advent of hyperthreading and multicore commodity processors, core specialization was an important feature that was added that allows applications, on a per job launch basis, to ask that much of the background kernel activity, including some types of interrupts, be confined to only one or several specific hardware threads on a multithreaded/multicore processor, while the application ran on the rest of the hardware threads (Oral et al. 2010). Doing so removed much of the OS noise and resulting application jitter, and allowed collectives running across many nodes in an application to complete in a more timely fashion. This was introduced around the time of only four to eight hardware threads per node (normally two-socket nodes in XT5 and beyond) but really began to shine as thread counts increased, thereby reducing the percentage "tax" of stealing threads from the application. The Linux community has slowly been considering some of these issues, and may soon provide equivalent functionality, allowing Cray to stop maintaining this feature separately. Figure 7.2 shows the time to do an 8-byte `MPI_Allreduce()` on a Cray XC40 equipped with Intel Xeon Phi Knights Landing (KNL) 68-core processor nodes, with and without core specialization. The bottom line shows very good scaling with core specialization turned on, and up to 4.7 times worse performance without it at over 1,800 nodes with 130,000 ranks.

Some other functional advancements including improved COW page fault handling in the presence of pinned pages. Since the NICs of the time did not support demand paging, memory pages exposed to the NIC for RDMA needed to be "pinned" in the sense that they could not be moved, paged out, or otherwise modified while the NIC pointed to them. Forking such pages normally causes COW faults when the parent or child touches that page (that is initially shared in normal *fork*/vfork style handling). Linux, by default, always allocates a new page to the first process that attempts to write the page, but if that is the parent, then the original page ends up inherited by the child which is not the desired behavior. Cray added the capability to mark pinned regions as unavailable for the child, or alternatively, as copied eagerly at the time of *fork*, or some combination of the two.

Another significant issue that was addressed was that of the page sizes used in the virtual memory system. The standard 4 Kbyte Linux page size is fairly small when considering large memory systems (gigabytes) and the size of typically commodity TLBs. Sparse reference patterns would essentially cause TLB misses on every reference, significantly degrading performance. Similar behavior could also occur in NIC address translation. The solution was to use large page allocation and mapping sizes. Linux provided some support for this, but the choice of page size was restricted that supported natively by the commodity processors. This was fairly limiting, especially given that the network address translation hardware in the NIC was more flexible with more page sizes to choose from. The solution to this was to divorce the page allocation size from the processor native mapping sizes, to allow pages sizes more natural for the NIC. A lingering problem with huge page support is the inability to coalesce fragmented pages and keep a set of huge pages available. A reboot of a node is required to restore huge pages, which is a problem for applications, resource management, and a waste of system cycles.

Providing for system-level resiliency was another challenge addressed with extensions to CLE. A mechanism called the Resiliency Communication Agent (RCA) was written to allow processes in Linux to access the publish/subscribe event bus provisioned on Cray's Hardware Supervisory System (HSS). This allows service daemons to register with RCA and potentially publish important events. During registration, the daemon can also optionally specify that a heartbeat would be provided by the daemon for additional confidence that the service is healthy. If either the heartbeat stops (if specified) or if the registered daemon or process exits, a failure event is generated. Clients of the service can register for these events. This allows the provisioning of various resiliency failover schemes for CLE services. In addition, RCA is used to provide a low-level kernel heartbeat to the supervisory system so that it could detect the failure of nodes without needing explicit notification. Some services also subscribed to these events to detect various forms of peer failures, though care needed to be taken to not overwhelm the out-of-band event bus. An example of this is the job launcher, where each node in the launch fanout tree subscribes for the failures of its ancestors and descendants in the tree. These failures are then propagated up and down the tree internally to the launcher as needed for cleanup or recovery.

Some of the work done on BSD-based systems from both BBN and Tera MTA also still applied to Linux, though many of the implementations were now different. Many of the features addressing scalability were brought over in some form.

Many different systems were shipped by Cray using the CLE software base including XT3 (same hardware as Redstorm), XT4 (multicore Opterons), XT5 (two-socket Opteron nodes), XE6 (two-socket Opteron nodes with new Gemini interconnect), and XK6 (nodes with an Opteron and Nvidia GPU with Gemini). Note that the previously described XMT used the XT5 package and CLE on the commodity processors.

7.9.1   CLE Today

Cray XC systems today are built with several different types of Intel processors along with Nvidia GPUs in some configurations, all on the new Aries based proprietary network. ARM processors are also supported. They use a CLE that is fairly similar, though evolved and improved from the OS used on Cray XT, XE, and XK systems. Various additional features have been added including the DataWarp I/O acceleration system, support for multiple different workload managers via published interfaces, and advanced power management, to name a few.

One key piece of technology used heavily in current CLE deployments is the Data Virtualization Service (DVS). This service provides remote access to any VFS compliant file system by provisioning servers to project such file systems to clients on other nodes. This service is used to project root file system and shared library content from a set of service nodes to the compute nodes in a hierarchical fan out.

Another important feature recently added to CLE is support for user-level container, specifically Docker and the related Shifter containers (Jacobsen and Canon 2015). These technologies allow for the packaging of an application and its supporting environment in an easy to use, portable image. Docker support is focused on single-node jobs and those that use TCP/IP for communication. Shifter adds the capability for native device access so that HPC protocols can be run directly, such as that provided by the proprietary interconnects in these systems, and so is appropriate for multi-node jobs.

There are several very large deployments of CLE in the field today. NCSA Blue Waters has the largest of the Cray XE/XK systems, with 26,868 compute nodes (mix of CPU and GPU nodes). ORNL Titan is also a very large Cray XK system with 18,688 GPU based compute nodes. LANL Trinity is currently the largest Cray XC system with 19,420 compute nodes (mix of Haswell and Knights Landing nodes).

7.9.2   CLE Tomorrow

Cray is currently designing its next generation of systems, code named "Shasta". CLE will be a significant part of that design and is expected to provide the OS support required to get to exascale-class supercomputing. However, Cray does recognize that some customers may not want CLE, both those that prefer non-Unix/Linux compute node OSs and those that may prefer a Linux deployment with a different derivation than Cray CLE. Cray is embarking on a plan to support such alternatives with a more flexible system management implementation.

There are two major issues to contend with for such non-Cray provided OS deployments: network access and interaction with the management system. For the former, Linux device drivers from the relevant network vendors should suffice for Linux-based implementations. Non-Linux alternatives may be harder and vendor dependent (easier if the network interfaces are open source). Interaction with the management system on Shasta will be handled with new open and published interfaces that will be plumbed through standard Ethernet-based management networks. This includes an Ethernet-based replacement for RCA. Given that these interfaces will be open and published, integration should be straightforward regardless of the OS base.

There are several other interesting technologies that Cray sees as having value for future OS environments. First, containers provide a means to isolate applications and their supporting libraries from other software stacks. Extending containers to include kernels is an interesting way to completely isolate applications and also reduce the supporting software stack to a minimum. For highly scalable applications this could be a big advantage, although there are security and other concerns that need to be resolved if containers have uncontrolled access to the system interconnect. For the analytic and artificial intelligence (AI) frameworks that use a more fully featured OS and software stack, using a container with an OS kernel might also be of interest. Under these fully featured containers, HyperVisors or VMs might ease both security and reliability concerns. The alternatives here need to be considered and experimented with, but there are good alternatives that can support a variety of existing and new applications.

7.9.3 CLE/CNL Lessons Learned

The main takeaway from the CLE experience is that Linux can be made to work at scale. This allows users to enjoy the benefits of a mature ecosystem in the context of highly scalable computers. But there are trade-offs. Work is required to make Linux scale, and while the community is starting to pay attention, it remains to be seen whether they will eventually have sufficient focus to allow vendors to avoid doing extra work on scalability. And even then, for some applications, the broad ecosystem is not as important as raw performance and keeping the OS out of the way. But for other applications, the ecosystem needs will likely continue to dominate.

Another lesson is that using an industry standard OS creates significant customer expectations. And these expectations are often at odds with the desire for scalability. The continuing strategy of providing services on nodes separate from where most of the computation occurs can help, but can also introduce issues on how those services are accessed.

The choices of OSs were most often trade-offs between the pursuit of raw performance and the need to develop and grow communities of users. The arguments about complexity, ease of development and support, and near-religious fervor over how a microsecond should be used, were proxies for the larger question of how to make trade-offs. Unix and Linux were productivity plays. But the need to make those productivity plays perform was real and took a great deal of time and effort. In the future, there is no obvious synthesis of this dialectic. The growing complexities of hardware and software in HPC systems will be a Gordian knot for some time to come.

Acknowledgements The authors would like to thank several people for their contributions to this document in specific areas. Carl Howe, Dan Tappan, Dave Barach, and Steve Blumenthal all provided important information on BBN's efforts. Rich Korry contributed information on MTK. Dean Roe provided details for CLE/CNL. Steve Reinhardt provided data and corrections on the Cray Research history, and provided the ideas for lessons learned from that experience.

References

(1995). UNICOS MCPF-2580394. Cray Research.

Alverson, G. A., Kahan, S., Korry, R., McCann, C., & Smith, B. J. (1995). Scheduling on the Tera MTA. In *Proceedings of the Workshop on Job Scheduling Strategies for Parallel Processing*, IPPS '95 (pp. 19–44). London: Springer.

Alverson, R., Callahan, D., Cummings, D., Koblenz, B., Porterfield, A., & Smith, B. (1990). The Tera computer system. In *Proceedings of the 4th International Conference on Supercomputing*, ICS '90 (pp. 1–6). New York: ACM.

Barach, D. R., Wells, R., Uban, T., & Gibson, J. (1990). Highly parallel virtual memory management on the TC2000. In *Proceedings of the 1990 International Conference on Parallel Processing*, ICPP '90 (pp. 549–550).

Baskett, F., Howard, J. H., & Montague, J. T. (1977). Task communication in DEMOS. In *Proceedings of the Sixth ACM Symposium on Operating Systems Principles*, SOSP '77 (pp. 23–31). New York: ACM.

Beeler, M. (1990). Inside the TC2000 computer.

Black, D. L., Tevanian, A., Jr., Golub, D. B., & Young, M. W. (1991). Locking and reference counting in the mach kernel. In *Proceedings of 1991 ICPP, Volume II, Software* (pp. 167–173). Boca Raton: CRC Press.

Brooks, E. D., Gorda, B. C., Warren, K. H., & Welcome, T. S. (1991). BBN TC2000 architecture and programming models. In *Compcon Spring '91. Digest of Papers* (pp. 46–50).

Brugger, S., & Streletz, G. (2001). Network livermore time sharing system (NLTSS). http://www.computer-history.info/Page4.dir/pages/LTSS.NLTSS.dir/pages/NLTSS.pdf.

Crowther, W., Goodhue, J., Gurwitz, R., Rettberg, R., & Thomas, R. (1985). The butterfly parallel processor. *IEEE Computer Architecture Newsletter*, 18–45.

Edmond, W., Bumenthal, S., Echenique, A., Storch, S., & Calderwood, T. (1986). The butterfly satellite IMP for the wideband packet satellite network. In *ACM SIGCOMM Computer Communication Review* (Vol. 16, pp. 194–203). New York: ACM.

Howe, C. D. (1988). An overview of the butterfly GP1000: a large-scale parallel Unix computer. In *Proceedings of the Third International Conference on Supercomputing*, ICS '88.

Jacobsen, D. M. & Canon, R. S. (2015). Contain this, unleashing Docker for HPC. In *Proceedings of the Cray User Group*.

Kaplan, L. S. (1991). A flexible interleaved memory design for generalized low conflict memory access. In *Proceedings of the Sixth Distributed Memory Computing Conference, 1991* (pp. 637–644).

Laboratory, C. D. G. L. A. N. (1982). *CTSS Overview*. Los Alamos National Laboratory, la-5525-m, Vol. 7 edition.

LeBlanc, T. J., Scott, M. L., & Brown, C. M. (1988). Large-scale parallel programming: Experience with BBN butterfly parallel processor. In *Proceedings of the ACM/SIGPLAN Conference on Parallel Programming: Experience with Applications, Languages and Systems*, PPEALS '88 (pp. 161–172). New York: ACM.

Morton, D. (2015). IBM mainframe operating systems: Timeline and brief explanation for the IBM System/360 and beyond.

Oral, S., Wang, F., Dillow, D., Miiler, R., Shipman, G., Maxwell, D., et al. (2010). Reducing application runtime variability on Jaguar XT5. In *Proceedings of Cray User Group*.

Partridge, C., & Blumenthal, S. (2006). Data networking at BBN. *IEEE Annals of the History of Computing, 28*(1), 56–71.

Rettberg, R., Wyman, C., Hunt, D., Hoffman, M., Carvey, P., Hyde, B., et al. (1979). Development of a voice funnel system: Design report. Technical report. Cambridge: Bolt Beranek and Newman Inc.

Sheltzer, A., Hinden, R., & Haverty, J. (1983). The DARPA internet: Interconnecting heterogeneous computer networks with gateways. *Computer, 16*, 38–48.

Unknown. (1996). Folklore: An innovative approach to a user interface. *Cryptolog - The Journal of Technical Health, XXII*(4), 11–16.

Various (1955–1989). Control data corporation records. Product literature. Charles Babbage Institute Archives, University of Minnesota.

Chapter 8
SCore

Atsushi Hori, Hiroshi Tezuka, Shinji Sumimoto, Toshiyuki Takahashi,
Hiroshi Harada, Mitsuhisa Sato and Yutaka Ishikawa

Abstract SCore is a software package for high- performance clusters. It includes a low-level communication layer named PM(v2), a user-level, global operating system called SCore-D, an MPI implementation, an OpenMP compiler that enables OpenMP programs to run on distributed memory clusters, as well as other cluster management utility programs. SCore was developed by the Real World Computing Partnership project during 1992–2002. SCore provided state-of-the-art technologies at the time. Some of the technologies became obsolete but some of them, e.g., gang scheduling and checkpoint with parity are still unique.

A. Hori (✉) · H. Harada · M. Sato · Y. Ishikawa
Riken R-CCS, 7-1-26 Minatojima-minami-machi, Chuo-ku, Kobe, Hyogo 650-0047, Japan
e-mail: ahori@riken.jp

H. Harada
e-mail: hiroshi.harada@riken.jp

M. Sato
e-mail: msato@riken.jp

Y. Ishikawa
e-mail: yutaka.ishikawa@riken.jp

H. Tezuka
Department of Creative Informatics Graduate School of Information Science and Technology,
The University of Tokyo, 7-3-1 Hongo, Bunkyo-ku, Tokyo 113-8656, Japan
e-mail: tezuka.hiroshi@ci.i.u-tokyo.ac.jp

S. Sumimoto
Fujitsu Ltd., 4-1-1 Kamikodanaka, Nakahara-ku, Kawasaki 211-8588, Japan
e-mail: sumimoto.shinji@jp.fujitsu.com

T. Takahashi
METAHACK Japan, K.K., 2-4-4-201 Honkugenuma, Fujisawa, Kanagawa 251-0028, Japan
e-mail: toshi@metahack.jp

© Springer Nature Singapore Pte Ltd. 2019
B. Gerofi et al. (eds.), *Operating Systems for Supercomputers
and High Performance Computing*, High-Performance Computing Series,
https://doi.org/10.1007/978-981-13-6624-6_8

8.1 Background

SCore (pronounced as [*es-core*]) is the name of a software package for high-performance clusters. It includes a middleware global OS, a low-level communication library, an MPI implementation, etc. SCore was developed in the Real World Computing Partnership (RWCP) project funded by Japanese government from 1992 to 2002, a 10-year project. Shortly after the beginning of the project, a variety of user-level communication libraries were developed, e.g., U-Net (von Eicken et al. 1995), AM (von Eicken et al. 1992), FM (Pakin et al. 1997). The Myrinet network (Boden et al. 1995), which had a programmable processor in the network interface card (NIC), played a big role in these developments. The SCore development team was no exception, so the PM(v2) communication library on Myrinet had been developed (Tezuka et al. 1997). Unlike other user-level communication libraries, however, the PM(v2) was designed with OS support in mind.

Another dominant trend of the time was the increasing prevalence of Beowulf clusters (Sterling et al. 1995). Thomas Sterling et al., developed a parallel machine, the so-called *Beowulf Cluster*, combining commodity parts and software, e.g., x86-based PCs, Ethernet, and Linux. As opposed to the Beowulf clusters, the SCore software package aimed at higher performance clusters.

In the early 90s, clusters were called COWs (Cluster of Workstations) or NOWs (Network of Workstations). SCore was first developed on SunOS (BSD) as the global OS for COWs or NOWs (Fig. 8.1), then moved to NetBSD. Finally, SCore was ported to Linux.

Fig. 8.1 Workstation cluster of 36 Sun workstations connected with Myrinet installed at RWCP, 1996. This cluster was used to develop the first version of SCore

8.2 Technical Details

8.2.1 SCore Overview

SCore is the name of a software package for HPC clusters. SCore-D is the global operating system to manage clusters (Hori et al. 1998). Since SCore-D runs on top of Unix (SunOS, NetBSD or Linux) on each node, it can be considered a middleware operating system. The SCore software package also includes the *scout* parallel shell environment, *PM(v2)*, a low-level communication library for Myrinet, Ethernet, InfiniBand and Shmem for intra-node communication, *MPC++*, (a multi-threaded C++ for distributed memory machines), an MPI implementation utilizing PM(v2), *SCASH*, a software-distributed shared memory implementation, and *OMNI*, an OpenMP compiler on top of SCASH. All of these programs and libraries were developed in the RWCP project. Most of them were unique and state of the art at the time.

8.2.2 SCore-D and PM(v2)

PM was originally developed as a communication library for Myrinet. Later, it was enhanced to support multiple protocols including Ethernet and Shmem, and it was renamed to PM(v2). PM(v2) supports zero-copy communication and proposed the pin-down cache (Tezuka et al. 1998), which has been widely used in other communication libraries.

We believed that for ease of use there was a need for time-sharing scheduling that gives users shorter response times than that of batch scheduling. At the time of the SCore development, the RWCP project obtained a CM-5 machine which supported time-sharing scheduling (i.e, gang scheduling). Another part of our motivation came from experiences of using Cray-1, which also switched from batch scheduling to time-sharing.

SCore-D, as an OS, had to guarantee the soundness of user jobs and PM had to provide a mechanism for that. PM(v2)'s endpoints were created by SCore-D and then passed to user processes. The routing table of PM was set by SCore-D to prevent user processes from sending messages to nodes outside of the set allocated to a particular job. The functions needed for the gang scheduling were privileged and only accessible from SCore-D. Thus, each endpoint had two ports, a privileged one for SCore-D and another one for user processes.

Among various user-level communication libraries, PM(v2) was the only one that supported these global OS functionalities. However, these ideas did not widely spread and SCore would face problems with the forthcoming InfiniBand NIC (Fig. 8.2).

Local Scheduling

Unix operating systems (including Linux) support time-sharing scheduling. Each process is assigned a time slot, often several 10 milliseconds, which renders the

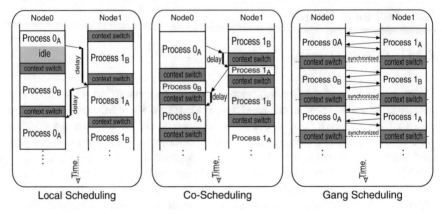

Fig. 8.2 Comparison of local scheduling, co-scheduling, and gang scheduling. "Process NX" means it is the N-th process of job X. Process 0_A and 1_A, or 0_B and 1_B communicate with one another in the same job

process eligible to run for the given period, unless it blocks on a system call. When the time slot is exhausted or the process is blocked for some reason, the OS scheduler selects another process to run and stops the execution of the current process, i.e., it switches the context and resumes execution of the new process.

This time-sharing scheduling of Unix (or Linux) works well on sequential processes. However, usually a parallel job consists of multiple processes running on different nodes. This means that context switches on different nodes may happen independently, not in a synchronized fashion. Let us consider the case where process 0 of a job sends a message to process 1 of the same job running on different nodes and process 0 waits for the answer of the message. If process 1 is not scheduled, then process 0 must wait until process 1 is scheduled and sends back a reply. Thus, waiting time of process 0 is wasted. This asynchronous scheduling in a cluster (i.e., over a set of compute nodes) is called *local scheduling*. To reduce waste, schedulers running on cluster nodes must be synchronized in some way.

Co-scheduling

When a process waits for an incoming message, the OS can block its execution and switch to another process, eligible to run. When a message arrives to one of the descheduled processes, which is waiting for incoming message(s), then the process becomes eligible to run. All processes eligible to run in a cluster are processes not waiting for incoming messages. This scheduling method is called *co-scheduling*. Co-scheduling can hide the communication latency by scheduling other processes.

Note that the communication latency must be larger than the time needed for context switching. Otherwise the communication latency cannot be hidden and the context switch overhead can hinder the execution of a parallel job. In general, this co-scheduling is effective when communication happens infrequently and communication latency is high. However, most HPC applications communicate very frequently and the latency of high-performance networks is low. Another problem of co-scheduling is that a process must wait for a message by a blocking system call and kernel drivers usually control the NIC by utilizing interrupts. However, user-level communication aims at eliminating the overhead of system calls and interrupt handling to achieve high communication performance. Thus, there is a disconnect between concepts of co-scheduling and user-level communication.

Gang Scheduling

Gang scheduling is a time-sharing scheduling technique where all processes of a parallel job are scheduled in a fully synchronized way. Let us assume that a job consists of process 0 and 1, running on different nodes. Gang scheduling synchronizes execution and all processes of a job are either in running or blocking states. There is no additional latency but the context switch overhead of gang scheduling. Thus, gang scheduling and user-level communication are well suited to each other.

Which one is the best approach?

Uncoordinated local scheduling results in low performance of job execution. In co-scheduling, processes are naturally coordinated by message reception, but high overhead, system-level communication must be applied. Gang scheduling may suffer from higher overhead because of global synchronization. Which one is better between co-scheduling and gang scheduling? The answer depends on many system parameters, e.g., the communication latency (system-level communication in co-scheduling, user-level communication in gang scheduling), process context switch duration, the overhead of global co-ordination in gang scheduling, etc. Co-scheduling works well if coordination by messaging does not depend on the communication pattern of the job. In contrast, the overhead of gang scheduling does not depend on the applications' communication pattern.

8.2.3 Network Preemption

To enable efficient time-sharing, our parallel and global operating system, named SCore-D, and the low-level communication layer, first called PM and later renamed to PM(v2), were codesigned from the beginning. The most important technical issue here was the handling of inflight messages. When a job is scheduled, all inflight messages at the time of the previous context switch must be restored. If a network is a direct network, i.e., where NICs are attached to a router and there are no network switches, it is possible for the CPU to save and restore inflight messages in the NIC and instruct the router when to switch jobs. If a network is indirect, i.e., where there are other switches or router boxes apart from compute nodes, it is very hard for the CPU to access the switch status. CM-5, which was the first commercial and parallel machine supporting practical gang scheduling, had an indirect network and inflight messages were rerouted to go to the nearest nodes at the time of context switching (Leiserson et al. 1996). PM was first developed on Myrinet which is categorized as an indirect network, and had no support for saving or restoring switch status.

Myrinet and *Network Preemption*

Myrinet network interface card (NIC) was a PCI device and it consisted of a CPU (called *LANai*), static RAM (SRAM), and a DMA engine which could move data between the SRAM and the host memory. To send a message, first the LANai processor triggered the DMA to copy the message from the host memory to the NIC memory, then the message was injected to the network. To receive a message, it followed the reverse sequence. Thus, the messages had to be stored in the SRAM in any case. Here, *endpoint* is defined as a object from which a user program can send and receive messages. Endpoints over nodes are logically connected with the others so that an endpoint can send and receive messages to/from any connected endpoints. Here, this set of connected endpoints is called a *channel*. One cannot communicate with the another one belonging to the other channel.

Consider the case, where two independent parallel jobs running on the same cluster use the Myrinet network. A message sent from a job must not be received by the other job. To realize this, each job must have a different channel. So the number of channels means the maximum number of jobs running at the same time. Indeed the size of SRAM in the NIC was very small, only 512 KiB, at the time of SCore development, and our PM(v2) could provide 13 channels on it. This might sound enough to run 13 jobs at the same time, but for symmetric multiprocessor (SMP) clusters a job could consume the same number of channels with the number of CPU cores (see Sect. 8.2.7). So the number of channels was not enough to run multiple jobs. Instead, we implemented a *virtual channel* where a *physical* channel was multiplexed by saving and restoring the channel status to/from the host memory. This is what we call *network preemption* inspired from the context switching of CPUs for scheduling multiple tasks.

Nowadays a NIC (or often called HCA) can send and receive messages directly from/into the host memory. And a larger number of channels can also be supported (e.g., in InfiniBand). So users do not have to care about the number of the channels and no network preemption is needed any more.

PM's endpoint had a receive message buffer. When a message came in and there was room for the message, the receiver would send back and ACK packet to the sender. When there was no room, it would send back a NACK packet. In normal operation, the sender receiving NACK packets resends the corresponding message. Otherwise, the sender releases the send buffer occupied by the message. When context switching begins, first all message sending is blocked, and then senders would wait for all ACK or NACK packets. When all ACK and NACK packets are received, endpoints are ready for context switching. SCore-D initiated this network preemption on all nodes of a job and waited for these events in a barrier. In this way, it was guaranteed that the preempted job had no inflight messages.

One could argue that the network preemption is unnecessary if every process to be context-switched has independent end-point(s). PM had several "channels" to be associated with endpoints. When an endpoint is associated with a channel, then it becomes active and it is ready to send and receive. When network preemption takes place, the channels in use are also switched to other endpoints allocated to other processes. If there was the same number of channels with the number of endpoints and each job exclusively owns its channels, then network preemption would not be needed because no messages would be delivered to the wrong endpoint at the time of context switching. By doing so, however, the program running on the Myrinet NIC should poll all send buffers when the doorbell flag is set to indicate a message is ready to be sent. The processor on the Myrinet NIC was slower than that of the host processor, and this would have added extra latency in message sending. Thus, we eventually decided to have a smaller number of channels than that of endpoints.

Before and after network preemption, user processes of a given job must be stopped and processes of the new scheduled job must be resumed. Since SCore-D was implemented at user level, user processes were stopped by sending the SIGSTOP signal and resumed by SIGCONT.

The network preemption was applied not only for gang scheduling but also for deadlock detection and for checkpoint-restart described in the following paragraphs.

Global State Detection

There was a shared memory region between the SCore-D process and a user process to communicate that a user process may request a service to SCore-D. In this shared memory region, there was a flag to indicate the state of the user process whether it was idle or busy. When a user process had nothing to do but waiting for incoming messages, then the upper level communication layer, i.e., MPI, would set the flag. If the PM(v2) library detected an incoming message the flag was reset.

During job context switching, the saved network context was inspected and if there were no inflight messages found in the network context and all flags of the currently running job indicated idle, the job was considered to be in a deadlock. If there was at least one outstanding request to SCore-D, then the job was considered to be idle waiting for a request and the job would not be scheduled until the request was done (Hori et al. 1997). By detecting user jobs status, idle or deadlocked, SCore-D could avoid wasting valuable computational resources.

Real-Time Load Monitor

In user-level communication, polling is often used to wait for incoming messages. Thus, it is very hard to see from outside of a process if the process is busy for computation or idle just waiting for messages. The idle flag used for detecting the global state of a job could also be used to monitor if a process was busy or idle. SCore-D could display the job's business in real time by sampling the idle flags (shown in Fig. 8.3).

8.2.4 High Availability

The SCore operating system was also designed to be fault resilient. There were two technologies developed; support for checkpoint-restart of user jobs as well as automatic restart of SCore-D global OS.

Computing Phase

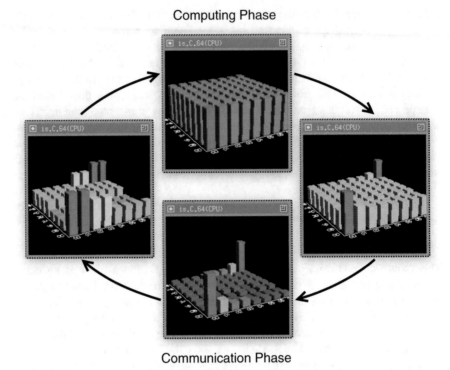

Communication Phase

Fig. 8.3 Example of SCore real-time load monitor showing the status of each process. The tall (and red) bar represents the business of a process and the low (and blue) bar represents the idleness of a process. In this example, NPB IS.C.64 was running. Alternations of communication phase and computation phase can be seen

Checkpoint and Parity

A consistent checkpointing mechanism can be implemented by using network preemption because network consistency is assured (Nishioka et al. 2000). SCore-D assumed that each node has a local disk, there was no reliable and scalable parallel file system at that time, so process contexts and network contexts were saved to local disks. In case of a node failure, the local disk of the node became inaccessible. To ensure survival from this condition, a unique parity was introduced.

RAID systems having parity are widely used. However, RAID systems require an extra disk for parity. In case of clusters with local disks on each compute node there was no extra disk and RAID-like parity system could not be applied. In the SCore checkpointing system, the idea of parity blocks was very similar to that in RAID systems, however, without the requirement of an extra disk (Kondo et al. 2003).

Figure 8.4 shows how parity was computed and stored into local disks. Every node wrote the process image and network context to its local disk. When a node wrote the first block to the disk, it would send the block to its neighboring node. On the neighbor, the received parity block and the second block to write were XORed

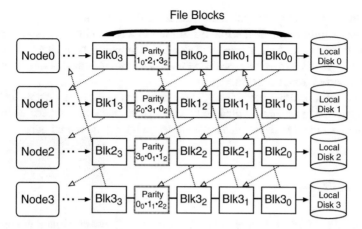

Fig. 8.4 Example of checkpoint parity

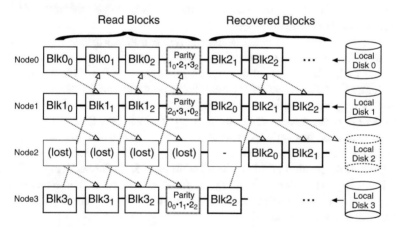

Fig. 8.5 Example of recovery when local Disk2 was lost in Fig. 8.4. The lost file was treated as zero-filled and the procedure for saving checkpoint data with parity was used to reproduce the lost blocks

and this parity block was sent to its neighbor. This procedure was repeated $N - 1$ times, where N is the number of participating nodes, and the received parity block was written to the disk. Similar procedure can also reproduce a lost file (shown in Fig. 8.5).

Automatic Restart of Jobs

Since SCore-D was a global OS, a node failure could result in a deadlock. Fortunately, SCore-D was programmed with MPC++, a multithread C++ extension described in the next subsection and SCore-D had a watch dog timer running as a dedicated thread. A token was passed around among compute nodes periodically. When a time out was detected, all SCore-D processes were shut down. Since this shutdown was done by the Scout environment (see Sect. 8.2.6), all SCore-D processes running on each node were successfully terminated without resulting in any zombie processes. The jobs running at the time of a shutdown were also killed, however, when the SCore-D was restarted by an operator, those jobs were restarted from the checkpointed images, if any, or restarted from the beginning.

The system operator could specify some nodes in the cluster as spares. If SCore-D was restarted to replace a failed node with a spare node, then processes from the failed node were migrated to the new node set including the spare node.

8.2.5 MPC++

SCore-D was a fairly complex system because each process frequently communicated with others to control and monitor user jobs. From the beginning, we decided to develop a parallel language to write SCore-D. This language was called MPC++, a multithreaded extension to C++.

MPC++ version 1.0 was designed for parallel/distributed programming (Ishikawa, 1996). Instead of setting several language extensions, we have designed a number of low-level parallel description primitives and the MPC++ meta-level architecture to realize an extendable/modifiable programming language system. The parallel description primitives were designed to make the development of the SCore-D operating system as well as complex user applications easy. These primitives were: (a) remote method invocation, (b) synchronization objects, and (c) global pointers.

MPC++ Version 2.0 was designed in two levels, level 0 and level 1. Level 0 specified parallel description primitives realized by the Multi-Thread Template Library (MTTL), C++ templates without any language extensions to define the MPC++ basic parallel execution model. Level 1 specified the MPC++ meta-level architecture and application specific extensions.

There was a user-level multithreaded runtime system implemented for MPC++, named User-Level Thread (ULT), which utilizes the PM communication library. MPC++ and ULT were designed not only for SCore-D but also users to write application programs. Since SCore-D processes ran with user processes, ULT for SCore-D was waiting for incoming messages in blocking operations to avoid consuming CPU time for polling.

8.2.6 Scout Parallel Shell Environment

Scout was a parallel shell execution environment, which was also used to boot up SCore-D processes. Figure 8.6 shows an example of the scout parallel shell execution. The scout command with the -g option followed by a hostname list separated by the "+" symbol creates a scout session on the listed hosts. On the front-end host where the scout command is invoked, a new shell is created. If the scout command followed

Fig. 8.6 Example of `scout` parallel shell execution. In this example, the value of the SHLVL environment is printed for readers to see the increased SHLVL value, indicating a new shell is created in the scout session

```
user$ echo $SHLVL
1
user$ scout -g comp0+comp1+ ... +comp6+comp7
SCOUT: session started.
user$ echo $SHLVL
2
user$ scout date
[comp0-3]:
Mon Jan 15 10:10:12 GMT 2018
[comp4]:
Mon Jan 15 10:10:11 GMT 2018
[comp5-7]:
Mon Jan 15 10:10:12 GMT 2018
user$ ^D
SCOUT: Session done.
```

by a normal command is typed in the scout session, the command is executed on every host. The unique feature of the scout command is that the STDOUT messages of each command were merged if the messages of adjacent nodes (see below) were the same. If the created shell terminates, the scout session is also terminates.

When a scout session is created, scout processes are created on each node and they are connected with TCP/IP connections forming a ring topology (shown in Fig. 8.7). The `scout` command invoked by a user becomes a front-end process and forks another shell. Each `scout` process receives the output via STDOUT of the executed command and the output is buffered. The scout process also receives the output of the previous scout process of the ring, and it is compared with the buffered output. If they are the same, then the buffered output is discarded and the received previous output is sent to the next node. If they are not the same, first the local buffered output is sent and then the previous output is sent to the next node. Once this is done, then the previous output is merely forwarded to the next `scout` process until it receives the output of the last node. Merging adjacent messages can reduce the network traffic, and user can easily identify nodes having the same output.

This message merging did not take place when SCore-D was running in a scout session. In that case, the output messages of every SCore-D process were merely forwarded to the front-end scout process.

8.2.7 *From PM to PM(v2)*

After the successful development of SCore-D and PM, the SCore development team decided to expand PM to support Ethernet devices and Shmem for intra-node communication.

Ethernet Device

Beowulf clusters used normal Ethernet drivers and the TCP/IP protocol. There is significant overhead in the protocol layers defined by OSI on top of physical protocol

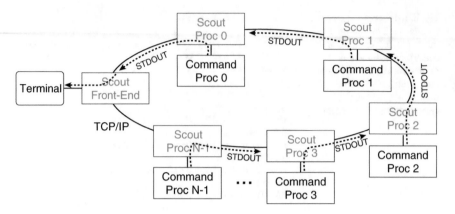

Fig. 8.7 Scout process structure

layer. Our goal was to have a new thin protocol layer optimized for HPC communication. The first implementation was to modify the firmware of the Ethernet NIC. This implementation, called *Giga-E PM*, could roughly double the communication performance, however, the availability of the NIC capable of modifying its firmware was very limited. So we decided to develop a new Linux kernel driver for the thin protocol. This was not a user-level communication because users had to call a system call to send messages and the driver required interrupts raised by Ethernet NIC. However, this approach still doubled the performance on the same Ethernet NIC. This PM device implemented as a kernel driver was named *PM Ethernet* (Sumimoto et al. 1999, 2000a, b).

Intra-Node Communication Device

The first version of the PM(v2) intra-node device used shared memory. However, to send a message, two memory copies must have taken place; one for copying message to the shared memory region and another one to copy the message form the shared memory region to the target buffer. So, we decided to develop a Linux kernel module that allowed a process to expose a memory region to another process resulting in one memory copy to send an intra-node message (Takahashi et al. 1999). This technique is known as kernel-assisted intra-node messaging nowadays. KNEM (Buntinas et al. 2006) and LiMIC (Jin et al. 2005) are implementations of the same idea.

Multi-protocol Support

PM(v2) had a routing table. Although the name might be confusing, this routing table had PM(v2) devices indexed by node number to choose which PM(v2) device to send messages to, not the pass to get the destinations. This routing table is a pseudo PM(v2) device supporting all PM(v2) functions and was named as *PM Composite* (Takahashi et al. 2000). Figure 8.8 shows an example of this routing table.

Routing Table of Rank0

Rank # of job	PM Device	Channel #	Node # of device	MTU
0	-	-	-	-
1	Shmem	-	1	8192
2	Myrinet	0	1	4096
3	Mryinet	1	1	4096
4	Ethernet	0	2	1500
5	Ethernet	1	2	1500
6	Ethernet	0	3	1500
7	Ethernet	1	3	1500

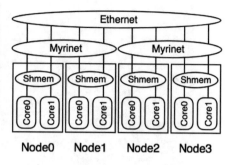

Fig. 8.8 This figure shows a routing table of a small cluster consisting of 4 nodes. Each pair of nodes are connected with Myrinet, and all nodes are connected with Etherent. Left table shows the example of routing table of the rank 0 process

SMP Cluster Support

To support SMP clusters, which was called *CLUMP (CLUster of sMPs)'* at that time, PM(v2) had a unique feature. Assume that we have two 4-way SMP nodes and running 8 processes in total, one process running on each core. A naive way, which is still used in many cases nowadays, was to have 16 internode connections in whole, with each process having 4 connections to communication with other nodes. Instead of having this all-to-all connection layout, only 4 channels were required in PM(v2).

PM(v2) provided connection-less communication and a channel could send messages to any nodes listed in the routing table. Assuming those channels were numbered as *chan0* to *chan3*. *chan0* was used to send message to the first process of each node. *chan1* was used to send messages to the second process, and so on. The channels were shared by sender processes on the same node. So, the maximum number of channels required by a process was limited by the maximum number of CPU cores in a node. Figure 8.8 also shows how the channels were allocated for a CLUMP. This idea was introduced because memory capacity of Myrinet was very limited at that time. In this way, the receiver process was required to poll on only one channel. In contrast, in the naive way, all 16 connections must be polled and this increases communication latency. The number of connections grows rapidly when the number of nodes and the number of processes per node increase.

8.2.8 Heterogeneous Cluster Support

MPC++ was enhanced to support a cluster consisting of different CPU types (Ishikawa et al. 1999). Data marshaling methods were added to the template library. A heterogeneous cluster having 16 x86 CPUs and 16 DEC Alpha CPUs connected with Myrinet and 1G Ethernet was build and SCore was running on it (Fig. 8.9).

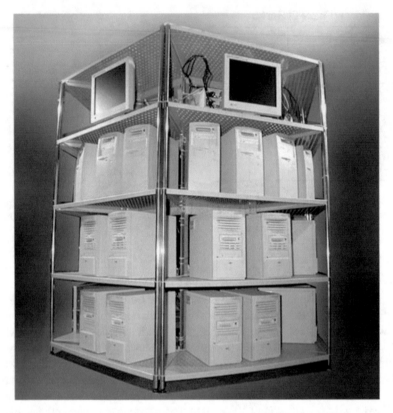

Fig. 8.9 Heterogeneous cluster consisting of 16 x86 CPUs and 16 DEC Alpha CPUs. This cluster was demonstrated at the SC'99 exhibition

8.2.9   Upper Software Layer

MPICH-CLUMP

MPICH-CLUMP (Takahashi et al. 1999) was an MPI implementation that had the capabilities of running flat-MPI on SMP clusters (Cappello et al. 2001) as well as zero-copy message transfer (O'Carroll et al. 1998).

SCASH and OMNI OpenMP

The SCore team also developed a distributed shared memory system, named SCASH. SCASH moved memory pages by using PM's RDMA functions (Harada et al. 2000). It was the first time in the world that the Omni OpenMP compiler and SCASH allowed OpenNP programs to run on a distributed memory cluster (Sato et al. 2001).

8.3 Subsequent Developments

On the TOP 500 list released in June 2001, the cluster made by the SCore development team was ranked as 35th. We emphasize, however, that all the faster machines on the list were made by big companies such as IBM, Cray, NEC, Fujitsu, Hitachi, etc.

The RWCP project ended in 2002 and the SCore development team was dismissed, but the SCore software development and maintenance continued by volunteers. The SCore software package and the OMNI OpenMP compiler package were inherited and distributed by the PC Cluster Consortium.[1]

After the end of the RWCP project, SCore was installed on some of the major Japanese cluster computers. Streamline Computing, a company based in the UK, also sold SCore clusters in Europe. The DDT parallel debugger developed by Allinea Software, a subsidiary company of Streamline Computing, supported SCore. Most notably, the RIKEN Super Combined Cluster (RSCC) (Kumon et al. 2004), which consisted of a Myrinet cluster and an InfiniBand cluster,[2] and these two clusters were connected with Gigabit Ethernet. The PM(v2) composite device could utilize Myrinet, InfiniBand and Gigabit Ethernet. The combined cluster was ranked 7th of TOP 500 list in June, 2004.

These look like success stories of SCore, however, the power of research and development of SCore was obviously weakened. The biggest technical issue was the rise of InfiniBand which took over Myrinet eventually. The InfiniBand API known as Verbs does not allow to share an endpoint between processes. Remember that PM(v2)'s endpoint was shared between the SCore-D process and the user processes for gang scheduling. We could not ignore InfiniBand simply because it was dominating HPC. The SCore software structure had to be redesigned to support InfiniBand. SCore Version 7 which is the last major version of SCore series was developed to have InfiniBand support. A newAPI PM, named PMX (Atsushi Hori, 2009), was also developed. Gang scheduling, the most unique feature of SCore, was sacrificed for having InfiniBand supported.

The author's instinct that time-sharing scheduling was necessary for easy-to-use computers was wrong. In most cases, the SCore-D gang scheduler was not used

---

[1] PC Cluster Consortium: https://www.pccluster.org, the SCore package software series can be still downloaded from https://www.pccluster.org/en/score-download.html.

[2] The RSCC cluster was developed by Fujitsu and the InfiniBand made by Fujitsu was used. They also developed their proprietary PM(v2) InfiniBand device, named PM/InfiniBand-FJ (Sumimoto et al. 2004). SCore as an open-source software package did not support InfiniBand at that time.

on big clusters and jobs were scheduled by batch schedulers instead. One reason of using batch scheduling is that users want to solve bigger problems on faster machines. Another reason is that current supercomputers are unable to run jobs in the execution time in which users can patiently watch the execution. The jobs running hours cannot run in minutes on a faster and bigger machine. The benefits of having shorter response time due to gang scheduling were abrogated because of long execution times.

In the 2000s, most computer vendors released HPC cluster products and software packages. In contrast to the situation of SCore, many commercial companies, research firms, and universities were and still are propelling cluster research and development for HPC. SCore's technical advantages were diminished.

8.4 Lessons Learned

One may say the SCore project succeeded in developing new software technologies for HPC cluster computing. Unfortunately, it cannot be said that it succeeded in dominating cluster software. One of the major reasons for this was that the RWCP project ended just before the commercial rise of HPC clusters.

The communication model of InfiniBand is connection oriented. It was obvious for the SCore development team that this would have resulted in having huge number of connections for large clusters. Although later InfiniBand introduced Shared Receive Queues (SRQ) to fix this issue in a limited way. Major MPI implementations also introduced dynamic connections to avoid all connections and use only the connections frequently utilized. This is an example where the technology design in upper stream requires complex treatment in lower stream technologies. Unfortunately, in general, technologies are getting more complex and having deeper layers than ever, which became very hard to optimize as a whole.

The second lesson learned is the importance of international research collaborations. In light of competition among various researchers in the world, only a few software packages with the same objectives could survive at the time of the SCore development. Now the HPC software stack is bigger and deeper than ever and research and development is getting more and more difficult. International research collaboration is getting more active than in the past. We believe this is a good trend.

References

Boden, N. J., Cohen, D., Felderman, R. E., Kulawik, A. E., Seitz, C. L., Seizovic, J. N., et al. (1995). Myrinet: A gigabit-per-second local area network. *IEEE Micro, 15*(1), 29–36.

Buntinas, D., Mercier, G., & Gropp, W. (2006). Design and evaluation of Nemesis, a scalable, low-latency, message-passing communication subsystem. In *Sixth IEEE International Symposium on Cluster Computing and the Grid, 2006. CCGRID 2006.* (vol. 1, p. 530, pages 10).

Cappello, F., Richard, O., & Etiemble, D. (2001). Understanding performance of SMP clusters running MPI programs. *Future Generation Computer Systems, 17*(6), 711–720. PaCT. II: HPC applications.

Harada, H., Ishikawa, Y., Hori, A., Tezuka, H., Sumimoto, S., & Takahashi, T. (2000). Dynamic home node reallocation on software distributed shared memory. In *HPC Asia 2000*.

Hori, A. (2009). *PMX Specification –DRAFT–*. Allinea Software.

Hori, A., Tezuka, H., & Ishikawa, Y. (1997). Global state detection using network preemption. In *JSSPP* (pp. 262–276).

Hori, A., Tezuka, H., & Ishikawa, Y. (1998). Highly efficient gang scheduling implementation. In *Proceedings of the 1998 ACM/IEEE conference on Supercomputing (CDROM), Supercomputing 1998* (pp. 1–14). USA: IEEE Computer Society.

Ishikawa, Y., Hori, A., Tezuka, H., Sumimoto, S., Takahashi, T., & Harada, H. (1999). Parallel C++ programming system on cluster of heterogeneous computers. In *Heterogeneous Computing Workshop* (pp. 73–82).

Ishikawa, Y. (1996). MPC++ approach to parallel computing environment. *SIGAPP Applied Computing Review, 4*(1), 15–18.

Jin, H. W., Sur, S., Chai, L., & Panda, D. K. (2005). LiMIC: support for high-performance MPI intra-node communication on Linux cluster. In *2005 International Conference on Parallel Processing (ICPP 2005)* (pp. 184–191).

Kondo, M., Hayashida, T., Imai, M., Nakamura, H., Nanya, T., & Hori, A. (2003). Evaluation of checkpointing mechanism on score cluster system. *IEICE Transactions on Information and Systems, 86*(12), 2553–2562.

Kumon, K., Kimura, T., Hotta, K., & Hoshiya, T. (2004). RIKEN Super Combined Cluster (RSCC) system. Technical Report 2, Fujitsu.

Leiserson, C. E., Abuhamdeh, Z. S., Douglas, D. C., Feynman, C. R., Ganmukhi, M. N., Hill, J. V., et al. (1996). The network architecture of the connection machine CM-5. *Journal of Parallel and Distributed Computing, 33*(2), 145–158.

Nishioka, T., Hori, A., & Ishikawa, Y. (2000). Consistent checkpointing for high performance clusters. In *CLUSTER* (pp. 367–368).

O'Carroll, F., Tezuka, H., Hori, A., & Ishikawa, Y. (1998). The design and implementation of zero copy MPI using commodity hardware with a high performance network. In *International Conference on Supercomputing* (pp. 243–250).

Pakin, S., Karamcheti, V., & Chien, A. A. (1997). Fast messages: Efficient, portable communication for workstation clusters and MPPs. *IEEE Transactions on Parallel and Distributed Systems, 5*, 60–73.

Sato, M., Harada, H., Hasegawa, A., & Ishikawa, Y. (2001). Cluster-enabled OpenMP: An OpenMP compiler for the SCASH software distributed shared memory system. *Scientific Programming, 9*(2,3), 123–130.

Sterling, T., Becker, D. J., Savarese, D., Dorband, J. E., Ranawake, U. A., & Packer, C. V. (1995). Beowulf: A parallel workstation for scientific computation. In *Proceedings of the 24th International Conference on Parallel Processing* (pp. 11–14). CRC Press.

Sumimoto, S., Naruse, A., Kumon, K., Hosoe, K., & Shimizu, T. (2004). PM/InfiniBand-FJ: A high performance communication facility using InfiniBand for large scale PC clusters. In *Proceedings of Seventh International Conference on High Performance Computing and Grid in Asia Pacific Region* (pp. 104–113).

Sumimoto, S., Tezuka, H., Hori, A., Harada, H., Takahashi, T., & Ishikawa, Y. (1999). The design and evaluation of high performance communication using a Gigabit Ethernet. In *International Conference on Supercomputing* (pp. 260–267).

Sumimoto, S., Tezuka, H., Hori, A., Harada, H., Takahashi, T., & Ishikawa, Y. (2000a). GigaE PM: A high performance communication facility using a Gigabit Ethernet. *New Generation Computing, 18*(2), 177–186.

Sumimoto, S., Tezuka, H., Hori, A., Harada, H., Takahashi, T., & Ishikawa, Y. (2000b). High performance communication using a commodity network for cluster systems. In *HPDC* (pp. 139–146).

Takahashi, T., O'Carroll, F., Tezuka, H., Hori, A., Sumimoto, S., Harada, H., et al. (1999). Implementation and evaluation of MPI on an SMP cluster. In *IPPS/SPDP Workshops* (pp. 1178–1192).

Takahashi, T., Sumimoto, S., Hori, A., Harada, H., & Ishikawa, Y. (2000). PM2: A high performance communication middleware for heterogeneous network environments. In *SC*.

Tezuka, H., Hori, A., & Ishikawa, Y. (1997). PM: a highperformance communication library for multi-user parallel environments. In *Usenix 1997*.

Tezuka, H., O'Carroll, F., Hori, A., & Ishikawa, Y. (1998). Pin-down Cache: A virtual memory management technique for zero-copy communication. In *Proceedings of the 12th International Parallel Processing Symposium on International Parallel Processing Symposium, IPPS 1998* (p. 308). USA: IEEE Computer Society.

von Eicken, T., Basu, A., Buch, V., & Vogels, W. (1995). U-Net: A user-level network interface for parallel and distributed computing. *SIGOPS Operating System Review*, 29, 40–53.

von Eicken, T., Culler, D. E., Goldstein, S. C., & Schauser, K. E. (1992). Active messages: a mechanism for integrated communication and computation. In *Proceedings of the 19th Annual International Symposium on Computer Architecture, ISCA 1992* (pp. 256–266). USA: ACM.

Chapter 9
NEC Earth Simulator and the SX-Aurora TSUBASA

Teruyuki Imai

Abstract The Earth Simulator (ES) is a parallel supercomputer based on the NEC SX vector computer system. The first-generation ES started its operation in 2002, the second generation started in 2009, and the third started in 2015. The ES system is a cluster of shared memory vector multiprocessor nodes connected via a high-speed network called the internode crossbar switch (IXS). Each node has a remote access control unit (RCU) to connect them to the IXS with memory protection, which enables Remote Direct Memory Access (RDMA) in user space. The operating system (OS) of ES is based on SUPER-UX, the OS for the SX series, which is based on System V Unix, with extensions for high-performance computing including an API for RDMA. Scalability in the OS of ES is enhanced to support a large-scale system than the previous multiple node SX systems. SX-Aurora TSUBASA was developed as a successor of the SX series and SUPER-UX. The hardware of SX-Aurora TSUBASA consists of x86 Linux hosts with vector engines (VEs) connected via PCI express (PCIe) interconnect. No OS kernel runs on the VE; instead, the VE OS modules (VEOS), user processes on the x86 host provide the functionality of an OS for the VE by controlling it via PCIe.

9.1 Introduction

The Earth Simulator (ES) is a parallel vector supercomputer system developed by the Earth Simulator Research Center (ESRDC) (JAMSTEC 2017) and is based on the NEC SX-6 vector supercomputer system.

ES was developed to create a "virtual planet earth". The original ES was the fastest supercomputer in the world for 2 years after it started its operation. Its high performance contributed to large-scale simulation for science and technology, e.g., a global atmosphere simulation (Shingu et al. 2002) and fusion science (Sakagami et al. 2002). Even after losing the number one ranking, ES was still useful and efficient for

T. Imai (✉)
NEC Corporation, Tokyo, Japan
e-mail: t-imai@cp.jp.nec.com

© Springer Nature Singapore Pte Ltd. 2019   139
B. Gerofi et al. (eds.), *Operating Systems for Supercomputers*
and High Performance Computing, High-Performance Computing Series,
https://doi.org/10.1007/978-981-13-6624-6_9

running scientific applications, especially for traditional legacy applications since they were memory-intensive and able to be well vectorized.

The operating system for ES is an enhanced version of SUPER-UX, a Unix-like OS used for the NEC SX series. SUPER-UX has functions for using and managing a large-scale cluster.

NEC SX supercomputers, including the Earth Simulator, and SUPER-UX provided a highly sustained performance with ease of use for decades for high-performance computing (HPC) applications. However, users from non-HPC domains, who used more modern Unix-like environments, faced difficulties using the SUPER-UX/SX environment because they were usually unfamiliar with its old Unix environment. Recently, Linux has become the de-facto standard environment for users in HPC. Open source software (OSS) has been growing for use not only in the non-HPC, but also in the HPC domain. However, it was difficult to provide the newer functions of the Linux environment to the users in the HPC domain. SX-Aurora TSUBASA, the successor of the SX series, was designed to overcome this difficulty.

In this chapter, we describe the hardware and OS of the original Earth Simulator and its successors, lessons learned from the hardware and operating system. We then describe SX-Aurora TSUBASA, the successor of ES, built from the experience of those lessons.

9.2 History

The original, Earth Simulator (ES1) started its operation in March 2002. ES1 consisted of 640 processor nodes connected by a high-speed crossbar (Shinichi et al. 2003). ES1 was ranked number one in the TOP500 (Meuer et al. 2005) from June 2002 to June 2004.

The second-generation Earth Simulator (ES2) started its operation in March 2009. ES2 consisted of 160 nodes connected by a fat-tree network.

The third-generation Earth Simulator (ES3) started its operation in March 2015. ES3 is an NEC SX-ACE system that consists of 5120 nodes connected by a fat-tree network.

9.3 Architecture of Earth Simulator

The architecture of ES is shown in Fig. 9.1. The ES system is a cluster of processor nodes (PNs) connected to an interconnection network. A PN is a multiprocessor node with shared memory for the execution of computational jobs. The interconnection network between PNs is a crossbar switch for ES1 and fat-tree for ES2 and ES3.

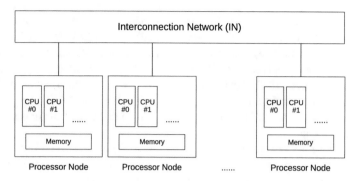

Fig. 9.1 Configuration of Earth Simulator

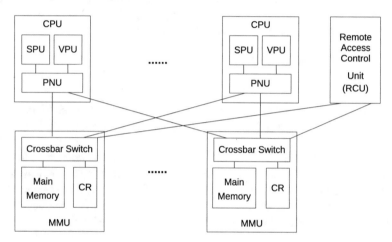

Fig. 9.2 Processor node of ES1

9.3.1 Processor Node and CPU

A node consists of multiple CPUs, main memory, and an interface to the interconnection network and I/O devices. The CPUs of a node are one-chip vector processors, based on the NEC SX series used in each generation. Nodes of the first ES were developed based on SX-6; those of ES2 were based on SX-9; and those of the ES3 were based on SX-ACE.

9.3.1.1 ES1

A processor node of ES1 is shown in Fig. 9.2.

Each node consists of 8 CPUs called arithmetic processors (APs), a main memory system, and a remote access control unit (RCU).

Each CPU consists of a scalar processing unit (SPU) and a vector processing unit (VPU) connected to a processor network unit (PNU). An SPU is a 64-bit reduced instruction set computer to process scalar operations and to fetch and decode instructions with pipelining and out-of-order execution. The VPU handles vector operations of up to 256 elements. Each VPU has eight sets of vector pipelines to execute integer and floating point number operations. Since the VPUs run at 1 GHz, the peak performance of each CPU is 8 GFlops. The PNU is an interface to transfer data from/to main memory units.

The memory system consists of 32 main memory units. Each unit consists of a main memory, communication registers, and a crossbar switch to connect the PNU of CPUs to the main memory or the communication registers.

An RCU connects a memory network of a processor node and the interconnection network and transfers data between main memory of different processor nodes via the interconnection network. See Sect. 9.3.3 for details.

9.3.1.2   ES2

Each node of ES2 consists of 8 CPUs, which are based on the NEC SX-9 processor, and a main memory system. Each CPU of ES2 has its own RCU within the same chip.

The CPU of ES2 consists of an SPU, a VPU, and an RCU connected to a processor network unit. The microarchitecture of the SPU and VPU is enhanced. An assignable data buffer (ADB), a programmable cache memory, is implemented in a processor network unit to reduce memory traffic by putting frequently accessed data. An instruction for prefetching data is added for using ADB efficiently.

9.3.1.3   SX-ACE, PN of ES3

The processor node of ES3 is shown in Fig. 9.3.

The CPU of SX-ACE includes four cores, an RCU, and memory controllers connected via the memory crossbar. The evolution of LSI fabrication enabled these components to fit into a single chip.

9.3.2   Non-precise Exceptions

To achieve high performance for vector operations, almost all exceptions are not precise in the SX series CPUs. Precise exceptions require a buffer and/or extra register files (Smith and Pleszkun 1985) to store the history of architectural states and to restore the state on exception. In a classical vector CPU like those in the SX series, the overhead of implementing precise exception is large, especially in executing applications with load–store dependencies (Espasa et al. 1997). Consequently, NEC

Fig. 9.3 SX-ACE
(Processor node of ES3)

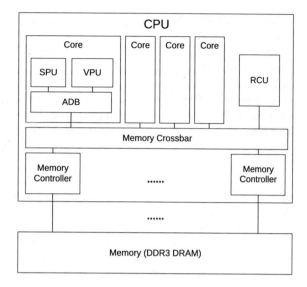

decided that CPUs would not support precise exceptions in the SX series except for the timer interrupt and the monitor call (MONC) instruction for system calls.

9.3.3   Interconnection Network

The interconnection network of ES is provided by an internode crossbar switch (IXS) (Noriyuki et al. 2008). Each processor node has a remote access control unit (RCU) to connect to the IXS.

The IXS was originally developed for an SX-4 multinode system (Hori 1997) and is composed of dedicated crossbar switches. Each switch has global communication registers that support atomic operations from CPUs connected to the IXS for synchronization, e.g., test-and-set and fetch-and-add.

A remote access control unit (RCU) is an interface that connects the main memory to the IXS on a processor node. Both the RCU and the internode switches provide the functionality of remote direct memory access. The RCU includes a data mover and a controller for the interconnection network. A data mover transfers data between local memory and remote memory. A controller accepts requests from CPUs to transfer data by a data mover. An SX CPU supports instructions for requesting data transfer known as internode access (INA) instructions in non-privilege mode, which enables a process to initiate an RDMA in user space, i.e., without issuing system calls. The INA instructions support synchronous and asynchronous transfers. For each job, the RCU has a pointer to a ring buffer in the main memory, which is used for queuing asynchronous transfer requests. Asynchronous transfer is usually used to avoid unpredictable stall time that occurs during synchronous transfers, and to use CPU time more efficiently by executing other instructions such as calculation in transferring.

To specify a target address of an INA instruction, a "global virtual address" is used, which consists of a logical node number and a virtual memory address of that logical node.

To allow multiple jobs to run on a system simultaneously, a CPU job ID (JID) and a multinode job ID are introduced. Internode access on the SX CPU uses JIDs for translating global virtual addresses. A multinode JID is used for translating incoming global virtual addresses in RDMA requests from the IXS to a physical address on the node.

The RCU has two address translation mechanisms that provide global virtual addressing for protection: a global node address translation buffer (GNATB) to translate node number and a global storage address translation buffer (GSATB) to translate memory addresses.

The GNATB enables a program to execute without modifying the program when the number of nodes has changed. It has a table to translate a logical node number into a physical node number and a multinode JID for each local JID. The GSATB protects physical memory on the node from remote access via IXS. It has a table to translate a virtual memory address into a physical memory address for each multinode JID. In RDMA, the node number and the virtual memory address are translated by the local GNATB and the remote GSATB, respectively.

9.4 Operating System of Earth Simulator

The operating system (OS) for the Earth Simulator is an enhanced version of NEC's SUPER-UX operating system (Yanagawa and Suehiro 2004), a variant of Unix specialized for NEC SX supercomputers. In this section, SUPER-UX and its enhancements for large-scale, high-performance computing (HPC) clusters are described.

9.4.1 SUPER-UX

SUPER-UX is based on Unix System V. To improve the portability of applications and usability, BSD features, TCP/IP, socket API, ftp, telnet, etc. are implemented in SUPER-UX. Some enhancements are also implemented to meet the requirements of HPC, which include

- support for multiprocessor nodes of up to 32 CPUs in a single node, and a multinode system up to 128 nodes (in the generation of SX-6);
- support for larger sizes of main memory, up to 8 TB; and
- the functionality of controlling IXS for OS-bypass communication.

To realize these enhancements, NEC investigated other well-known Unix environments, such as BSD, and implemented some functionality useful to the SUPER-UX/SX environment with hardware-dependent code.

9.4.2   Distributed Shared Memory Support

SUPER-UX supports distributed shared memory via IXS. Distributed parallel programs running on multiple nodes, hereafter referred to as "multinode programs", use the extensions for message passing and controlling. The NEC message-passing interface (MPI) library uses RDMA   via IXS. The extensions of SUPER-UX for distributed shared memory provide appropriate protection for MPI applications.

New concepts and functions that support multinode programs in SUPER-UX include

- Message-passing process group,
- Global Memory,
- Logical node, and
- New system calls for managing Global Memory.

A message-passing process group (MPPG) is a set of processes on SUPER-UX to handle a multinode program such one that uses MPI, high-performance Fortran (HPF), etc. Processes in an MPPG can run on multiple nodes. SUPER-UX provide functions to send a signal to a remote process in the MPPG to which the sender belongs, to terminate all processes in an MPPG when one process of the MPPG aborts, etc., for multinode programs.

"Global Memory" is a memory area mapped from both a process address space, which a CPU uses on load and store operations, and a global virtual address space, which an RCU uses to access remote memory   via the internode crossbar switch. SUPER-UX permits remote access to Global Memory from processes which belong to the MPPG of the owner of the Global Memory by managing GSATB in an RCU. SUPER-UX maintains CPU JIDs and multinode JIDs to allow internode access transfer between processes in the same MPPG. SUPER-UX also counts the usage of Global Memory for memory protection, to prevent memory areas accessible via IXS from being freed.

A logical node is a domain in which a multinode program can share a memory area. SUPER-UX maps a logical node to a physical node. Processes in the same logical node are required to run on the same node. Different logical nodes are permitted to be mapped to a single physical node, i.e., processes in different logical nodes can share a node. SUPER-UX realizes the mapping from a logical node to a physical node by setting the GNATB on nodes where a multinode program runs. This function is useful, for example, when debugging a multinode program on a single node, or on the development of a multinode program for a large-scale supercomputer in a small test environment.

SUPER-UX implements new system calls for handling MPPGs: *dp_create* creates an MPPG, *dp_join* joins an existing MPPG specified by an argument, and *dp_exit* leaves the joining MPPG.

SUPER-UX provides the following system calls for a multinode program:

- *dp_xmalloc* allocates a Global Memory, a process memory area that can be shared among processes in the MPPG, not mapped to global virtual address space, however;
- *dp_xmfree* frees a Global Memory;
- *dp_xmshare* maps an allocated Global Memory to global address space to make the area accessible from remote processes; and
- *dp_xmatt* attaches a Global Memory of other processes in the MPPG for RDMA.

The MPI library for the SX series uses internode access operations via IXS and the mapping of Global Memory for data transfer. This enables communication in user mode; no system call is necessary for data transfer. When an MPI program starts, mpirun invokes mpid on nodes, a daemon to manage process creation and communication. The mpid process prepares MPPG by using *dp_create* or *dp_join* on each node and then prepares child processes to run the MPI program. The created processes drop privileges and execute the MPI program. In the MPI program, the MPI library prepares communication buffers by using *dp_xmalloc* and *dp_xmshare*, and uses *dp_xmatt* to access the remote buffer.

RDMA functions, such as those for MPPG and Global Memory, are available for implementing a lower communication layer of MPI and partitioned global address space (PGAS) languages such as coarrays. Only NEC MPI is implemented directly using the functions. SUPER-UX/SX also supports high-performance Fortran (HPF), a Fortran-based PGAS language. NEC HPF utilizes the RDMA functions through the NEC MPI library for its communication operations.

The RDMA functions on SX are similar to unreliable datagram (UD) or reliable datagram (RD) services via InfiniBand, although the interfaces are different in that the SX series supports the functions as part of the instruction set, not an abstract interface as in the case of InfiniBand verbs: a memory area for RDMA communication is to be registered to GSATB like a memory region (MR), and a ring buffer for requests for each job is registered to RCU. The differences are listed below.

- Each process has a single ring buffer used for requests corresponding to a send queue (SQ), no queues corresponding to a receive queue (RQ), and a completion queue (CQ), while a process using InfiniBand (IB) has a queue pair (QP), a pair consisting of a SQ and RQ, and a CQ. The RCU supports commands to store the status of preceding requests to local memory instead of a CQ.
- The SX series only supports RDMA read/write, and atomic (test-and-set) operations, while IB supports RDMA read/write, atomic, and send/receive operations.
- The RCU on the SX series is able to access remote memory specified by a global address which includes a logical node number, corresponding to local identifier (LID), which enables transparent checkpoint/restore and process migration. IB requires the LID, QP number, and MR key of a peer upon data transfer.

From the viewpoint of software, differences between SUPER-UX on the SX series and IB are as follows. SUPER-UX does not provide API functions for RDMA for user space since only the NEC MPI is expected to use user-level RDMA communication. In protection, RDMA is permitted between processes in the same MPPG, which is specified by privileged MPI daemon, on SUPER-UX. Using IB communication, a process protects its memory areas from remote access by using a protection domain and R_key of a memory region: a peer process is permitted to access remote memory in the protection domain where the memory region is registered; a correct R_key is required on RDMA. On SUPER-UX, only an area allocated by using *dp_-xmalloc* can be accessed by calling *dp_xmshare*. Using IB, a process needs to register a buffer for RDMA from remote processes by *ibv_reg_mr* after the allocation, and needs to notify a remote process of the R_key.

9.4.3 Enhancements for Large-Scale Cluster

The original Earth Simulator system consists of 640 processor nodes (PN), an interconnection network, and several peripheral components as shown in Fig. 9.4.

The number of nodes in the Earth Simulator system is much larger than that of prior SX systems. To achieve high performance on such a large-scale parallel system, the scalability of SUPER-UX was enhanced from the viewpoint of both performance of applications and system management. The enhancements include

- redesign of functions from algorithms for improvement,
- reduction of overhead for managing parallel processes, and

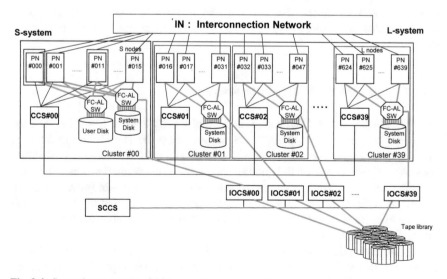

Fig. 9.4 Supercluster system of ES1

- the reduction of system management overhead and control data size by introducing the supercluster system.

The supercluster system (Yanagawa and Suehiro 2004; Shinichi et al. 2003) was introduced to the operating system for ES1 to manage many nodes as a single system image (SSI) (Riesen and Maccabe 2011).

The ES1 system is divided into 40 units called clusters. Each cluster consists of 16 PNs, a cluster control station (CCS) that controls all its resources, e.g., nodes and disks, an input–output control station (IOCS) and system disks via a storage area network. The IOCS controls file recalls and migration between system disks and a tape library (see Sect. 9.4.4.1).

All clusters are managed as a single cluster from the supercluster control station (SCCS), which is connected to all CCSs in the system. From the SCCS, the system administrator can manage the whole system by sending commands to processor nodes via the CCSs. The system administrator can also monitor the whole system by gathering system information from all PNs and CCSs. This two-level cluster system realizes SSI system management.

While the ES1 system consists of 40 clusters from the viewpoint of system management, it consists of an S-system, a cluster for interactive use and small-sized jobs, and a single large L-system, the other 39 clusters for large batch jobs, from the viewpoint of end users.

9.4.4   File System

SUPER-UX implements the supercomputing file system (SFS) as a local file system, and the network file system (NFS) as a shared file system. However, the Earth Simulator has also used other file systems and a staging mechanism for the large-scale cluster.

9.4.4.1   Automated File Recall and Migration

For I/O performance on ES1, each L node, a processor node in L-system, uses the work area on a local file system instead of accessing the shared file system, e.g., home directories, for executing jobs. End users could not have individual data areas on system disks connected to L nodes. The users were required to place data and programs on a tape drive or in a home directory of the S-system. Instead of being cached or prefetched, files used by an application were required to be transferred from tapes or home directories to a local file system of each L node explicitly before the application was run.

For the convenience of users, the job scheduler (JS) provided the function of automated file recall and migration. JS also provided a new type of job scheduling with the required number of nodes and the assignment of necessary user files as scheduling parameters for the automated file recall and migration: prior to executing a distributed parallel job on each L node, JS requests the IOCS to transfer the file to be used from the tape drive or other storage area to the system disk of the L node for the job (file recall); and after the execution of the job, the JS requests that the IOCS move necessary files to a specified place (file migration).

This function enabled the system disk connected to each node to be used easily and efficiently, requiring the end user to only specify the file necessary for the job when the job was submitted. It was unnecessary to change the application program running on ES.

9.4.4.2 GStorageFS

ES2 used automated file recall/migration by using the job scheduler and NEC GStorageFS (Hiroko et al. 2008) for a high-speed I/O performance.

GStorageFS is a shared file system that uses a fiber channel (FC) storage area network (SAN). GStorageFS is based on SGI's XFS for storing data, and NFS3 for requests via TCP/IP network (Saini et al. 2007). A GStorageFS server and clients are connected via a TCP/IP network and the FC SAN. The client sends an NFS request to the GStorageFS server via the TCP/IP network. On a small I/O transaction such as file creation, only the NFS via the TCP/IP network is used. On a large I/O request, the GStorageFS server sends a list of disk blocks to the client and transfers data between storage media (disks) and the client directly using third-party transfer, thereby improving performance. GStorageFS supports a single file system consisting of multiple volumes each consisting of multiple logical units (disks). To avoid congestion, GStorageFS distributes files created by different clients on different volumes.

9.4.4.3 ScaTeFS

ES3 used an automated file recall/migration by using the job scheduler and the NEC scalable technology file system (ScaTeFS). Since a node of SX-ACE only has a 10 Gigabit Ethernet interface card, it requires a high-speed shared file system because it cannot depend on an FC SAN shared among clients and servers.

ScaTeFS is a shared file system accessed via TCP/IP network. A system using ScaTeFS is composed of multiple clients, multiple I/O servers, and disk arrays connected to FC switches. Multiple clients and I/O servers are connected via TCP/IP. I/O servers provide the service of a distributed shared file system and manage the metadata of the file system. ScaTeFS supports multiple I/O servers to provide a single large file system. Both data and metadata are distributed to multiple I/O servers for large capacity and load balancing purposes. Data and metadata caches on clients are supported. This improves small I/O performance and access to metadata such as opening a file and retrieving attributes of a file.

9.5 Lessons Learned

From the development and maintenance of the SX series and SUPER-UX, we learned the importance of staying current with the latest de-facto standards and the importance of a good design and implementation to facilitate this.

In 1980s and 1990s, when the early SX series were released and ES1 was studied and designed, the System V Unix and its variants were standard. At that time, SUPER-UX was accepted by both end users and system administrators as a variant of the Unix environment.

However, the de-facto standard environment has changed in the decades since. Linux has now become the de-facto standard at the time of writing this chapter. Exploiting open source software (OSS) on SUPER-UX/SX was difficult because many OSS programs were developed, tested, and assumed to be in a Linux environment.

NEC developed some proprietary technologies for addressing the challenge of constructing a large-scale cluster of vector processors, e.g., IXS, automatic staging, and shared file systems. Maintaining such proprietary technologies is costly and migrating them to the latest standards can be difficult or near-impossible.

It is difficult to port newer operating systems such as Linux, which became the de-facto standard environment, to the SX series. SUPER-UX was not updated to be based on System V Release 4 (SVR4) where the virtual memory system was changed to that based on SunOS (Balan and Gollhardt 1992) supporting memory-mapped files. This is because the virtual memory system of such newer operating systems, with demand paging and copy-on-write features, depends on precise page faults.

As a result, NEC needed to implement new features to follow standards or de-facto standards such as POSIX, and to port de-facto standard tools, such as bash and OpenSSH, on SUPER-UX with a high cost of development and maintenance. Some newer standard features on Unix, e.g., memory-mapped files, had never been supported on the SX series. In addition, device drivers, network protocols, file systems, etc. had been limited due to the cost of porting.

On the basis of the SX series, including the Earth Simulator systems, and the lessons learned from the experience, the architecture of the SX series' successor was designed. See Sect. 9.6.

9.6 SX-Aurora TSUBASA

SX-Aurora TSUBASA (NEC Corporation 2018) was announced in 2017 and launched in 2018 as a successor of the NEC SX series supercomputer.

The system architecture of SX-Aurora TSUBASA was changed significantly from the prior SX series to provide the user a Linux compatible environment on a vector processor without precise page faults. The design concepts of the processor were unchanged.

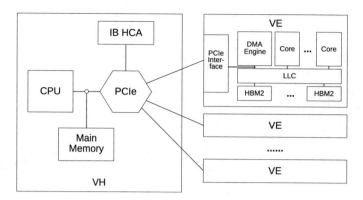

Fig. 9.5 SX-Aurora TSUBASA (V island)

9.6.1 Architecture

The architecture of SX-Aurora TSUBASA is shown in Fig. 9.5.

SX-Aurora TSUBASA consists of an x86 host called the vector host (VH) and one or more vector engine (VE) nodes. VE nodes are connected to the VH via the PCI express (PCIe) interconnect.

The VH is a commodity off-the-shelf server running Linux operating system. It has one or more x86 CPUs with main memory, I/O devices such as local storage, and a network interface.

A VE node is newly designed hardware, a PCIe card with a vector CPU module. The instruction set architecture (ISA) and microarchitecture of the CPU are based on those of the prior SX series to achieve high performance. See Sect. 9.6.2 for more details.

A set consisting of VH and one or more VE nodes connected to it is called a V island. A single V island with a single VE node is the smallest type of SX-Aurora TSUBASA system. A single V island with multiple VE nodes is supported for a small system. For a large-scale SX-Aurora TSUBASA system, configurations using an InfiniBand (IB)-connected cluster of multiple V islands are supported (shown in Fig. 9.6). SX-Aurora TSUBASA no longer has IXS or other proprietary interconnects. Each V island is connected via an IB network with one or more IB host channel adapters (HCA).

9.6.2 Vector Engine

A VE node consists of eight VE cores, a Direct Access Memory (DMA) engine, a last level cache (LLC) shared among the VE cores and the DMA engine, main memory, and a PCIe interface (Fig. 9.5). The VE cores, DMA engine, and LLC are

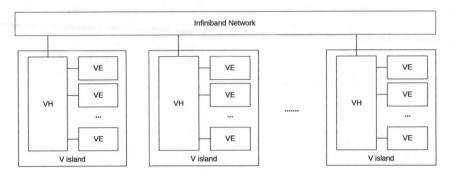

Fig. 9.6 SX-Aurora TSUBASA cluster

implemented in a single VE LSI. High bandwidth memory 2 (HBM2) is used for the main memory of a VE. A VE LSI and 6 HBM2 are integrated on a silicon interposer.

A VE core is a classical vector processor like the prior SX series, which has a scalar processing unit (SPU) and a vector processing unit (VPU) with improved microarchitecture. A VE core supports almost all instructions of a prior SX CPU as well as some extended instructions, such as fused multiply-add (FMA) and packed operations. However, there are significant differences:

- All registers of the VE cores and the DMA engine are accessible via PCI express; hence, the registers on a VE node are visible in PCI memory space from the host. Main memory of a VE node is accessible by the DMA engine on it. Some main memory areas are also mapped from PCI memory space. The mapping is configurable.
- A VE core does not have any privileged or kernel mode for operating systems. However, for protection, a VE core still supports the monitor call (MONC) instruction for invoking a system call and other exceptions. The instructions raise an interrupt to the host and stops the VE core itself instead of entering privileged mode. Each VE core has an exception status (EXS) register to control its execution. A host process is able to start and stop execution of a VE core by setting the EXS register via PCIe.
- All privileged registers, e.g., a register to set a page table, are only accessible via PCI memory space; no instruction of a VE core may read or write to privileged registers.
- Instructions to access PCI memory space are supported: load host memory (LHM) loads data from PCI memory space to a scalar register, and store host memory (SHM) stores data in a scalar register to PCI memory space. A VE core may access host memory, and I/O devices, etc., via the PCIe interconnect. A VE has an address translation mechanism. On LHM and SHM, the DMA address translation buffer (DMAATB) translates addresses into PCI memory space for the VE cores to access, which enables a VE task to access resources via the PCIe interconnect safely. The address translation mechanism is shared with the DMA engine. Since

the DMA engine provides the DMA descriptor table with address translation for the VE cores, a VE task can also use the DMA (or RDMA) engine safely.
- The endianness changed from big-endian to little-endian; integer and pointer representation in memory is now compatible with the host.

The functions mentioned above enable a VE node to be controlled from the host machine. The differences that were designed and implemented provide OS functionality on the host. See Sect. 9.6.3 how the differences are utilized.

9.6.3 VEOS

The software stack of SX-Aurora TSUBASA is shown in Fig. 9.7.

In SX-Aurora TSUBASA, VE OS modules (VEOS) using a VE driver on the host provide the functionality of an operating system for the vector unit.

VEOS consists of a *ve_exec* and a VE OS service. The *ve_exec* program loads a VE program, requests the creation of a VE process for the program, and serves system calls of the process. See Sect. 9.6.4 for details. The VE OS service runs on each VE node and manages the resources of each VE node. It accepts requests from *ve_exec* and other requests for information from the VE processes as well as requests for controlling VE processes and/or VE resources.

A VE driver is installed in kernel space of the host Linux and is used for accessing VE nodes. A VE driver is a PCI device driver that provides an *mmap* routine to map VE registers to VE OS services and an *ioctl* routine to wait for an interrupt notification from a VE core when an exception occurs. The VE driver is a loadable kernel module. Modification of the Linux kernel running on the VH is not required to support the VEs.

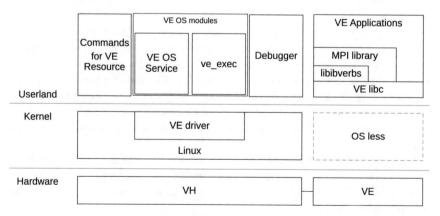

Fig. 9.7 Software stack of SX-Aurora TSUBASA

There is no OS kernel on a VE. Instead, a C library (libc) compliant with standards, e.g., ISO C99, C11, and POSIX including pthreads, has been ported to the VE CPU to provide the needed services. A user space InfiniBand verbs library (libibverbs), and an MPI library were also developed for VEs and run on top of libc. Application programs for VEs can use the standard libc, MPI library, etc., which enables developers to write application programs in standard programming languages such as C, C++, and Fortran without special programming models.

Commands to show and/or handle the status of VE resources, e.g., ps, vmstat, strace, sar, and accton, were ported. These commands communicate with the VE OS service instead of directly reading and writing to procfs or using special system calls such as *ptrace* and *acct*.

The GNU debugger, gdb, has also been ported for debugging VE programs. The VE OS service accepts trace requests like *ptrace*. The debugger for VE makes requests to the VE OS service instead of *ptrace* system calls. The command strace for VE also, uses the requests to trace system calls on VE.

9.6.4 Execution of a VE Program

To execute a VE program, *ve_exec* loads the VE program, creates a VE process, and handles system calls from it.

9.6.4.1 Starting a VE Process

To execute a program on VE, a user invokes the *ve_exec* command with path to the program. The *ve_exec* process makes a request to the VE OS service to create a VE process. The service then sets up data structure for the new VE process and initializes its context.

The *ve_exec* process reads the VE program and sets up the VE process's memory space: *ve_exec* reads the ELF header and program header in the program, and requests the VE OS service to map the loadable segments, i.e., the parts of the executable file to be loaded, e.g., text and data. The service allocates VE memory, transfers the contents of the file from the VH to the VE, and creates a mapping from the process. *ve_exec* also creates the image of the main stack of the process by copying the arguments and building an auxiliary vector, and then sends that image to the process.

After the VE process memory is set up, *ve_exec* requests the VE OS service to start the process and then waits for a system call request. The service sets the process to the RUNNING state and appends it to a run queue. The service then starts the execution of the process (see Sect. 9.6.5.2).

9.6.4.2 Offloading System Calls

When a VE process is running, the *ve_exec* process corresponding to the process, hereafter referred to as *pseudo-process* (Shimizu and Yonezawa 2010), waits for notification of exceptions on the VE, and handles the exceptions.

A system call on the VE is implemented as follows: a VE process writes a system call number and arguments of the system call in the corresponding VH process memory using SHM instructions. After storing the system call number and the arguments, the process invokes a MONC instruction, which stops the VE core and sends an interrupt to the VH. When an interrupt from the VE is received, the Linux kernel on the host invokes an interrupt handler of the VE driver. An interrupt request (IRQ) is allocated for each VE core. The interrupt handler finds the pseudo-process corresponding to the process that is on the VE core and wakes it up.

When woken up, the pseudo-process determines the cause of the exception and handles the exception. When an exception is caused by an illegal operation such as a page fault or division-by-zero, the pseudo-process sends an appropriate signal, e.g., SIGSEGV for a page fault, to itself and aborts both the VE process and the corresponding pseudo-process. If the cause is a MONC instruction, the pseudo-process reads the system call number and arguments and determines which system call was requested. The pseudo-process handles the requested system call and returns the result to the process. System calls are handled by the following two methods.

Simple Offloading A pseudo-process invokes the same system call in the Linux kernel on the host. To handle a system call with one or more pointers specified, the pseudo-process copies in data before invoking the system call on the host or copies out data after returning from the system call on the VH. System calls regarding I/O (e.g., *open*, *read*, and *write*), handling a file system information (e.g., *stat*, and *unlink*), handling a socket (e.g., *socket*, and *getsockopt*), getting process, user, and group IDs (e.g., *getpid*, *getuid*, and *getgid*) are implemented using the simple offloading method.

Specific Implementation Other system calls have a VE-specific implementation in the pseudo-process. A pseudo-process requests a VE OS service via an interprocess communication (IPC) socket, and the VE OS service handles the request. For example, system calls regarding memory management such as *mmap*, *munmap*, and *brk* and process/thread management such as *fork* and *clone* have a specific implementation method for handling them.

Simple offloading provides high compatibility with low development and maintenance cost because it invokes the Linux system call itself. The system call numbers on the VEOS are based on version 3.10 for x86-64 in VEOS version 1.0: the version when SX-Aurora TSUBASA was launched. The numbers from 0 to 316 are used (315 is used for extending the stack and 316 is used for VEOS-specific functions). In VEOS version 1.0, 110 system calls are implemented in simple offloading.

9.6.5   Process/Thread Management

VE OS supports multiprocessing and multi-threading by using a context switch.

9.6.5.1   Fork and Clone Task

On SX-Aurora TSUBASA, each VE process or thread has its corresponding process or thread on the VH to handle exceptions.

When the *fork* system call is invoked, the pseudo-process also forks. The child requests the VE OS service to create a VE process, and the parent waits for the completion of creating the child VE process. The service creates a child VE process, copies a context from the parent process, and creates the VE process memory. The service also builds the page table of the child: since copy-on-write is unavailable due to non-precise page fault, new pages are allocated for private mapping, and the contents of the new pages are copied from the parent process. For shared mapping pages, the service clones the page table entries to share the pages with the parent. After the procedure of creating the child process, the parent and the child request the service to restart their corresponding VE processes.

The VEOS supports the *clone* system call with only flags used for creating a POSIX thread. When the *clone* system call is invoked, the pseudo-process creates a thread using pthread_create() in the libc of the VH. The child thread requests the VE OS service to create the child VE thread, and the parent thread waits for the completion of creating the VE thread. The service then creates a child VE thread and copies a context and the page table from the parent VE thread. After the procedure of creating the child thread, the parent and the child request the service to restart their corresponding VE threads.

9.6.5.2   Context Switching

The VEOS supports context switching for multiprocessing and multi-threading of tasks. The VE OS service manages data structures representing tasks (process and thread). The service treats a process and a thread in the same manner as the Linux kernel does. Processes and threads, referred to as tasks, are managed through a data structure that represents each task. The service has run queues and wait queues to manage tasks.

The VE OS service has a scheduler and performs context switching similar to other operating systems. The differences are that the VE OS service uses a timer in the Linux kernel on the host. When the timer expires, the service checks if the time slice is expired. When the time slice is expired, the service stops the VE core by modifying the EXS register via PCI memory space. The service saves the current context from the VE core registers to host memory in the VE OS service process by memory-mapped I/O (MMIO) read operations and DMA, and restores the context of the next task to the core registers by MMIO write operations and DMA because a VE node does not have hardware for context switching. After the context is replaced, the service restarts the execution of the VE core.

9.6.6   Memory Management

On SX-Aurora TSUBASA, the Linux kernel of the host and pseudo-process manages the virtual address space of a VE process, and the VE OS service manages physical memory.

The virtual address space of a VE process is embedded in the corresponding pseudo-process as shown in Fig. 9.8.

The pseudo-process reserves 16 TB of virtual address space for a VE process starting from 0×600000000000, which is unlikely to conflict with other libraries on the host. The reserved area is used for the text segment, the data segments, the heap, and the main thread stack. The pseudo-process maintains the usage of the fixed area. When a VE process invokes the *brk* system call or the *grow* system call (a VE-specific system call for extending stack area), the corresponding pseudo-process updates the top of the heap or stack, respectively, and requests the VE OS service to map the updated area to physical pages.

Dynamically allocated virtual address space is primarily managed by the Linux kernel on the host. However, the pseudo-process manages areas allocated by the kernel to deal with the limitation of no mixed page sizes in the VE page table.

The pseudo-process handles dynamic areas requested by *mmap* in the following two steps. The pseudo-process manages a set of 512 MB-sized and 512 MB-aligned

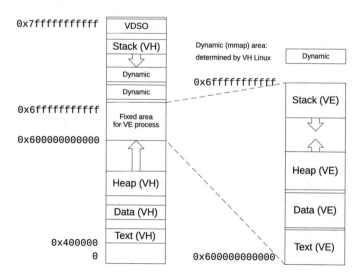

Fig. 9.8 Virtual address space layout

chunks for 2 MB pages, and a set of 16 TB-sized and 16 TB-aligned chunks for 64 MB pages. On the request of *mmap*, the pseudo-process finds a contiguous free area of the requested number of pages in the chunks: when the size of pages requested is 2 MB or 64 MB, the pseudo-process searches a 512 MB set or a 16 GB set, respectively. If no contiguous free area to be mapped is found, the pseudo-process allocates a new chunk using *mmap* on the VH and allocates an area from the new chunk. After allocating an area in the VE process address space, the pseudo-process requests the VE OS service to map the allocated area to physical pages.

The VE OS service manages VE main memory in a buddy system similar to other operating systems such as Linux. When a pseudo-process requests to map memory, the service allocates physical pages and registers a mapping from the requested area to the allocated pages by creating new page table entries.

Memory-mapped file support is a challenge for VEOS because there is no file system on a VE. VEOS supports mapping a regular file to virtual address space, but with some limitations. When a VE application requests to map a file to memory, the VEOS allocates VE memory and transfers the content of the file from the host to the VE memory. When a VE application requests to unmap a file-mapped area, the VEOS transfers the contents of the file from the VE to the VH. The VEOS supports shared mapping by creating a mapping to the memory area where the content of the file has been loaded. Memory-mapped file support enables applications to be ported more easily to the VE.

9.6.7 OS-Bypass Communication on Aurora

On SX-Aurora TSUBASA, OS-bypass zero-copy communication is available in both the cases where the VE processes are in the same V island, communicating via PCIe, and where the VE processes are in different V islands, communicating via InfiniBand (IB).

To communicate with VE nodes in the same V island, VEOS provides a VE shared memory (VESHM) function. VESHM provides the following two functions: the function `veshm_open()` registers a VE process memory area to permit VE processes on the other VE nodes to attach, and the function `veshm_attach()` attaches an opened VE process area on a remote VE node. When a `veshm_open()` call is made, the VE OS service maps the VE memory area from PCI memory space. When a `veshm_attach()` call is made, the service checks whether the requesting process is running as the user of the requested process and whether the requested area is registered. If both are true, the service maps from the requested process to the VE memory area in PCI memory space; otherwise, it returns an error.

A VE process can access attached remote memory areas. An attached area is accessible using the load host memory (LHM) and store host memory (SHM) instructions and/or the DMA engine. A VE process can also communicate directly via IB by using IB verbs. The libibverbs user space library has been ported to VE: a VE process maps an area of HCA registers and accesses the registers with LHM and

SHM; areas of queue pairs and control data on VE memory are mapped from PCI memory space.

The MPI library supports both VESHM for communication with VE processes in the same V island and IB verbs for communication across V islands.

9.6.8   Related Work

The system architecture, i.e., computing nodes dependent on a host connected via PCIe, is similar to general-purpose GPUs (GPGPUs) and other accelerators. The VE in SX-Aurora TSUBASA supports standard programming modes where a program starts with the `main()` routine and performs I/O using standard functions. It is necessary to divide a program into a main routine on a host and kernel functions written in a special language such as CUDA and OpenCL to use an accelerator.

The design and implementation of VEOS are inspired by microkernel operating systems such as Mach and prior HPC operating systems for heterogeneous systems. Mach (Accetta et al. 1986) handles Unix system calls and file systems in a user space service. In a Mach system, the Mach microkernel runs on all nodes. A process performs I/O and system calls by communicating with the servers via the IPC mechanisms provided by the microkernel. In SX-Aurora TSUBASA, a VE node does not run a kernel. Instead, a VE process invokes a system call by using a lower level method: a special instruction via PCI express and an interrupt on the VH.

In the heterogeneous OS for the Cell/B.E. cluster system (Shimizu and Yonezawa 2010) and IHK/McKernel (Gerofi et al. 2016), system calls by an application process are offloaded to its corresponding *pseudo-process* on another Linux host or core. There is no kernel on VE nodes for computing in an SX-Aurora TSUBASA system, while there are lightweight kernels on computing nodes in Cell/B.E. cluster system (Shimizu and Yonezawa 2010) and application cores in the IHK/McKernel system (Gerofi et al. 2016).

Acknowledgements The author would like to thank Takashi Yanagawa for his help regarding the operating system and the supercluster system of ES1. The author would like to thank the colleagues of the SX-Aurora TSUBASA development group in NEC for their many comments, suggestion, and assistance in writing this article.

References

Accetta, M. J., Baron, R. V., Bolosky, W. J., Golub, D. B., Rashid, R. F., Tevanian, A., et al. (1986). Mach: A new kernel foundation for UNIX development. In *Proceedings of the USENIX Summer Conference*.
Balan, R., & Gollhardt, K. (1992). A scalable implementation of virtual memory HAT layer for shared memory multiprocessor machines. In *Proceedings of USENIX Summer 1992 Technical Conference*.

Espasa, R., Valero, M., & Smith, J. E. (1997). Out-of-order vector architecture. In *Proceedings of the 30th Annual ACM/IEEE International Symposium on Microarchitecture (MICRO 30)*.

Gerofi, B., Takagi, M., Hori, A., Nakamura, G., Shirasawa, T., & Ishikawa, Y. (2016). On the scalability, performance isolation and device driver transparency of the IHK/McKernel hybrid lightweight kernel. In *2016 IEEE International Parallel and Distributed Processing Symposium (IPDPS)* (pp. 1041–1050).

Hiroko, T., Emiko, M., Atsuhisa, O., Koji, S., Satoshi, S., & Toshiyuki, K. (2008). Outline of the SUPER-UX, operating system for the SX-9. http://www.nec.com/en/global/techrep/journal/g08/n04/pdf/080410.pdf.

Hori, K. (1997). Supercomputer SX-4 multinode system. *NEC Research and Development, 38*(4), 461–473.

JAMSTEC (2017). Earth simulator.

Meuer, H., Strohmaier, E., Dongarra, J., & Simon, H. (2005). Top500 supercomputer sites. www.top500.org.

NEC corporation (2018). SX-Aurora TSUBASA. http://www.nec.com/en/global/solutions/hpc/sx/index.html.

Noriyuki, A., Yasuhiro, K., Masaki, S., & Takahito, Y. (2008). Hardware technology of the SX-9 (2) - internode switch. http://www.nec.com/en/global/techrep/journal/g08/n04/pdf/080404.pdf.

Riesen, R., & Maccabe, A. B. (2011). Single system image. In D. A. Padua (Ed.), *Encyclopedia of parallel computing* (pp. 1820–1827). US: Springer.

Saini, S., Talcott, D., Thakur, R., Rabenseifner, P. A. R., & Ciotti, R. (2007). Parallel I/O performance characterization of Columbia and NEC SX-8 Superclusters. In *IEEE International Parallel and Distributed Processing Symposium (IPDPS)*.

Sakagami, H., Murai, H., Seo, Y., & Yokokawa, M. (2002). 14.9 TFlops three-dimensional fluid simulation for fusion science with HPF on the earth simulator. In *Proceedings of the 2002 ACM/IEEE Conference on Supercomputing*, SC '02 (pp. 1–14). IEEE Computer Society Press.

Shimizu, M., & Yonezawa, A. (2010). Remote process execution and remote file I/O for heterogeneous processors in cluster systems. In *Proceedings of 2010 10th IEEE/ACM International Conference on Cluster, Cloud and Grid Computing (CCGrid)* (pp. 145–154). Melbourne, VIC.

Shingu, S., Takahara, H., Fuchigami, H., Yamada, M., Tsuda, Y., Ohfuchi, W., et al. (2002). A 26.58 TFlops global atmospheric simulation with the spectral transform method on the Earth simulator. In *Proceedings of the 2002 ACM/IEEE Conference on Supercomputing*, SC '02 (pp. 1–19). IEEE Computer Society Press.

Shinichi, H., Mitsuo, Y., & Shigemune, K. (2003). The development of the Earth simulator. *IEICE Transactions in Information and Systems, E86-D*(10), 1947–1954.

Smith, J. E., & Pleszkun, A. R. (1985). Implementation of precise interrupts in pipelined processors. In *Proceedings of the 12th Annual International Symposium on Computer Architecture (ISCA'85)*.

Yanagawa, T., & Suehiro, K. (2004). Software system of the Earth simulator. *Parallel Computing, 30*(12), 1315–1327. The Earth Simulator.

Chapter 10
ZeptoOS

Kamil Iskra, Kazutomo Yoshii and Pete Beckman

Abstract The goal of the ZeptoOS project was to explore fundamental limits and advanced designs required for petascale operating system suites, focusing on ultrascale and collective OS behavior. Within the project, the Linux kernel was ported to the IBM Blue Gene's compute nodes. Major research activities included work on HPC-specific memory management (called Big Memory) and on extensible I/O forwarding infrastructure (called ZOID). The project demonstrated excellent performance and scalability of the Linux kernel, comparable to the IBM lightweight kernel, at the same time attracting novel use cases.

10.1 History and Timeline

The ZeptoOS research project was launched in 2004 under the U.S. Department of Energy (DOE) FastOS program. It was a collaboration between Argonne National Laboratory and University of Oregon, led by Pete Beckman and Allen D. Malony, respectively (since this chapter discusses a subset of the work carried out within the project, only the authors most relevant to that part of the effort are included in the authors list). The project aimed to explore fundamental limits and advanced designs required for petascale operating system suites, focusing on ultrascale and collective OS behavior, as well as methods to gather and study performance data on very large systems. The name of the project is based on the metric unit prefix *zepto* (10^{-21}) and reflects our original desire to build a very small kernel. The project was renewed in 2007 under the DOE FastOS2 program and formally ended in 2010.

K. Iskra (✉) · K. Yoshii · P. Beckman
Argonne National Laboratory, Lemont, USA
e-mail: iskra@mcs.anl.gov

K. Yoshii
e-mail: kazutomo@mcs.anl.gov

P. Beckman
e-mail: beckman@mcs.anl.gov

© Springer Nature Singapore Pte Ltd. 2019
B. Gerofi et al. (eds.), *Operating Systems for Supercomputers
and High Performance Computing*, High-Performance Computing Series,
https://doi.org/10.1007/978-981-13-6624-6_10

161

10.1.1   Major Activities

The major approach we took to achieve the project's research goals was to port Linux to the compute nodes of the IBM Blue Gene massively parallel supercomputers in order to study the pros and cons of running it there, especially in comparison with the vendor-provided lightweight kernel.

10.1.1.1   Initial Work on Blue Gene/L

Around the start of the ZeptoOS project, Argonne purchased a single-rack IBM Blue Gene/L (BG/L) (Ritsko et al. 2005) system. We were interested in exploring in depth its software capabilities, but doing so turned out to be harder than expected. The system consisted of 1,024 compute nodes and 32 I/O nodes. The compute nodes ran a lightweight BLRTS kernel (Moreira et al. 2006), which was proprietary and closed, whereas the I/O nodes ran Linux and were relatively open. Each node had two PowerPC 440 cores, which were not cache coherent, limiting Linux on the I/O nodes to just one core. The system featured multiple interconnects (Gara et al. 2005), among them a 3D torus for point-to-point communication between the compute nodes, a tree-like collective network for collective operations, a global interrupt network for barrier-style synchronization, and a Gigabit Ethernet on I/O nodes for communication with other systems. The architectural design of BG/L had each job run in an isolated partition comprising compute nodes and their associated I/O nodes, and the nodes were rebooted for each new job. Compute nodes and I/O nodes could communicate over the collective network (see Fig. 10.6 later in this chapter); compute nodes would forward I/O operations to the I/O nodes, where they would be executed. The system was designed primarily for running parallel MPI jobs. Other supported application interfaces (APIs) included POSIX file I/O and BSD socket (client-side-only) interfaces. Extensibility was not part of the design.

Our initial explorations focused on the more open I/O node stack. We created a new infrastructure on top of IBM's stack that made it easier to configure and build customized I/O node kernels and ramdisks (root file system images), with easy integration of other software components such as the PVFS file system (Carns et al. 2000) or the Cobalt job scheduler (Tang et al. 2009). The fact that nodes within partitions were rebooted for each job and that kernels and ramdisks could be configured separately for each partition, made our development work easy and low risk, since we could experiment with our stack in one partition while other users could run their jobs undisturbed on the rest of the system using the standard software stack. ZeptoOS was made publicly available (ZeptoOS 2005) and was in active use at multiple BG/L sites around the world.

Our ambition, however, went further. We wanted to run a custom OS stack on the BG/L compute nodes. Linux was already running on the I/O nodes, and we knew that compute nodes and I/O nodes used basically the same hardware, so running Linux on the compute nodes seemed within reach. The closed nature of the system, however, precluded us from achieving our goal. For example, we had limited information about the boot process or the initialization of the hardware. The proprietary torus network used for communication between compute nodes was not available on I/O nodes, so there was no available Linux driver for it. In the end, with some assistance from IBM engineers, we modified the IBM BLRTS kernel to perform all initialization and then transfer control to a Linux kernel image loaded into memory as part of the job. We managed to demonstrate this worked, but we failed to make it *useful* because we were still missing BG/L support in MPICH so we could not run regular parallel applications.

In parallel, we began working on a custom I/O forwarding solution because we wanted to experiment with certain POSIX I/O extensions, and the vendor-provided solution was not extensible. We discuss the details in Sect. 10.3. This effort also kick-started a fruitful collaboration with researchers from ASTRON in the Netherlands, who were facing difficulties with real-time data streaming; we expand on this effort in Sect. 10.4.

We also studied OS jitter. We developed a custom Selfish benchmark (Beckman et al. 2006b) to measure the timing and duration of jitter events on a variety of platforms. We developed infrastructure to inject artificial jitter on BG/L compute nodes in order to study its effect on the performance of a representative set of MPI collective operations (Beckman et al. 2006a, 2008; Nataraj et al. 2007). We do not discuss this work here in detail because of space constraints, but interested readers may consult the referenced publications.

10.1.1.2 Project's Heyday: Blue Gene/P

The purchase of Intrepid, a 40-rack IBM Blue Gene/P (BG/P) (IBM Blue Gene team 2008) system, allowed Argonne to negotiate a significantly more open software stack. Full source code was released for the CNK lightweight kernel (Giampapa et al. 2010), along with IBM's modifications to MPICH. These enabled us to develop a "native" Linux for the compute nodes. The upgraded node hardware also made running Linux more relevant; each node featured four cache coherent cores, so the Linux kernel could fully utilize them.

Booting a different kernel on the compute nodes necessitated a reimplementation of the I/O forwarding software running on the I/O nodes; thankfully, we could reuse much of the prior work from BG/L. The software had to be extended to handle not just the I/O forwarding, but also job management (including application launch), as well as the communication with the control system running on the service node. The latter was relatively straightforward, thanks to the availability of the source code of IBM's I/O forwarding implementation that could serve as a reference.

External interest in running Linux on BG/P compute nodes was surprisingly quick. As soon as we had anything working, and long before MPI jobs would run reliably, we were approached by researchers from the University of Chicago who wanted to run many-task computing workloads on the massively parallel Argonne BG/P systems, but were previously unable to on the standard CNK kernel. We will discuss the resulting collaboration in more detail in Sect. 10.4.

Our own interest, though, was to get MPICH to work under Linux on BG/P and to fully utilize the available native interconnects (torus, collective, and global interrupts). Getting the torus network to work under Linux was a major challenge. As already mentioned, there was no Linux driver for it, only the reference code in the lightweight CNK kernel source. What made it more difficult was that the torus was upgraded on BG/P with a DMA engine for improved performance. That engine required physically contiguous memory buffers. This worked fine in CNK, which had a simple, static virtual-to-physical memory mapping; but it was a nonstarter when using regular Linux paged memory. Because we wanted to use IBM's BG/P patches to MPICH with as few modifications as possible (so that we could make a more accurate comparison of application performance under different kernels), we opted to implement a static memory mapping area in Linux, which we called *Big Memory* (Yoshii et al. 2009, 2011a). This work will be discussed in detail in Sect. 10.2. In addition to providing Big Memory, we also needed to port to Linux IBM's low-level dependencies, specifically the deep computing messaging framework (Kumar et al. 2008) and the system programming interface libraries. Once this was accomplished, most of the OS-specific details were contained in the lower level components, enabling IBM's BG/P patches to MPICH to compile under ZeptoOS with minimal modifications. Big Memory also eliminated a major performance bottleneck of Linux on BG/P: its PowerPC 450 CPU cores necessitated that all translation lookaside buffer (TLB) misses had to be handled in software. Thus, active use of paged memory could result in large overheads. Due to Big Memory, we were able to compare individual aspects of different OS kernels in isolation, without the results being overshadowed by the fundamental differences in memory management. The results of the scalability studies we ran under these circumstances challenged established assumptions about the source and influence of OS jitter on the performance of highly parallel applications.

10.1.1.3 Blue Gene/Q and the Project's Demise

By the time Argonne received its first IBM Blue Gene/Q (BG/Q) system, the ZeptoOS project was formally over. Nevertheless, we intended to port the BG/P ZeptoOS stack to BG/Q, if only as a limited-scope skunkworks project. This, unfortunately, turned out to be impractical given the changes to the I/O nodes on BG/Q. As discussed in Sect. 10.1.1.1, on earlier Blue Gene systems, each compute node partition had its own set of I/O nodes that would boot at job launch time together with the compute nodes. On BG/Q, however, I/O nodes became shared and persistent: a single I/O node could be responsible for the handling of multiple independent jobs, potentially belonging to different users, and I/O nodes were not rebooted between jobs. This change made us unable to run our custom software stack on the I/O nodes without affecting other users, and our compute node stack depended on the custom I/O stack to be of practical use. Hence, ZeptoOS on BG/Q unfortunately never happened.

10.2   Memory Management

Like other general-purpose operating systems, the Linux kernel employs paged virtual memory, which provides multiple benefits, including process isolation, copy-on-write optimization, and simplicity of the physical memory allocation. For HPC workloads, however, the overhead of such memory management can be considerable (Moreira et al. 2006). Paged virtual memory degrades memory access performance as a result of page faults and TLB misses, and it requires additional memory for page table maintenance. Furthermore, there may be no contiguity of physical addresses across page boundaries (in fact, the virtual-to-physical mapping is not guaranteed to be constant, since the OS kernel can remap pages at run time). This last characteristic turned out to be particularly problematic for us on BG/P when we worked on enabling the use of the DMA engine of the torus network under Linux, prompting us to develop Big Memory, an alternative memory management infrastructure for HPC workloads.

The PowerPC 450 processor used on BG/P (IBM Blue Gene team 2008) consisted of four cache coherent, 32-bit cores. While the processor featured HPC-specific extensions such as dual-pipeline floating-point units, the CPU cores were not optimized for high performance with paged memory under Linux. In particular, the TLB on each core had only 64 entries and TLB misses had to be handled in software because the cores did not have a hardware page walker. Consequently, using regular 4 KiB pages under Linux would cause significant slowdowns in case of random-access patterns, as we will show in Sect. 10.2.2.1. On the other hand, PowerPC 450 had some advantages compared to, for example, regular x86-64 cores. The processor supported multiple page sizes ranging from 1 KiB to 1 GiB, and pages of different sizes could be freely used simultaneously. Any number of TLB entries could be configured statically; and in fact a subset of the available 64 entries was reserved for the OS kernel, firmware, and BG/P-specific memory-mapped I/O devices.

We experimented with increasing the page size to 64 KiB in order to reduce the TLB pressure; but, as we will show later, the resulting improvements were limited. A better solution in Linux would have been to use the *hugetlb* mechanism which can use pages in the megabyte range (or today even gigabyte). Shmueli et al. (2008) successfully used it to evaluate the performance of Linux on BG/L nodes. Because hugetlb support in Linux was not transparent at the time, they used a wrapper library called libhugetlbfs that would semi-transparently map application's text, data, and

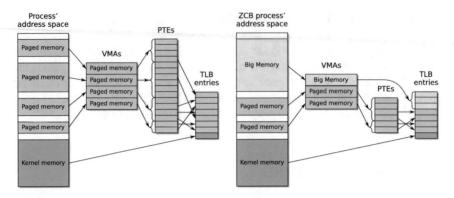

Fig. 10.1 Overview of Linux memory management: paged memory (*left*) vs Big Memory (*right*)

heap to a memory area backed by hugetlbfs. While their approach allowed Linux to achieve performance comparable to that of CNK on a number of workloads, it did not eliminate TLB misses completely; so for highly irregular memory access patterns significant performance degradation could still occur. It also was not the right solution to solve the Linux issues with the DMA engine on BG/P. Since then, transparent support for huge pages has been introduced in the Linux kernel (starting with version 2.6.38 (Arcangeli 2010)), but it remains limited; for example, it is not supported for file-backed regions such as the application text and data sections, and it is an opportunistic mechanism without performance guarantees.

10.2.1 Big Memory Architecture

Figure 10.1 compares and contrasts the standard Linux paged memory management and our Big Memory extension.

In Linux (Fig. 10.1, left), the address space of each process consists of a set of virtual address ranges called virtual memory areas (VMAs). VMAs have access permissions associated with them; access attempts outside of VMAs result in memory faults. VMAs are created on process startup but are also added later when *mmap* is called. Each VMA is backed by a set of page table entries (PTEs) used to translate virtual memory addresses to physical ones. PTEs are created by the kernel based on the VMAs and are stored in memory in advance or upon request. To reduce the overhead of accessing PTEs during address translation, modern processors cache recent translations in the TLB. TLB entries associated with paged memory are flushed by the kernel when switching context to another process. Physical memory backing the virtual address space is normally allocated lazily, on the first memory access to each page. The standard page size is 4 KiB.

In contrast, Big Memory was a special, reserved region of physically contiguous memory. As can be observed in Fig. 10.1, right, it was mapped into the virtual address space of a process by using a single VMA that was *not* backed by PTEs. Instead, simple offset-based mapping was used, which was backed by very large TLB entries of 256 MiB each that were statically pinned. This effectively eliminated TLB misses on accesses to Big Memory, ensuring maximum memory performance.

Unlike hugetlb-based approaches, our solution was fully transparent, required no code changes to the application, worked with static executables, and covered all the application segments. We achieved this by modifying the ELF binary loader in the kernel. For applications that were to use Big Memory, we set a custom flag in the ELF header of the executable file (we created a simple command line tool to manage the flag). We referred to such executables as ZeptoOS Compute Binaries, or ZCBs. On loading a ZCB during the *execve* system call, the kernel initialized the Big Memory region, constructed the initial stack frame, and preloaded the application's text and data sections there. The kernel could not use regular file mappings because Big Memory, not being paged, could not support them. A flag was also set in the task structure in the kernel so that other kernel functions could easily determine that they were dealing with a ZCB process.

Processes using paged memory and Big Memory could coexist on one node. In fact, even the address space of a ZCB process was hybrid, containing VMAs backed by regular paged memory and by Big Memory. File-backed memory mappings—as used, for example, to support shared libraries—ended up in paged memory, whereas anonymous, private requests (as used for large `malloc()` calls) went to Big Memory. To keep track of the different memory chunks within the Big Memory region, we added a custom memory manager to the kernel, utilizing the kernel's self-balancing red-black tree structure. Hybrid memory layout was also challenging in terms of organizing the TLB efficiently: several TLB entries were permanently reserved, more had to be statically pinned to support Big Memory, yet enough entries needed to be left available for regular caching duties or the performance of applications utilizing paged memory could significantly degrade.

Figure 10.2 shows the control flow in the kernel page fault handler. If a PTE was found for a faulting address, the handler simply filled in a TLB entry from the PTE. Big Memory had no PTEs; in that case, if the faulting task was a ZCB, the added code checked whether the faulting address was within the Big Memory area; if so, it installed the TLB entries covering the whole Big Memory region. Essentially, we would get a single TLB miss on the first access to Big Memory after the process had been scheduled in; the entries would normally remain in place until the process was scheduled out again. With context switches being fairly rare on the compute nodes, the entries were semi-static.

The physical memory area used by Big Memory was reserved at boot time to avoid complicated physical memory management and was thus not available for use by the kernel as regular, paged memory. This dramatically reduced the complexity of the implementation. The size of Big Memory could be specified by using Linux kernel parameters. BG/P compute nodes were normally rebooted between jobs, so the reservation could be set for each job.

Initially, we implemented a single Big Memory region per node, which limited the number of MPI tasks to one per node (Yoshii et al. 2009, 2011a), forcing the

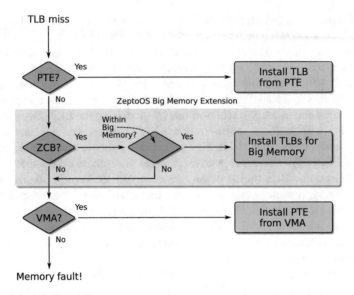

Fig. 10.2 ZeptoOS page fault handler. The shaded region highlights the modifications we made to support Big Memory

use of multithreading to take advantage of all the available CPU resources (this was known in the BG/P nomenclature as the *SMP mode*). We later extended the support to four separate Big Memory instances (Yoshii et al. 2011b), which enabled the use of one MPI task per *core*, also known as the *virtual node mode*. Each Big Memory area was local to a particular core; a task using Big Memory was bound to a core by using strict CPU affinity controls, which is a common technique in HPC to reduce performance variability.

10.2.2 Performance

We evaluated the performance of our solution using a variety of benchmarks and applications. Below we present a subset of these experiments.

10.2.2.1 Memory Benchmarks

We used custom microbenchmarks to evaluate the performance of the memory subsystem. The streaming copy benchmark copied data sequentially from one half of a memory buffer to another. The random memory access benchmark read data from a memory buffer in a semi-random order. Both benchmarks were single-threaded.

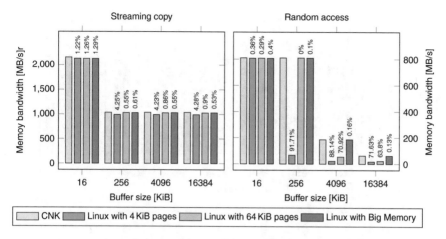

Fig. 10.3 Memory bandwidth under CNK and Linux: streaming copy (*left*) and random access (*right*). The percentage numbers indicate slowdown compared with CNK

The results are shown in Fig. 10.3. We conducted the experiments on BG/P compute nodes, running under the standard lightweight kernel CNK, Linux with regular 4 KiB pages, Linux modified to use 64 KiB pages, and Linux with Big Memory. The bars show the absolute memory bandwidth, and the labels above the Linux bars show the percentage of slowdown relative to CNK. Standard error was under 1% in all the experiments, so we omitted the error bars.

As shown in the streaming copy results (Fig. 10.3, left), with a 16 KiB buffer size, which fit well in the 32 KiB L1 cache, the Linux kernel incurred approx. 1.2% performance loss. Since no TLB misses occurred in this case, we suspect that the periodic Linux timer interrupts would thrash the L1 cache. With a 256 KiB buffer size, which was the maximum size that the 64 TLB entries of 4 KiB each could cover, the performance under Linux with 4 KiB pages dropped by over 4%. As expected, 64 KiB pages helped here, keeping the performance loss to under 1%, even at the largest buffer sizes. The reason is that the overhead of a TLB miss became relatively small: updating a TLB entry took approx. 0.2 μs, while loading a 64 KiB page took approx. 60 μs. The performance with Big Memory was similar to that with 64 KiB pages.

Big Memory showed its advantages when the memory was accessed randomly (Fig. 10.3, right). The results with 4 KiB pages show an order-of-magnitude performance degradation at a 256 KiB buffer size. Increasing the page size to 64 KiB improved the situation, but only temporarily: at a 4 MiB buffer size, we could still see a performance degradation by a significant factor. In contrast, Big Memory essentially eliminated the performance gap, tracking the performance of CNK within well under 1%.

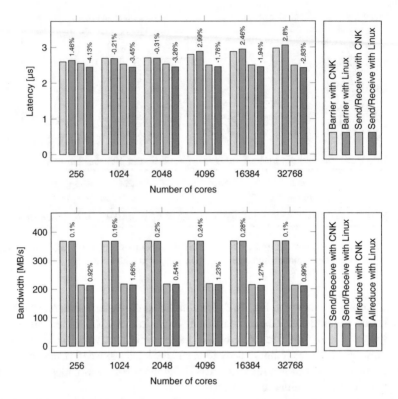

Fig. 10.4 Performance with MPI microbenchmarks: latency (*top*) and bandwidth (*bottom*). The percentage numbers indicate slowdown compared with CNK (negative numbers indicate speedup)

10.2.2.2   MPI Benchmarks

We ran a set of custom microbenchmarks to compare the performance and scalability of ZeptoOS and CNK. All experiments were run on between 64 and 8,192 BG/P compute nodes in virtual node mode (four MPI tasks per node).

Figure 10.4, top, shows the results of latency measurements with `MPI_Barrier()` and `MPI_Send()`/`MPI_Recv()` ping-pong benchmarks. With the barrier, the latency gap between ZeptoOS and CNK would grow slightly with increasing core count. This could be an indication of "OS noise," but the effect was minor and would likely not be observed in real applications (as they do not normally invoke `MPI_Barrier()` 400,000 times per second). Interesting, in the send/receive benchmark, where a pair of processes located in the opposite corners of a compute node partition exchanged messages back and forth, Linux with Big Memory outperformed CNK. The message size used was 4 bytes. The performance discrepancy was due to the fact that the low-level user space library, which converted the virtual-to-physical memory addresses for the DMA unit, had less overhead under ZeptoOS than under CNK. Again, this probably would not be a significant effect in real applications.

Figure 10.4, bottom, shows the bandwidth measurements with the MPI_Send()/-MPI_Recv() ping-pong benchmark and with MPI_Allreduce(). With the send/receive benchmark, the performance gap between ZeptoOS and CNK was small (0.1–0.3%) and did not exhibit any scalability degradation. The message size used in this case was 16 MiB. With allreduce, the performance gap was slightly larger (0.9–1.7%), but again there were no signs of any scalability problems. We believe that the larger gap could be attributed to the fact that allreduce used the collective network here, which—unlike the torus network used in send/receive—did not have a DMA engine, so the CPU itself had to take care of copying the data from the main memory to the network device and back. Thus, allreduce was likely to be more sensitive to jitter.

10.2.2.3   HPC Applications

In addition to the microbenchmarks, we also compared the performance of ZeptoOS and CNK on two real, highly scalable parallel applications.

Parallel Ocean Program (POP) (Jones et al. 2005; Kerbyson and Jones 2005) is a well-known HPC application for studying the ocean climate system. POP is known for being sensitive to jitter, so it seemed like an excellent candidate for our study.

We used unmodified POP version 2.0.1 and the X1 benchmark data set. We ran it at the scale of 64 to 4,096 nodes, in SMP mode (one MPI task per node). The results are shown in Fig. 10.5, left, and they are surprising: we found POP to scale better under Linux than under CNK. Our subsequent investigation revealed that POP, being extensively instrumented, would call the *gettimeofday* system call as much as 100,000 times on each node during the application execution. System call overhead is generally lower under Linux than under CNK; additionally, *gettimeofday* benefits from the presence of the periodic clock tick in Linux, which simplifies time calculations. Consequently, the cost of the *gettimeofday* call under Linux on BG/P compute nodes was nearly an order of magnitude lower than under CNK. Since this was a strong-scalability experiment, this overhead became ever more significant with increasing node counts, eventually enabling Linux to overtake CNK. When we replaced the *gettimeofday* system call with a user space implementation and repeated the experiment on 4,096 nodes, we observed Linux being around 1% slower than CNK, as expected.

NEK5000 (Nek5000 2008) was another application we used for comparing performance. It is a computational fluid dynamics solver developed at Argonne National Laboratory. We ran it simulating fluid flow in a T-junction, using up to 8,192 nodes in virtual node mode (four MPI tasks per node). Figure 10.5, right, shows the results. As can be observed, the application ran under Linux with Big Memory at 32,768 cores with a 1.16% performance loss compared with CNK.

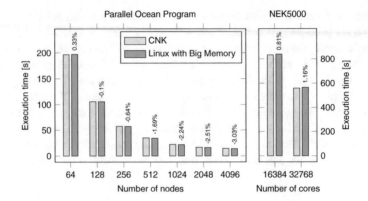

Fig. 10.5 Performance of HPC applications: Parallel Ocean Program (*left*) and NEK5000 (*right*). The percentage numbers indicate slowdown compared with CNK (negative numbers indicate speedup)

Fig. 10.6 I/O architecture of BG/L and BG/P systems (simplified)

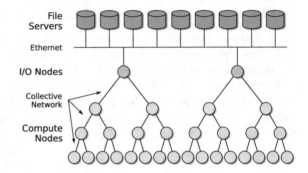

10.3 Input/Output Architecture

Often, the importance of I/O to the success of an HPC system is not appreciated. Surprisingly then, interest in our software by some of its most successful users (see Sect. 10.4) was triggered by the promises of a more flexible I/O support. Thus, we feel that this retrospection of the ZeptoOS project would be incomplete without touching on the I/O aspects as well.

A simplified view of the I/O architecture of BG/L and BG/P systems (Gara et al. 2005) is depicted in Fig. 10.6. Compute nodes, running a lightweight kernel, did not perform I/O locally. Instead, the kernel would forward I/O operations over the tree-like collective network to an I/O node, where a user space daemon (CIOD) would retrieve the operations from the network and issue the requests against the Linux kernel running on the I/O node. I/O nodes had traditional Ethernet interfaces (Gigabit on BG/L, 10 Gigabit on BG/P IBM Blue Gene team (2008)) that they could use to communicate with file servers or the outside world.

The overall architecture was sound; however, on BG/L, I/O operations were serialized both on the dual-core compute nodes and on the I/O nodes (which serviced between 8 and 64 compute nodes each, depending on system configuration (Gara et al. 2005)). This was addressed on BG/P, but another major issue for us was that the design was not easily extensible. Only fixed subsets of POSIX file I/O and BSD socket operations were supported by the standard I/O forwarding infrastructure (Moreira et al. 2005).

To address this, we developed the ZeptoOS I/O Daemon (ZOID) as an alternative (Iskra et al. 2008) to the standard CIOD infrastructure on BG/L. Since the inner workings of CIOD were not documented, reproducing it in its entirety would have been challenging. We opted, therefore, to use it for nonperformance-critical operations such as job initialization and termination. A job that wanted to use our ZOID infrastructure needed to be linked with our modified C library, which, at initialization time on the compute nodes, would notify the ZOID daemon running on the I/O node, using a separate virtual channel of the collective network. ZOID would then deactivate the standard CIOD by sending it a signal and would assume I/O forwarding responsibilities. A custom communication protocol over the collective network was implemented entirely in user space on the compute node side, cutting down on the latency by eliminating the overhead of a system call. At job termination time, ZOID would reactivate the standard CIOD to perform the expected message exchanges with the compute node kernel and the service node as part of the job cleanup (the service node was responsible for managing the whole BG/P system and ran no ZeptoOS-specific components (Moreira et al. 2005)).

Unlike the standard infrastructure, ZOID was multithreaded: it could handle forwarded operations from multiple compute node clients in parallel, using a pool of worker threads. More important from a research point of view, it was extensible: it featured a plugin interface, enabling advanced users to extend the set of operations that could be forwarded between compute nodes and I/O nodes. A base plugin, called `unix`, provided the forwarding of POSIX file I/O and BSD socket calls while CIOD was deactivated. Another plugin, called `zoidfs`, implemented an I/O protocol specifically designed with parallel file I/O in mind: it was stateless, NFSv3-like, with maximally expressive read/write operations that could modify multiple regions of a file within a single call. It was the desire to implement that protocol on Blue Gene that motivated the development of ZOID. The custom protocol over the collective network was optimized with bulk data transfers in mind, including support for zero-copy data transfers, provided that user-supplied buffers met alignment requirements imposed by hardware.

As indicated in Sect. 10.1.1.2, when ZeptoOS moved to using a Linux-based compute node kernel on BG/P, the responsibilities of ZOID increased significantly; Fig. 10.7 shows an overview of all the major components on compute nodes and I/O nodes. The figure may seem complex, especially on the compute node side, but in reality, much of that complexity had to do with our desire to provide applications with a range of flexible options to best match their needs. The OS kernel on the compute node side is not drawn at the traditional bottom, to indicate that the compute nodes were not fully independent, but instead depended on the I/O nodes for certain functionality. In this case, the Linux kernel would call back to the user space FUSE and IP forwarding components in certain situations, which is why those components were drawn under the kernel. The only new component was the node management daemon, launched on the compute nodes at boot time. Its primary responsibility was job management (launching application processes, handling termination, etc.). A corresponding job management component was also added to the ZOID daemon running on I/O nodes, which communicated with the service node. A regular application using POSIX file I/O calls, if linked with a ZOID-enabled `libc` version that forwarded data directly via the `unix` plugin, could achieve throughput of up to 760 MB/s. To maximize the flexibility, however, we also provided a FUSE client on top of the same plugin so that unmodified binaries using regular system calls would still work, albeit at a performance penalty, as the overhead of going through the Linux kernel would reduce throughput to 230 MB/s. MPI (specifically, MPI-I/O) could use the `zoidfs` plugin for maximum performance, or it could go through `libc`, utilizing either of the two already discussed options. The `zoidfs` plugin on the I/O node side either could communicate with the PVFS client library directly or could use POSIX file I/O to support any file system implementation, just like the `unix` plugin. In addition to BSD socket calls forwarded using the `unix` plugin, we added the IP packet forwarding capability using the Linux TUN/TAP driver. It was implemented as part of the node management daemon on the compute node side. While the throughput of that approach was low (22 MB/s), it provided unparalleled flexibility, including the ability to open an interactive terminal session on a compute node for ease of experimentation or debugging. The remaining component in Fig. 10.7, `libzoid_cn`, is a low-level library coordinating simultaneous access to the collective network from multiple compute node clients.

In addition to providing the core functionality, we implemented a number of tools and features on top that made the infrastructure easier to use for a broader range of workloads and by power users. For example, we implemented an optional IP forwarding capability between compute nodes using the Linux TUN/TAP driver. This was built on top of the MPI stack and thus took advantage of the torus network. Its performance was surprisingly good; we measured speeds of up to 287 MB/s,

Fig. 10.7 I/O and job management-related components of ZeptoOS on BG/P systems. Components that communicate with each other within a node are stacked vertically

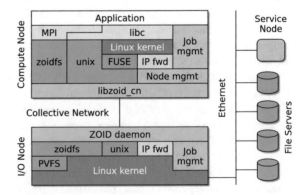

compared with 357 MB/s that we saw with MPI benchmarks. That rate was a lot better than what we saw over the collective network between I/O nodes and compute nodes. We also added the capability for a user-supplied script to be launched on each I/O node at job startup and termination. We provided a file broadcasting utility that could efficiently (with a speed in excess of 300 MB/s) transfer a file to each compute node managed by a particular I/O node, for example, to stage large input data at job startup.

10.4   Major Users

LOFAR (LOw-Frequency ARray) (Butcher 2004) is a radio telescope built by the Netherlands Institute for Radio Astronomy (ASTRON). It consists of thousands of geographically distributed antennas; data from these antennas needs to be processed centrally, in real time (Romein et al. 2006). At the time that ASTRON researchers got in touch with us, they were using a BG/L system and were facing significant difficulties streaming the input data into the system with the throughput required by the workload. While standard I/O forwarding software supported a subset of BSD socket calls, it worked only with TCP sockets, not with UDP, which was how data arrived from the antennas. Hence, an input conversion step was required before the data could be fed to the compute nodes for further processing, forcing the use of a separate input cluster performing buffering and conversion. I/O nodes could not prefetch data; and since the single-threaded standard CIOD serialized all I/O, periodic writing out of the output data could delay the input data streaming, placing the real-time requirements of data processing in jeopardy.

Switching to ZOID solved many of these problems. An application-specific ZOID plugin made it possible to run custom code on the I/O nodes, which enabled the handling of UDP sockets and the buffering of input data directly there. This eliminated the need for a separate, expensive input cluster. Utilizing the I/O nodes, the output data volume was also significantly reduced by integrating the data from individual compute nodes before sending it out to the file system. Previously that step had to be done in postprocessing.

What enabled these optimizations was not only the flexibility of ZOID but also its efficiency. Many of these improvements could in theory have been implemented with the standard CIOD by running custom input and output daemons on the I/O node that CIOD would communicate with using local sockets. This approach would have, however, required multiple additional memory copies when switching context between user space processes and the kernel. Dual-core I/O nodes on BG/L utilized only one core because the cores were not cache coherent (Moreira et al. 2005). That single functional PowerPC 440 CPU core, running at 700 MHz, had to manage both the kernel IP stack and the BG/L collective network. Any extraneous memory copies would have resulted in a significant decrease in performance and, eventually, a failure to meet the real-time requirements. ZOID was optimized to support zero-copy data transfers, including to and from a plugin-provided memory location on the I/O node side. Hence, input UDP data from the antennas, once stored in the input buffer, would stream to compute nodes without any intermediate copies. Nevertheless, overburdening the CPU remained a concern. Therefore, in a collaboration driven by ASTRON, we experimented with enabling the second CPU core on the I/O nodes. We thought that we could offload the management of the collective network to it. The initial experiments were encouraging: write throughput to the PVFS parallel file system jumped over 30%, approaching the theoretical Gigabit NIC bandwidth. Managing noncoherent memory turned out to be a significant problem, however, triggering a large number of difficult to diagnose bugs, so at least at Argonne we never put this feature into production.

CPU utilization on I/O nodes remained a challenge for ASTRON even after moving to a BG/P system, with its four active cores on each I/O node. The main bottleneck turned out to be the performance of paged memory with Linux due to TLB misses—something that our Big Memory work was likely to help. It had, however, been designed for use on the compute nodes and ASTRON needed it on the I/O nodes (Romein et al. 2010). This demonstrates the benefits of building flexible, open solutions—other researchers can find unexpected uses for them that the original authors have never envisioned. Allocating the critical ring buffer structure in Big Memory reduced the memory copy overhead by over 200%. With additional optimizations, the overall CPU utilization dropped to 66.5%, where originally it was estimated at 151% (i.e., exceeding by half the CPU capacity of the node) (Yoshii et al. 2011a).

Falkon and Swift Raicu et al. (2007), Zhao et al. (2007) are many-task computing (MTC) systems that were developed by researchers from the University of Chicago and Argonne National Laboratory. The researchers wanted to take advantage of the massively parallel Argonne BG/P systems to run their large workloads. MTC workloads consisted of large numbers of loosely coupled tasks (frequently sequential) that were executed over short periods of time on highly parallel systems (Raicu et al. 2008a). BG/P's standard CNK lightweight kernel was optimized for a different use case: massively parallel MPI jobs where all tasks started simultaneously, ran for a relatively long time, and finished at the same time. Initially, no provisions were made for running different binaries on different nodes, or for restarting individual nodes, etc. Thus, porting existing MTC systems, from what we would today call cloud environments, to BG/P would have been exceedingly hard. It would have required embedding the scheduling logic, scripting, caching, etc., as well as the code of all the target applications, within a single binary. It would have had to work reliably, because if one process crashed, the control system would terminate all the others as well. Furthermore, there were practical problems such as the fact that Falkon was originally written in Java, which was not a supported runtime environment under CNK.

ZeptoOS made running such workloads not only possible but practical. Because of the scale of the system (40,960 compute nodes), a centralized task dispatcher would not scale, so a hierarchical architecture was developed, with dispatchers running on each I/O node and communicating over the collective network with executors running on the compute nodes. The availability and ease of use of ramdisks on both compute nodes and I/O nodes made it simple to cache application binary files, shared static input, and intermediate output files, using simple scripting mechanisms. This aspect turned out to be critical to the eventual success, since uncoordinated I/O from massive numbers of nodes would overwhelm the file servers. Data staging became a necessity.

Once the initial problems were overcome, the researchers were able to perform experiments at a previously unprecedented scale. For example, in one experiment with a molecular dynamics application, around 1 million tasks were successfully executed on over 118,000 CPU cores during a two-hour window (Raicu et al. 2008b). The system was able to sustain utilization of 99.6%, completing over 100 tasks per second on average, peaking at around 400.

To make such experiments practical, we had to provide additional functionality in ZeptoOS. For example, we added a performance-monitoring capability to the ZOID daemon so that researchers could study the effectiveness of their caching strategies, load-balancing mechanisms, etc. At one point, we were asked to help solve a problem of an application that needed an input data set that was several times too large to fit within a cache of a single BG/P node. Using the IP forwarding over torus mechanism discussed in Sect. 10.3 plus a few standard Linux kernel subsystems (Multiple Device driver, Network Block Device), we dedicated four compute nodes as caching nodes and exported the contents of their ramdisks to the remaining compute nodes, where it was mounted as a single file system capable of holding all the required data. While we do not know if this was put into production, the fact that a working prototype could be put together quickly demonstrates the power and effectiveness of the open software stack we provided.

10.5   Lessons Learned

The impact of the ZeptoOS project can be analyzed from several angles.

From the research point of view, the key contribution was the study of the performance of HPC applications under a full kernel (Linux) versus a lightweight one (CNK). We were, of course, not the first ones to conduct such a study (Petrini et al. 2003; Jones et al. 2003; Brightwell et al. 2003). What made our work different was a conscious attempt to keep the Linux environment as close to the lightweight kernel one as possible. Thus, rather than relying on some existing enterprise Linux distribution, as many HPC centers did for their production Linux clusters, in ZeptoOS, the compute node image was built from the ground up to be as minimal as possible, and only a few most critical daemons would run alongside an HPC application. We also made a concerted effort to run the native BG/P communication stack under ZeptoOS with as few modifications as possible, rather than getting TCP/IP to work and running regular MPICH on top of that. To do that, we had to implement Big Memory in the Linux kernel. Our goal was to ensure that the environments surrounding each kernel were as similar as possible and thus that any observed discrepancies in application performance could be attributed accurately to the differences between the kernels themselves. The resulting experiments demonstrated that, when suitably configured, running on an HPC-optimized hardware, and with an HPC-optimized communication stack, Linux *can be* performance competitive against a state-of-the-art lightweight kernel, even when running at a scale of tens of thousands of nodes. Of course, one could argue that ZeptoOS was not a regular Linux, because Big Memory was significantly different from a regular Linux paged memory. But that in itself was an important research contribution. By replacing *just* the memory manager, we demonstrated that the bulk of the slowdown seen as "OS noise" could be attributed to that particular component and not, say, to the task scheduler, or to the interrupt handler. In fact, we experimented with modifying other aspects of Linux as well, for example, we disabled the periodic clock tick timer (that work predated the tickless effort in the mainline Linux kernel), but that failed to make any significant difference in the experiments we ran. In terms of impact, while Cray implemented Compute Node Linux (CNL) on their own, they were aware of our research and our positive results fit their experience and expectations. These results helped encourage them to use Linux on their systems and switch from the lightweight Catamount kernel (Kelly and Brightwell 2005; Wallace 2007).

So, can Big Memory, which was inspired by the memory management from lightweight kernels, be considered an early example of a multikernel architecture? Not really, because apart from that one component, the rest of the kernel *was* Linux. Its use did, however, result in certain additional constraints common to lightweight kernels. Without paged memory, there was no lazy file reading or copy-on-write; *mmap* did not support file mappings; and, more significantly, *fork* was not supported. As a result, an HPC application running in Big Memory under ZeptoOS could not launch an external command in a subprocess, which prevented some interesting potential use cases.

Thus, the majority of users who ran traditional HPC applications stayed with the standard lightweight kernel since it met their needs. As indicated in Sect. 10.4, the most interesting use cases of our software stack were from *nontraditional* users: real-time data streaming and many-task computing workloads. We consider support for such workloads to be the second important contribution of our work. It taught us that making our software as flexible as possible is the key to attracting new users, and it showed us that there were whole communities out there who were not well served by the existing HPC software stacks that were optimized for a different use case.

While we do not dispute that support for standard APIs is critical, HPC is at the forefront of system performance, and thus there will always be cases where standard APIs are not enough (plus, there are many standards, and vendors cannot be expected to support them all). OS software stacks must be easily extensible to enable power users to cater to their own needs. That extensibility needs to be provided at a level where using it will be *efficient*. For example, any communication protocol can be tunneled over a TCP socket; but if such tunneling decreases throughput by an integer factor, then it is unlikely to be an acceptable extension mechanism for many problems.

With regard to MTC workloads, IBM extended its software stack to provide a rudimentary support for them as well (Peters et al. 2008). A compute node would launch a local executor that would determine the name of the application binary to subsequently launch on that node; once the application finished, the executor would be invoked again for the next iteration. CNK had to reboot between the launches of different binaries. The control system was extended to be more tolerant of individual process crashes. A special memory region was implemented that could survive a reboot and could thus function as a persistent cache; it was initially a raw memory buffer but in time was extended to be accessible as a local ramdisk. While the critical infrastructure pieces were thus eventually provided, we thought that, in comparison, ZeptoOS benefited from the ecosystem that came with the use of Linux. One should not underestimate the value of a solution that encourages quick prototyping by cobbling together a few scripts. A successful environment not only needs to make complex things possible but also should strive to keep simple things simple.

Acknowledgements We thank the rest of the ZeptoOS core team: Harish Naik and Chenjie Yu at Argonne National Laboratory and the University of Oregon's Allen D. Malony, Sameer Shende, and Aroon Nataraj. We thank our colleagues at Argonne who offered their expertise and assistance in many areas, especially Susan Coghlan and other members of the Leadership Computing Facility. We also thank all our summer interns, in particular Balazs Gerofi, Kazunori Yamamoto, Peter Boonstoppel, Hajime Fujita, Satya Popuri, and Taku Shimosawa, who contributed to the ZeptoOS project. Additionally, we thank ASTRON's John W. Romein and P. Chris Broekema and the University of Chicago's Ioan Raicu, Zhao Zhang, Mike Wilde, and Ian Foster. In addition, we thank IBM's Todd Inglett, Thomas Musta, Thomas Gooding, George Almási, Sameer Kumar, Michael Blocksome, Blake Fitch, Chris Ward, and Robert Wisniewski for their advice on programming the Blue Gene hardware.

This work was supported by the Office of Advanced Scientific Computer Research, Office of Science, U.S. Department of Energy, under Contract DE-AC02-06CH11357. This research used resources of the Argonne Leadership Computing Facility, which is a DOE Office of Science User Facility.

References

Arcangeli, A. (2010). Transparent hugepage support. *KVM Forum.* https://www.linux-kvm.org/images/9/9e/2010-forum-thp.pdf.

Beckman, P., Iskra, K., Yoshii, K., & Coghlan, S. (2006a). The influence of operating systems on the performance of collective operations at extreme scale. *IEEE International Conference on Cluster Computing, Cluster.*

Beckman, P., Iskra, K., Yoshii, K., & Coghlan, S. (2006b). Operating system issues for petascale systems. *ACM SIGOPS Operating Systems Review, 40*(2), 29–33.

Beckman, P., Iskra, K., Yoshii, K., Coghlan, S., & Nataraj, A. (2008). Benchmarking the effects of operating system interference on extreme-scale parallel machines. *Cluster Computing, 11*(1), 3–16.

Brightwell, R., Riesen, R., Underwood, K., Bridges, P. G., Maccabe, A. B., & Hudson, T. (2003). A performance comparison of Linux and a lightweight kernel. *IEEE International Conference on Cluster Computing, Cluster* (p. 251–258).

Butcher, H. R. (2004). LOFAR: First of a new generation of radio telescopes. *Proceedings SPIE, 5489,* 537–544.

Carns, P. H., Ligon III, W. B., Ross, R. B., & Thakur, R. (2000). PVFS: A parallel file system for Linux clusters. *4th Annual Linux Showcase and Conference* (pp. 317–327). GA: Atlanta.

Gara, A., et al. (2005). Overview of the Blue Gene/L system architecture. *IBM Journal of Research and Development, 49*(2/3), 189–500.

Giampapa, M., Gooding, T., Inglett, T., & Wisniewski, R. (2010). Experiences with a lightweight supercomputer kernel: Lessons learned from Blue Gene's CNK. *International Conference for High Performance Computing, Networking, Storage and Analysis, SC.*

IBM Blue Gene team. (2008). Overview of the IBM Blue Gene/P project. *IBM Journal of Research and Development, 52*(1/2), 199–220.

Iskra, K., Romein, J. W., Yoshii, K., & Beckman, P. (2008). ZOID: I/O-forwarding infrastructure for petascale architectures. *13th ACM SIGPLAN Symposium on Principles and Practice of Parallel Programming, PPoPP* (pp. 153–162). UT: Salt Lake City.

Jones, T., Dawson, S., Neely, R., Tuel, W., Brenner, L., Fier, J., et al. (2003). Improving the scalability of parallel jobs by adding parallel awareness to the operating system. *ACM/IEEE Conference on Supercomputing, SC.* Phoenix: AZ.

Jones, P. W., Worley, P. H., Yoshida, Y., White III, J. B., & Levesque, J. (2005). Practical performance portability in the parallel ocean program (POP). *Concurrency and Computation: Practice and Experience, 17*(10), 1317–1327.

Kelly, S. M. & Brightwell, R. (2005). Software architecture of the light weight kernel, Catamount. *47th Cray User Group Conference, CUG.* NM.

Kerbyson, D. J., & Jones, P. W. (2005). A performance model of the parallel ocean program. *International Journal of High Performance Computing Applications, 19*(3), 261–276.

Kumar, S., Dozsa, G., Almasi, G., Heidelberger, P., Chen, D., Giampapa, M. E., et al. (2008). The Deep Computing Messaging Framework: Generalized scalable message passing on the Blue Gene/P supercomputer. *22nd Annual International Conference on Supercomputing, ICS* (pp. 94–103).

Moreira, J. E. et al. (2006). Designing a highly-scalable operating system: The Blue Gene/L story. *ACM/IEEE Conference on Supercomputing, SC.* FL.

Moreira, J. E., et al. (2005). Blue Gene/L programming and operating environment. *IBM Journal of Research and Development, 49*(2/3), 367–376.

Nataraj, A., Morris, A., Malony, A., Sottile, M., & Beckman, P. (2007). The ghost in the machine: Observing the effects of kernel operation on parallel application performance. *ACM/IEEE Conference on Supercomputing, SC.*

Nek5000 (2008). NEK5000: A fast and scalable high-order solver for computational fluid dynamics. https://nek5000.mcs.anl.gov/.

Peters, A., King, A., Budnik, T., McCarthy, P., Michaud, P., Mundy, M., et al. (2008). Asynchronous task dispatch for high throughput computing for the eServer IBM Blue Gene® supercomputer. *IEEE International Symposium on Parallel and Distributed Processing, IPDPS.*

Petrini, F., Kerbyson, D. J., & Pakin, S. (2003). The case of the missing supercomputer performance: Achieving optimal performance on the 8,192 processors of ASCI Q. *ACM/IEEE Conference on Supercomputing, SC.*

Raicu, I., Foster, I. T., & Zhao, Y. (2008a). Many-task computing for grids and supercomputers. *Workshop on Many-Task Computing on Grids and Supercomputers, MTAGS.*

Raicu, I., Zhang, Z., Wilde, M., Foster, I., Beckman, P., Iskra, K., & Clifford, B. (2008b). Toward loosely coupled programming on petascale systems. *ACM/IEEE Conference on Supercomputing, SC.*

Raicu, I., Zhao, Y., Dumitrescu, C., Foster, I., & Wilde, M. (2007). Falkon: A fast and light-weight task execution framework. *ACM/IEEE Conference on Supercomputing, SC.*

Ritsko, J. J., Ames, I., Raider, S. I., & Robinson, J. H. (Eds.). (2005). IBM Journal of Research and Development. IBM Corporation. *Blue Gene* (Vol. 49).

Romein, J. W., Broekema, P. C., Mol, J. D., & van Nieuwpoort, R. V. (2010). The LOFAR correlator: Implementation and performance analysis. *15th ACM SIGPLAN Symposium on Principles and Practice of Parallel Programming, PPoPP* (pp. 169–178).

Romein, J. W., Broekema, P. C., van Meijeren, E., van der Schaaf, K., & Zwart, W. H. (2006). Astronomical real-time streaming signal processing on a Blue Gene/L supercomputer. *ACM Symposium on Parallel Algorithms and Architectures, SPAA* (pp. 59–66). Cambridge.

Shmueli, E., Almási, G., Brunheroto, J., Castaños, J., Dózsa, G., Kumar, S., et al. (2008). Evaluating the effect of replacing CNK with Linux on the compute-nodes of Blue Gene/L. *22nd ACM International Conference on Supercomputing, ICS* (pp. 165–174). Greece: Kos.

Tang, W., Lan, Z., Desai, N., and Buettner, D. (2009). Fault-aware, utility-based job scheduling on Blue Gene/P systems. In *IEEE International Conference on Cluster Computing and Workshops, Cluster*.

Wallace, D. (2007). Compute Node Linux: Overview, progress to date and roadmap. *Cray User Group Conference, CUG*.

Yoshii, K., Iskra, K., Naik, H., Beckman, P., & Broekema, P. (2009). Characterizing the performance of "Big Memory" on Blue Gene Linux. *2nd International Workshop on Parallel Programming Models and Systems Software for High-End Computing, P2S2* (pp. 65–72).

Yoshii, K., Naik, H., Yu, C., & Beckman, P. (2011b). Extending and benchmarking the "Big Memory" implementation on Blue Gene/P Linux. *1st International Workshop on Runtime and Operating Systems for Supercomputers, ROSS* (pp. 65–72).

Yoshii, K., Iskra, K., Naik, H., Beckman, P., & Broekema, P. C. (2011a). Performance and scalability evaluation of "Big Memory" on Blue Gene Linux. *International Journal of High Performance Computing Applications, 25*(2), 148–160.

ZeptoOS (2005). ZeptoOS: Small Linux for big computers. http://www.mcs.anl.gov/research/projects/zeptoos/.

Zhao, Y., Hategan, M., Clifford, B., Foster, I., von Laszewski, G., Nefedova, V., et al. (2007). Swift: Fast, reliable, loosely coupled parallel computation. *IEEE Congress on Services* (pp. 199–206).

Chapter 11
K Computer

Takeharu Kato and Kouichi Hirai

Abstract The K Computer secured the number one spot on the TOP500 list in June 2011. Since then it has been awarded first place in various high-performance computing (HPC) benchmarks, such as HPCG, Graph 500, and the HPC Challenge Class 1. The K Computer is a large-scale parallel supercomputer with several Fujitsu developed unique hardware components, e.g., the SPARC64 VIII fx CPU, and the Tofu interconnect. The software architecture supports high levels of parallelism, provides Reliability, Availability, and Serviceability (RAS) functions for stable operation and a large-scale distributed file system called FEFS to handle huge amount of data. We developed a special operating system environment based on Linux with additional drivers and kernel functionality to make efficient use of SPARC64 VIII fx's HPC extensions. In this article, we describe the background of our development, as well as the design and implementation of the operating system running on the K Computer. We also describe our current outlook for the software architecture of the next-generation high-performance computer systems succeeding the K Computer.

11.1 Introduction

11.1.1 Overview of the K Computer System

Thedevelopment of the K Computer[1] started at RIKEN in 2005 as part of the Ministry of Education, Culture, Sports, Science and Technology (MEXT)'s next-generation supercomputer project. It was jointly developed by RIKEN and Fujitsu.

---

[1] K Computer is a registered trademark of the Institute of Physical and Chemical Research (RIKEN). It is named for the Japanese word "kei", meaning 10 quadrillion.

T. Kato (✉) · K. Hirai
Fujitsu Ltd., (Company Mail No. H1883), Software Development
Div. Next Generation Technical Computing Unit, 4-1-1 Kamikodanaka, Nakahara-ku
Kawasaki-shi, Kanagawa, Kawasaki 211-8588, Japan
e-mail: kato.takeharu@jp.fujitsu.com

K. Hirai
e-mail: k-hirai@jp.fujitsu.com

© Springer Nature Singapore Pte Ltd. 2019
B. Gerofi et al. (eds.), *Operating Systems for Supercomputers
and High Performance Computing*, High-Performance Computing Series,
https://doi.org/10.1007/978-981-13-6624-6_11

This system has been awarded first place in many benchmarks such as HPCG, Graph 500, and HPC Challenge Class 1 since it earned the number one spot on the TOP500 list in June 2011. The K Computer provides top-level performance not only for benchmark programs but also for practical applications. It is a supercomputer system with high execution efficiency. In this section, we provide an overview of the K Computer, describe the design of its operating system (OS), and discuss successor systems.

11.1.2   System Architecture of the K Computer

The overall system of K Computer is shown in Fig. 11.1. The system is divided into four main components: (1) compute node group, (2) local file system, (3) global file system, and (4) the peripheral equipment group.

The K Computer has more than 80,000 computation nodes. Each compute node consists of an 8-core Fujitsu SPARC64 VIII fx CPU (Maruyama et al. 2010), an Interconnect Controller (ICC) network chip, and 16 GiB of memory. The SPARC64 VIII fx CPU has a number of HPC-specific features, such as the on-chip CPU core barrier and a cache control mechanism called sector cache.

Each compute node is connected via ICC to Fujitsu's proprietary Tofu interconnect (Ajima et al. 2012), a six-dimensional mesh/torus network. The Tofu interconnect has four RDMA engines and can process four packets simultaneously.

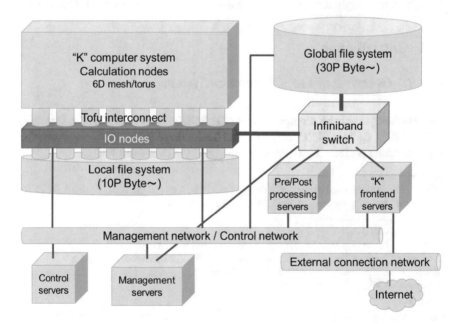

Fig. 11.1 Overview of the K Computer system

In addition, it has a hardware supported barrier synchronization function between nodes. By using this function, synchronization of system daemons operating in each compute node can be realized at low cost.

As shown in Fig. 11.1, the K Computer has a two-tier file system of a local file system and a global file system. The local file system is a temporary storage area dedicated to applications executing on compute nodes. The local file system is supported by designated I/O nodes. The global file system is a permanent storage area that can be directly accessed by users.

11.1.3   Software Architecture of the K Computer

The software configuration of K Computer is shown in Fig. 11.2. Although some of the software components were developed based on open source software (OSS), most components are exclusive to the K Computer. In particular, software components that utilize unique features of the CPU and the Tofu interconnect are very specific to the K Computer. However, the OS and the communication layer, i.e., MPI, have

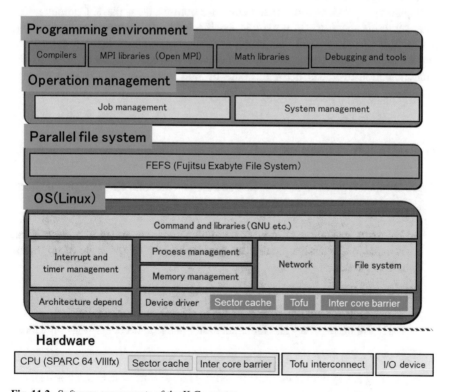

Fig. 11.2   Software components of the K Computer

been designed to emphasize portability and to provide a general-purpose application execution environment.

The entire operation management software used in K Computer was developed by Fujitsu. For batch job operation, in order to make good use of the Tofu interconnect, compute nodes for a job are allocated as close to each other as possible. In addition, to avoid low performance due to the shape of the allocation, various job shapes are explored to obtain optimal allocations. This is a necessary feature of large-scale systems.

Both the global and local file systems utilize Fujitsu's own FEFS (Sakai et al. 2012), which is based on the open source Lustre file system. We enhanced Lustre according to the characteristics of both file systems, and realized two objectives with one implementation.

In order to make seamless use of both file systems, we introduced file staging. File staging takes care of the data transfer between file system hierarchies. During *stage-in*, data moves from the global to the local file system before a job begins execution. Transfer from the local to the global file system after job execution is called *stage-out*. Staging functions are executed automatically. In addition, by executing data staging on dedicated I/O nodes, data transfers can take place asynchronously during the execution of another job.

Fujitsu also provides a dedicated compiler optimized for the K Computer. The compiler is designed to fully exploit specific hardware features available in the K Computer. In large-scale computing systems, "MPI everywhere" usually leads to poor memory and communication efficiency. We reduce memory pressure and communication overhead between nodes by multi-threading and relying on MPI exclusively for internode communication.

11.2   Design Principles

The K Computer system was implemented based on the following design principles.

1. Scalability

    - To assure execution of large-scale applications, we aimed at a system that is capable of massive parallelism supporting jobs on the scale of up to one million nodes.

2. High availability

    - The overall system must not stop due to single-component failures.
    - Early failure recovery and fault isolation must support continuous operation.

3. High occupancy rate

    - Aiming at a system operating availability rate of 80% or higher, allocate compute nodes to jobs without wasting resources.
    - Early recovery from failures ensures avoiding interrupted operation.

4. Operability

- Support for general-purpose APIs, such as POSIX compliance, provides inter-operability for applications with other architectures.
- Monitoring and operation are automated as much as possible and made easy for system administrators.

5. High performance

- In order to fully exploit hardware performance capabilities, system software must stay out of the way of applications as much as possible.
- In order for applications to achieve sufficient performance, hardware resources must be utilized as efficiently as possible.

Based on the design principles listed above, the K Computer introduced enhancements at the OS level to ensure a high operating ratio in a large-scale environment. Specifically, the K Computer is equipped with high availability features to minimize the influence of system noise and system failures. It also provides support to utilize the CPU's HPC features, e.g., SIMD operations, large page-based Translation Lookaside Buffer (TLB), etc. In the next section and beyond, we will describe the design and implementation of the OS running on the K Computer.

11.3 Design and Implementation of K OS

The OS on the K Computer was designed and implemented to achieve the following four objectives: application portability, scalability of parallel applications, high reliability and availability, and reduction of OS overhead. We now describe these objectives in more detail.

11.3.1 Application Portability

Since the K Computer is the Japanese flagship supercomputer, it should be a general-purpose machine and enable many academic/industrial users to utilize their existing applications with minimal migration effort from other machines. When development started, around 2015, most Japanese domestic supercomputers were already commodity-based clusters running various Linux OS distributions. In order to provide source-level compatibility with existing applications, Linux was adopted as the K Computer OS.

K OS is based on Linux kernel version 2.6.25.8 with libc 2.7 and libgcc 4.2.4. Employing a Linux kernel with its software stack, K OS supports the POSIX interface and a standard management environment.

11.3.2 Improving the Scalability of Parallel Applications

Most applications on the K Computer are parallel applications that run on a set of compute nodes in bulk synchronous parallel (BSP) execution mode. However, in order to operate the system properly, we need various system daemons like the job scheduler, system managers, and so on. These components may induce system noise in a parallel computing system, because they run asynchronously regardless of the behavior of user jobs.

In a parallel application, it is often assumed that the processing time from the beginning of a computation phase until synchronization takes the same amount of time across compute nodes. If computation time is prolonged by system daemons, synchronization will be also prolonged, which can cause performance degradation in massively parallel cluster systems that consist of over tens of thousands of compute nodes (Ferreira et al. 2008).

One way to solve this problem is to assign a specific core in multicore CPUs for the OS daemons. This can reduce interference with job processes that run on other CPU cores. However, the K Computer has only eight CPU cores on each compute node. If we applied this approach, one core out of the eight cores in each CPU would be allocated for system daemons, limiting overall compute power to 87.5% of the theoretical peak. This would pose a serious performance limitation. For this reason, we did not adopt the core specialization approach in the K Computer.

Instead of using OS specific CPU cores, we reduced the number of system daemons and made their execution synchronous among compute nodes. We reduced system noise in the K Computer by improving node monitoring daemons and the distributed file system. We describe our modifications in Sects. 11.3.2.2 and 11.3.2.3, respectively. We also improved the way how file system state is monitored in Lustre clients. It was necessary to improve the scalability of the file system so that requirements of the K Computer could be met. Section 11.3.2.4 describes the improvements to Lustre state monitoring.

11.3.2.1 Global Daemon Execution

System daemons of the original Linux environment had been eliminated as much as possible. Additionally, to ensure that system daemon interference occurs on all compute nodes at the same time, the remaining daemons are activated synchronously, i.e., at the same time across the compute nodes, synchronized by a global clock. Figure 11.3 illustrates this mechanism. We did not only eliminate the unnecessary system programs in the OS, but we also modified the behavior of the required ones, so that the duration of periodic activities remains constant across compute nodes. Table 11.1 demonstrates these improvements.

We use the network time protocol (NTP) for time synchronization among nodes in K Computer. There are designated management servers (called Service Processors) in the K Computer, and each compute node belongs to a particular service processor,

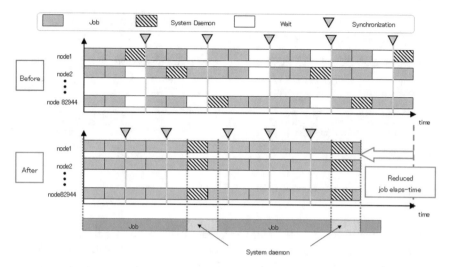

Fig. 11.3 Synchronized execution of system daemons

Table 11.1 Improvement of system daemons' periodic processing in K

Daemon	Before		After		Component
	T (cycle)	Duration	T (cycle)	Duration	
ntpd	64 s	110 μs	64 s	85 μs	OS Daemon
init	5 s	42 μs	5 s	10 μs	OS Daemon

with whom it synchronizes. Thus, each compute node needs to synchronize with its service processor only. However, typically NTP daemons synchronize with both the local node and remote nodes. We omitted the code for synchronization with the local node in K Computer to reduce the duration of NTP's periodic processing loop.

We also reduced the duration of the init daemon. The init daemon checks its command FIFO periodically to communicate with utilities like the shutdown command. In our system, to reduce interference by the init process, we extended the interval between these checks, since response time to the shutdown command is not important. The init process is also monitoring terminals for logins. Since our system does not have TTY terminals, we completely removed this check.

11.3.2.2   Noiseless Node Observation

In HPC clusters, the system activity data collector (sadc) is often used for collecting statistical information on CPU and memory usage. Sadc can also be used for performance analysis. The sadc command is invoked periodically from the cron daemon in standard Linux environments. It obtains statistical information from the kernel and writes them into a log file. Typically, sadc is a long running process.

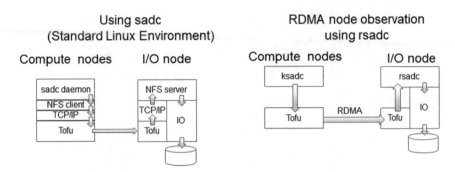

Fig. 11.4 Noiseless usage data collection

To solve the issue of `sadc` interference, we developed a new node observation daemon called `ksadc`. `Ksadc` runs on I/O nodes and uses the RDMA mechanism of the Tofu interconnect on the K Computer. By using the RDMA mechanism, we can collect statistical information from remote memory to I/O nodes directly. As a result, we were able to completely eliminate the periodic invocations of `sadc` on computing nodes. Figure 11.4 shows the reduced overhead of collecting usage data.

11.3.2.3 Scalability of Distributed File System

We use an improved version of the Lustre file system for K Computer. The default Lustre file system client holds server-side locks on object storage targets (OSTs) when it accesses files. The client needs to manage data structures for locks to reduce the communication cost between servers and clients. These data structures grow by the number of servers, i.e., the number of OSTs, in the cluster.

Lustre file system clients keep track of lock state by periodically checking and updating its status against all OSTs, which is performed on the granularity of seconds by default. This noise is proportional to the number of OSTs, and thus it can amplify interference in large-scale clusters, as shown in Fig. 11.5.

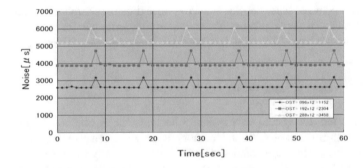

Fig. 11.5 Noise in the Lustre file system

In K Computer, we improved Lustre'slock management mechanism as follows:

- If there is no change in the number of locks used or in the lock status, do not perform periodic processing.
- By setting an upper limit on the number of locks to check at a given time, process duration is constrained within a certain period of time.

Through the above improvements, noise length is shortened from 41 to $10\,\mu s$ irrespective of the number of OST servers.

11.3.2.4   File System State Monitoring

As we mentioned already, the FEFS distributed file system adopted in K Computer is based on the Lustre file system. Lustre has a mechanism to notify the activation of client nodes (called ll_ping).

In Lustre, the server is notified about client status by periodically reporting client activity to the server. This increases the amount of traffic and prevents scalability in large-scale clusters such as the K Computer due to the large number of clients under each file system server.

Since the operation management software for monitoring the state of each node is already present in K Computer, it is not necessary for the file system to periodically monitor the state of the clients. Therefore, updating the state of the clients is needed only when the file system modifies consistency information of the stored data or metadata. Thus periodic checks can be omitted in our system.

Based on the above idea, we eliminated the periodic client status notification processing by ll_ping in the K Computer. In our file system, only when the client accesses data and metadata on the server does the server confirm the state of each client which holds that particular piece of information. This reduces noise on compute nodes as well as the amount of communication needed.

11.3.3   Reliability and High Availability

K Computer is a large-scale cluster exceeding 80,000 nodes. In the design phase, we estimated that memory failure will occur once every 3 days, because load on the memory is very high in HPC workloads.

We introduced a mechanism to analyze the cause of a memory failure in detail by the OS. This is to avoid wrong execution results and to minimize the influence of memory failures on applications. When a memory failure occurs, the memory area is marked to prevent allocations to applications.

If the given memory area is used by an application, the OS terminates the application forcefully and it notifies the job manager. When the job manager receives this notification, it terminates processes of the job on all nodes which are used by the given application. The job manager then checks the cause of the crash and if the reason was a memory failure, it reallocates healthy nodes to the job and reruns it automatically.

Memory failures do indeed occur once every few days in the K Computer, just as we assumed during the design phase. The K Computer memory protection functionality has prevented wrong results from memory faults during the production phase.

We also developed an automatic memory reload mechanism for file system data. Since we adopted a diskless system for compute nodes in the K Computer, processes on each compute node always access file data that is cached on the compute node from remote nodes. When a memory failure occurs, reloading data from the file system degrades file access latency. To prevent this issue, when the OS detects that memory failure occurred on file system cache, it automatically reloads the data to reduce file access time later during application execution. With this function, data on previously corrupted memory can be accessed immediately when the application accesses the data again, hiding the impact of a memory failure from the application.

Although we designed memory RAS functionality from memory failure rates of our former machines and some consideration about conditions of memory failure, including file access time reduction during memory failures, we rarely see memory failure conditions where we could apply this function effectively. We now think this mechanism provides little improvement in effectiveness.

11.3.4 Reducing OS Overhead

We added the following functionalities to standard Linux in K Computer in order to improve numerical calculation performance by reducing the overhead of the kernel:

1. Improvements to saving and restoration of floating-point registers.
2. Reduction of TLB misses by transparent large pages.

11.3.4.1 Floating-Point Registers

In K Computer, Linux processes and processes in computation jobs share the same core and its FPU. Since saving and restoring, the FPU context is generally a costly. It reduces performance of computation kernel in the job. Therefore, we consider a mechanism to reduce the cost of FPU context switches in computation kernel execution. Recent CPUs provide mechanisms to notify the OS when accesses to floating-point registers occur. The following methods are well known for reducing the cost of saving and restoring floating-point registers using this notification mechanism.

- FPU owner approach (Intel Corporation 2009)
  FPU owner is a method to reduce the number of registers saved and restored by tracking the thread's usage of floating-point registers. When context switches

occur, the OS confirms whether the current thread (the current thread means the thread which yields the CPU resource to another thread) has used the FPU. If the current thread has used the FPU, the OS marks the thread as FPU owner on the given CPU core. After that the OS instructs the CPU to raise an exception when another FPU register access occurs. An exception is issued from the CPU when a non-FPU owner thread uses FPU registers. The OS then configures the CPU exception not to be issued when accessing the FPU register after updating the FPU context. By this method, unnecessary saving and restoring of floating-point registers can be avoided at thread switches, which reduces context switching cost. The method was originally recommended by Intel.

- Lazy FPU approach (Mauerer 2010)

Lazy FPU is a mechanism to reduce the associated costs to floating-point register handling adopted by Linux. The OS checks whether the current thread has used FPU registers at context switch time and if the current thread has used the FPU, the OS saves the FPU context into its task control block. The OS then configures the CPU exceptions to be issued. After that, the CPU exception occurs when threads which run after the current thread has accessed the FPU. By catching the FPU exception, the exception handler in the Linux kernel restores the FPU context, and then the exception handler will reset FPU exception issues. Compared with FPU owner method, this method can shorten thread switching time for the general case. This method also simplifies OS implementation compared to the FPU owner method because FPU register handling routines can be confined into architecture dependent portions of the OS.

The FPU owner method, on the other hand, requires additional FPU handling routines in the architecture independent portions of the OS, e.g., thread-exit, thread-migration, and so on. That is an undesirable characteristic for OSs like Linux which support many CPUs types.

In HPC systems, it is favorable to grant FPU ownership to user jobs because floating-point registers are necessary resources to execute numerical calculations. However, in the Lazy FPU method, the arithmetic processing in the application may be disturbed by context switch handling of the OS, which would cause performance problems in floating-point intensive loops in the application.

Thus, we adopted an improved version of the FPU owner method for our OS. At first, in order for the OS kernel to distinguish between numerical calculation jobs and other processes, we introduced a mechanism that notifies the OS of the creation of numerical calculation job processes from the job management system. Next, we minimized the number of FPU context switches by using the FPU owner method. Last, in order to suppress the FPU register handling during numerical calculation in application space, the OS kernel checks whether the current thread is part of a numerical calculation job when the thread returns to user space from the OS kernel. If so, the OS kernel restores the FPU context for the thread and indicates the thread as the FPU owner. Table 11.2 summarizes the differences the different FPU context switching methods.

Table 11.2 Comparison of floating-point register handling methods

Timing	FPU owner	Lazy FPU	K Computer
Context switch back to previous process	—	Save	Restore or save and restore
FPU access	Save and restore	Restore	—

11.3.4.2 Large Page Support in the K Computer

Using the virtual memory management system of SPARC64, Linux manages memory in units of 8 KiB pages. Although SPARC64 CPU has a cache (TLB) to speed up the address translation performed by hardware, the number of TLB entries is limited. When using 8 KiB as page size, it is impossible to store the whole address translation table in the TLB for an application that may use several megabytes or gigabytes of memory. Under such condition, address translation overheads cause performance degradation. In order to avoid this problem, large page-based mappings are often used in HPC systems. Large pages provide a mechanism to translate from virtual address to physical address in larger units.

At the time of the K Computer development, the Linux kernel community also discussed the necessity for supporting large pages transparently in the kernel, e.g., Transparent Huge Pages (THP) or Linux Superpages, as well as memory resource reservation features, e.g., memory cgroups, in order to solve the problem described above. However, there was no implementation available yet.

Thus, we implemented our own large page mechanism in order to ensure availability and quality before K Computer shipping. It consists of a job memory management mechanism in the OS kernel and a large page library for job processes. See Fig. 11.6.

We added a new memory pool exclusive for application jobs in the kernel. In order to guarantee the amount of available memory pages for jobs, the OS reserves memory

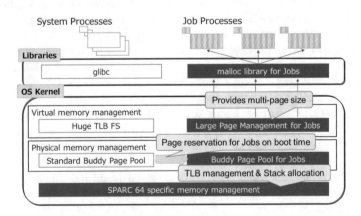

Fig. 11.6 Large page mechanism in K Computer

pages at boot time and the reserved pages are stored in the memory pool designated for user jobs. We also implemented a `malloc()` library to allocate memory from the memory pool for jobs by calling the standard `malloc()` routine. Memory from the user job pool is transparently mapped by large pages so that existing applications can take advantage of this feature without program modifications.

This large page mechanism is designed for parallel applications, and compared to THP in standard Linux, it has the following characteristics:

Heap allocation method optimized for parallel application
General-purpose modern memory allocation libraries, e.g., `jemalloc()`, libc, `malloc()`, etc., create separate heaps dynamically for each thread using the *mmap* system call. This works well for general-purpose applications because it can avoid lock contentions among threads. However, from our experience of K Computer development, we found that this method is inappropriate for HPC environments from a scalability point of view because it can introduce system noise. Specifically, the method described above allocates data to different virtual addresses on different compute nodes because the timing of memory allocations depends on the order of execution among threads. This can cause differences in the number of TLB misses among nodes which leads to scalability issues for parallel applications. However, it is hard to completely synchronize the behavior of thread execution order because modern OSs consist of various subsystems which operate asynchronously. To avoid the above issue, we introduced an option to suppress the creation of thread-specific heaps.

Supporting multiple page sizes
At the time of the K OS' development, standard Linux environments supported only one-page size for large pages. In large-scale parallel computers, the amount of memory in each compute node is usually smaller than that in general servers. Nevertheless, both memory access performance and memory usage efficiency are important in HPC systems. To fulfill these requirements, we added support to indicate large page sizes per memory area in applications. The reason was that attributes of different memory areas, e.g., data, heap, and stack, which need large page-based mappings, depend on the characteristics of the given application.

11.4 Lessons Learned

We described our implementation of a specialized OS for SPARC64 VIII fx based on the Linux kernel. However, both application behavior and typical use cases, as well as operation of HPC systems, have changed substantially since the development of the K Computer. Some of our design criteria and implementation approaches, e.g., strict resource management, large page mechanism with strict reservation, might not be suitable for modern HPC systems anymore. While we took a closed development approach for the K Computer's OS, we might take a more open development method for our next machines so that we can more easily catch up with current trends in HPC systems.

We demonstrated how we reduced system noise on the K Computer with modification to software systems including the base OS and the file system. But we found that it was hard to maintain our software with this approach. We intend to try to reduce system noise on HPC systems with a more comprehensive approach including firmware and hardware, e.g., taking advantage of many-core CPUs, and improve maintainability.

11.5   Future Plans and Towards Post-K

In this section, we describe future directions based on trends and our insights gained through the development of the K Computer.

At the time of development of the K Computer, Linux did not support basic functionalities necessary for HPC, such as memory resource management mechanisms for computation jobs and transparent large page support that could have been used without program modifications. Therefore, we implemented resource management functions and large page support manually.

On the other hand, in recent years, we realized that improvements in resource management functions have become available, accompanying the widespread usage of container technologies and better interoperability due to support for transparent large pages in other OSs, such as FreeBSD. Many of the functions that we implemented are now available in standard OSS/Linux environments. For this reason, many of the problems we faced at the time of K Computer development are now practically solved. Based on issues and technological trends with OS development and operation of the K Computer, the following initiatives were implemented on the PRIMEHPC FX100, the system that came two generations after the K Computer.

1. Adoption of assistant CPU core(s)
   Each compute node now has two extra cores called *assistant cores*, which are dedicated to system activities. This contributes to cost reduction of the entire system and further reduction of OS noise.
2. Adoption of CMG, i.e., NUMA
   A configuration in which the core and the memory are grouped in a chip called Core Memory Group (CMG) is adopted in the CPU. As multicore technology progresses, access conflicts from each core to memory are likely to occur. Therefore, by adopting CMG, it was decided to form a NUMA configuration. As a result, even if multiple processes are executed on the CPU (assuming one process per CMG), memory accesses do not conflict among processes, contributing to performance improvements.
3. Improvement of large page function
   In the K Computer, the system memory and the application memory were separated to some extent, and a mechanism to guarantee the number of large pages available to applications was introduced. However, in actual operation, application memory can run short when sudden demand for system memory rises.

Therefore, FX100 strictly separates memory for system and application use at node startup. But when strictly separating, there are cases where it is not possible to meet system memory demands. Therefore, we added a function that can limit the cache of the file system and release the file cache at an early stage. With that, we were able to adopt strict separation and made avoiding problems easier.

Without striving for completeness, we describe some of the measures we are considering as we look toward the post-K Computer.

1. Adoption of ARM-v8 and SVE architecture
   We decided to adopt ARM-v8, which is a general-purpose architecture widely used in various application areas. Furthermore, we adopt the Scalable Vector Extension (SVE), a vector instruction extension designed for HPC. By these means, it is possible to realize a general-purpose and high-performance system. Therefore, we are hoping that the software developed for post-K Compute can be widely utilized all over the world, improving the distribution of our software. For this purpose, we are currently focusing on building the HPC software ecosystem using ARM-v 8 and SVE. Through these efforts, we are hoping that many ARM-v8 applications will be able to operate efficiently on the post-K Computer without modifications.

2. Generic large page support and resource management
   Since HPC-specific functionalities in Linux are being enhanced day-by-day, our fundamental policy is to rely on these general-purpose functions as much as possible. In addition, through this measure, we are also planning to improve some of these functionalities.
   Specifically, we will utilize the generic large page functions in Linux, such as THP and general resource management functions such as container based on cgroups. In addition, we are considering to implement a flexible application execution environment that is not bound to a specific Linux distribution.

References

Ajima, Y., Inoue, T., Hiramoto, S., Takagi, Y., & Shimizu, T. (2012). The Tofu interconnect. *IEEE Micro, 32*(1), 21–31.

Ferreira, K. B., Bridges, P., & Brightwell, R. (2008). Characterizing application sensitivity to OS interference using kernel-level noise injection. In *Proceedings of the 2008 ACM/IEEE Conference on Supercomputing, SC '08* (pp. 19:1–19:12). Piscataway, NJ, USA: IEEE Press.

Intel Corporation (2009). *Intel® 64 and IA-32 Architectures Software Developer's Manual*.

Maruyama, T., Yoshida, T., Kan, R., Yamazaki, I., Yamamura, S., Takahashi, N., et al. (2010). Sparc64 VIIIfx: A new-generation octocore processor for petascale computing. *IEEE Micro, 30*(2), 30–40.

Mauerer, W. (2010). *Professional Linux Kernel Architecture* (1st ed.). Wrox Press.

Sakai, K., Sumimoto, S., & Kurokawa, M. (2012). High-performance and highly reliable file system for the K Computer. *Fujitsu Scientific and Technical Journal, 48*, 302–309.

Chapter 12
Argo

Swann Perarnau, Brian C. Van Essen, Roberto Gioiosa, Kamil Iskra, Maya B. Gokhale, Kazutomo Yoshii and Pete Beckman

Abstract Argo is an ongoing project improving Linux for exascale machines. Targeting emerging production workloads such as workflows and coupled codes, we focus on providing missing features and building new resource management facilities. Our work is unified into *compute containers*, a containerization approach aimed at providing modern HPC applications with dynamic control over a wide range of kernel interfaces.

12.1 A Brief History of Argo

Argo is an ongoing project of the U.S Department of Energy to design and develop low-level system software for future exascale systems. Inspired by the recommendations of the International Exascale Software Project Roadmap (Dongarra et al. 2011), the project started in 2013 as a comprehensive initiative to adapt, extend, and

S. Perarnau (✉) · K. Iskra · K. Yoshii · P. Beckman
Argonne National Laboratory, Lemont, IL, USA
e-mail: perarnau@mcs.anl.gov

K. Iskra
e-mail: iskra@mcs.anl.gov

K. Yoshii
e-mail: kazutomo@mcs.anl.gov

P. Beckman
e-mail: beckman@mcs.anl.gov

B. C. Van Essen · M. B. Gokhale
Lawrence Livermore National Laboratory, Livermore, CA, USA
e-mail: vanessen1@llnl.gov

M. B. Gokhale
e-mail: maya@llnl.gov

R. Gioiosa
Oak Ridge National Laboratory, Oak Ridge, TN, USA
e-mail: gioiosar@ornl.gov

© Springer Nature Singapore Pte Ltd. 2019
B. Gerofi et al. (eds.), *Operating Systems for Supercomputers
and High Performance Computing*, High-Performance Computing Series,
https://doi.org/10.1007/978-981-13-6624-6_12

improve the low-level HPC system software stack, based on the current expectations of exascale architectures and workloads.

On the hardware side, we expect exascale systems to feature tens of thousands of compute nodes with hundreds of hardware threads and complex memory hierarchies with a mix of on-package and persistent memory modules. On the software side, the increasing resource density on HPC nodes, combined with the growing relative cost of internode communications, provides a strong motivation for new kinds of HPC applications. In particular, we expect the trend of coupling computation components with data analytics or visualization components to continue.

12.1.1 Argo 1.0

During its first phase, which ended in 2016, Argo grew into a project involving up to 40 researchers, redesigning from the ground up the operating system and runtime software stack to support extreme-scale scientific computations. At the heart of this phase were four key innovations: dynamic reconfiguring of node resources in response to workload changes, allowance for massive concurrency, a hierarchical framework for management of nodes, and a cross-layer communication infrastructure that allows resource managers and optimizers to communicate efficiently across the platform. Those components span all levels of the machine: a parallel runtime sits on top of an HPC-aware operating system on each node, while a distributed collection of services manage all nodes by using a global communication bus.

The **NodeOS**, the focus of this chapter, is the operating system running on each node of the machine. It is a based on the Linux kernel and tuned and extended for HPC needs on future architectures.

Argobots (Seo et al. 2017) is the runtime component of Argo. It implements a low-level threading and tasking framework entirely in user space, giving users total control over their resource utilization. It also provides a data movement infrastructure as well as tasking libraries for massively concurrent systems.

GlobalOS is a collection of services implementing a distributed, dynamic control of the entire machine. It divides the system into *enclaves*, groups of nodes sharing the same configuration and managed as a whole (Perarnau et al. 2015). These enclaves can be subdivided, forming a hierarchy, with dedicated nodes (masters) at each level to respond to events. Among the provided services, the GlobalOS includes distributed algorithms for power management (Ellsworth et al. 2016) and fault management (Bautista-Gomez et al. 2016) across the enclave tree.

The Global Information Bus (GIB) is a scalable communication infrastructure taking advantage of modern high-performance networks to provide efficient reporting and resource monitoring services to applications and system services.

This phase of the project resulted in many of its components growing into projects of their own or being adopted by community efforts. In particular, Argobots is now being used to provide a more efficient OpenMP implementation (Seo et al. 2018).

12.1.2 Argo 2.0

Now in its second phase, the project is focused on the NodeOS and GlobalOS components. As the architecture of exascale became clearer, the project has increased its efforts in the area of management of new byte-addressable memory devices, such as on-package and persistent memory, while continuing the development of our resource management infrastructure, both inside a node and across nodes. Another area of increased attention is the power management. We are working on enabling the management of advanced power control mechanisms from user space (primarily by the runtime) and integrating it across the hierarchy with the help of a global resource manager (GRM); a full solution will also include cooperation with the system job scheduler. The global and node-local resource partitioning mechanisms provide convenient abstractions to implement such infrastructure.

Most of the work presented in this chapter focuses on the NodeOS components and reflects their status at the end of the first phase of Argo (Perarnau et al. 2017). Nevertheless, it matches our current thinking and as we approach exascale, our understanding of future platforms.

12.2 A New Role for Operating Systems in HPC

In the context of Argo, we believe that the role of a multitasking OS such as Linux is transitioning away from managing access to shared resources on the node (CPU, memory, NIC, etc.) by using multiplexing techniques such as time sharing and swapping. Instead, we assume the availability of a lightweight runtime and a more complex global resource manager; and we argue that the operating system should coarsely *partition* the numerous resources available, offer a unified interface—*containers*—for users to express their resource and system services requirements, and provide the mechanisms to manage those partitions dynamically.

Lightweight runtimes (Wheeler et al. 2008; Seo et al. 2017), forming part of comprehensive parallel programming frameworks, will then be given exclusive control of resources to perform custom redistribution according to their knowledge of the application and its inner parallelism. Such an approach ensures a more deterministic execution and noticeably lower overheads. Across the machine, the global resource manager is given a peer to connect to on each node, enabling comprehensive and dynamic control policies to be enforced.

Still, care must be taken to ensure that HPC applications, including new workloads such as coupled codes and workflows containing multiple components competing for resources, actually benefit from running in close proximity to each other instead of grinding to a halt because of unintended interference.

12.2.1 Example Workload

Figure 12.1 presents an overview of a complex application workflow and the inter-action between its processes. The simulation application in the workflow is Gromacs (Pronk et al. 2013), a standard molecular dynamics simulation package in the biology community. In biology, visualization is a key tool for understanding the func-tions of molecular systems. Isosurface extraction using the Quicksurf (Krone et al. 2012) algorithm is being used here for rendering. This algorithm is implemented in situ (Dreher and Raffin 2014) to avoid the high cost of I/O between components.

The coupling is managed by FlowVR, an in situ middleware designed for building asynchronous workflows. The Gromacs simulation code runs multiple processes on each node, in MPI-only mode, and has been modified to extract atom positions at runtime rather than writing them to a file. The in situ visualization component (VDA) is a pipeline consisting of five sequential processes on each node. Three of them are compute modules: (1) distributing the atoms in a regular grid, (2) computing a density value for each cell based on the atoms in the cell and its neighborhood, and (3) computing a marching cube on the density grid. The two remaining steps perform redistribution of atom positions. Data exchanges between modules are performed by using a shared-memory space managed by the FlowVR daemon hosted on each node. If the sender and receiver modules are on the same node, the daemon simply passes a pointer to the receiver; otherwise, it uses MPI to send the data to the remote daemon hosting the destination module. The daemon is heavily multithreaded, consisting of four internal threads plus a thread for each module running on the node; none of them are computationally intensive.

Correct placement of application processes on the node is critical to obtaining optimal performance. The five in situ analytics processes together require at most 20% of the CPU cycles of a single core, but they must be kept apart from the Gromacs processes, which are highly sensitive to perturbations.

Fig. 12.1 Process interaction of a coupled application

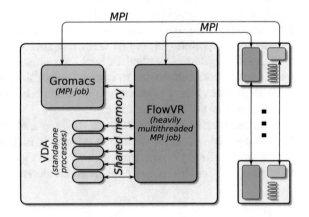

This workflow exemplifies the complexity of future production jobs on exascale systems from a resource management standpoint. Inside a single batch job, three types of processes share the same nodes, with distinct requirements and optimization opportunities. First, the simulation component (Gromacs) is a typical MPI application, capable of using OpenMP internally. As parallel programming runtimes are transitioning to user-level threads and internal dynamic load balancing (Wheeler et al. 2008; Seo et al. 2017), this group of threads could benefit from an improved system scheduling policy. Second, visualization stages are single threaded and involve low overhead but must be kept apart from the simulation for performance reasons. At the same time, the communication between the simulation and the visualization requires shared-memory access and might also use a shared NVRAM device in the future. Third, the FlowVR daemon must share memory and cores with both Gromacs and the visualization and is implemented through Pthreads. Fourth, system services will run on the nodes and should also be isolated from the user processes. With standard Linux interfaces, satisfying all these requirements is tedious at best and prone to errors.

12.2.2 An Argo Node Operating System

Driven by this growing complexity of HPC workloads, we envision a containerization approach focused on providing modern HPC applications with a unified interface for resource partitioning and other kernel features. This approach will also be compatible with popular container frameworks. Built on top of the Linux kernel, our *compute containers* simplify the management of complex workloads and provide users with a single API to further customize the environment of each component.

We complement this approach on several fronts. First, we provide a node resource manager (NRM), an active user space component that manages the resources attributed to containers and that can communicate with the GlobalOS to report application performance and enforce power limitations. Second, we extend the memory management of Linux to be able to subdivide NUMA memory nodes. Third, we add support for memory-mapped access to node-local, PCIe-attached NVRAM devices. Fourth, we introduce a new scheduling class targeted at parallel runtimes supporting user-level load balancing. We evaluate these features using a set of parallel benchmarks running on a modern NUMA platform. The experiments show that our NodeOS enables better utilization of the hardware, with less effort than would be required in a fully "manual" approach.

Fig. 12.2 Example
configuration of the Argo
NodeOS

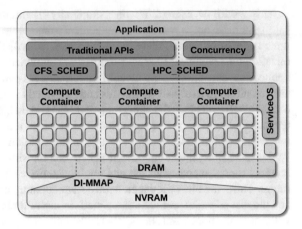

12.3 Compute Containers as a Unified Interface to Kernel Facilities

We introduce the concept of *compute containers* to provide integrated control over individual hardware and software resources on each node of an exascale machine. Our compute containers have a different purpose from that of popular containerization frameworks such as Docker (Merkel 2014). Our goal is to accommodate divergent needs of different components of complex applications. As an example, Fig. 12.2 shows a node configured with three compute containers. Each application component has a partition of node resources (CPU cores, memory) allocated to it (see Sect. 12.4). In one container, a portion of the memory is used as a DRAM cache for on-node NVRAM to accommodate out-of-core computations (see Sect. 12.5). Our containers can use different task-scheduling policies; traditional HPC workloads as well as those using lightweight, user space threading ("Concurrency" in the figure) can benefit from an HPC-specific scheduler (see Sect. 12.6), whereas highly oversubscribed workloads (e.g., for hiding the NVRAM access latency) tend to run better under the default Linux CFS scheduler.

12.3.1 Containers for Future HPC Systems

Containers have been broadly adopted for hassle-free packaging deployment and as a replacement for hypervisor-type virtualization. They quickly gained popularity for their lightweight nature and their bare-metal performance (Xavier et al. 2013; Beserra et al. 2015). In HPC, container technologies are being studied as a dependency management and packaging solution, for example, the NERSC's Shifter work (Jacobsen and Canon 2015). Unlike popular technologies such as Docker (Merkel 2014), we focus on hardware resource management, an effort that is distinct from, but complementary to, packaging. We intend to be compatible with existing technologies, starting with the use of standard container description formats (APPC) (APP 2017). We list here the aspects of our solution that reflect our focus on providing a containerization solution for HPC platforms.

No namespaces: Our containers do not use namespaces or `chroot`. As is common in HPC, we expect all the user processes on a compute node not only to belong to the same user but also to be part of the same job and thus communicate with one another. Erecting barriers in the form of separate process or file system namespaces would be counterproductive to this goal. This approach also removes considerable complexity and overhead from container management.

Runtime/Batch system awareness: We envision our node resource manager as an intermediary between the job scheduler and the MPI runtime implementation, allowing us to set up containers, enter them during the launch sequence, and clean up afterward. We aim to avoid triggering additional system noise for each contained MPI rank.

Scheduling policies: Our containers allow a user to specify that all the contained processes should be under a configurable scheduling policy. We apply this policy when creating new processes inside containers, and it is inherited automatically by any Linux process spawned within, as per the regular Linux forking semantics. If necessary, new processes can change their scheduling policy from inside the container.

Module loading and configuration: Our containers can request the loading and configuration of custom modules, to allow platform-specific features to be accessed dynamically inside containers. We use this feature for our support of DI-MMAP (see Sect. 12.5).

We also provide partitioning of node resources, as explained in the next section.

12.3.2 Implementation

From a user's point of view, a compute container is described by using a manifest file providing the information needed by our container launcher. Thus, a user can specify in the container description the amount of resources required by the application; indicate whether a particular scheduling policy should be in place; and identify what subsystems, such as a high-performance DRAM cache for node-local NVRAM, are to be configured. Figure 12.3 shows an example of such a container manifest, using the APPC standard manifest format.

Our implementation is split into several components. First is the node provisioning. As we explain in Sect. 12.4, we partition off resources for system services. In order for this partition to contain all the system services, including the dynamically created processes, either the system `init` process must be modified or all existing processes must be moved to this partition later in the lifetime of the node but before an application is launched.

Fig. 12.3 Example of a
container spanning 48
hardware threads and using
the HPC scheduler

```
{
    "acKind": "ImageManifest",
    "acVersion": "0.6.0",
    "name": "mycontainer",
    "app": {
        "isolators": [
            {
                "name": "scheduler",
                "value": {
                    "policy": "SCHED_HPC",
                    "priority": "0"
                }
            },
            {
                "name": "container",
                "value": {
                    "cpus": "48",
                    "mems": "1"
                }
            }
        ]
    }
}
```

Second is the container scheduling. The compute container matching the high-level description provided by the user must be created before the application can run. We call this process *scheduling* a container. The container description lists the size of necessary resources but not which resources to use. This issue is handled by the container manager component of our NRM, using information about the system topology to select appropriate resources. Additionally, the container manager sets the selected scheduling policy and performs the necessary steps to set up a DRAM cache for node-local NVRAM on behalf of the application. This component also allows privileged operations (for the ServiceOS) and non-privileged ones (user actions) for manipulating compute containers. It reuses the Linux uid mechanisms to apply ownership to partitions, thus preventing undue task and resource migrations or deletion by other uids. There is also a comprehensive reporting tool for node configuration.

Third is the application launching. On Linux, a newly created process inherits the current container of its parent. We leverage that fact to launch an application directly inside the right container. Similarly, all processes and threads created by the application later on will share the same container. In the case of MPI applications, we ask the user to provide a container manifest to mpirun instead of an application executable to run. The manifest is then distributed to all nodes, where local containers are scheduled before executing the application. Since our compute containers do not modify the environment of the application or its view of the file system, most features work without change.

12.3.3 The Node Resource Manager

As mentioned earlier, an active node resource manager is deployed on compute nodes to handle container and resource management. This NRM has several critical features.

First, it acts as a single entry point for all requests coming from the job scheduler or the GlobalOS. This upstream API provides both a receiving endpoint, listening for new commands from the upper layers of the resource management stack, and a sending endpoint, providing a stream of management events (container creation/deletion, stdio streams) and current resource consumption metrics.

Second, the NRM does not create containers itself. Instead, when it receives a request for the creation of a new container or a new command launch inside an existing container, the NRM dispatches the request to an available container runtime like those provided by industry container solutions or our own lightweight implementation. Nevertheless, the NRM is still in charge of tracking those containers and the resources they use, and matching new requests with the appropriate container. Additionally, if the container runtime being used does not provide some of the features we support, the NRM first launches a small wrapper inside the created container to perform the necessary operations (such as changing the scheduler policy).

Third, the NRM actively monitors resource utilization of the node, as well as the performance of each active application, and uses this information to enforce resource management limits requested by the GlobalOS (Ellsworth et al. 2016). For example, the NRM retrieves at regular intervals information from the temperature and power sensors in the system. This information includes the location of the sensors (e.g., fan, CPU), the current reading, and the hardware limits (critical levels). If needed, architecture-specific interfaces such as Intel RAPL (Intel 2019) are also used. The NRM can also monitor the performance of the applications currently running on the system, using hardware performance counters. This monitoring information is communicated to the GlobalOS through our event stream, and is used locally to enforce resource limits. Indeed, the GlobalOS can send requests asking for a power consumption limit to be enforced at the node level. The NRM can then communicate with the application runtime to lower its core count if the runtime supports it, reduce the size of a container by itself, or use power management facilities of Linux to reduce the frequency of the cores, for example.

12.4 Partitioning

We extend the Linux kernel with additional resource control capabilities to maximize resource utilization with HPC workloads. We take advantage of the control groups (*cgroups* Kernel.org 2004) resource isolation infrastructure that is a foundation of most containerization frameworks, ours included.

The resources are first partitioned during node boot. A small subset of CPU and memory resources is bundled into a *ServiceOS* partition (see Fig. 12.2), which is subsequently populated with system services as well as non-HPC tasks running on the node. The bulk of the resources is thus left unused so as to be allocated to compute containers at job launch time in order to host the HPC application processes. Partitions ensure a perfect separation of user space processes, although some kernel activities may still use resources allocated to the compute containers.

12.4.1 Linux Control Groups

Linux offers the ability to control groups of processes as a single unit and to tune many of its internal resource management policies based on those groups. The interface to this group control facility is a virtual file system similar to sysfs, called *cgroup*. This file system presents a hierarchy of groups, in the form of directories, each group/directory containing a special file with the list of process IDs inside it. The Linux kernel enforces by default that any process is created in the same group as its parent, but new groups can be created and processes moved into them independently of their process creation hierarchy.

While the behavior and capabilities of this control group facility have changed over time, the principles have stayed the same. At its core, this facility relies on *resource controllers*, a set of components modifying the internal policies of Linux to take into account groups of processes and often offering additional tuning parameters. All resource controllers also respect the principle of sharing the resources they control fairly among groups at the same level of the hierarchy.

The resource controllers range from fair timesharing between groups (cpu controller), to quality of service tuning of the network (net_prio), or suspend/resume facilities (freeze). Interestingly, most container solutions use only the namespacing capability of these control groups (as a way to easily track all the processes associated with a given container) and utilize the resource control capabilities only if the user explicitly provides the necessary parameters.

12.4.2 CPU and Memory

The CPU resources are partitioned by using the existing cpusets resource controller, which associates a set of CPU cores (or hardware threads, to be more precise) with a cgroup. To ensure the most predictable runtime behavior, we partition CPU cores such that each is allocated to only a single partition. The ServiceOS is normally allocated a single CPU core (typically consisting of multiple hardware threads). The remaining cores can all be allocated to a single compute container or, at the request of the application, can be divided among multiple containers to accommodate complex workflows (see Sect. 12.2.1).

Partitioning the system memory is a more complex operation. In principle, the
cpusets controller can also associate a memory node with a cgroup; however,
the granularity is at the NUMA node level, which is too coarse for our purposes
(ServiceOS does not typically need a whole NUMA node, and not all systems use
NUMA architecture). Linux does offer a memory controller that can set a limit
at byte granularity; but it lacks control over physical memory location, making it
an unattractive option in the face of deepening memory hierarchies consisting of
multiple tiers of DRAM in addition to node-local, PCIe-attached NVRAM.

To solve this problem, we implemented fine-grained memory nodes (FGMNs).
Physical NUMA nodes are partitioned into arbitrary logical blocks at a user-defined
granularity, based on a specification supplied at boot time. These partitions are presented to the rest of the system as separate NUMA nodes, enabling their use by the
cpusets controller. FGMNs are a reimplementation of the *fake NUMA* feature of
the standard Linux kernel, with significant enhancements in terms of flexibility and
robustness. We normally allocate under 5% of memory to the ServiceOS and leave
the rest to be allocated to the compute containers. The kernel is not bound by memory
partitioning and can satisfy its internal dynamic allocations (such as the page cache)
with memory from any node. The cache of DI-MMAP, however, is NUMA-aware
and so can be constrained as desired (see Sect. 12.5).

12.4.3 Evaluation with a Complex Workflow

We are using the Gromacs workflow outlined in Sect. 12.2.1. It is run on nodes consisting of dual-socket, 12-core Intel Xeon E5-2670 v3 processors, 128 GiB of RAM,
and 10 Gbps Ethernet NIC. Hyperthreading is enabled. The nodes are booted with
48 FGMNs of approximately 2.6 GiB each. Figure 12.4 shows the tested container
configurations.

Because of constraints in its internal decomposition algorithm, Gromacs works
well only with certain process counts. For consistency, we opted to run it with 21 processes in all configurations, even if in some cases that choice leaves an idle core. Data
is extracted every 10 iterations of the simulation. In the first configuration (Fig. 12.4,
top left), a ServiceOS is confined to a single core (two hardware threads) and two
FGMNs (only one depicted for simplicity), while the application workflow as a whole
is executed in a single compute container using the rest of the resources. This is the
default configuration for conventional single program multiple data (SPMD) HPC
jobs, but we do not expect it to provide a sufficient isolation for Gromacs inside the
overall workflow. The second configuration (Fig. 12.4, top right) is meant to address
that; it creates a separate compute container for the in situ visualization and data analysis (VDA), with one CPU core and two FGMNs, leaving the rest for the Gromacs
simulation container. Because the FlowVR management daemon communicates with
all the components of the workflow, we allow it to run unconstrained. While the tasks
running in each container allocate memory from their assigned FGMNs, there is pur-
posely no restriction for cross-container memory access, the reason being the need

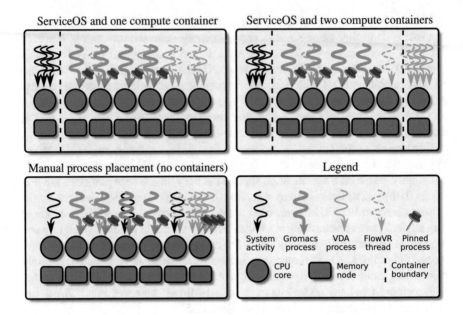

Fig. 12.4 Different node configurations for the coupled application

Fig. 12.5 Performance of the coupled application under different node configurations

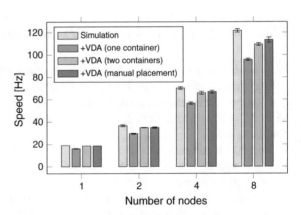

to allow shared-memory communication. The third configuration (Fig. 12.4, bottom left) reproduces the second one manually by setting affinities for the processes on a vanilla node with no partitioning; it is meant to serve as a baseline when assessing the overhead introduced by NodeOS configurations.

We ran Gromacs and the in situ Quicksurf pipeline with the three configurations described above on up to eight nodes; the results are shown in Fig. 12.5. Performance is reported in Hz: the number of iterations the simulation managed to perform in a given time period. Also included in the figure is a run labeled *Simulation* that gives a performance baseline for Gromacs modified to use FlowVR but without the in situ pipeline running. The *+VDA (one container)* run denotes the configuration from the top left of Fig. 12.4. Each of the Gromacs processes is pinned to a single core. The container has an extra core where the in situ processes could run, but the kernel scheduler is not constrained to run them only there, which leads to a 21% increase in Gromacs execution time compared with the baseline in the worst case at eight nodes, as well as an increased performance variability. The *+VDA (two containers)* run denotes the configuration from the top right of Fig. 12.4. In this case, the performance impact of the concurrent execution of the in situ modules is reduced to only 2.2% over the baseline at one node and 10% at eight nodes, an improvement of 16.45% at one node and 11% at eight nodes over the one-container run. The performance penalty indicated by the two-container run over the baseline is due to an increase in the synchronization rate between Gromacs and FlowVR. While a single synchronization has a fixed cost, as the simulation speed improves, more synchronizations occur in the same time period. Note that we deliberately chose a high output frequency to amplify the perturbations on the system, which explains the 10% cost over the baseline at eight nodes; a normal production run would output data every 1,000 iterations or less. The *+VDA (manual placement)* run, which corresponds to the configuration from the bottom left of Fig. 12.4, reproduces the same process placement as the two-container run, but using the `taskset` command manually rather than using containers. The performance is essentially the same up to four nodes, but a slight overhead of 3% arises at eight nodes. We limited the experiments to eight nodes because the chosen high output frequency overflows the in situ pipeline with more nodes. These experiments demonstrate that using the containers can free the user from the burden of process placement, for a limited performance penalty.

12.5 Incorporating Solid-State Drives

The preceding sections addressed resource management of CPU cores and associated main memory regions. We now discuss extending resource management to data accessed from node-local solid-state drives (SSDs), which are included in many proposed exascale node architectures.

To efficiently use node-local, PCIe-attached NVRAM SSD, we integrated the data-intensive memory-map (DI-MMAP) runtime into NodeOS. DI-MMAP has been optimized for data-intensive applications that use a high-performance PCIe-attached SSD for extended memory or for access to persistent data structures via the memory–map interface. Prior work (Van Essen et al. 2015) demonstrated that DI-MMAP can outperform the traditional Linux memory–map by significant margins for memory-constrained, data-intensive applications. We integrated DI-MMAP into NodeOS to provide similar performance benefits, as well as to provide additional tuning knobs for controlling the effects of I/O within the HPC node.

DI-MMAP has been integrated with containers in order to give the user maximal control over allocation and management of the HPC compute node persistent memory resources, particularly in their interaction with CPU cores and main memory. DI-MMAP provides an explicit buffer and page management strategy that has been optimized for out-of-core memory-mapped I/O usage that requires page eviction on almost every page fault. To access the DI-MMAP buffer, users first have to ask for its allocation using virtual configuration files (sysfs). Users can also control the memory location of the buffer using `numactl`. Our compute containers execute those steps directly during the launch of a container with the appropriate configuration.

In this section, we present a series of experiments showing the performance of DI-MMAP with and without compute containers. The experiments were run on an Intel CPU E7-4850 @2.00 GHz (quad-socket Westmere) with 512 GiB memory, 40 cores (80 threads), PCIe Gen 2 x16 slot, with a 1.2 TB Intel SSD (P3700 NVMe card, PCIe Gen3 x4). This node uses RHEL7 with a 4.1.3 Linux kernel. Our first experiment used a synthetic I/O benchmark—the Livermore Random I/O Toolkit (LRIOT) (Van Essen et al. 2015) designed to test I/O to high-performance storage devices, especially PCIe-attached SSDs. The benchmark generates tests that combine multiple processes and multiple threads per process to simulate highly concurrent access patterns. Sequential and random patterns can be tested at user-specified read-to-write ratios using memory-mapped, direct, or standard I/O.

Figure 12.6 reports the performance of a single LRIOT process mapping a 384 GiB file from the SSD using DI-MMAP. The number of threads per core was varied from 32 to 256 (x-axis). DI-MMAP used the buffer size of 8 GiB, preallocated when the kernel module was loaded. This configuration is consistent with the use case of data-intensive applications using all available memory for dynamic data structures in their heaps. The runtime to complete 12,582,912 4 KiB read ops is shown on the y-axis. Three setups are reported. For the baseline, the benchmark and DI-MMAP run unconstrained across the whole machine. In the second setup, LRIOT is constrained to a single socket with `taskset`, while the DI-MMAP buffer is still allocated across all NUMA nodes. The third test uses compute containers to constrain cores and associated memory regions to a single NUMA node for LRIOT and DI-MMAP. It shows DI-MMAP with higher performance under compute containers than using `taskset` or the unconstrained case. Compared with `taskset`, DI-MMAP under containers is 20% faster for 32 threads, 23% for 64 threads, 19% for 128, and 4%

Fig. 12.6 Comparison between runtimes of LRIOT accessing a file through DI-MMAP. Application and buffers: unrestricted, limited to a single socket with `taskset`, and limited to a single socket with containers, respectively

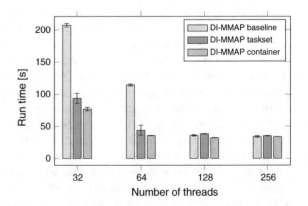

for 256. The diminishing differences between the three experiments are due to the NVMe device reaching saturation (maximum number of IOPs it can service).

These results show that for highly concurrent, threaded applications with read-heavy I/O (e.g., analyzing a visualization dataset generated by simulation or querying a database), DI-MMAP with compute containers is significantly faster than with standard `taskset`; thus, compute containers provide a convenient isolation mechanism to improve performance.

The LRIOT benchmarks tested highly multithreaded, read-only, memory-mapped I/O. To extend testing to use cases more representative of future HPC workflows, we ran these scenarios on a workload with an HPC miniapp and an analysis benchmark. The LULESH miniapp was used as the simulation code. In parallel, we ran a streamline-tracing (Jiang et al. 2014) visualization and data analytics application that traverses an out-of-core dataset, data from a $3,072^3$ Rayleigh-Taylor instability simulation from Lawrence Livermore National Laboratory. This dataset is the simulation of the evolution of two fluids mixing, creating a turbulent mixing layer that yields a complex flow field. The streamline-tracing code searches for flow streamlines in the flow field. The code has been adapted to access the dataset through memory-mapped I/O.

We first measured the performance with LULESH running by itself on the entire compute node, as would be done in a traditional simulation workflow. The next case had the two applications run concurrently without any restrictions under standard Linux, with the streamline benchmark using standard memory-mapped I/O to access files on the SSD. Then we used two compute containers, one for each application, partitioning the available node resources between the two. This setup also made use of DI-MMAP for streamline tracing. In order to mimic the interaction of coupled codes in this setup, the applications were launched concurrently and coarsely tuned to have runtimes similar to a first-order approximation.

The LULESH simulation was configured to run using 64 processes, one thread per process, on a $size = 30$ (*modest test size*) and $size = 45$ problem (*large test size*). There were $size^3$ elements per domain and one domain per process. The streamline code ran as a single process with 64 threads, each tracing a streamline using uniform seeding. The streamline length was set to 4,096, and seed points were uniformly sampled from each 3-D region. The sampling density was either $2 \times 2 \times 2$ per region for the modest test size or $4 \times 4 \times 4$ per region for the large test size.

The results of the experiment are summarized in Fig. 12.7. The leftmost bar shows the run time of LULESH by itself. The next set of bars is the runtime of each application as the applications run concurrently in unconstrained Linux without core affinity or regard to placement. The rightmost set of bars shows performance when the two applications are run in two separate containers. As the figure shows, performance of LULESH is greatly reduced when the visualization and data analysis streamline code runs with it in standard Linux, while the performance is the same or slightly better when each application is constrained to a separate container. LULESH performance degrades by 36.1% and 46.4% over the baseline with standard Linux for the modest and large experiments, respectively. Running in a container prevents the streamline code from taking resources from LULESH. Thus, the simulation performance is

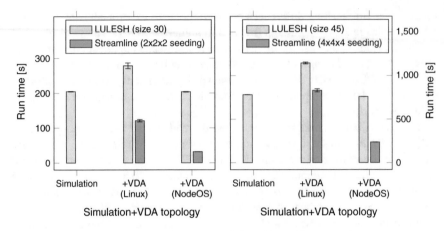

Fig. 12.7   LULESH + streamline VDA: modest (left) and large (right) test sizes

not impacted by having a concurrent "in situ" application running on the compute node. Note that the performance of the streamline-tracing VDA application with DI-MMAP (in NodeOS) is 3.78× and 3.53× faster than the standard Linux environment for the modest and large tests, respectively. This performance improvement for the streamline-tracing VDA application is due largely to improvements DI-MMAP offers beyond standard *mmap* that were previously published (Van Essen et al. 2015), with some contribution due to the performance isolation of containers illustrated in Fig. 12.6.

12.6   Scheduling

In user mode, the CPUs and memory resources are partitioned by using control groups and FGMNs, respectively. In kernel mode, however, a single Linux kernel image is still shared by all the cores in the systems. Thus, when an application thread enters the kernel, either voluntarily through a system call or involuntarily through an interrupt, the HPC application effectively competes with the other user and kernel daemons in the system to access hardware and software resources. For example, an application thread can spin on its runqueue lock in a timer interrupt as long as the lock is held by another function (e.g., a process migration or load balancing).

Full-fledged OS kernels such as Linux can introduce OS noise during the execution of HPC applications (Gioiosa et al. 2004; Morari et al. 2011, 2012). In our approach, we limit the number of interruptions and cycles spent in kernel mode to the detriment of HPC applications. To this extent, we need to limit process preemptions as well as the execution of kernel activities that are not directly related to the HPC application.

Figure 12.8 shows the execution of a conjugate gradient OpenMP application on a system with eight compute cores using CFS. The trace was obtained from ftrace

Fig. 12.8 NPB CG execution trace. Each color in the trace represents a different task while vertical bars represent kernel activities. The figure shows that (1) tasks are generally migrated from CPU to CPU even if there is an equal number of CPUs and tasks and (2) kernel activities often interrupt computation

(Rostedt 2009), a lightweight kernel-tracing system available in recent versions of the Linux kernel. In the trace, the *x*-axis shows the execution time, each row represents a processor core, and each OpenMP thread is assigned a specific color. As we can see, application threads are continuously migrated from CPU to CPU, depending on the particular task load of each processor at the time load balancing is performed. Note that although in this experiment we ran eight application threads on an eight-core system, not all threads are necessarily runnable at the same time. In fact, the system load may show an imbalance because a thread is blocking on a long-latency operation or because a user or kernel daemon has woken up. When the load becomes imbalanced, the CFS load balancer will attempt to redistribute the load by migrating tasks. High bars in each CPU row denote kernel activities performed, while application threads are running.[1]

We modified the Linux kernel to provide performance isolation *and* increased throughput. We developed a new task scheduler (HPC_SCHED) that simplifies the scheduling of HPC application processes and threads. This new scheduler is an OS kernel component and orthogonal to user-level containers. Thus, the scheduler can be used in conjunction with containers (i.e., the HPC application running in a computing container could leverage our new scheduler) or in isolation (if containers are not used). The advantages of the new scheduling algorithm are threefold. First, HPC application tasks are scheduled by a specific scheduler and do not increase the CFS load. Thus, HPC tasks are not considered during CFS bookkeeping operations, such as the load balancing in the previous example. Second, we prioritize the HPC_SCHED scheduling class over the regular CFS scheduling class. Thus, tasks in the CFS class cannot preempt HPC tasks and can run on a CPU only if no runnable HPC tasks are assigned to that CPU at the time. Third, HPC_SCHED implements a set of scheduling algorithms that are designed for HPC applications. Specifically, HPC_SCHED can be configured with the following options.

---

[1] Because of pixel resolution, threads seem to be in kernel mode for long intervals. However, zooming in on the trace reveals many independent, short kernel activities, such as timer interrupts, that appear as one block in the trace.

User.   The OS does not perform any assignment of threads to CPUs; the user-level
            runtime is in charge of setting the affinity of each application thread. This mode of
            operation is intended for intelligent runtimes that implement their own scheduler.
Round-Robin.   Tasks in the HPC_SCHED scheduling class are assigned to CPUs
            in a round-robin order. If the number of tasks in the HPC_SCHED class is larger
            than the number of available CPUs, some CPUs will be oversubscribed.
Topology-Aware.   Tasks are assigned to CPUs in a way that maximizes perfor-
            mance by reducing hardware resource contention, typically by employing a
            breadth-first approach.

In all cases, the scheduling of HPC tasks on the same CPU is supposed to be
cooperative; in other words, tasks voluntarily release the CPUs to other tasks to offer
them a chance of making progress. Currently, HPC_SCHED does not implement
time sharing and preemption among HPC tasks in the same run queue. This design
choice follows the general execution strategy of one thread per CPU traditionally
employed in HPC environments. Even when using the round-robin and topology-
aware policies, HPC_SCHED will still honors user-defined CPU affinity and will not
schedule a task on a CPU that is not set in the task's CPU affinity mask. This design
ensures seamless integration with the rest of the NodeOS components, especially
containers.

We also analyzed many kernel control paths that are normally executed on each
CPU to ensure the correct functioning of the system and a fair sharing of hardware
resources among the active processes. Many of these activities are unnecessary in
HPC environments, where compute nodes are typically assigned to a single user. We
identified the most common kernel activities that can be removed without impacting
the correctness of running applications. We traced several applications and ranked
the most common kernel activities and those with the largest variance, which have the
highest probability of being harmful. To limit the number of code modifications, we
followed an iterative approach, removing unnecessary kernel control paths until we
achieved satisfactory performance. Removing just a few activities, such as the CFS
load balancing operations, already provides considerable advantages. We also rely
on specific configuration options of the Linux kernel, like fully dynamic scheduler
interrupts (also called tickless).

We performed our evaluation on a dual-socket AMD Opteron 6272 equipped
with 16 cores per socket, 64 GiB of RAM divided into four NUMA domains, and
an InfiniBand interconnection network. We analyzed the impact of HPC_SCHED
when running parallel OpenMP applications. test We ran 32 OpenMP threads, one
per CPU core. We selected several NPB kernels (BT, CG, LU), HPC applications
(LULESH), and data analytics workloads (Graph 500) and compared HPC_SCHED
with the standard CFS scheduler and with execution when application threads are
statically bound to cores ("CPU Affinity"). This execution was achieved by setting
the GOMP_CPU_AFFINITY environment variable used by the OpenMP runtime. For
Graph 500, the speedup was computed in terms of TEPS (harmonic mean across
64 searches). Figure 12.9 shows the results in terms of speedup with respect to the
execution with CFS. The graph shows that applications with good locality (BT and

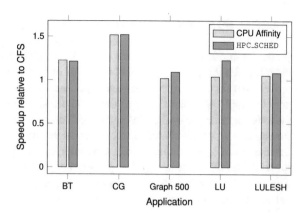

Fig. 12.9 Speedup of OpenMP with statically set affinity and HPC_SCHED compared with standard CFS

CG) benefit primarily from reusing data in the processor caches and are sensitive to unnecessary process migrations often performed by CFS. For these applications, statically setting the CPU affinity of each thread provides considerable performance improvements, up to 1.5× for CG. Both HPC_SCHED and the static CPU affinity achieve this performance. In other cases, however, simply statically binding application threads to cores does not provide much benefit, if any. This situation happens for applications with poor locality or whose dataset does not fit in the processor caches. As shown in Fig. 12.9, HPC_SCHED achieves considerably better performance for Graph 500, LU, and LULESH—respectively, 1.09×, 1.20×, and 1.10×—while statically binding threads to cores in the OpenMP runtime achieves measurable performance improvements only for LULESH (1.06×) and marginally for LU (1.03×).

Interestingly, and perhaps counterintuitively, HPC_SCHED also provides performance improvements for data analytics. In fact, as explained above, HPC_SCHED not only prevents application threads from moving from one CPU to another (increasing cache locality) but also favors HPC tasks over CFS tasks and reduces the amount of OS noise on the CPU running the HPC application tasks. These advantages still hold when using containers, as several user and kernel daemons may be running in the CFS scheduling class, and the CFS scheduler could decide to move threads from one CPU to another within the same container. The result is a higher responsiveness of the data analytics tasks that are able to find an available CPU as soon as they become runnable.

12.7 Lessons Learned

Overall, the conducted experiments confirm the viability of our lightweight approach to resource management, which retains the benefits of a full OS kernel that application programmers have learned to depend on, yet at the same time offers additional HPC-specific extensions. Rather than providing a constricted "one size fits all," our extensions are a toolset that can be freely mixed and matched, resulting in an abundance of possible node-local or even process-local configurations to best benefit particular application components or workflow management middleware. We consider this flexibility to be a critical aspect of our approach.

We also focus on more complex experiments using coupled codes, including a coupled application consisting of the Gromacs simulation and the Quicksurf in situ data visualization, as well as simulated workloads consisting of LULESH as a simulation component and streamline tracing as a data analysis component. Unfortunately, these types of applications are still somewhat rare on production HPC systems, and most of the HPC software stack is slow to adopt features to ease their development. The lack of flexibility in MPI process management and batch schedulers in particular is limiting the growth of container technologies, and the applicability of our work at larger scale.

In the end, modification to the Linux kernel is still proving to be difficult to deploy on production systems. Most system administrators are still cautious about offering boot options to users, and as a research group we lack the manpower to upstream and maintain complex features in the kernel. These difficulties pushed the Argo project to aim for the migration of most of our work into low-level userspace software with minimal and upstreamable changes to kernel and root-only codes. For example, our container management is being split between a facility-provided runtime and a userspace daemon without any privileges. We are also moving memory management features into user-installable libraries.

12.8   Future of Argo

The capabilities offered by the Argo approach also have an impact on the entire ecosystem around the NodeOS. Changing the HPC ecosystem to support containers is enabling many new opportunities for resource management across the machine by collaborating with the job schedulers and the parallel runtimes. Offering to users an active interface to communicate their resource requirements and act on resource management events also enables new developments in workload managers. The Flux job scheduler (Ahn et al. 2014) in particular is working with the Argo project to take advantage of our features.

Argo is an ongoing project, and we will continue this work through the first exascale systems and beyond. Our current focus includes better management of novel byte-addressable memory technologies like persistent memory and on-package memory. We are also working to extend the capabilities of the node resource manager to enable complex power control policies based on regular monitoring of application progress and dynamic resource allocation across all the containers running on a node.

It is good for exascale projects to consider the consequences of the end of Moore's law and Dennard scaling. While the consequences are hard to predict, we believe that they will force designers to place increasing numbers of more specialized components within each node. One of the key challenges in such a system will be the ability of the application software running on top to indicate and negotiate how to best manage the underlying hardware resources in a manner that is conflict-free and efficient for application performance. We believe that the best approach to address this challenge will be by introducing an intermediate layer of *resource arbitration*: a comprehensive and more complex version of the node resource manager, able to arbitrate resource requirements both of the complex applications running on the node and of the heterogeneous hardware available.

Acknowledgements Results presented in this chapter were obtained using the Chameleon testbed supported by the National Science Foundation. Argonne National Laboratory's work was supported by the U.S. Department of Energy, Office of Science, Advanced Scientific Computer Research, under Contract DE-AC02-06CH11357. Part of this work was performed under the auspices of the U.S. Department of Energy by Lawrence Livermore National Laboratory under contract No. DE-AC52-07NA27344. This research was supported by the Exascale Computing Project (17-SC-20-SC), a collaborative effort of the U.S. Department of Energy Office of Science and the National Nuclear Security Administration.

References

Appc: App container specification and tooling (2017). https://github.com/appc/spec.

Ahn, D. H., Garlick, J., Grondona, M., Lipari, D., Springmeyer, B., & Schulz, M. (2014). Flux: A next-generation resource management framework for large HPC centers. In *2014 43rd International Conference on Parallel Processing Workshops (ICCPW)* (pp. 9–17). IEEE.

Bautista-Gomez, L., Gainaru, A., Perarnau, S., Tiwari, D., Gupta, S., Cappello, F., et al. (2016). Reducing waste in large scale systems through introspective analysis. In *IEEE International Parallel and Distributed Processing Symposium (IPDPS)*.

Beserra, D., Moreno, E. D., Endo, P. T., Barreto, J., Sadok, D., & Fernandes, S. (2015). Performance analysis of LXC for HPC environments. In *International Conference on Complex, Intelligent, and Software Intensive Systems (CISIS)*.

Dongarra, J., Beckman, P., et al. (2011). The international exascale software project roadmap. *International Journal of High Performance Computing Applications*.

Dreher, M., & Raffin, B. (2014). A flexible framework for asynchronous in situ and in transit analytics for scientific simulations. In *IEEE/ACM International Symposium on Cluster, Cloud and Grid Computing (CLUSTER)*.

Ellsworth, D., Patki, T., Perarnau, S., Seo, S., Amer, A., Zounmevo, J., et al. (2016). Systemwide power management with Argo. In *High-Performance, Power-Aware Computing (HPPAC)*.

Gioiosa, R., Petrini, F., Davis, K., & Lebaillif-Delamare, F. (2004). Analysis of system overhead on parallel computers. In *IEEE International Symposium on Signal Processing and Information Technology (ISSPIT)*.

Intel. Running average power limit – RAPL. https://01.org/blogs/2014/running-average-power-limit---rapl.

Jacobsen, D. M., & Canon, R. S. (2015). Contain this, unleashing Docker for HPC. In *Proceedings of the Cray User Group*.

Jiang, M., Van Essen, B., Harrison, C., & Gokhale, M. (2014). Multi-threaded streamline tracing for data-intensive architectures. In *IEEE Symposium on Large Data Analysis and Visualization (LDAV)*.

Kernel.org (2004). Linux control groups. https://www.kernel.org/doc/Documentation/cgroup-v1/cgroups.txt.

Krone, M., Stone, J. E., Ertl, T., & Schulten, K. (2012). Fast visualization of Gaussian density surfaces for molecular dynamics and particle system trajectories. In *EuroVis Short Papers*.

Merkel, D. (2014). Docker: Lightweight Linux containers for consistent development and deployment. *Linux J., 2014*(239).

Morari, A., Gioiosa, R., Wisniewski, R., Cazorla, F., & Valero, M. (2011). A quantitative analysis of OS noise. In *2011 IEEE International, Parallel Distributed Processing Symposium (IPDPS)* (pp. 852–863).

Morari, A., Gioiosa, R., Wisniewski, R., Rosenburg, B., Inglett, T., & Valero, M. (2012). Evaluating the impact of TLB misses on future HPC systems. In *2012 IEEE 26th International, Parallel Distributed Processing Symposium (IPDPS)* (pp. 1010–1021).

Perarnau, S., Thakur, R., Iskra, K., Raffenetti, K., Cappello, F., Gupta, R., et al. (2015). Distributed monitoring and management of exascale systems in the Argo project. In *IFIP International Conference on Distributed Applications and Interoperable Systems (DAIS), Short Paper*.

Perarnau, S., Zounmevo, J. A., Dreher, M., Van Essen, B. C., Gioiosa, R., Iskra, K., et al. (2017). Argo NodeOS: Toward unified resource management for exascale. In *IEEE International Parallel and Distributed Processing Symposium (IPDPS)*.

Pronk, S., Pall, S., Schulz, R., Larsson, P., et al. (2013). GROMACS 4.5: A high-throughput and highly parallel open source molecular simulation toolkit. *Bioinformatics*.

Rostedt, S. (2009). Finding origins of latencies using ftrace. In *Real Time Linux Workshop (RTLWS)*.

Seo, S., Amer, A., & Balaji, P. (2018). BOLT is OpenMP over lightweight threads. http://www.bolt-omp.org/.

Seo, S., Amer, A., Balaji, P., Bordage, C., Bosilca, G., Brooks, A., et al. (2017). Argobots: A lightweight low-level threading and tasking framework. *IEEE Transactions on Parallel and Distributed Systems, PP*(99), 1–1.

Van Essen, B., Hsieh, H., Ames, S., Pearce, R., & Gokhale, M. (2015). DI-MMAP: A scalable memory map runtime for out-of-core data-intensive applications. *Cluster Computing, 18*, 15.

Wheeler, K. B., Murphy, R. C., & Thain, D. (2008). Qthreads: An API for programming with millions of lightweight threads. In *2008 IEEE International Symposium on Parallel and Distributed Processing* (pp. 1–8).

Xavier, M. G., Neves, M. V., Rossi, F. D., Ferreto, T. C., Lange, T., & De Rose, C. A. F. (2013). Performance evaluation of container-based virtualization for high performance computing environments. In *Euromicro International Conference on Parallel, Distributed and Network-Based Processing (PDP)*.

Part IV
Multi-kernels

Chapter 13
A New Age: An Overview
of Multi-kernels

Rolf Riesen, Balazs Gerofi, Yutaka Ishikawa and Robert W. Wisniewski

In the previous two parts of this book, we studied various lightweight kernel (LWK) projects, learned why they have been largely replaced by Linux on production systems, and looked at efforts to make Unix/Linux more suitable for highly parallel High-Performance Computing (HPC) systems. In this part, we present projects that combine a full-weight Operating System (OS) with an LWK on a single compute node (Gerofi et al. 2016).

We saw that despite LWKs' excellent scalability, the lack of full Linux compatibility and limited availability of device drivers have inhibited their widespread deployment. Although Linux dominates the TOP500 list now, there is concern in the research community and industry that its use is holding back progress and limits performance, scalability, and innovation. Extreme-scale architectures are evolving quickly with hierarchical memories, complex Nonuniform Memory Access (NUMA) structures, and accelerators of various kinds forcing, changes in programming models and usage of these systems.

Because of its broad user base and therefore required generality, Linux does not tend to adapt quickly to new demands or deliver optimal performance for each community. For example, because extreme-scale HPC is a small portion of the Linux market, and some of the required changes to obtain optimal performance would be

R. Riesen (✉)
Intel Corporation, Hillsboro, OR, USA
e-mail: rolf.riesen@intel.com

B. Gerofi · Y. Ishikawa
RIKEN Center for Computational Science, Kobe, Japan
e-mail: bgerofi@riken.jp

Y. Ishikawa
e-mail: yutaka.ishikawa@riken.jp

R. W. Wisniewski
Intel Corporation, New York City, NY, USA
e-mail: robert.w.wisniewski@intel.com

© Springer Nature Singapore Pte Ltd. 2019
B. Gerofi et al. (eds.), *Operating Systems for Supercomputers
and High Performance Computing*, High-Performance Computing Series,
https://doi.org/10.1007/978-981-13-6624-6_13

intrusive to the Linux kernel and may even hamper more mainstream use cases, other OS architectures may be better able to meet the needs of HPC.

Still, it is clear that Linux is vitally important to today's supercomputing. Since it is ubiquitous and offers a wide range of tools and programming environments, it has brought productivity enhancements to the HPC community that few would be willing to give up for improved machine performance (Hammond et al. 2010).

It is perhaps then not surprising that several projects have been initiated that build on the HPC OS work done in the 1990s and the beginning of this century, and aim to combine the ease-of-use and familiarity of Linux with the nimbleness and performance characteristics of an LWK. By combining an LWK with Linux, most of these multi-kernel projects also demonstrate how Linux device drivers can be transparently utilized, and thus address standalone LWKs' device driver shortcomings.

Combining different OS kernels on the same CPU or compute node only makes sense when there are sufficient cores. That means efforts to do so are fairly new and there is not a lot of experience that points to the most effective methods. This, in turn, leads to a diverse spectrum of ideas and implementations, and multi-kernels are enjoying a renaissance.

In this part of the book, we provide information on seven such projects. While there are similarities, the differences between the projects might be of more interest since they highlight the differing goals and compromises each team had to consider.

FusedOS by an IBM Research team is a descendant of the Compute Node Kernel (CNK) from the Blue Gene era, based on experiences with K42 (Krieger et al. 2006), and is described in Chap. 14.

Hobbes (Brightwell et al. 2013; Kocoloski et al. 2015) at Sandia National Laboratories and associated universities, is a project to look beyond the compute node OS and manage an extreme-scale system as a whole and configure it for particular use cases, including, when needed, running the Kitten LWK (Lange et al. 2010). Details are in Chap. 15.

The NIX OS (Minnich and Mckie 2009) in Chap. 16 is unique in this group because it builds on the capabilities and the streamlined elegance of Plan 9 (Pike et al. 1995), and targeted thousand-core nodes long before they became available. The chapter describes the ideas behind NIX and provides a good explanation why current HPC OS projects attempt to provide Linux compatibility. The description also shows why that is difficult and that it may not be in the best interest of performance, scalability, and maintainability.

The Interface for Heterogeneous Kernels (IHK)/McKernel project (Gerofi et al. 2013; Shimosawa et al. 2014) at the RIKEN Advanced Institute for Computational Science is a project that inserts an LWK as a Linux kernel module into the compute node OS. It has the obvious advantage of being able to operate inside an unmodified Linux kernel, thus enhancing its chances for adoption in production environments. Chapter 17 explains how it works, shows the techniques that make it possible, and presents performance comparisons to Linux.

The Multi-OS project for HPC (*mOS*) (Wisniewski et al. 2014) at Intel had as its original target the many cores of the Xeon Phi Knights Landing processor. The Intel team has been collaborating closely with the IHK/McKernel team from RIKEN with the result that there are many similarities between the two OSs. However, they have meaningful and pedagogical differences, and Chap. 18 explains what is different and why.

The Technical University of Dresden in Germany has a long history with L4 micro-kernels (Liedtke 1995). They are continuing these efforts with the Fast Fault-tolerant MicroKernel (FFMK) project (Lackorzynski et al. 2016; Weinhold et al. 2016) and have novel ideas on how work can be distributed among the available cores of a system in a dynamic fashion. The authors describe their work in Chap. 19.

The final chapter in this part of the book presents one of the most recent projects in this field: HermitCore (Lankes et al. 2016, 2017) in Chap. 20. While it shares several characteristics with the other OSs in this part, HermitCore has as one of its main goals the support of cloud computing. An LWK is appealing because of the smaller attack surface and because cloud workloads run inside virtual machines that supply the full-weight features required.

None of these OSs are in production yet. Adopting new OSs or kernel features takes time and it will be interesting to see where the projects, and their progenitors, will be in a decade when exascale computing has been firmly established.

References

Brightwell, R., Oldfield, R., Maccabe, A., & Bernholdt, D. (2013). Hobbes: Composition and virtualization as the foundations of an extreme-scale OS/R. In *Proceedings of the 3rd International Workshop on Runtime and Operating Systems for Supercomputers, (ROSS).*

Gerofi, B., Ishikawa, Y., Riesen, R., Wisniewski, R. W., Park, Y., & Rosenburg, B. (2016). A multi-kernel survey for high-performance computing. In *Proceedings of the 6th International Workshop on Runtime and Operating Systems for Supercomputers, ROSS '16* (pp. 5:1–5:8). New York, NY, USA: ACM.

Gerofi, B., Shimada, A., Hori, A., & Ishikawa, Y. (2013). Partially separated page tables for efficient operating system assisted hierarchical memory management on heterogeneous architectures. In *13th International Symposium on Cluster, Cloud and Grid Computing (CCGrid).*

Hammond, S., Mudalige, G., Smith, J. A., Davis, J. A., Jarvis, S., Holt, J. et al. (2010). To upgrade or not to upgrade? Catamount versus Cray Linux environment. In *2010 IEEE International Symposium on Parallel Distributed Processing, Workshops and Phd Forum (IPDPSW).*

Kocoloski, B., Lange, J., Abbasi, H., Bernholdt, D., Jones, T., Dayal, J. et al. (2015). System-level support for composition of application. In *Proceedings of the 5th International Workshop on Runtime and Operating Systems for Supercomputers, (ROSS).*

Krieger, O., Auslander, M., Rosenburg, B., Wisniewski, R. W., Xenidis, J., Silva, D. D. et al. (2006). K42: Building a real operating system. In *Proceedings of EuroSys'2006* (pp. 133–145). ACM SIGOPS.

Lackorzynski, A., Weinhold, C., & Härtig, H. (2016). Decoupled: Low-effort noise-free execution on commodity system. In *Proceedings of the 6th International Workshop on Runtime and Operating Systems for Supercomputers, ROSS '16.* New York, NY, USA: ACM.

Lange, J., Pedretti, K., Hudson, T., Dinda, P., Cui, Z., Xia, L. et al. (2010). Palacios and Kitten: New high performance operating systems for scalable virtualized and native supercomputing. In *Proceedings of the 24th IEEE International Parallel and Distributed Processing Symposium, (IPDPS).*

Lankes, S., Pickartz, S., & Breitbart, J. (2016). HermitCore: A unikernel for extreme scale computing. In *Proceedings of the 6th International Workshop on Runtime and Operating Systems for Supercomputers, ROSS '16* (pp. 4:1–4:8). New York, NY, USA: ACM.

Lankes, S., Pickartz, S., & Breitbart, J. (2017). *A Low Noise Unikernel for Extrem-Scale Systems* (pp. 73–84). Cham: Springer International Publishing.

Liedtke, J. (1995). On micro-kernel construction. In *SOSP '95: Proceedings of the Fifteenth ACM Symposium on Operating Systems Principles* (pp. 237–250). New York, NY, USA: ACM Press.

Minnich, R. G., & Mckie, J. (2009). Experiences porting the Plan 9 research operating system to the IBM Blue Gene supercomputers. *Computer Science - Research and Development, 23*(3), 117–124.

Pike, R., Presotto, D. L., Dorward, S., Flandrena, B., Thompson, K., Trickey, H., et al. (1995). Plan 9 from bell labs. *Computing Systems, 8*(2), 221–254.

Shimosawa, T., Gerofi, B., Takagi, M., Nakamura, G., Shirasawa, T., Saeki, Y. et al. (2014). Interface for heterogeneous kernels: A framework to enable hybrid OS designs targeting high performance computing on manycore architectures. In *21th International Conference on High Performance Computing, HiPC*.

Weinhold, C., Lackorzynski, A., Bierbaum, J., Küttler, M., Planeta, M., Härtig, H. et al. (2016). FFMK: A fast and fault-tolerant microkernel-based system for exascale computing. In *Software for Exascale Computing - SPPEXA 2013-2015* (Vol. 113, pp. 405–426).

Wisniewski, R. W., Inglett, T., Keppel, P., Murty, R., & Riesen, R. (2014). mOS: An architecture for extreme-scale operating systems. In *Proceedings of the 4th International Workshop on Runtime and Operating Systems for Supercomputers, ROSS '14* (pp. 2:1–2:8). New York, NY, USA: ACM.

Chapter 14
FusedOS

Yoonho Park, Bryan Rosenburg and Robert W. Wisniewski

Abstract FusedOS was started in 2011 as part of the IBM Blue Gene/Q effort to explore the possibility of providing HPC applications a rich operating environment on heterogeneous systems. FusedOS's design objectives were to address both core heterogeneity and the need for a rich and familiar operating environment for more applications. We generalized the types of compute elements to cores optimized for power efficiency (power-efficient cores or PECs), and cores optimized for single-thread performance (single-thread-optimized cores or STOCs). We envisioned that PECs may have limited capability to run traditional kernels (such as GPUs do today), and that applications running on a chip with PECs and STOCs will desire to fully utilize the capability of the chip in a Linux environment. Before FusedOS, there were two approaches to providing an operating environment for High-Performance Computing (HPC). A Full-Weight Kernel (FWK) approach starts with a general-purpose operating system and strips it down to better scale up across more cores and out across larger clusters. A Lightweight Kernel (LWK) approach starts with a new thin kernel code base and extends its functionality by adding more system services needed by applications. In both cases, the goal is to provide end users with a scalable HPC operating environment with the functionality and services needed to reliably run their applications. To achieve this goal, we propose a new approach, called FusedOS, that combines the FWK and LWK approaches. FusedOS provides an infrastructure capable of partitioning the resources of a multicore heterogeneous system and collaboratively running different operating environments on subsets of the cores and memory, without the use of a virtual machine monitor. With FusedOS, HPC applications can enjoy both the performance characteristics of an LWK and the rich functionality of an FWK through cross-core system service delegation. This

Y. Park (✉) · B. Rosenburg
IBM Research, Yorktown Heights, NY, USA
e-mail: yoonho@us.ibm.com

B. Rosenburg
e-mail: rosnbrg@us.ibm.com

R. W. Wisniewski
Intel Corporation, New York City, NY, USA
e-mail: robert.w.wisniewski@intel.com

© Springer Nature Singapore Pte Ltd. 2019
B. Gerofi et al. (eds.), *Operating Systems for Supercomputers and High Performance Computing*, High-Performance Computing Series,
https://doi.org/10.1007/978-981-13-6624-6_14

227

chapter describes the FusedOS architecture and a prototype implementation on Blue Gene/Q. The FusedOS prototype leverages Linux with small modifications as a FWK and implements a user-level LWK called Compute Library (CL) by leveraging CNK. We present CL performance results demonstrating low noise and show micro-benchmarks running with performance commensurate with that provided by CNK. We present CL performance results demonstrating low noise provided by CNK. We also present micro-benchmarks and an HPC benchmark running with performance commensurate with that provided by CNK.

14.1 Introduction

As processor frequencies leveled out and faded as a major contributor to continued performance improvement, there was a shift toward using multiple cores to design "faster" computers. While multicore counts continued to increase, heterogeneous technology such as GPUs was seen as a way to address the challenges inherent in the drive toward exascale. In addition, there was an increased need for system software to provide richer environments to allow disparate applications to utilize the hardware on the largest supercomputers. This resulted in the need to support the capabilities provided by a general-purpose operating system, such as Linux, including libraries, file systems, and daemon-provided services. We explicitly call out that the application cares about the *operating environment* Linux provides, not the Linux kernel itself. We refer to a collection of Linux APIs, personality, etc., as a Linux environment.

FusedOS was started in 2011 as part of the IBM Blue Gene/Q effort to explore the possibility of providing HPC applications a rich operating environment on heterogeneous systems. FusedOS's design objectives were to address both core heterogeneity and the need for a rich and familiar operating environment for more applications. We generalized the types of compute elements to cores optimized for power efficiency (power-efficient cores or PECs), and cores optimized for single-thread performance (single-thread-optimized Cores or STOCs). We envisioned that PECs may have limited capability to run traditional kernels (such as GPUs do today), and that applications running on a chip with PECs and STOCs will desire to fully utilize the capability of the chip in a Linux environment.

Before FusedOS there were two approaches to providing an operating environment for HPC. A Full-Weight Kernel (FWK) approach starts with a general-purpose operating system, typically Linux, and strips down the environment to better scale up across more cores and out across larger clusters. In contrast, a Lightweight Kernel (LWK) approach starts with a new thin kernel code base and extends its functionality by adding more system services needed by applications. In FusedOS, rather than choosing either an LWK or an FWK approach, we combined both. FusedOS uses a Linux kernel as the FWK and implements a user-level LWK called Compute Library (CL) by leveraging CNK (Giampapa et al. 2010) from Blue Gene/Q. The FusedOS design goal is for HPC performance-critical code to run without interference on the PECs and for requests requiring a full Linux environment to be delegated to the STOCs. Applications should achieve similar performance in FusedOS as in an LWK (we chose performance in CNK as our baseline) and, at the same time, be able to make use of the richer functionality of a FWK. We introduce FWK functionality but do not expose applications to the interference and jitter of FWKs (Ferreira et al. 2008).

There were two main issues in understanding whether a FusedOS strategy would be viable. They are (i) whether Linux is sufficiently malleable to allow the fusion and (ii) whether the interactions between CL and Linux introduce too much latency and hurt performance. We believe that if we needed to make substantial Linux modifications, the effort of maintaining them would be prohibitive. Examining the frequency and types of interactions between CL and Linux should help determine the feasibility of our approach and may influence the design of future architectural features that improve the performance of the paths between CL and Linux.

The concept of FusedOS, in general, has advantages beyond heterogeneity. Historically, Linux developers have been reluctant to adopt changes specific to the HPC community. This is in part because the Linux community tends to accept changes that matter for the general population, while HPC architectures have tended to push technology limits in order to achieve the highest performance for scientific and engineering applications. FusedOS can support a variety of applications with legacy requirements while providing the ability to leverage a more nimble LWK to effectively incorporate new technologies.

In order to study both the extent of the required modifications to Linux and the performance impact of our approach, we implemented a prototype of FusedOS on Blue Gene/Q. Although Blue Gene/Q has homogeneous cores, we simulate heterogeneous cores by assigning a set of cores to act as PECs. In that role, cores run almost exclusively in user mode executing application code. A small supervisor-state monitor is used only to simulate the hardware we would expect to exist on true PECs. This prototype provides the additional ability to accurately trace and monitor events. It represents a conservative view of how the actual hardware would perform as its capabilities need to be simulated by the prototype software.

14.2 Architecture

In this section, we present an architectural description of FusedOS, an approach for combining FWK and LWK code bases to provide a complete operating environment with LWK performance for HPC code while providing FWK functionality.

The FusedOS architecture is shown in Fig. 14.1. STOCs and PECs represent the potential heterogeneity that FusedOS will need to manage. STOCs are best suited for serial computation and any required system processing, while PECs are targeted for parallel computation. STOCs and PECs will have similar instruction set architectures. However, STOCs will have features found in high-performance, general-purpose processors while PECs will be optimized for power and space. PECs will have a subset of STOC features and may not contain capabilities such as supervisor mode. The FusedOS design assumes coherent shared memory between and across STOCs and PECs. Current research has shown that heterogeneous nodes with non-coherent

Fig. 14.1 FusedOS architecture

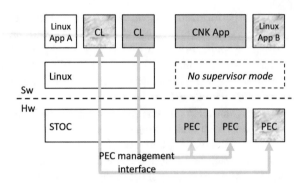

shared memory can be quite difficult to program. Examples include GPUs and IBM Cell processors. Indications are that these types of architectures are moving toward a more tightly coupled approach. Today, GPUs are typically treated as functional units controlled by a CPU. In contrast, PECs are independent processors, having their own independent flow of execution. In our FusedOS prototype, the Compute Library (CL) manages PECs. CL is a Linux application that encapsulates LWK functionality. Specifically in our prototype, it is built from CNK source code and runs as a user process on Linux, but it could be derived from any LWK.

Linux applications will run on a subset (or all) of the STOCs like the *Linux App A* in Fig. 14.1. Applications that run on CNK or another LWK will run unmodified on the PECs like the *CNK App*. While Linux is not an LWK, the FusedOS approach can provide a Linux environment on a PEC. This is represented by *Linux App B*.

The CL manages the PECs and applications through the PEC management interface as illustrated in Fig. 14.2. To run an LWK application, the CL requests a PEC, loads the LWK application into the memory region assigned to the PEC, stores startup information in a memory area shared with the PEC, then tells the PEC to start the application. When an LWK application thread makes a system call or encounters an exception, the PEC stores the system call or exception information in the shared memory area and then passes control to the CL thread. After the CL thread services the system call or handles the exception, it resumes the LWK application thread.

A *clone* system call will result in a new thread being started. The thread will run either on the same PEC or another PEC. This approach allows FusedOS to support any thread-based runtime such as OpenMP. A CL instance is started for each CNK application, with one CL thread started per application thread. CL threads handle system calls and exceptions generated by the corresponding application threads.

The partitioning of cores and memory is configurable to meet the application's needs. For an HPC application, most of the memory is allocated to the CL-managed PECs. The CL can utilize some of the STOCs to run sequential portions of the application more efficiently. The CL can utilize the STOCs with an additional FWK system call that executes application code on the STOC. Of course, the application must be compiled for both the STOC and PEC if the STOC and PEC instruction set architecture (ISAs) are different. Pragmas could be used to direct the execution of

Fig. 14.2 PEC management interface

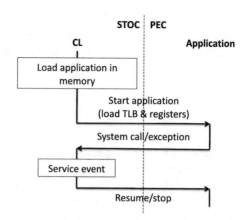

application code on the STOCs or PECs. For Linux applications, all the STOCs and most of the memory is managed by Linux. This configuration would be used to run an application that requires Linux services not provided by CL such as *Linux App A* and *B*. The application would run under Linux and not utilize CL or the PECs.

FusedOS is able to provide Linux on compute nodes while providing LWK performance for HPC applications by partitioning both cores and memory—a strategy that allows us to address scalability issues of multicore systems and potential functional limitations of future heterogeneous core architectures. FusedOS removes operating system jitter by eliminating preemption as well as system code on application cores. The only exceptions and interrupts are those generated by the applications themselves. There is still potential for architectural jitter because conflicts can arise in the caches or other shared resources. However, in Sect. 14.4, we show jitter from these conflicts to be quite small in comparison with other operating system jitter such as TLB and cache pollution and noise from daemons.

FusedOS and CNK both function-ship system calls to a proxy process running in a Linux system. The difference is that with CNK the proxy process runs on an entirely different node (an I/O node) from the application, while in FusedOS the proxy is running on the same node. FusedOS can exploit this difference to provide functionality beyond what CNK can offer. For example, FusedOS can allow Linux processes and CNK processes to share memory and to interact via Unix pipes or SysV semaphores.

FusedOS minimizes changes to Linux by encapsulating the LWK as a Linux process. Changes in Linux proper are limited to hooks in bootstrap code and exception handlers. Hooks in bootstrap code allow us to partition the cores and memory. Hooks in the exception vectors allow us to pass control to the CL. All other kernel codes are placed in a loadable file system module, which is independent of Linux. Of course, the file system module must respect the Linux module API.

For our implementation of the FusedOS CL, we leveraged Blue Gene/Q's CNK code. We reused and enhanced large portions of the CNK code including application loading, memory management, and thread management. Our architecture allows a different LWK to be fused with Linux in a similar manner. Because CL is running as a Linux process, FusedOS avoids the use of a virtual machine monitor. We believe that modest modifications to Linux will allow us to provide the necessary mechanisms to run CL.

14.3 Prototype

We have implemented a prototype of FusedOS on the IBM Blue Gene/Q system. Our prototype consists of five components: the Compute Library (CL), the PEC FS Linux kernel module, the PEC monitor, an RoQ network driver, and clustering support.

Blue Gene/Q features homogeneous cores, and therefore does not follow our STOC/PEC model by itself. Thus, we artificially partition cores into STOCs and PECs. On each core designated a PEC, we run a minimal system software layer (the PEC monitor) that mimics a PEC's control interface. It thereby allows our Compute Library (CL) to control applications remotely on the PECs, while itself running on a STOC. Thereby, we mimic the heterogeneity that we expect on future exascale systems.

A Blue Gene/Q node has 17 cores, each providing 4 hardware threads. We currently use 1 core as a STOC, 15 cores as PECs, and 1 core for the RoQ network driver. Like Linux, we treat each hardware thread as a separate CPU, and therefore consider each PEC core as 4 PECs. A Blue Gene/Q node has 16 GB of physical memory. We allocate 4 GB for Linux and 12 GB for PECs. See Haring et al. (2012) and Gschwind (2012) for more details on Blue Gene/Q.

We modified Linux to partition cores and memory and to export the PEC monitor's control interface to CL. In order to minimize the changes to Linux and to modularize our code, we added minimal hooks only where necessary and placed the bulk of our code in a loadable file system kernel module (PEC FS). Using this module, CL can control the execution of processes on PECs and access these processes' virtual address spaces via *ioctl* and *mmap* system calls.

In the remainder of this section, we describe the components of our prototype and their interaction in greater detail.

14.3.1 PEC Monitor

The PEC monitor is the only supervisor-mode code that runs on the PECs. It provides a control interface to CL, but does not itself implement any OS functionality for the processes running on the PEC. PEC monitor and CL communicate via a shared memory area called the PEC context.

After the monitor is started, it waits in a loop for a command from the CL. The polling loop makes use of a hardware feature that puts the processor in a low-power wait state until the polled memory location changes (see Haring et al. 2012 for details).

When instructed by the CL, the PEC monitor loads register content and TLB entries from the PEC context and starts the execution of a user process. On an exception or a system call, the PEC monitor stores the process's state back into the PEC context and notifies the CL on the STOC. Our current prototype uses inter-processor interrupts (IPIs) for these signals.

14.3.2 Linux Hooks and PEC FS Module

We have added hooks to the core initialization code (`smp_init()`), the kernel initial-ization code (`start_kernel()`), and the IPI handler code (`bgq_ipi_dispatch()`) of the Linux kernel. These hooks implement the partitioning of cores and memory by skipping the initialization of the PEC resources in Linux. Further, they forward signals from the PEC monitor to CL by notifying a CL thread when an IPI arrives from a PEC.

The PEC FS kernel module exports the PEC monitor's control interface to CL. It provides *ioctl*s to send commands to the PEC monitor. These *ioctl* system calls block until the PEC monitor acknowledges the command. Some commands such as loading TLB entries return immediately and others such as start or resume a PEC process return when the process has raised an exception or invoked a system call.

The PEC FS module further provides access to the PEC monitor, the PEC context, and the PEC application memory through *mmap*. CL uses this interface to access the virtual address space of processes running on the PECs (e.g., for initial program loading).

14.3.3 Compute Library (CL)

The Compute Library (CL) is a Linux application that encapsulates the functionality of the CNK lightweight kernel. It provides OS functionality for CNK applications running on PECs. CL itself runs on a STOC and behaves like a regular user-space application under Linux. It uses the interface of the PEC FS kernel module to access PEC memory and to control process execution on the PECs by issuing commands to the PEC monitor.

Like CNK, CL calculates static TLB entries when loading an application. As it cannot install these TLB entries on the remote cores by itself, it stores them in the PEC context and instructs the PEC monitor to load the TLB on the target PEC core. Similarly, CL writes the designated initial register state of a process in the PEC context. Instead of switching to user mode, like a traditional OS, it instructs the PEC monitor to start the application on the PEC. For this purpose, it issues a blocking *ioctl* system call to PEC FS in Linux.

When the application on the PEC makes a system call or raises an exception, the PEC monitor stores the register state and sends an IPI to the STOC, where PEC FS unblocks the corresponding CL thread. CL services the system call or exception and then asks the PEC monitor to resume the application, blocking once again in an *ioctl* system call. When the system call is an exit or the exception is fatal, the CL asks the monitor to exit the application.

As in any OS, we have two alternatives for mapping application threads to threads in the OS—in our case to CL threads, which are user-space threads in Linux: We can (1) create a CL thread for each hardware thread, or (2) create a CL thread for each CNK application thread. Alternative (1) requires fewer threads in CL, but each CL thread must multiplex several application threads. In contrast, alternative (2) allows for a simple 1:1 mapping, but requires more threads in CL (and thus in Linux). We opted for alternative (2), creating a CL thread for each CNK application thread to avoid the complexity of multiplexing. CNK system calls can be directly mapped to Linux system calls this way; blocking system calls simply block the CL thread and, thereby, the CNK application thread as well.

The virtual address space layout for applications in FusedOS resembles that of CNK: a 16-MB lower region contains system code and data (PEC monitor and PEC context). The upper region starting at 16 MB contains the application's text, data, and heap segments. CL uses *mmap* system calls to PEC FS to recreate this address space layout in its own virtual address space. We thereby avoid address translation in the OS services provided by CL (e.g., for buffers in FS system calls), because an application's virtual addresses map 1:1 to CL addresses.

14.3.4 RoQ Network Driver

Both the Linux and the CNK side of our prototype use the Blue Gene/Q torus network. Parallel CNK applications employ an unmodified MPI stack and reach performance close to a production CNK system. Linux utilizes RoQ for TCP/IP networking and RDMA over the torus. CNK applications on Blue Gene/Q usually use a modified MPICH 2 stacked on the PAMI messaging library.

The interface to the Blue Gene/Q torus on each node has several hundred FIFO queues used for transfer commands to the hardware and for addressing a communication partner. Despite that abundance, their use needs to be coordinated. We modified RoQ and adjusted the FIFO numbers it uses for communication to avoid overlaps with the FIFOs that the PAMI library uses by default. By changing RoQ instead of PAMI, we maintain compatibility with the unmodified build environments of regular Blue Gene/Q systems. Unmodified CNK application binaries can be run on the FusedOS prototype.

14.3.5 Clustering Support

The prototype ties together individual nodes running FusedOS into a cluster with a unified view of network file systems outside Blue Gene/Q and employs the SLURM resource scheduler as the infrastructure for launching jobs on several nodes.

The I/O nodes of a Blue Gene/Q system typically access external storage systems via InfiniBand or 10G Ethernet and provide CNK on the compute nodes with access to these file systems. Similarly, FusedOS I/O nodes mount external file systems (via NFS) and re-export them to compute nodes. The Linux instance on FusedOS compute nodes mounts the external file systems from the compute nodes. When a CNK application performs an I/O system call, CL delegates them to Linux. Thereby, both Linux and CNK applications have the same view of the file system. They both see the virtual file system (VFS) of the Linux on their node, with mounted external network file systems and node-local parts.

We employ a variant of the 9P protocol (from the research operating system Plan 9) over TCP/IP to access an I/O nodes' file system from a compute node. On the I/O node, we run the distributed I/O daemon (diod) as the server for the 9P protocol. On the client, we use the 9P client included in the mainline Linux kernel. Both client and server communicate using TCP/IP sockets. The IP packets are transferred by RoQ, using the RoQ Ethernet front end.

14.4 Results

We evaluated FusedOS against Linux and CNK on the Blue Gene/Q platform. We used Linux kernel version 2.6.32-220.4.2 from the RedHat Enterprise Linux 6 distribution with modifications for running on both the Blue Gene/Q I/O and compute nodes. These modifications were made by the Blue Gene development group at IBM Rochester (Minnesota) and the IBM Watson Blue Gene Active Storage group. We used CNK from the March 2012 general availability (GA) distribution (branch V1R1M0). We disabled the Kernel Flight Recorder of CNK, a tracing facility, in order to measure the performance without instrumentation disturbance.

We use two Sequoia benchmarks, LAMMPS (Plimpton 1995) and Fixed Time Quanta (FTQ), to show that FusedOS can provide the same low-noise environment and performance as CNK. By comparing FusedOS to Linux, we show that our approach can potentially provide both LWK performance and FWK features at the same time.

14.4.1 Interference

Studies have shown that destructive interference caused by OS noise can dramatically impact run times of HPC applications, particularly bulk-synchronous applications (Ferreira et al. 2008). LWKs such as CNK have excellent noise properties, showing almost completely deterministic runtimes, with only slight deviations caused by architectural noise, not OS interference.

In FusedOS,we designate STOC cores as *noise cores*, as they handle all the OS functionality. This approach has the advantage that applications on the PECs are iso-

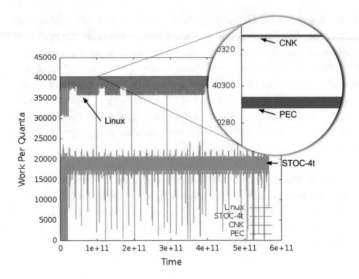

Fig. 14.3 Performance of FTQ benchmarks in different operating environments

lated from OS noise and interrupt overhead. As a result, PECs maintain the noise characteristics of LWKs, thereby allowing more deterministic HPC application behavior.

To show that FusedOS provides a low-noise environment, we used the FTQ benchmark, which is one of the standard mechanisms for both measuring and analyzing noise signatures. FTQ counts the number of times a loop completes during a fixed amount of time determined by a hardware clock. In our evaluation, we chose the tightest FTQ loop. In contrast to variants that do more pseudo-work in the loop body, this variant tends to accentuate more high-frequency architectural noise. This provides higher fidelity when looking at CNK and FusedOS results.

Figure 14.3 shows the results we gathered running FTQ on Linux, CNK, and FusedOS over a period of around 6 min. The Y-axis shows the number of iterations accomplished during a time quantum while the X-axis shows time. Since we are running an FTQ instance per core, we concatenate the output of all instances in order to graph a single line per OS.

The red line shows the results of FTQ running on Linux. There is a set of large noise spikes at the beginning while the executable is paged in and migrated to lightly loaded cores. Linux displays both large amounts of high-frequency noise and occasional large spikes. Such spikes, particularly aperiodic ones, are the anomalies that have been shown to be the most destructive to performance on large-scale clusters. It should be noted that the Linux we tested has already been tuned somewhat for an HPC environment and is running a minimal set of daemons.

The lines for PEC (in purple) and CNK (in blue) are on top of the Linux result line. The circle inset zooms in on the Linux and CNK results. As expected, CNK is a flat line, with only a slight deviation in results due to architectural noise amounting to +/- a single loop iteration. The FusedOS PEC iterations report a similar straight line, with a slightly higher high-frequency variation of approximately $+/-10$ loop iterations. Neither CNK nor FusedOS displays any spikes or variation outside of the high-frequency variation for the entire run. Thus, one would expect deterministic application behavior in both CNK and FusedOS.

The fourth line in the figure labeled STOC-4t shows the results from running 4 FTQ instances on the Linux STOC at the same time the FusedOS PECs were running their FTQ instances in parallel. First, this shows the heavy noise impact of saturating all hardware threads of a Linux instance with an increase in the number and duration of spike events. The absolute performance of each four-way SMT FTQ run is also about half that of a single-threaded instance because hardware threads share resources that are sufficient to fully satisfy only two threads, with the other two threads available to hide memory latency. Since FTQ has no memory dependence, all four hardware threads contend for the resources resulting in half the performance per instance. Considering that the FTQ PEC results were generated while also running FTQ on the STOC, this shows that no matter what the load is on the STOC, the PECs are unaffected, proving the effectiveness of noise isolation in FusedOS.

14.4.2 LAMMPS

LAMMPS is an HPC benchmark that simulates "particle-like" systems such as molecular dynamics. Comparing results between FusedOS and CNK, we see that FusedOS provides HPC application performance similar to CNK.

We employed the *3d Lennard-Jones melt* benchmark script from LAMMPS version *1jul12*. The LAMMPS documentation recommends running several processes per multicore node in a hybrid manner, each process using OpenMP to exploit several threads and coordinating with other processes via MPI. Figure 14.4 shows LAMMPS running on up to 256 compute nodes on FusedOS, CNK with 16 cores (CNK), and CNK with 14 cores (CNK*). CNK normally uses 16 cores. However, to understand the performance difference between FusedOS and CNK we also used CNK with 14 cores.

LAMMPS used one MPI rank per node. On FusedOS and CNK with 14 cores, LAMMPS used 28 threads. On CNK with 16 cores, LAMMPS used 24 threads. FusedOS is 6–8% slower than CNK with 16 cores. However, FusedOS is only 1–3% slower than CNK with 14 cores. While the core count explains some of the performance difference, the remaining difference is due to the overhead of the OpenMP system calls.

14.4.3 System Call Latency

To measure the performance of system call handling, we used lat_syscall from the lmbench micro-benchmark suite. Lat_syscall measures the performance of several

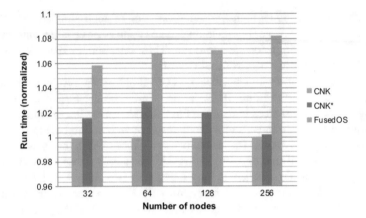

Fig. 14.4 Performance of LAMMPS in different operating environments

system calls including *null* and *getpid*. The *null* system call is *getpid* with its result cached by the C library, which avoids calls to the kernel.

Because *null* is just a call into the C Library, the times for Linux, CNK, and CL are similar, approximately 44 cycles. Both CNK and Linux handle *getpid* with just a kernel entry and kernel exit. As expected, *getpid* is faster in CNK than in Linux. CL is more expensive for several reasons. It requires an IPI for inter-core communication and potentially a thread switch to CL on the STOC. Table 14.1 summarizes those results.

As a direction for exploration, we changed the way CL waits for system calls. We replaced IPIs and process unblocking with a polling loop based on the memory reservation/waitrsv mechanism. This version is significantly faster, as the results in the "CL w/waitrsv" column show. However, using the waitrsv mechanism requires a dedicated hardware thread, and therefore removes a CPU from Linux.

14.5   Discussion

The benchmarks we presented in this chapter indicate that there are performance and noise advantages to our approach even on a homogeneous system. A clear area of exploration would be to look at what changes we would make in our approach, if we were designing for homogeneous hardware. Results from our micro-benchmarks suggest that we may want to service some system calls entirely on the application

Table 14.1 Linux, CNK, and CL system call latency

	Linux	CNK	CL	
			IPI	waitrsv
null	0.0277	0.0275	0.0269	0.0269
getpid	0.4014	0.2500	8.9082	2.2801

cores from which they originate, or perhaps split individual services between the PEC and the STOC.

Enabling asynchronous system calls for PEC I/O operations would help hide latency. We can potentially improve service times on the STOC by moving request handling from user space into the kernel, eliminating some of the latency associated with waking up the handling process. An alternate approach would be to consolidate CL service routines into a single thread so that we can afford to keep that thread ready and not have to wake it up with IPIs. Even in a heterogeneous system, we may be able to explore some of these design trade-offs by using specialized libraries on the PECs to limit the frequency and granularity of system call requests to the STOC.

There are definite similarities between our PEC FS control system and the facilities provided by a virtual machine monitor such as the Linux Kernel Virtual Machine (KVM). We opted to not use a VMM as part of the implementation of FusedOS due to concerns over the availability of hardware virtualization features on exascale systems. It stands to reason that if supervisor mode is eliminated for density and power reasons, then hypervisor mode will not be available, either. However, it would be interesting to quantify the trade-offs of such an approach to understand the overhead of using a VMM to control PECs.

Acknowledgements We would like to thank the following people for providing the Linux kernel and build environment used with FusedOS: Blake Fitch (IBM Watson Blue Gene Active Storage group), Heiko Schick, Peter Morjan (IBM Boebligen Exascale Innovation Center), and Thomas Gooding (IBM Rochester Blue Gene kernel team).

The Blue Gene/Q project has been supported and partially funded by Argonne National Laboratory and the Lawrence Livermore National Laboratory on behalf of the U.S. Department of Energy under subcontract no. B554331. This work is also supported by the U.S. Department of Energy under Award Numbers DE-SC0005365 and DE-SC0007103.

References

Ferreira, K. B., Bridges, P., & Brightwell, R. (2008). Characterizing application sensitivity to OS interference using kernel-level noise injection. In *International Conference for High Performance Computing, Networking, Storage and Analysis, 2008. SC 2008*.

Giampapa, M., Gooding, T., Inglett, T., & Wisniewski, R. (2010). Experiences with a lightweight supercomputer kernel: Lessons learned from Blue Gene's CNK. In *International Conference for High Performance Computing, Networking, Storage and Analysis (SC), 2010*.

Gschwind, M. (2012). Blue Gene/Q: Design for sustained multi-petaflop computing. In *Proceedings of the 26th ACM International Conference on Supercomputing* (pp. 245–246). ACM.

Haring, R., Ohmacht, M., Fox, T., Gschwind, M., Satterfield, D., Sugavanam, K., et al. (2012). The IBM Blue Gene/Q compute chip. *IEEE Micro, 32*(2), 48–60.

Plimpton, S. (1995). Fast parallel algorithms for short-range molecular dynamics. *Journal of Computational Physics, 117*(1), 1–19.

Chapter 15
Hobbes: A Multi-kernel Infrastructure for Application Composition

Brian Kocoloski, John Lange, Kevin Pedretti and Ron Brightwell

Abstract This chapter describes the Hobbes OS/R environment, which was designed to support the construction of sophisticated application compositions across multiple system software stacks called enclaves. The core idea of the approach is to enable each application component to execute in the system software environment that best matches its requirements. Hobbes then provides a set of cross-enclave composition mechanisms enabling the individual components to work together as part of a larger application workflow. Unique aspects of Hobbes compared to other multi-kernels include its emphasis on supporting application composition, its focus on providing cross-enclave performance isolation, and its use of hardware virtualization to enable the use of arbitrary OS/Rs. In particular, Hobbes leverages distributed, user-level resource management and hardware virtualization to allow underlying OS kernels to be largely agnostic of the multi-kernel environment, making it straightforward to add support for new OS kernels to Hobbes. We demonstrate Hobbes using a modern

This contribution has been co-authored by Sandia National Laboratories, a multimission laboratory managed and operated by National Technology & Engineering Solutions of Sandia, LLC, a wholly owned subsidiary of Honeywell International Inc., for the U.S. Department of Energy's National Nuclear Security Administration under contract DE-NA0003525, and by UT-Battelle, LLC under Contract No. DE-AC05-00OR22725 with the U.S. Department of Energy. The United States Government retains and the publisher, by accepting the contribution for publication, acknowledges that the United States Government retains a non-exclusive, paid-up, irrevocable, and worldwide license to publish or reproduce the published form of this manuscript, or allow others to do so, for United States Government purposes.

B. Kocoloski (✉)
Washington University in St. Louis, St. Louis, MO, USA
e-mail: brian.kocoloski@wustl.edu

J. Lange
University of Pittsburgh, Pittsburgh, PA, USA
e-mail: jacklange@cs.pitt.edu

K. Pedretti · R. Brightwell
Sandia National Laboratories, Albuquerque, NM, USA
e-mail: ktpedre@sandia.gov

R. Brightwell
e-mail: rbbrigh@sandia.gov

© Springer Nature Singapore Pte Ltd. 2019
B. Gerofi et al. (eds.), *Operating Systems for Supercomputers and High Performance Computing*, High-Performance Computing Series,
https://doi.org/10.1007/978-981-13-6624-6_15

Cray XC30m machine, showing the generality of OS/R configurations it supports, as well as its ability to leverage existing unmodified HPC system management tools.

15.1 Introduction

Large core counts and increasingly heterogeneous node architectures pose significant challenges for system software in large-scale High-Performance Computing (HPC) environments. Additionally, HPC jobs themselves are becoming more complex, with performance, energy, and power constraints forcing more of the application pipeline to be consolidated onto the same system. Instead of simply executing a single large-scale simulation, future supercomputing systems will likely need to support more complex workflows composed into a single job; the examples of these compositions include simulation and analytics pipelines (Lofstead et al. 2009; Zheng et al. 2013; Dayal et al. 2014), coupled HPC applications (Slattery et al. 2013), and introspective toolkits (Boehme et al. 2016). As the complexity of hardware and applications continue to grow, it is unlikely that a single operating system and runtime (OS/R), derived from commodity software, will be fully capable of effectively satisfying all that is asked of it.

For this reason, significant work has been undertaken to provide multiple specialized OS/R environments on a single node, wherein individual workload components can be selectively deployed into environments designed specifically for them. Recent years have seen significant efforts in the design of lightweight kernels (Giampapa et al. 2010; Lange et al. 2010), aero-kernels (Hale and Dinda 2015; Hale et al. 2016), and multi-kernels (Liu et al. 2009; Rhoden et al. 2011), each of which provides some capability for deploying specialized OS/R architectures to support a particular class of workloads. This chapter describes how we build off of these efforts to provide a core set of interfaces and resource management principles that make it straightforward to (1) leverage other new/experimental OS/Rs in future supercomputers and (2) orchestrate jobs, workflows, and other system activities across "multi-enclave" environments that span multiple OS/Rs.

While the mechanisms for deploying alternative OS/Rs in multi-enclave systems have been described elsewhere (Wisniewski et al. 2014; Ouyang et al. 2015; Gerofi et al. 2016), these systems have each focused on ad-hoc architectures designed around a single specific lightweight kernel OS. We claim that as the complexity of supercomputing systems grows along with the computational resources of each local node, there will be a greater need for the ability to support multiple arbitrary OS/R environments simultaneously, based on the mix of workloads in a given job composition. As an example, a future supercomputing job could be a multistage workflow consisting of a MPI based BSP application running in an optimized lightweight co-kernel, that feeds its results as input for a second simulation application running in a specialized many-task runtime OS/R environment, with the final data output flowing into a MapReduce style analytics code running in a VM. While the capabilities of instantiating and deploying each of these OS/R instances exist today, there is yet no way to effectively orchestrate all of these separate environments such that they can be deployed and managed effectively, and there is no core underlying infrastructure to deploy additional, perhaps yet undeveloped, OS/Rs in a multi-enclave system. In this chapter, we describe the system architecture necessary to make this possible.

At the heart of our work is a distributed user-level resource management framework that allows independent system software components to allocate and manage raw physical resources. Each software component with resource management capabilities is a first class "entity" in our framework and is able to directly allocate hardware resources from a distributed database. This database is stored externally from any OS on the system, is directly accessible through shared memory, and provides access to hardware resources through the use of abstract identifying handles. In this way, hardware resources can be directly assigned to components at any layer in the software stack, including operating system kernels, application runtimes, and even individual applications themselves. Instead of implementing allocation policies, the underlying system software is instead only required to provide *mapping* functions that translate abstract resource identifiers to underlying physical hardware resources, thereby making these resources accessible to the allocating entity.

In this chapter, we leverage the publicly available Hobbes OS/R project infrastructure (Brightwell et al. 2013; Kocoloski et al. 2015). The Hobbes project proposed that future exascale supercomputing systems should feature extensive support for combining multiple applications into a composed job that could be simultaneously executed across a single exascale system, with each application component executing inside its own dedicated enclave. In this work we extend the Hobbes model through the addition of new resource management interfaces, APIs for cross-OS/R communication and coordination, and services to integrate job management tools with arbitrary multi-OS/R infrastructures. The contributions of our work are:

- We present a set of design principles, based on abstract resource representations and user-level resource management, that make it possible to leverage specialized OS/R instances in supercomputers.
- We discuss our node management service, Leviathan, which provides system services and APIs for composing applications across OS/R instances in a modern multi-enclave HPC system infrastructure. These APIs are designed and implemented at user-level and require only limited kernel-level support.
- We discuss the system requirements needed to launch multi-enclave applications with existing HPC management tools (e.g., Cray ALPS tools).
- We demonstrate that our system based on these principles can support the deployment of unmodified applications using unmodified tools in an OS/R-agnostic fashion.

15.2 The Hobbes Exascale OS/R

The vision for the Hobbes Exascale OS/R (Brightwell et al. 2013; Kocoloski et al. 2015), illustrated in Fig. 15.1, is to compose HPC application workloads across multiple system software stacks called enclaves. In this chapter, we perform research

Fig. 15.1 High-level
overview of the Hobbes
OS/R supporting a composed
in-situ application

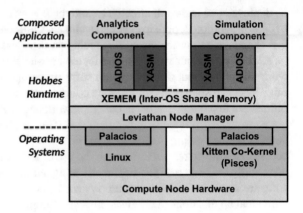

in the context of Hobbes-enabled systems, based on a Cray Linux operating system coupled with a set of HPC-tailored OS/Rs that have been previously incorporated into the Hobbes framework. Sections 15.3 and 15.2.6 will discuss the design criteria and implementation, respectively, of the Leviathan node management service in the context of Hobbes- enabled systems. In this section, we briefly discuss the capabilities of the existing core system software components for deploying multi-enclave OS/Rs.

15.2.1 Kitten

Kitten (Lange et al. 2010) is a special-purpose OS kernel designed to provide a simple, lightweight environment for executing massively parallel HPC applications. Like previous lightweight kernel OSs, such as Catamount (Kelly et al. 2008) and CNK (Giampapa et al. 2010), Kitten uses simple resource management policies (e.g., physically contiguous memory layouts) and provides direct user-level access to network hardware (OS bypass). A key design goal of Kitten is to execute the target workload—highly scalable parallel applications with nontrivial communication and synchronization requirements—with higher performance and more repeatable performance that is possible with general-purpose operating systems.

15.2.2 Pisces

Pisces (Ouyang et al. 2015) is a co-kernel architecture designed to allow multiple specialized OS/R instances to execute concurrently on the same local node. Pisces enables the decomposition of a node's hardware resources (CPU cores, memory blocks, and I/O devices) into partitions that are fully managed by independent system software stacks, including OS kernels, device drivers, and I/O management layers.

Using Pisces, a local compute node can initialize multiple Kitten (Lange et al. 2010) OS instances as co-kernels executing alongside an unmodified Linux host OS. Full co-kernel instances may be created and destroyed in response to workload requirements (e.g., application launch and termination), or individual resources may be revoked from or added to running instances. Specific details of these operations are presented elsewhere (Ouyang et al. 2015).

15.2.3 Palacios

Palacios (Lange et al. 2010) is an open-source VMM designed to be embeddable into diverse host OSs and currently fully supports integration with Linux and Kitten host environments. When integrated with Kitten co-kernel instances supported by Pisces, Kitten and Palacios act as a lightweight hypervisor providing full system virtualization and isolation for unmodified guest OSs. The combination of Kitten and Palacios has been demonstrated to provide near-native performance for large-scale HPC applications using lightweight VMs running atop a Kitten host environment (Lange et al. 2011).

15.2.4 XPMEM

The XEMEM shared memory architecture (Kocoloski and Lange 2015) supports application-level shared memory communication across enclaves (co-kernels and/or Palacios VMs). XEMEM exports a user-level API that is backward compatible with the API exported by SGI/Cray's XPMEM shared memory implementation for Linux systems (Woodacre et al. 2003), which allows processes to selectively export regions of their address space to be mapped by other processes. Because the XEMEM API is supported across each enclave OS/R environment, any application targeting the API can be deployed across any multi-enclave topology without modification. XEMEM provides a single global shared memory address space through the use of globally unique memory segment IDs managed by a global name service. In addition to naming, the name service also provides global discovery of shared memory regions allowing applications to transparently map memory regions from any other OS/R instance.

15.2.5 HPMMAP

HPMMAP (Kocoloski and Lange 2014) is a specialized memory manager for Linux kernels, designed to provide lightweight memory management functionality through a guaranteed large page mappings and pre-allocated memory allocations for regular Linux processes. HPMMAP is implemented as a Linux kernel module and provides transparent memory management for HPC applications by interposing system calls for memory allocation (e.g., *brk*, *mmap*, etc.) HPMMAP is thus an example of a specialized entity that manages resources at the kernel-level for HPC workloads.

15.2.6 Leviathan

The Leviathan Node Manager provides system services and APIs for managing to compute node resources and orchestrating multiple OS/R instances running on the Hobbes NVL. Leviathan runs as a service daemon in the bootstrap OS/R environment and is responsible for initializing the system, collecting resource information, "offlining" the set of resources that will be managed, and exporting the system state via an in-memory database stored on a shared memory segment. Leviathan follows a distributed management model, so the majority of the management activities take place in independent client service processes that execute in each separate OS/R instance. Software components become "Leviathan enabled" by linking against the Leviathan client library. Beyond providing a centralized storage location for the whole system state, Leviathan also exports a set of common APIs and mechanisms available to each OS/R and application running in the system. Each of these capabilities is included in the client library and are accessible to any application that wishes to use them. During application component process creation, the Leviathan library automatically executes a series of initialization functions that map the Leviathan database into the application's local address space, and then enables a set of APIs and interfaces for the application to use.

15.3 Orchestrating Specialized OS/Rs

Exascale system software is trending toward specialized OS/R architectures (Wisniewski et al. 2014; Ouyang et al. 2015; Gerofi et al. 2016; Hale and Dinda 2015; Hale et al. 2016; Kocoloski and Lange 2014; Zounmevo et al. 2015). In this work, we build off of the recent efforts of the HPC systems software community in specialized OS/R architectures. Specifically, we provide a core set of interfaces and resource management principles that make it straightforward to (1) leverage these and additional arbitrary OS/Rs in future supercomputers and (2) orchestrate jobs, workflows, and other system activities across multiple enclaves in multi-OS/R based systems.

15.3.1 System Components

The primary motivation behind the majority of specialized OS/R architectures is the desire to provide customized resource management approaches that have been optimized to a specific subset of workloads. These systems allow low overhead access to hardware resources with a small set of abstractions tailored to the needs of the target applications. As such, deploying and managing a collection of these OS/Rs requires a unified approach to allocating and assigning resources for each system software layer. To provide this capability, we have implemented a node-level resource management framework that operates outside the context of an operating system. In our model, resources are dynamically assigned to system software instances via user-level operations that are independent of any other OS/R on the node.

Underlying our approach is a very thin set of abstractions that are used to represent and manage individual hardware resources. Our approach operates on two primary classes of objects: *Entities* which are defined as any software components capable of directly managing a set of hardware resources and *Resources* which are a set of hardware units capable of being independently managed by a given *Entity*.

Hobbes Entities

In Hobbes, *entities* are any piece of software that is able to directly manage a raw piece of physical hardware. This definition intentionally does not specify at what layer of the system software stack the entity is operating at. It is possible for a Hobbes entity to be an operating system kernel, a runtime environment, or even an application itself. This approach allows various software components to effectively bypass resource management policies of underlying system software layers when the features provided by those layers are not needed.

Hobbes Resources

A resource in Hobbes is any piece of hardware that is functionally "isolatable" from the other hardware resources on a node. In general, resources are coarse-grained components collected by decomposing the full set of hardware resources on a node. For example, a resource would consist of an entire CPU core or a large chunk of contiguous physical memory (the size is configurable, but is typically 128 MB). Resources do not "belong" to any given OS/R but are rather dynamically allocated to entities as they are needed.

In our system, all resources are represented in the node information database with an opaque and globally unique abstract resource ID. Database entries identify the relevant physical characteristics of the resource—e.g., for a memory region, its NUMA zone, size, etc.—as well as provide an abstract resource handle. When an entity allocates a resource, it receives the resource handle. While this handle has no direct utility to the allocating entity itself, it can be passed to its underlying OS kernel which is responsible for mapping the associated physical hardware into the entity's context. This abstraction allows a level of resource identity virtualization that becomes more necessary the higher up the system software stack an entity resides, which is especially true for VM-based environments where physical identities can often conflict with virtualized resources.

15.3.2 User-Level Resource Management

The primary resource management layer of Hobbes is a user-level service that provides distributed access for each *entity* on the system. This is accomplished using a node-level information service that tracks the state of each hardware resource and OS/R instance/entity. All of this state is collected and stored in a globally accessible in-memory database created by a user-level daemon. The database itself is stored in raw physical memory that is explicitly mapped into the address space of each entity that wishes to access it. The database allows distributed operations so entities are capable of directly manipulating the database state, which in turn allows entities to independently allocate certain resources directly as they are needed without having to go through a centralized service. While this model does assume that each entity is a trusted component, for the workloads we target this is acceptable as each component is assumed to be a cooperative member of a composition submitted as a single job. In addition, our system reserves a (configurable) subset of resources for use by a management OS/R instance (typically the booting OS), and also supports pre-allocations driven by a job control service.

Performing resource management at user level has two key advantages: (1) performance and (2) OS generality. HPC applications prefer to manage raw hardware resources with specialized, simplified operations for memory management, scheduling, and communication. Thus it is critical that Hobbes resources be units that are physically addressable and manageable directly by Hobbes entities. Additionally, user-level management makes it simpler to incorporate arbitrary specialized OS instances. Enclave OSs are only required to perform straightforward mapping operations that translate each Hobbes resource's abstract representation to a physically addressable object. This makes it simpler to integrate new OSs into our system as they do not need to directly negotiate access to hardware with other kernels in the system.

Figure 15.2 gives a high-level view of our approach. Each OS/R is managed by a single control process, or "init task", that connects to the node information database on behalf of the underlying operating system. These init tasks are responsible for performing the necessary user-level operations to track the state of its local OS/R entity (e.g., resources allocated, processes running). While it is not shown in the figure, any user-level task (application and/or runtime) is also capable of connecting to the database in order to directly allocate resources.

15.3.3 Role of Operating Systems

A key principle we have followed in our system design is that the user-level interfaces to our management service should be abstract, meaning that the protocols should be based on abstract data representations. This allows the protocol to be widely portable between different potential architectures by relying on this identity virtualization. At

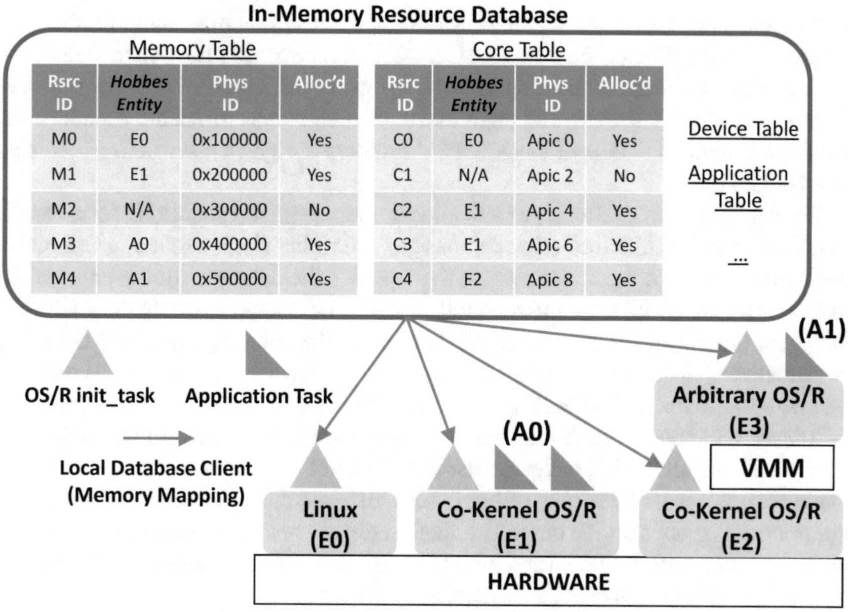

In-Memory Resource Database

Memory Table				Core Table				
Rsrc ID	*Hobbes Entity*	Phys ID	Alloc'd	Rsrc ID	*Hobbes Entity*	Phys ID	Alloc'd	
M0	E0	0x100000	Yes	C0	E0	Apic 0	Yes	Device Table
M1	E1	0x200000	Yes	C1	N/A	Apic 2	No	Application
M2	N/A	0x300000	No	C2	E1	Apic 4	Yes	Table
M3	A0	0x400000	Yes	C3	E1	Apic 6	Yes	
M4	A1	0x500000	Yes	C4	E2	Apic 8	Yes	...

(A1)

OS/R init_task   Application Task

Local Database Client
(Memory Mapping)

(A0)

Arbitrary OS/R
(E3)

VMM

Linux
(E0)

Co-Kernel OS/R
(E1)

Co-Kernel OS/R
(E2)

HARDWARE

Fig. 15.2 High-level view of resource management in an arbitrary multi-OS/R system

the same time, the *lower layer* protocols used by the underlying system software—
that is, the operating systems—are guided by different constraints. At this layer, in
order to facilitate easy integration of other alternative OS/Rs, resources should be
represented by their true underlying hardware IDs, as the hardware-level interfaces
are guaranteed to be shared between every OS kernel, and each OS should already
have support for operating on those resource representations.

The primary operation of an OS in our architecture is to provide a *mapping* of
those abstract resources IDs allocated by a local entity to the raw physical hardware
they reference. Conceptually, the act of mapping a resource can be thought of as a
two-step process: (1) conversion from the abstract identifier that uniquely identifies
the resource to a raw physical ID and (2) bootstrapping or otherwise configuring
privileged hardware state to physically enable the resource for access by the user-
level process.

The details of the mapping process depend on the underlying resource being
mapped. For memory, resource handles take the form of XEMEM (Kocoloski and
Lange 2015) segids, and by default each 128 MB region of physical memory in
the system is associated with a single segid. The mapping process consists of
translating a segid to a range of page frame numbers associated with the memory region, and then mapping these page frames into the entity's address space.
To perform the mapping, XEMEM leverages a distributed communication protocol
whereby OS kernels (including virtual machine and native operating systems) pass
messages via hardware primitives (hypercalls, interrupts) to communicate the list of

raw page frame IDs for the segment. Additionally, if virtual machines are involved, a hypervisor performs a final layer of translation, converting host page frame lists to guest page frames, and passing them to the guest OS. Once a list of page frames is received, the OS updates the page tables of the process to enable access to the memory. Extended details of the XEMEM protocol are given elsewhere (Kocoloski and Lange 2015).

To map CPU cores, after a process allocates an abstract resource ID for a core, it first queries the node information database to determine if it is executing in a native enclave or a VM. In the native case, it then queries the database for the physical ID of the core—its APIC ID—and then tells its local OS kernel to query the ACPI/MP tables for this ID and boot the core into the OS. In the latter case in which the entity is virtualized, instead of issuing this request to its own kernel, the entity sends a message to the init task executing in the host OS kernel, which performs the same ACPI/MP table querying to boot the core, and then adds a new virtual core to the VM where the allocating entity exists. The host init task sends a message back to the guest process with the new (virtual) APIC ID, and the guest process informs the guest kernel to boot up the core. The final hardware resources currently supported by our architecture, PCI devices, are supported in a similar fashion to CPU cores, with PCI addresses (bus:device:fn) replacing APIC IDs.

On the Complexity of OS Integration

While this resource management architecture adds several new components to the system in the form of abstract resource identifiers and resource mappings, we note that it is explicitly designed to push the complexities to user space as much as possible. This was an explicit design decision made in order to ease the adoption of new and alternative OS/Rs. As a result, in order to incorporate a new OS/R as a virtualized enclave in our system, there are only two features it must implement: the ability to dynamically add and remove hardware resources based on their physical IDs, and an XEMEM driver.

For the former, we note that Linux-based enclaves already support dynamic resource addition/removal via the "hotplug" APIs, which are defined for each of the CPU, memory, and PCI subsystems. For the latter, the XEMEM system provides Linux support in the form of a Linux kernel module. Thus, no modifications need to be made to the base Linux enclave kernel, and no modifications need to be made to guest OSs based on Linux either.

In order to gauge the effort required to provide these capabilities in other operating systems, we argue both qualitatively and quantitatively that the efforts are not overly significant. First, as discussed above, the OS-level interfaces required in our system (in order to support XEMEM) operate on physical hardware primitives, leveraging inter-processor interrupts (IPIs), hypercalls, and page frames in order to communicate across enclave boundaries. Thus, the majority of the XEMEM driver can likely be easily adopted from one OS to the other as these mechanisms almost certainly exist already, or can be easily added as they do not rely on any OS-specific subsystems. As to the complexity of performing dynamic hardware initialization, this could be more complex based on how the OS manages physical resources, but again we argue that

Table 15.1 New code written to enable integration of the Kitten LWK in Hobbes

Kernel subsystem		Lines of code added	
		OS neutral	OS specific
XEMEM		5,518	68
Resource hotplug operations	CPU	166	161
	Memory	104	71
	PCI	0	0
Total		5,788	300

physical resource discovery and teardown mechanisms are likely provided already by most OS kernels.

To provide a quantitative argument, we analyzed the lines of code that were added to the Kitten kernel to integrate into our system. Table 15.1 shows the lines of code for both the XEMEM kernel subsystem as well as for resource hotplug operations, and breaks each down by the number of lines we consider to be OS neutral, and those that are OS specific, meaning they invoke a separate kernel subsystem as opposed to direct hardware manipulation functions. For XEMEM, while the kernel driver consists of over 5,000 lines of code, only about 1% is OS specific, with most of the 1% being wrapper functions that invoke Kitten's existing utilities to walk and update process page tables. The resource hotplugging mechanisms are more evenly split between OS specific and OS neutral operations, but in both cases required minimal changes of only a few hundred lines of code. These functions essentially add or remove entries from accounting structures in the kernel, and then issue hardware operations to disable the device (e.g., disabling interrupts and halting the CPU, unmapping kernel page tables, etc.). Due to its nature as a lightweight kernel that by design does not provide much infrastructure beyond basic hardware configuration, we consider these measurements to be a reasonable upper bound on the effort needed to incorporate other alternative OS/Rs in our system.

15.3.4 Inter-Enclave Interfaces

Beyond tracking the state of resources and entities, our system also provides inter-faces and communication channels between enclaves. These mechanisms are used to enable high-level workflow compositions and system services. In order to increase portability between OS/Rs, these mechanisms are implemented on top of the raw resources that are already tracked by the system. The design follows the same paradigm we used for managing resources: communication channels are exposed as high-level interfaces executing at user level, however, they are implemented using low-level hardware features.

For example, our framework provides message passing communication channels between two endpoints running on any OS/R in the system. The operation of the channel is primarily performed in user space via shared memory operations that are implemented on top of raw physical memory allocated directly from the resource database. Each message queue is identified via an abstract identifier stored in the database, that can, in turn, be translated to a resource handle associated with a given region of physical memory. Therefore, whenever an endpoint wishes to establish a message queue it locates the identifier in the database, translates it to a memory resource handle, and passes that to the underlying OS to create a mapping for it. Once the mapping is complete at both endpoints, the shared memory channel is available in the address space of each user-level process. Blocking based communication is handled similarly by associating an interrupt resource (implemented using IPIs) with the shared memory region.

15.4 Leviathan Node Manager

Our node management system is implemented as a component in the Hobbes environment. The foundation of the system is the Leviathan Node Manager which runs as a service daemon in the bootstrap OS/R environment. The service daemon is responsible for initializing the system, collecting resource information, "offlining" the set of resources that will be managed, and exporting the system state via an in-memory database stored on a shared memory segment. As stated earlier, Leviathan follows a distributed management model, so the majority of the management activities take place in independent client service processes that execute in each separate OS/R instance. Software components become "Leviathan enabled" by linking against the Leviathan client library. Beyond providing a centralized storage location for the whole system state, Leviathan also exports a set of common APIs and mechanisms available to each OS/R and application running in the system. Each of these capabilities are included in the client library and are accessible to any application that wishes to use them. During process creation the Leviathan library automatically executes a series of initialization functions that map the Leviathan database into the application's local address space, and then enables a set of APIs and interfaces for the application to use.

15.4.1 Node Information Database

The core of Leviathan is an in-memory NoSQL database that is used to store all of the necessary state in the system. The database is based on a modified version of WhiteDB (2017), and provides lightweight access to every Leviathan entity on the node. The database is stored entirely in a single large contiguous memory allocation, which allows it to be easily exported via shared memory to other address spaces running in entirely separate OS/R instances. The NoSQL semantics of the database also allows low overhead concurrent access for each control process in the system. Database operations are applied directly by the invoking process, and are protected via a mutual exclusion mechanism embedded into the database storage structure

Table 15.2 Leviathan node information database row types

Database record	Description
HDB_ENCLAVE	Enclave record representing an OS/R instance
HDB_MEM	Memory resource (128 MB of contiguous RAM)
HDB_CPU	CPU resource (1 CPU core)
HDB_PCI	PCI device resource
HDB_XEMEM_SEGMENT	Exported shared memory region
HDB_XEMEM_ATTACHMENT	Remote attachment to a shared memory region
HDB_APP	Application record tracking the components of a composed job

itself. Thus, each client process need only map in the single shared memory segment in order to have full access to the database.

Table 15.2 shows the most significant database records stored by Leviathan. Each record corresponds to a resource, entity, or interface currently available on the system. All of the state information tracked by Leviathan is stored as a row in the database and thus provides a single point of integration for any new OS/R architecture. Because the database is managed at user level, an OS/R does not require extensive modification in order to support its interfaces. The engineering required for system integration is exported to user space control processes and is based on a set of interfaces already provided as part of the Leviathan client library.

15.4.2 Leviathan Interfaces

Leviathan provides a range of interfaces and communication mechanisms to each client process running on a system. These interfaces form the backbone of communication and coordination across the system, and allow the integration of each OS/R instance into a global management service. Leviathan provides a range of basic communication building blocks, as well as higher level interfaces built on top of them. The two fundamental interfaces on which Leviathan depends are shared memory segments and IPI-basednotifications.

Shared Memory

Fundamentally, all system communication is handled via shared memory operations. Leviathan leverages the XEMEM (Kocoloski and Lange 2015) cross-enclave shared memory architecture, which allows processes to selectively export regions of their address space. XEMEM segments allow exporting memory at the page granularity, and ensure that each exported segment is fully allocated and pinned to underlying physical memory. This approach allows each OS/R to map in a shared segment by simply adding the appropriate physical pages to its own internal page tables. This allows any OS/R in the system to support our shared memory interface by implementing basic page table operations that are most likely already available.

This also avoids interface complexity that would arise from each OS/R having to understand a higher level memory segment representation (such as a Linux vm_area_struct), and instead standardizes the interface semantics to match the underlying hardware representation.

Signals

In addition to raw shared memory, Leviathan also supports a signaling framework that allows asynchronous notifications to be associated with a given shared memory region. These signals allow the implementation of blocking semantics over a shared memory communication channel, in order to avoid the necessity of polling or other out of band notification mechanisms. Signals are implemented as a special type of shared memory segment stored in the Leviathan database. The memory segment is also allowed to be empty (or sized 0) to allow for bare signals without the overhead of an associated memory mapping. This approach allows Leviathan to maintain persistent notification channels using the same resource identifiers used for shared memory. The underlying implementation for Leviathan signals also follows the principle of hardware-level representation. At the OS-level, a signal is assumed to be a single IRQ vector assigned to a given core's APIC. This allows signal transmission to be triggered through a standard IPI send operation that can occur from any CPU in the system. Like the shared memory implementation, modern OS/Rs are likely to include IPI interfaces as well as interrupt handling mechanisms, so supporting these operations does not require extensive modifications. Signals are differentiated by the IRQ vector they are received at, and so also do not require extensive protocols for multiplexing/demultiplexing interrupts in order to decode the recipient.

Message Queues

Shared memory and asynchronous signals are the two fundamental communication channels on which the rest of the Leviathan interfaces are constructed. Here we will describe one such interface that is designed to allow message passing based communication between multiple entities running on the system (but potentially in separate OS/R environments). Message passing in Leviathan is achieved using a Message Queue abstraction that is provided by the Leviathan library. Message queues are essentially just a single shared memory segment exported by a process, and an associated reserved signal. These message queues are registered with the Leviathan database and so are discoverable by any other entity on the system. An entity wishing to send a message first attaches to the message queue of the intended recipient, which results in the mapping of the message queue memory segment into its own address space. The sender then adds its message to the tail of the queue, and then notifies the recipient by sending an IPI to the destination specified in the queue structure. At the receiver, the IPI is propagated up to the waiting process which dequeues the message and issues a reply or ACK indicating the message was received. Message queues implement a many-to-one communication model, in that multiple entities is allowed to simultaneously send messages to the same recipient's queue. The messages themselves contain the identity of the sender if it is needed. Concurrency between multiple senders is achieved through the use of memory based locks embedded into the queue data structures. Message queues are one of the core services used by enclaves in our system. Messages are sent between enclaves to create virtual machines, launch applications, and transfer files between enclaves.

Naming/Discovery

Finally, the Leviathan database also provides a key/value service to store arbitrary data for specific user-defined purposes. An example use of the key/value service is to provide "human-readable" XEMEM `segids`, storing a user-defined string as a key with the value being the `segid`. We use this service to query segids that are created for enclave command queues; if an enclave's unique ID is "X", it allocates a `segid` for its command queue and stores it with a key of "enclave-X-cmd-queue" in the key/value store. This interface also makes it simple for individual applications of a composed workflow to map each other's memory by registering named regions that map context-specific data. For example, simulation and analysis components of an in-situ workflow can map a special human readable `segid` and use it to transfer data between components.

15.4.3 Launching a Job with Leviathan

To illustrate some of the core capabilities of the Leviathan node manager, in this section we discuss how the process of launching an application leverages various Leviathan services.

A high-level view of the job launch process is illustrated in Figs. 15.3 and 15.4. The user launches their application with the standard Cray `aprun` utility, using standard `aprun` options to select node layouts and other relevant job parameters. However, instead of directly invoking the application, the user executes a Leviathan utility responsible for deploying the application into the Hobbes environment. Figure 15.3 illustrates the difference between a regular aprun and one that leverages the Leviathan infrastructure. The user passes a pointer to an XML file which contains the specification for the enclave in which the application will execute, which includes the resources (cores, memory blocks, PCI devices) that will be assigned to the new OS/R, as well as the OS/Rs kernel image and the Leviathan control process that will manage the enclave. The user also specifies resources for the application itself,

```
#!/bin/sh
# Regular Cray aprun
aprun -N 1 -n 1 -L 60 sh -c /tmp/hobbes_install/a.out
# Hobbes-capable Cray aprun
aprun -N 1 -n 1 -L 60 sh -c \
    ./hobbes_launch_app /tmp/hobbes_install/enclave_config.xml \
    --use-large-pages --heap_size=128 --stack_size=64 \
    /tmp/hobbes_install/a.out
```

Fig. 15.3 Example shell script to launch an application

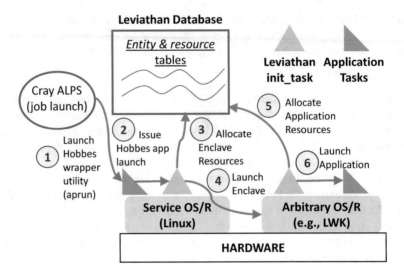

Fig. 15.4 The Leviathan infrastructure

including how much memory will be needed to map its process' address spaces (e.g., the heap and stack sizes). Finally, the user passes the path to the (unmodified) application executable.

The Hobbes utility parses the provided enclave configuration file and sends a message to the Leviathan service daemon, including the specification for the new enclave and the application to run. The service daemon allocates resources from the Leviathan resource database and launches the enclave on the requested resources. Note that the enclave can be launched as a lightweight "co-kernel" based on the Pisces architecture (Ouyang et al. 2015), or any arbitrary OS/R can be launched into a virtual machine via the Palacios hypervisor (Lange et al. 2010). Once the new enclave boots, its control process maps the Leviathan database into its address space, updates the state of the new enclave to be successfully initialized, and sends a message to the service daemon indicating it has booted.

At this point, the service daemon sends a message to the new enclave with the specification for the application. The enclave's control process then allocates the requested resources from the database, maps them into the local OS/R, creates the address space for the application's processes (heap, stack, etc.) on top of these resources, and launches the processes on the requested cores.

15.5 System Integration

One of the core tenets of our approach to orchestrating multi-enclave systems are to support full system integration with existing system management tools. Although we envision that composed workloads will be explicitly cognizant of the nature of multi-enclave systems, and that applications will be tailored to the specific capabilities of the underlying OS/R, it is nevertheless critical to provide a single system image (SSI) (Riesen and Maccabe 2011) for services that are unaware of the distributed nature of our multi-enclave system infrastructure. This section describes our approach to providing an SSI in the context of jobs compiled against Cray's MPI library and launched via Cray's ALPS (Application-Level Placement Scheduler) (Karo et al. 2006) software suite. We assume an infrastructure such as that described in Fig. 15.4. Specifically, we assume the "Service OS/R" is based on the Compute Node Linux (CNL) runtime environment (Kaplan 2007), with a target enclave based on an arbitrary specialized OS/R.

Though our efforts and resulting system capabilities are demonstrated in the context of these specific tools, we believe our approach and lessons learned from this experience are applicable to a broad range of system management tools, as our underlying infrastructure is not specifically tailored to the Cray runtime environment.

15.5.1 Shadow Processes

As Fig. 15.4 demonstrates, application components are launched by a set of Leviathan utilities that are not direct child processes of the Cray `aprun` utility. To provide compatibility and a single point of control in this system, each application launch thus needs to create a set of "shadow" processes in the native Cray service OS/R environment to provide a single point of control. These shadow processes have a one-to-one correspondence with each process that is launched into an external OS/R enclave. At the simplest level, these shadow processes are responsible for initialization and to provide a seamless notification to the Cray `aprun` daemon when the remote process terminates. Beyond these basic tasks, shadow processes are also responsible for propagating signals issued by the `aprun` process to destination processes, as well as for executing specific system calls on behalf of the associated application process. System call invocation is necessary whenever the application's OS/R does not implement a required piece of functionality. The most common scenario that requires this functionality is if a specialized OS/R does not include the necessary driver support for a specialized interconnect device.

System call invocation is enabled through the presence of a consistent one-to-one memory mapping between the actual application process and its associated shadow process. This shared memory layout is implemented using an address space unification approach where the shadow and application processes have identical virtual and physical address spaces. This allows for system calls to be executed from the shadow process context without requiring escape analysis for system call parameters or complex machinery to handle address space modifications. We discuss this approach further in Sect. 15.5.2.

In addition, we also ensure that the application environment is consistent across both the shadow and remote processes. Shadow process PIDs map one to one with the PIDs assigned to the application process running in a separate enclave. Whenever an application is launched in a specialized OS/R, it specifies the PID it needs to match the PID allocated for the shadow process in the service OS/R. This unification is required when a shadow process issues system calls on behalf of an application process to initialize network devices. Such calls are needed, for example, to initialize the Cray Aries network device (Alverson et al. 2012). Shadow processes also pass their full environment to the application processes. This allows the application process to access special environment settings specified by Cray's utilities, such as ALPS_APP_PE, which provides a process with its unique MPI rank.

15.5.2 Systemcall Forwarding

In cases where system calls are not supported by the application's local OS/R (e.g., network device drivers), shadow processes are required to execute system calls on behalf of the application. Our system implements a system call forwarding approach to provide these services. However, unlike the previous system call forwarding approaches (Gerofi et al. 2016), our approach is implemented using user-level mechanisms and so is not coupled to any specific co-kernel architecture.

Our approach to system call forwarding has two main components. First, forwarding of system calls is decoupled from any underlying co-kernel or OS-specific architecture. In our system, system calls that is unhandled by a local OS/R are first passed to the local OS/R's control process, and then forwarded to the shadow process running in the service OS/R via the Leviathan message queue interface (see Sect. 15.4.2). This approach allows Leviathan to export the same mechanism to multiple different OS/R environments, including OS/Rs that may be executing in virtual machines for which there is no available tightly coupled co-kernel interface. We note that while our approach requires several additional context switches as it relies on a separate user-level process to handle the necessary communication, most system calls are not performance sensitive in these applications (e.g., network devices such as the Cray Aries only use system calls to initialize devices and map device memory into process address spaces; all networking operations on the critical path is full OS bypass and performed via memory mapped I/O).

The second component of our infrastructure is the use of an address space unification approach that makes it possible to forward system call arguments without performing any data marshaling for parameters. Our approach is to unify the address spaces of the application and shadow processes with the XEMEM interface, as illustrated in Fig. 15.5. As the figure demonstrates, the address space for the application processes (the upper right-hand side of the figure) is mapped into the shadow processes at the same virtual addresses (upper left). Similarly, the virtual address spaces of the shadow processes (lower left) are mapped into the application processes at the same virtual addresses (lower right). We note that this approach is completely OS-agnostic, requiring only that the two OS/Rs can be configured to map process address spaces to nonoverlapping regions.[1]

---

[1]In Linux, address space layouts for the shadow processes can be set with the "–mcmodel" and "-pie" parameters to the gcc compiler.

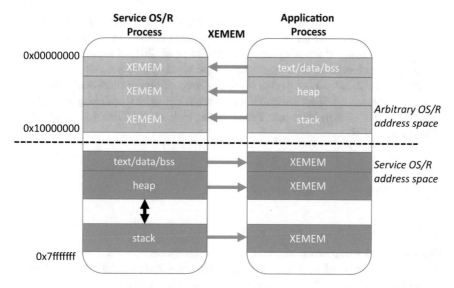

Fig. 15.5 Address space unification between a shadow process and an arbitrary OS/R process

15.5.3   Unix Signals

To orchestrate command and control of jobs in the Hobbes infrastructure requires the ability to forward signals between the service OS/R's shadow processes and the processes in the application's OS/R. Each shadow process registers a signal handler for core Unix signals, and when it receives them from the aprun utility (e.g., SIGINT to kill the application), it forwards them to the destination processes. The shadow processes also monitor the state of the application processes, and terminate themselves when the application completes to notify aprun of the job completion.

15.6   Evaluation

In this section, we present an experimental evaluation, leveraging the Leviathan node manager to demonstrate the capabilities of the Hobbes OS/R. The primary goals of our evaluation are to demonstrate the following three key ideas: (1) based on its OS-agnostic design, our infrastructure is sufficiently flexible to support a variety of different OS/R configurations; (2) our use of hardware virtualization to support non-co-kernel OS/Rs does not induce significant performance degradation of key target applications; (3) existing, unmodified job administration tools can launch unmodified applications in each enclave configuration we evaluate.

We emphasize that our evaluation is not designed to demonstrate the value of multi-enclave system architectures, but rather to demonstrate that our system supports them and can leverage unmodified toolchains on top of them. Results showing the performance benefits of these architectures have been demonstrated previously, both by designers of the Hobbes system (Kocoloski et al. 2015; Ouyang et al. 2015; Kocoloski and Lange 2015) using many of the same system software components we evaluate here, as well as by other research groups studying additional lightweight and experimental OS/R architectures (Wisniewski et al. 2014; Gerofi et al. 2016; Giampapa et al. 2010; Hale and Dinda 2015; Hale et al. 2016; Liu et al. 2009; Rhoden et al. 2011).

15.6.1 System Infrastructure

Evaluation Platform

Our evaluation was performed on a Cray XC30m testbed system. Each node of the system consists of dual-socket, 12-core 2.4 GHz "Ivy-Bridge" Intel Xeon E5-2695v2 processors with 32 GB RAM per socket. The compute nodes are interconnected with the CrayAries network (Alverson et al. 2012). Testing was performed during a three-day window in which we were given root access to 32 of the compute nodes to reboot into the Hobbes infrastructure.

Enclave Configurations

For each of our experiments, we measured the performance of the same application binary in three different system software environments: (1) the native Linux operating system provided by Cray, (2) a co-kernel environment leveraging Pisces (Ouyang et al. 2015) to create a single Kitten (Lange et al. 2010) co-kernel alongside the native Cray OS, and (3) a virtual machine environment in which the Kitten lightweight kernel runs as a guest VM hosted by the Palacios (Lange et al. 2010) VMM. For this final configuration, the virtual machine itself was hosted by a Pisces co-kernel. For each configuration, testing was performed on a single socket of each compute node with the workload running on eight cores of the socket.

   We note that while our evaluation is limited to a set of two different OS kernels (Linux and Kitten), the third configuration in which we boot Kitten as a guest OS leverages a build of Kitten in which no Pisces co-kernel interfaces are compiled into the kernel image. Thus, this configuration is arbitrary in the sense that the guest kernel has no explicit awareness of the multi-enclave system configuration. The only components of the guest OS required to support this configuration are the XEMEM driver and resource hotplug mechanisms as discussed in Sect. 15.3.3. Nevertheless, in future work, we plan to leverage additional specialized OS/Rs.

   Because our experiments are performed across a 32-node cluster, each OS/R must have the ability to access the Cray Aries network device. Furthermore, because the Kitten kernel lacks an Aries driver, we use shadow processes (see Sect. 15.5.1) to issue system calls to the network device on behalf of the application processes. This support is provided by the user-level system call forwarding mechanism described in Sect. 15.5.2. Importantly, the system call forwarding mechanism is exactly the same in both the native Kitten and VM Kitten configurations, as the interfaces are decoupled from any kernel-level message passing scheme.

15.6.2   Workloads

We designed experiments to measure both networking performance and the performance of two key HPC benchmarks. We evaluated the following workloads: (1) Intel MPI Benchmarks (IMB) (Intel Corporation (Intel Corporation 2018); (2) High Performance Linpack (HPL) (Petitet and Cleary 2008); and (3) High-Performance Conjugate Gradient (HPCG) (Dongarra et al. 2015).

IMB is a suite of microbenchmarks used to characterize MPI networking performance. We used IMB to measure internode bandwidth and latency as well as scalability of collective operations up to 32 nodes. HPL and HPCG are from the TOP500 (Meuer et al. 2005) suite and represent different extremes in application behavior. HPL is highly compute bound and typically achieves near the theoretical peak computational capability of the underlying hardware. The HPL input problem was configured for weak scaling with a memory footprint of approximately 800 MB per node (N = 10,000 for 1 node scaling to N = 56,000 for 32 nodes). In contrast, HPCG is highly memory bound and was recently added to the TOP500 suite to better represent modern sparse linear algebra workloads. HPCG's default $104 \times 104 \times 104$ problem size was used, resulting in a memory footprint of approximately 950 MB per node. The workloads were evaluated from 1 to 32 compute nodes (ranging from 8 to 256 total cores) with HPL and HPCG run in weak scaling configurations. HPL and HPCG were built with MPI+OpenMP support, and were run with one MPI process per node using OMP_NUM_THREADS = 8. All performance results in this section report the average of at least three runs of the associated benchmark.

15.6.3   Results

Networking Performance Results

We first ran the IMB benchmark to measure the performance of networking operations in each of our system configurations. Figure 15.6 illustrates two-node bandwidth measured by the IMB PingPong benchmark. The figure shows that the native Kitten configuration achieves that same bandwidth as the native Cray only configuration for all message sizes up to 1 MB. For the Kitten guest configuration, there is a dip in performance around the 1 KB message size, and then performance tracks with the two native environments albeit with a small degree of degradation until message sizes around 1 MB are reached, at which point the guest achieves native bandwidth.

Fig. 15.6 IMB PingPong
bandwidth in various OS/R
architectures

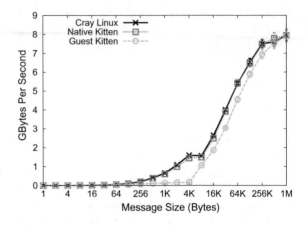

Fig. 15.7 IMB PingPong
latency in various OS/R
architectures

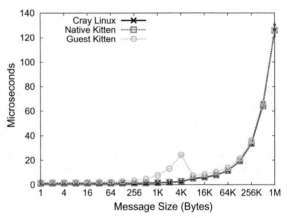

Figure 15.7 illustrates two node latency measured by the IMB PingPong benchmark. As in the bandwidth results, the native Kitten environment achieves native performance, while the guest Kitten incurs overhead around the 1 KB message size. In this case, however, the guest achieves native latency for all message sizes from 8 KB to 1 MB. Finally, Fig. 15.8 shows the latency of a 32 node MPI_Allreduce() in each OS/R configuration. Once more, the figure demonstrates native performance in the Kitten co-kernel, with overhead on the order of 20 μs for message sizes between 1 and 64 KB in the Kitten guest.

In each of these cases, we see that the guest VM incurs performance overhead for small- to medium-sized messages. We attribute these results to the fact that the Palacios hypervisor is not yet full capable of enabling the exact caching configurations for the device's PCI memory regions in the VMs Extended Page Table (EPT) and Memory Type Range Register (MTRR) settings. This leads to slightly different hardware operations in the native and virtualized cases, leading to performance degradation for a specific set of message sizes. We do not consider this to be a fun-

Fig. 15.8 IMB
`MPI_Allreduce()`
latency in various OS/R
architectures

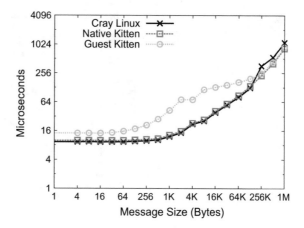

Fig. 15.9 HPL in various
OS/R architectures

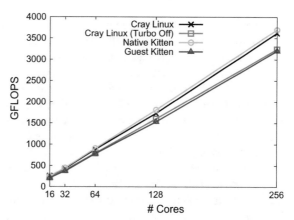

damental limitation of our approach, but rather a temporary lack of support in the hypervisor that could be addressed in the future.

In fact, we are rather encouraged by these results, because they illustrate that it is possible to provide near-native performance (for many message sizes) in a virtual machine for a network device that is not self-virtualizable. This is made possible by the unified address space organization and user-level system call forwarding scheme provided by the Hobbes infrastructure, as well as the full OS bypass nature of data movement on the Aries network device.

HPL and HPCG Performance Results

Next, we also ran the HPL and HPCG benchmarks to determine the ability of the Hobbes infrastructure to support representative HPC workloads in various OS/R configurations.

The results of the HPL experiments are shown in Fig. 15.9. First, the figure demonstrates that the Cray Linux environment and the native Kitten co-kernel environment

Fig. 15.10 HPCG in various OS/R architectures

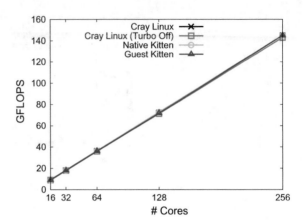

achieve comparable performance results from 16 to 256 cores (1–32 nodes), with the Kitten environment showing small performance gains (about 2%) at the largest scale run. On the other hand, we see a small degree of performance degradation in the Kitten VM environment, with performance roughly 13% lower at 256 cores. However, upon investigating this result we discovered that the Palacios VMM was configured to disable TurboBoost in the VM. To confirm this was the source of overhead, we ran an additional set of experiments in the native Cray environment with TurboBoost disabled, and the results were very similar to the Kitten VM configuration.

The results of the HPCG experiments are shown in Fig. 15.10. In this application, each configuration shows comparable performance. Given that HPCG is not as compute intensive of an application as HPL, it is intuitive to expect that TurboBoost will not have as significant of an effect on performance. This demonstrates that our system is capable of supporting arbitrary, virtualized OS/R architectures without sacrificing performance achievable in bare-metal only co-kernel configurations.

Finally, in addition to the promising performance results, each experiment in this section demonstrates that the Hobbes infrastructure can support the same unmodified binary using existing job management tools through its ability to expose a single system image to the Cray ALPS software suite, and through the generic cross-enclave interfaces provided by the Leviathan node management service.

15.7 Lessons Learned

Our work on the Hobbes OS/R taught us several lessons pertaining to extreme-scale OS/R design and implementation. First, we learned that a multi-stack OS/R approach is effective for providing performance isolation and eliminating system noise. Specifically, the Pisces framework proved effective at isolating BSP-style applications from potential interference from co-running workloads. We believe this finding is directly related to the fact that Pisces reduces both hardware interference, by space-partitioning most of the compute hardware, as well as software interference, by provisioning OS instances that have no cross-kernel dependencies.

In the context of multi-kernel operating systems, one of the unique components of Hobbes was our use of lightweight virtualization via the Palacios VMM. By leveraging virtualization and XEMEM shared memory, we designed communication interfaces for cross-stack communication and integration that are not tied to either the vendor-provided Linux kernel nor the lightweight Kitten kernel. The presence of such OS-agnostic interfaces makes it easier to adopt new/alternative OS/Rs into our system, including additional kernels that were not designed with multi-kernel capabilities in mind. In addition to this flexibility, virtualization also allows missing services not provided in the LWK, such as file systems and other I/O related subsystems/drivers, to be provided via virtual machines. Such an approach allows our system to provide drivers/subsystems that may not even be present in the vendor's Linux-based OS image.

However, while the flexibility to deploy alternative OS/Rs is valuable from a research perspective, we learned that it is quite challenging to support real application workflows in multi-kernel environments. Vendor-provided management libraries, such as Cray's ALPS, are often proprietary and only provided in binary form. This made it difficult for us to determine what system services needed to be present in the lightweight kernel environment to support Cray's utilities. Even forwarding all systems calls from the lightweight kernel to the shadow process, as described in this work, did not resolve all dependencies, as various environment variables as well as socket connections to a daemon on the Linux side needed to be present. We were able to resolve these requirements through a combination of system call forwarding, address space mirroring and signal propagation via the Leviathan infrastructure, but it is likely that further work will be needed to provide access to other proprietary services on future systems.

Finally, we have also come to learn that some of the initial motivating problems behind the Hobbes OS/R, including supporting flexible user environments have been solved to some extent by containerization technologies, including Docker, Shifter, Singularity, and the Spack package manager. We believe that future work in the context of HPC OS/Rs should consider how to provide compatibility with these frameworks in order to provide performance isolation along with the image customization that they already support.

15.8 Conclusion

Exascale system software is trending toward specialization. In this chapter, we presented the Hobbes OS/R and a set of design principles based on resource abstractions and user-level resource management that make it possible for HPC systems to deploy and manage arbitrary specialized OS/R instances. We designed a node manager called Leviathan that provides a set of user-level services to compose application workflows and support job management toolkits. Finally, we showed that the Hobbes

OS/R together with Leviathan is flexible to support a range of specialized OS/Rs, including those executed in virtual machines, without sacrificing performance, and without requiring any modifications to applications or existing system management tools.

References

Alverson, B., Froese, E., Kaplan, L., & Roweth, D. (2012). Cray Inc., white paper WP-Aries01-1112. Technical report, Cray Inc.

Boehme, D., Gamblin, T., Beckingsale, D., Bremer, P.-T., Gimenez, A., LeGendre, M., et al. (2016). Caliper: Performance introspection for HPC software stacks. In *Proceedings of the 29th ACM/IEEE International Conference for High Performance Computing, Networking, Storage and Analysis, (SC)*.

Brightwell, R., Oldfield, R., Maccabe, A. B., & Bernholdt, D. E. (2013). Hobbes: Composition and virtualization as the foundations of an extreme-scale OS/R. In *Proceedings of the 3rd International Workshop on Runtime and Operating Systems for Supercomputers, ROSS '13* (pp. 2:1–2:8).

Dayal, J., Bratcher, D., Eisenhauer, G., Schwan, K., Wolf, M., Zhang, X., et al. (2014). Flexpath: Type-based publish/subscribe system for large-scale science analytics. In *Proceedings of the 14th IEEE/ACM International Symposium on Cluster, Cloud and Grid Computing, (CCGrid)*.

Dongarra, J., Heroux, M. A., & Luszczek, P. (2015). HPCG benchmark: A new metric for ranking high performance computing systems. Technical Report UT-EECS-15-736, University of Tennessee, Electrical Engineering and Computer Science Department.

Gerofi, B., Takagi, M., Hori, A., Nakamura, G., Shirasawa, T., & Ishikawa, Y. (2016). On the scalability, performance isolation, and device driver transparency of the IHK/McKernel hybrid lightweight kernel. In *Proceedings of the 30th IEEE International Parallel and Distributed Processing Symposium, (IPDPS)*.

Giampapa, M., Gooding, T., Inglett, T., & Wisniewski, R. (2010). Experiences with a lightweight supercomputer kernel: Lessons learned from Blue Gene's CNK. In *2010 International Conference for High Performance Computing, Networking, Storage and Analysis (SC)*.

Hale, K., & Dinda, P. (2015). A case for transforming parallel runtimes into operating system kernels. In *Proceedings of the 24th International ACM Symposium on High Performance Parallel and Distributed Computing, (HPDC)*.

Hale, K., Hetland, C., & Dinda, P. (2016). Automatic hybridization of runtime systems. In *Proceedings of the 25th International ACM Symposium on High Performance Parallel and Distributed Computing, (HPDC)*.

Intel Corporation. (2018). IMB: Intel MPI Benchmarks. https://software.intel.com/en-us/articles/intel-mpi-benchmarks.

Kaplan, L. (2007). Cray CNL. In *FastOS PI Meeting and Workshop*.

Karo, M., Lagerstrom, R., Kohnke, M., & Albing, C. (2006). The application level placement scheduler. In *Proceedings of the Cray User Group Meeting*.

Kelly, S., Dyke, J. V., & Vaughan, C. (2008). Catamount N-Way (CNW): An implementation of the Catamount light weight kernel supporting N-cores version 2.0. Technical report, Sandia National Laboratories.

Kocoloski, B., & Lange, J. (2014). HPMMAP: Lightweight memory management for commodity operating systems. In *Proceedings of the 2014 IEEE 28th International Parallel and Distributed Processing Symposium, IPDPS '14* (pp. 649–658). Washington, DC, USA: IEEE Computer Society.

Kocoloski, B., & Lange, J. (2015). XEMEM: Efficient shared memory for composed applications on multi-OS/R exascale systems. In *Proceedings of the 24th International ACM Symposium on High Performance Parallel and Distributed Computing, (HPDC)*.

Kocoloski, B., Lange, J., Abbasi, H., Bernholdt, D., Jones, T., Dayal, J., et al. (2015). System-level support for composition of application. In *Proceedings of the 5th International Workshop on Runtime and Operating Systems for Supercomputers, (ROSS)*.

Lange, J., Pedretti, K., Hudson, T., Dinda, P., Cui, Z., Xia, L., et al. (2010). Palacios and Kitten: New high performance operating systems for scalable virtualized and native supercomputing. In *Proceedings of the 24th IEEE International Parallel and Distributed Processing Symposium, (IPDPS)*.

Lange, J., Pedretti, K., Dinda, P., Bridges, P., Soltero, C. B. P., & Merritt, A. (2011). Minimal-overhead virtualization of a large scale supercomputer. In *Proceedings of the 7th ACM SIG-PLAN/SIGOPS International Conference on Virtual Execution Environments, (VEE)*.

Liu, R., Klues, K., Bird, S., Hofmeyr, S., Asanovic, K., & Kubiarowicz, J. (2009). Tessellation: Space-time partitioning in a manycore client OS. In *Proceedings of the 1st USENIX Conference on Hot Topics in Parallelism, (HotPar)*.

Lofstead, J., Zheng, F., Klasky, S., & Schwan, K. (2009). Adaptable, metadata rich IO methods for portable high performance IO. In *Proceedings of the 23rd IEEE International Parallel and Distributed Processing Symposium, (IPDPS)*.

Meuer, H., Strohmaier, E., Dongarra, J., & Simon, H. (2005). Top500 supercomputer sites. www.top500.org.

Ouyang, J., Kocoloski, B., Lange, J., & Pedretti, K. (2015). Achieving performance isolation with lightweight co-kernels. In *Proceedings of the 24th International ACM Symposium on High Performance Parallel and Distributed Computing, (HPDC)*.

Petitet, A., & Cleary, A. (2008). HPL: A portable implementation of the high-performance linpack benchmark for distributed-memory computers. http://www.netlib.org/benchmark/hpl/.

Rhoden, B., Klues, K., Zhu, D., & Brewer, E. (2011). Improving per-node efficiency in the datacenter with new OS abstractions. In *Proceedings of the 2nd ACM Symposium on Cloud Computing, (SOCC)*.

Riesen, R., & Maccabe, A. B. (2011). Single system image. In D. A. Padua (Ed.), *Encyclopedia of parallel computing* (pp. 1820–1827). New York: Springer.

Slattery, S., Wilson, P. P., & Pawlowski, R. (2013). The data transfer kit: a geometric rendezvous-based tool for multiphysics data transfer. In *Proceedings of the International Conference on Mathematics & Computational Methods Applied to Nuclear Science & Engineering, (M&C)*.

WhiteDB. (2017). Whitedb. http://whitedb.org.

Wisniewski, R. W., Inglett, T., Keppel, P., Murty, R., & Riesen, R. (2014). mOS: An architecture for extreme-scale operating systems. In *Proceedings of the 4th International Workshop on Runtime and Operating Systems for Supercomputers, ROSS '14* (pp. 2:1–2:8). New York, NY, USA: ACM.

Woodacre, M., Robb, D., Roe, D., & Feind, K. (2003). The SGI Altix 3000 global shared-memory architecture. Technical report, Silicon Graphics International Corporation.

Zheng, F., Yu, H., Hantas, C., Wolf, M., Eisenhauer, G., Schwan, K., et al. (2013). GoldRush: Resource efficient in situ scientific data analytics using fine-grained interference aware execution. In *Proceedings of the 26th ACM/IEEE International Conference for High Performance Computing, Networking, Storage and Analysis, (SC)*.

Zounmevo, J., Perarnau, S., Iskra, K., Yoshii, K., Giososa, R., Essen, B. V., et al. (2015). A container-based approach to OS specialization for exascale computing. In *Proceedings of the 1st Workshop on Containers, (WoC)*.

Chapter 16
NIX

Ron Minnich

Abstract The NIX project targeted manycore architectures in which only a small subset of the cores could run kernel code. Consider N cores on a die arranged in a grid, with an on-die network providing a totally symmetric network and access to common memory. Let us assume that only $\sqrt{N}$ of the cores can run a kernel and the rest can only run user mode code. NIX was intended to provide a kernel for such a system. The hypothetical target was a 1,024 core system, as several vendors hinted that was reasonable in the 2016 time frame. We picked this number as it was large enough to far exceed any possible number of user processes: the Plan 9 systems on which NIX was based use only a small fraction of this number. Further, the realities of memory bandwidth will limit the number of active cores to small single digits. We also wanted to have a system with good support for Go, the then-new language from Google. At the time, Go was a statically linked language and a typical binary was about 1 MiB. This influenced the design of the virtual memory system in NIX. The base page size was expanded from 4,096 bytes to 2 MiB. We further extended Plan 9's virtual memory model to transparently support GiB pages, but via a simple heuristic that made it far less complex than existing systems. The target system had a 32:1 ratio of application cores to kernel cores (a close match to the Blue Gene/Q system at 16:1), and it was designed for space sharing, not time sharing, and had a minimum page size of 2 MiB; supported GiB pages; and yet, at the same time, looked in all other ways like a standard Plan 9 system.

16.1 Introduction

NIX is an operatingsystem built for HPC, but with a distinct flavor of Plan 9. We started the project as an exploration in April 2011, and did most of the implementation in May 2011, with only minor changes past that point, and continued test and measurement work for another year.

R. Minnich (✉)
Google LLC, Menlo Park, CA, USA
e-mail: rminnich@gmail.com

© Springer Nature Singapore Pte Ltd. 2019
B. Gerofi et al. (eds.), *Operating Systems for Supercomputers and High Performance Computing*, High-Performance Computing Series, https://doi.org/10.1007/978-981-13-6624-6_16

269

The most significant aspect of NIX is its provision of dedicated cores for applications, so-called Application Cores (ACs). The notion of ACs comes from our discussions with processor vendors as well as implementations of supercomputers such as Blue Gene/Q. In 2011, most supercomputers provided a Symmetric Multiprocessing Model (SMP), in which a sea of homogeneous cores was managed by a kernel, and interrupts were routed to all cores, with any core being able to service any interrupt. Processes on these cores flitted in and out of the kernel continuously, in response to system calls and interrupts: every core had to be able to run the kernel. This is the basic model of Unix: processes have an identity in both kernel and user mode.

It was clear in 2011 that this model was on its last legs: future systems with thousands of cores on a die would stretch it to the breaking point. We decided to explore a nonsymmetric system in which most cores could not run the kernel. Applications would be scheduled on application cores by a kernel, but the full kernel would never run on application cores. We hence partitioned the cores into traditional Time-sharing Cores or TCs; and Application Cores or ACs. Applications would get near-bare-metal performance on ACs, and would never suffer interference due to interrupts and other kernel activities.

We were hardly the first to do this: both commercial products (Drobo) and HPC products (Blue Gene/Q, and any number of GPU systems) implement this model.

But we decided to take our model further by implementing *operational transparency*. We assume that all cores have a common memory space, which has several consequences as given below:

- Processes always run correctly, whether they are on an AC or TC. In other words, save for performance impact, the process could run equally well on an AC or TC.
- Starting a process on an AC is not special in any way, and, in fact, can even be best effort, i.e., AC can be preferred, but not required.
- A process is a process, be it on an AC or a TC. All process controls work, as well as all system calls.
- *Any* command, including interactive commands such as debuggers and editors, can run correctly on an AC or a TC.

We further made it allowable for a process to jump back and forth between an AC and a TC. Processes, once started on an AC, are not stranded there. As a consequence:

- Commands can move from AC to TC at any time and will still run correctly.
- Very complex activities not appropriate for an AC can be handled on the TC, which greatly simplifies what we need to do on an AC.
- Programs can even be written to have phases, which run on the most appropriate resource, be it an AC or a TC.

The result is that on NIX, any program can be started on a dedicated application core and can, as needed, transition back to a time-sharing core. Process status commands will show all active processes on all cores. Debugging, process control, monitoring— none of these need to change. We did extend the shell syntax a bit to make it easy, from the command line, to start a process on an AC.

These requirements, as far as we know, are still not common for asymmetric systems. It is far more common, when providing bare metal access to applications, to view the application cores as external devices which must be treated specially.

While NIX was successful in its own terms, it was also overtaken, as were so many other efforts, by the Linux tsunami—as of this writing, all of the supercomputers on the TOP500 run Linux, as compared to zero 20 years ago. Further, the envisioned dedicated application processors did come into existence—but they were GPUs. That we did not anticipate. Nevertheless, the NIX work lives on in Harvey-OS.

In order to understand NIX, one must first understand basic Plan 9 concepts. Hence, we will begin our NIX discussion with an overview of the resource sharing environment provided by Plan 9; the Plan 9 port to the Blue Gene supercomputers, known as 9k, NIX itself, and the lessons learned from that effort.

16.2 Plan 9, a Resource Sharing Operating System

Plan 9 (Pike et al. 1995) is a resource sharing operating system. Unix and its intellectual descendants, such as Linux, are remote access systems.[1] Resource sharing systems allow resources, such as files and I/O devices, to be accessed without concern for where they are in the world. Remote access systems, such as Unix, require that you know the identity of the host containing a resource before gaining access to it. Resource sharing systems provide *location transparency*.

This distinction is essential to understanding the rest of the discussion of this work. Further, we have found that it is easy to confuse Plan 9's similarities to Unix and assume that they are basically the same. The similarity is intentional, so as to ease use. But the differences are profound and, therefore, it is essential to at least be aware of those differences.

16.2.1 Plan 9 Name Spaces

The key to the use of Plan 9 is the concept of a *name space*. A namespace consists of files and directories used by a group of one or more processes. Name spaces are constructed by adding 9p servers and kernel devices to a process by a *mount* system call. Name spaces are not global, as in Unix; rather, they are set up by the init process and inherited. Children of init can break the connection to the init namespace, modify it, and pass the changed namespace to their children.

In Fig. 16.1, we show the init process and a shell, and the way in which a subprocess can modify a shared name space. In this case, the subprocess is the mount command, and it is adding /dev to the namespace shared by init and rc. This is a mode of mounting familiarity to any Unix user.

---

[1] A good explication of the two types of systems can be found in (Padlipsky 1985).

Fig. 16.1 Namespace with
`init`, showing use of the
`mount` command to mount
`/dev` into a shared name
space

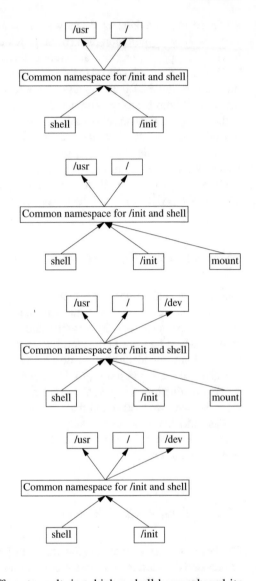

In the next figure, we show a different result, in which a shell has unshared its namespace and then run the `mount` command. This is similar to what happens on Linux with the unshare command[2]; a new namespace is created and modifications to it are not seen by `init` (Fig. 16.2).

Every resource in Plan 9, be it a file server or a kernel device, presents itself as resource that can be bound into a name space. Because of this uniform model, drivers and 9p servers can be mutually recursive: there is a special driver, called *mnt*,

---

[2]Not surprising since the idea for unsharing came from Plan 9 to Linux.

Fig. 16.2 Namespace with `init`, showing the result of an unshared name space

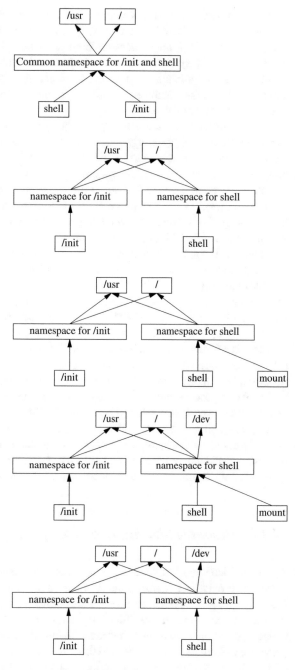

which is used to connect a 9p server into a process name space; some 9p servers aggregate both drivers and servers into a composite name space to be presented as a single entity to 9p clients, including remote kernels.

The Plan 9 model is in sharp contrast to Linux or Unix, in which resources are presented by all kinds of things: files by file systems in the kernel; network stacks by socket system calls, Inter-Processor Communication (IPC) channels, and synthetic files; processes by system calls and file systems. In contrast to Plan 9, even Linux name spaces lack a basic consistency: there are almost a dozen different types of namespaces in Linux; namespaces are not so much a unifying mechanism in Linux as they are an additional set of APIs.

Traditional Unix has one namespace, the global one created on boot or during normal operation by mounting, e.g., the root file system and user home directories. Once a file system is mounted in Unix, it is globally visible to all processes, even those currently running. The file system mounts are maintained in a global table in the kernel. In contrast, Plan 9 changes the Unix model by making mount points an attribute of a process, or set of process, not of the entire system. This change is similar to the change from languages which supported only global variables to languages which supported lexical scoping for variables.

Unlike in Unix, the Plan 9 mount operation is not privileged; any process can attempt to modify its namespace by mounting new servers or drivers. Processes can inherit a namespace or start with an empty namespace; modify it in a way visible to its parent (which is how the `mount` command works; it makes a change which is visible to its parent, usually the shell); modify it in a way not visible to the parent; and pass none, some, or all of the namespace to children.

There is a further essential distinction to Plan 9 name spaces: the set of operations they support can be implemented by a 9p server or a kernel driver. The `/net` directory, for example, is traditionally where the kernel network stack is mounted. It began life in Plan 9 as a process, and was migrated to the kernel for performance. Not a single program that used /net needed to be changed. The server for /net can be anything, as long as it follows the conventions for /net. It is easy and common, when testing new network stack ideas, to use a process that implements /net and use it instead. No programs need change when using a different provider of /net.

By way of illustration, we provide a resource sharing example in the next section.

16.2.2   Resource Sharing Example: /proc

`/proc` on Plan 9 is a synthetic file system that contains information about processes, as well as providing a control point for them so they can be managed and debugged. Plan 9 has no *ptrace* system call, as it does not need one: all the operations provided by *ptrace* are implemented as "files" in the `/proc` file system. Debuggers on Plan 9 hence operate on `/proc` files, instead of using the *ptrace* system call. To debug a program, a debugger needs access to the `/proc` file system.

It is easy to see how one might write a debugger to use a file in `/proc` as opposed to the *ptrace* system call. But let us consider the problem of debugging a process on a different system. How can this be accomplished?

On remote access systems, we need to log into the node and run the debugger, i.e., we would ssh to the node, and run gdb there. Or, we might ssh to the node, and run gdbserver, and connect to the node from gdb. In either case, we have to independently arrange to get the files to where the debugger is, via rsync or some other tool, because remote access to a system does not guarantee that the source code is there too. For this and other reasons, gdb has had to define a remote debugging protocol. This protocol is not like any other protocol and, in fact, is ill defined and difficult to implement: its definition is driven by need and the programming fashion of the day, which explains the use of XML in several message types.

On Plan 9, we have a number of choices, and they all work because of location transparency. We show them in Fig. 16.3.

One might take the traditional path of logging into the target node, and running a debugger. Even in Plan 9, this model differs, as the namespace of the process on the users node[3] is imported to the target node. Hence, when the debugger opens source code files, it will open the version of those files used to compile the binary. The system looks like one system, although it is two.

Another option is to have "remotely" run the debugger on the system started from the shell on the user's machine. In this case, the remote debugger still inherits the namespace of the users shell process node, and all its file I/O will occur in the user namespace. Again, there is no need to move source around; by dint of the resource sharing model, the source code is always present in the namespace, without regard to its actual physical location.

A third option is to import /proc from the remote node to the local shell's namespace and run the debugger. In other words, a user might (in one shell) replace the local /proc with the remote /proc via a mount[4] and then run the debugger as though the process were running on the local machine.

This third option works even if the remote system and the local system are different architectures. For example, the /proc/pid/regs file contains the process register values. This file presents the data in an endian-independent, word-sized independent format.

There is no special remote debug protocol needed on Plan 9, as in Unix, because the /proc device implements a standard interface, and data is presented in an endian- and wordsize-independent format over a common wire protocol. The wire protocol is 9p, in all cases, so no new protocols need to be defined for the different cases of logging into the node; running a remote debugger instance with access to the source code; or importing the remote /proc. The debugger in Plan 9, acid, has 5,000 lines of C, and 100 of those lines relate to architecture; one reason the architecture-specific part is so small is that the /proc file system does the endian- and word-size conversion for the /proc files.

---

[3]*Not* the namespace of the node; the namespace of the process on the node. Again, the distinction is crucial.

[4]As mentioned above, mounts are not privileged operations in Plan 9, as they are not global. In Linux terms, every login process runs as though it had been started with a CLONE_NEWNS option.

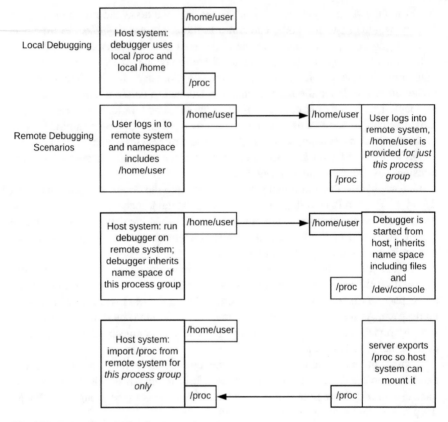

Fig. 16.3 Debugging on Plan 9 using namespaces

This last scenario is what we used to control and debug processes on Blue Gene when we ported Plan 9. We were able to control and debug processes on the PowerPC CPUs in the Blue Gene from our x86 laptops. All this worked because, on Plan 9 and its successor systems such as NIX, every component, be it a user level server or a kernel driver, is required to implement a standard interface to support the resource sharing model. This interface looks like a file server.

In the next section, we provide a brief overview of file server operations.

16.2.3 File Operations

We show the file operations in Table 16.1.

There are some subtleties worth noting.

- *attach* is like *mount* and provides a handle which can be used for *walk* operations. An *attach* modifies the state of the current process namespace, not any global state.

Table 16.1 File operations

Function	Action
attach	Connect to a server and return a communications handle to it
walk	Given a handle to a server and a path, create a new handle resulting from walking to the new path
stat and *wstat*	Given a handle, return (*stat*) or modify (*wstat*) a handle's metadata (*wstat* implements operations including *chmod*, *times*, and so on)
open	Given a handle, open it
create	Given a handle and path, create a file/directory relative to that handle
close	Given a handle, close it
read	Given a handle to an opened file or directory, read it
write	Given a handle to an opened file, write it
remove	Given a handle, remove it

An *attach* is, therefore, like an environment variable: inherited, and not global. Unlike Unix, an *attach* is authenticated to the user, not the machine; an *attach* cannot change other users namespaces; and an *attach* cannot result in privilege elevations via access to setuid files or device files; for that reason, *attach* is not itself a privileged operation.

- *walk* uses handles from *attach* or *walk* and can walk to files or directories.
- *open*, *stat*, and *remove* do not operate on paths; they operate on handles which have been walked to. In the case of *stat*, it means we do not need both *stat* and *fstat* system calls.
- *open* can open any handle which is walked to, providing permissions allow it.
- There is no *readdir* operation; directories are read by reading the handle from an open.
- *stat* and *readdir* return an endian- and word-size independent blob which is unmarshaled in a user library. This blob is opaque to the kernel. This model is quite unlike the Unix model, in which the kernel returns an architecture-dependent structure.

The standard resource sharing protocol for Plan 9 is 9p, which is used for I/O on everything—files and devices. Unlike most file system protocols, 9p has no embedded information about file types; packets for directory and file reads have the same format, for example. 9p manages client communications with servers and that is all. Hence, the set of operations used inside the kernel for devices has an equivalent set in 9p. This equivalence is key to making location-independence work. A read of a directory always provides the same result whether the directory is local or provided by a 9p server at a distance. A *stat* operation returns the same result for local files or remote files, regardless of architecture. In terms of data formats and operations, there are no differences between local and remote operations. No extra translations or conversions are performed on metadata.

With that in mind, we can provide an overview of the Plan 9 system calls (Table 16.2).

Table 16.2 Plan 9 system calls

Name	Function
bind, *mount*	Operate on namespace. *mount* is as described above; *bind* is like the Linux bind mount (which it inspired)
chdir	Change directory
open, *close*, *pread*, *pwrite*, *dup*, *create*, seek	Classic Unix system calls for files, save that *dup* on Plan 9 is like *dup2*
pipe	Convenience system call that uses the Plan 9 pipe device to create a bidirectional pipe (like socketpair in Unix)
rfork, *exec*, *exits*, *await*	Standard Unix-like system calls with namespace inheritance control (on *rfork*). Inspired *rfork* in BSD and *clone* in Linux. *Exits* exits with a string, not an integer as in Unix. The *exits* string can be read in `/proc/<pid>/status`; processes on one node can wait for processes on another node to exit by opening and blocking on a read of this file. *Await* returns a process exit string value
`notify`, `noted`	These are like Unix signal handlers, save that in Plan 9 signal handlers receive strings, not integers
(w)*stat*, (f)*wstat*	Like the Unix *stat* and *fstat* calls; the *wstat* variants allow changing of metadata, and replace the chmod and other system calls from Unix
`errstr()`	Plan 9 errors are strings, not integers. `Errstr()` retrieves the error string
Other miscellaneous system calls	There are a few other system calls for getting time, managing semaphores, and implementing rendezvous but they are not needed for this discussion

16.3　Why We Chose Plan 9 as an HPC System

The Plan 9 kernel has a simple, regular, and small set of interfaces. There is no file system support in the kernel: there is support for namespace management and for converting a textual file name to a connection to a 9p server or kernel device. We had built embedded systems with Plan 9 in which there was no local file system media at all. All local "mounts" were devices, and all "file system mounts" were to 9p servers on the network.

Plan 9 could thus have a very compact memory footprint, with many resources provided by off-node devices. At the same time, the user environment would be the same on a small embedded node as on a user's workstation, since the user could compose a namespace on each system that was identical, without having to find a sysadmin to beg for another mountpoint or automounter configuration. This flexibility promised to be highly useful in HPC systems, where the only local resource can be devices, and all files are provided over a network. Plan 9 looked like a perfect match to Blue Gene.

Further, measurements with the Fixed Time Quantum (FTQ) (Sottile and Minnich 2004) benchmark had shown that Plan 9 had incredibly low "OS noise", in fact, it could almost equal purpose built kernels like Blue Gene's Compute Node Kernel (CNK), and was one to two orders of magnitude lower than Linux. Multiuser Plan 9 systems had less OS noise than single-user Linux systems.

Finally, users had to make no sacrifice to use Plan 9 on an HPC system, we could provide the same environment on a Blue Gene node as was provided on a desktop. The system calls are the same, and the capabilities are too. All that changed was the set of resources: HPC systems have networks desktop users can only dream about; desktop users have many terabytes of local disk, and HPC systems typically have none.

Plan 9 was a general-purpose kernel, but very compact compared to Linux, not because it could do less, but because it had a better (in our eyes) design. It was as compact as most lightweight kernels, but did not share their limitations. For these reasons, we coined the term "Rightweight kernels" to describe how we thought Plan 9 fit into HPC. As port of this work, we ported Plan 9 to the Blue Gene L, P, and Q machines starting in 2006 and ending in 2010. We were the first non-IBM kernel to run on Blue Gene.

16.3.1 The Blue Gene Port

The main participants in the Blue Gene port were Eric Van Hensbergen of IBM, Jim Mckie of Bell Labs, Charles Forsyth of Vita Nuova Ltd, and the author. We started the Blue Gene port in 2006 (Minnich and Mckie 2009).

Blue Gene/L was built around 65,536 Power PC 405 CPUs, 32-bit processors. Each board had 2 GiB of memory and several novel networks (Forsyth et al. 2010).

Plan 9 is so portable that even now, the time it took for Blue Gene/L surprises the author. The port to the simulator took a few days. The port to real hardware took a few weeks, including the creation of a port to the very high bandwidth (multi-Gbytes/second) 3D torus. Plan 9 has a structure that makes porting very easy (the author recently did the first RISC-V port in a few days).

We had a working port to Blue Gene/L in a few weeks in 2006 after making the decisions to try it out. The author wrote the first version of the memory management unit (MMU) code in one evening in a hotel room and it worked, unchanged, the next day. For this version of the MMU code, we used 1 MiB pages. The change from 4 kiB to 1 MiB pages, which is pervasive in most Unix systems, required about 10 lines of changes in one file in Plan 9.

One of the continuing problems, however, that would also catch up with us on NIX, was the unique Plan 9 toolchain, written by Ken Thompson. It was not standard enough to make bringing over HPC software easy.

As the Blue Gene project reached the end of its days, and it moved to a more Linux-centric model, we took the exploration in a new direction, which we call NIX.

16.4   NIX

Now that we have outlined Plan 9 basics, we can discuss NIX. First, we give an overview of the target architecture model; then discuss the changes we made to Plan 9 to create NIX in response to that model, and then the implementation and results.

16.4.1   Architectural Model: Asymmetry is the Future

Until just a few years ago, the rule in HPC was that systems were composed of a sea of homogeneous components, each of which, in turn, was composed of a manycore system of identical components. Even systems which initially flouted this rule, such as the Blue Gene/L with its hybrid node containing four vector pipelines, quickly came into line: the successor systems to Blue Gene/L reverted to the standard model, culminating in the Blue Gene/Q: tens of thousands of CPU sockets populated with 17-core CPUs, in which each core was identical.

But even in Blue Gene/Q, the homogeneous CPUs have functional differences, while all CPU cores run IBM's CNK, the 17th core is reserved for system functionality running communication threads that handled function shipping, control commands, and optionally MPI progress. Further, since that time, specialization in hardware has become greater, as in the use of CPU/GPU systems.

Heterogeneity is the rule for systems from now on, from everything to HPC to ML systems at Google to bitcoin mining operations around the world.

But on the CPU side of these heterogeneous systems, homogeneity continues to rule: the CPUs on manycore dies are all the same. Even on systems with, e.g., hundreds of cores per socket, every core is fully capable of running Linux, containing all the support for all privilege modes, virtual machines, and I/O devices.

Starting in 2011, we began to hear that in some future manycore systems, only a small fraction of the cores would be able to run a kernel; the rest would be user mode cores only. This change would have many effects: the kernels themselves would not need to be as scalable, and the importance of scheduling and time sharing would decline as space sharing increased. In some cases, systems which had green threads, and hence relatively low numbers of processes, might be able to dedicate several cores to the kernel, and one core per process, and eliminate time sharing entirely.

In this scenario, when a green thread on core blocks, the process on that core can start a different thread; if there are no threads to run, the process can drop the core into a low power state, but remain on the core. Cores are never preempted. Since on manycore systems processes are always competing for memory bandwidth, only a few are active; the bandwidth and power saved by not context switching the core could be substantial, and given the increasing number of cores, leaving some idle is acceptable. When we have so many cores, keeping all cores running at all times is no longer a critical need.

NIX was designed for these heterogeneous CPU environments. Our starting assumption was that there would be systems in which a fraction of the cores would be capable of running a kernel; the rest of the cores would be limited to running user mode code.

16.4.2 The NIX Design

NIX is built on our Plan 9 kernel for Blue Gene, but modified for asymmetric systems. It has several additional changes which we felt would make it suitable for the Go language. In 2011, Go binaries were statically linked and the minimum size was one MiB. We decided to make user-space pages either 2 MiB or 1 GiB, and skip 4 kiB pages entirely. This change was in line with HPC kernels on Blue Gene, which had only 1 MiB pages; and the Sandia kernels for x86, which had 2- or 4-MiB pages.

In NIX, we divide the set of cores into fully capable Time-sharing Cores, named TCs; and Application Cores, i.e., cores restricted to only user code, named ACs. On systems which only consist of TCs, it is still possible to assign a set of TCs to function as ACs. That partitioning is done statically at boot time and does not change.

16.4.2.1 NIX Architecture

The architecture of NIX follows from the above discussion:

- *Asymmetry* Cores are for applications, not kernels. Only a small fraction of available cores run a kernel and their main function is to allocate applications to cores and move data to remote servers. At minimum, however, at least one core needs to be able to run a kernel.
- *ACs not required* Notwithstanding our assumption above, applications must always run even if no ACs are available. Further, applications must be able to easily transition back and forth from TCs to ACs as needed, on an instruction by instruction basis, if needed.
- *Convenience* The use of ACs must be convenient, both at startup time and while running. This implies that very few system calls be added, or extended; and, further, that specifying an AC be convenient from the command line as well as in programs.

- *Shared Memory* Because the cores were all on one die, we assumed that shared memory would still be available on each socket and between sockets. This has proved to be a durable assumption in platform architecture to the present time, even as the use of CPU/GPU systems has come to dominate HPC.
- *Large pages* Pages are by default 2 MiB, but the use of 1 GiB pages should be easy and, if possible, transparent; 4,096 byte pages are not available.

16.4.3   Changes to the Plan 9 Kernel for NIX

The main development of Plan 9 ended in 2012, and for that reason a detailed description of the changes we made for NIX is probably of little interest. Instead, we provide an overview of how these changes worked.

16.4.3.1   Application Cores

Kernels need to manage core startup and operation. Time-sharing Core (TC) management on NIX is not remarkably different from other Unix-like operating systems. On startup, a single Boot Strap Processor (BSP)[5] sends Startup Inter-Processor Interrupt (Startup IPIs, or SIPIs) to the other cores. As these cores start up, they register themselves in a set of data structures and indicate their presence to the BSP. Once the system is booted, these structures are used in assigning interrupt routing, scheduling, and housekeeping tasks, i.e., operational tasks.

When an AC is started, most parts of this kernel setup are skipped: ACs are not available for device interrupt servicing; they are not used to run kernel housekeeping tasks; and there is no timer interrupt on an AC, in order to minimize application interference. ACs are still registered but in a different set of structures.

ACs can be thought of as a processor, waiting on a hardware pipe connected to the TC, which is passed a function and its arguments by the TC and runs them. The AC periodically returns requests to the TC, which must be done on a TC, and which implements those requests. The most exceptional request is when the AC indicates it will no longer run the application.

This is very much a CSP (Hoare 1978) model, also used in Occam, Plan 9 threading and Go's goroutines. The CSP model was implemented in the Transputer in hardware, but no processors available today support it. Therefore, it is not possible, on conventional CPUs, for ACs to run entirely in user mode. Some CPU capabilities are necessarily higher priority than user mode, such as virtual memory setup. What is one to do if the user code makes invalid memory references, divides by zero, or traps for other reasons? In some future architecture, this might halt the AC and send a message interrupt to a TC; on today's CPUs, the AC traps to a higher privilege state and per-core code must handle the trap: there must be a kernel. It can be a very

---

[5]It is now a core, but the terminology was created long before multi-core CPUs existed.

```
struct ICC
{
     /* fn is kept in its own cache line */
     union {
          void     (*fn)(void);
          uchar    _ln1_[ICCLNSZ];
     };
     int     flushtlb;       /* on the AC, before running fn */
     int     rc;             /* return code from AC to TC */
     char*   note;           /* to be posted in the TC after
                                returning */
     uchar   data[ICCLNSZ];  /* sent to the AC */
};
```

Fig. 16.4 The inter-core call structure

simple kernel, however, the AC kernel consists of several dozen lines of C and about 200 lines of assembly. The main function of this kernel is to start application code and catch it when it exits. Direction of what to run, and management of exits, is done by the kernel running on the TCs.

ACs run a loop, waiting on a memory variable to change. TCs set up memory for the ACs to use, then change the memory variable. Once the AC has performed the function, the TC has directed it to do, it changes the memory variable back.

The memory variable implements pipe-like semantics, with the TC passing work down the pipe, and the AC passing results back. Sometimes, the AC passes a request back as a result, and the TC acts on that request. But from the point of view of the AC, returning work to do and returning a result are no different. In all cases, the AC returns a result, then re-enters a scheduling loop and waits for another assignment. ACs are in this sense stateless.

NIX has one more unique property: the requests made by an application *are implemented by the application itself, running on the TC*. NIX implements this by moving the application context to the AC, when the application wishes to run on an AC; and then back to the TC, when the application needs a service only a TC can provide. This work might be run in a kernel, as a system call; but it can also be run by a different phase of the program, in user mode.

AC startup code initializes the core and waits for a message telling it what to do. As mentioned, we implement these messages with a shared memory variable that provides pipe-like semantics. We call these messages Inter-Core Call, or ICCs, for short. We show the ICC in Fig. 16.4.

The ICC takes advantage of the fact that all cores share memory. It contains:

- a pointer to a function,
- a hint to flush the TLB before the function starts,
- a return code value,
- a pointer to a data area for more information to return to the TC and
- a parameter block to be passed to the function, when it is called on the AC, limited to an architectural value of a multiple of the cache line size.

Fig. 16.5 The AC scheduler, which runs continuously and performs work as the TC directs

```
void acsched(void)
{
    acmmuswitch();
    for (;;)
    {
        acstackok();
        mwait(&icc->fn);
        if(icc->flushtlb)
            acmmuswitch();
        DBG("acsched: cpu%d: fn %#p\n",
                machno, icc->fn);
        icc->fn();
        DBG("acsched: cpu%d: idle\n", machno);
        mfence();
        icc->fn = nil;
    }
}
```

TCs fill in the data and the function pointer, and do a memory fence; the AC sees the variable change, calls the function, and when the function returns, the AC fills in the return code (in the `rc` struct member) and potentially the note and sets the function pointer to nil (NULL pointer in Unix). This is the signal to the TC that the AC is waiting for more work.

We show the core AC kernel wait-for-work code in Fig. 16.5.

This kernel is quite simple: it waits to be told what to do, and does it. The wait is implemented via an `mwait()` function. The work is indicated by a function pointer. To call a function on an AC, the TC fills in the parameters, and sets the function pointer in the ICC.

The function in Fig. 16.5 consists of an initial setup call (acmmuswitch) and a loop. The acmmuswitch call is made at the entry as this is a new scheduler epoch and possibly the AC needs to switch page tables: acmmuswitch loads a new page table root, which has the side effect of clearing the TLB. The call to `acstackok()` at the start ensures our stack is not growing without end; it should always be the same at the top of the loop. Once the `mwait()` returns, the code checks `flushtlb()` and, if it is set, calls the acmmuswitch function again. The scheduler calls the function (which may not return); does an `mfence()`; then sets the pointer to nil. The TC, which is either watching this pointer via an `mwait()`, or checking it periodically, will then take action. Note that the TC rarely blocks on this pointer, unless it has nothing else to do; further, note, continuous iteration of this loop is not the common case. Usually, the function is called to run a user application, and the user application will exit to the TC in other ways—usually a system call.

How is application code started on an AC? There are three mechanisms: the *exec* system call, the *rfork* system call, and the proc file system. In all these cases, starting user code on an AC is implemented by resuming from a system call, and leaving user code is implemented via system call or other trap. We show an example flow in Fig. 16.6.

The first way to move to an AC is via a modified *exec* system call. NIX extends *exec* options to include a 'best effort' to run on an AC. NIX currently runs the process on

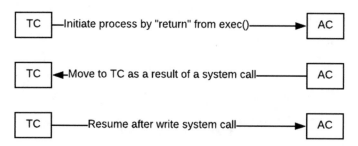

Fig. 16.6 Moving a process to an AC, managing a system call, and resuming it again

a TC if it cannot find an AC. Again, running on an AC is a best effort action, not an absolute. The extended *exec* replaces the standard *exec*, and is backward compatible.

The second is a change to the *rfork* system call. *Rfork* in Plan 9 has two behaviors: one is to start a new process and another is to modify the current process. We added a new option to *rfork*, RFCORE, which allows a child process or the current process to start on an AC. Again, the AC might not be selected, one is chosen as available. The process will work correctly in any event.

The third method, which does allow choosing an AC, is via /proc. In Plan 9, processes are controlled by writing to /proc/pid/ctl. We extend the command set to allow a process to move to an AC, either any AC (by choosing AC-1) or a specific AC by writing core <core> to the ctl file. The write can be done in a program or by a shell redirection, e.g., echo core 5 >/proc/pid/ctl will move pid to AC 5; this can even apply to the shell itself. The command will fail if the move is not possible. Once the process exits the *write* system call, assuming it succeeded, it is running on the AC.

Note that in all these cases, a process is started on an AC in a way that looks like a return from a system call: either *exec*, *rfork*, or *write*. In NIX, all processes start on an AC this way. This greatly simplifies the API for using an AC, as well as making the AC kernel very simple. We did not add any system calls to NIX to support ACs; we just made a few simple changes to existing ones and it all worked. The total amount of code to add these options is about 100 lines.

The last point of discussion is how a process starts on an AC and transitions back to a TC to implement system calls.

TCs direct ACs to run functions. The functions exist in shared memory, as does the process image. Further, processes on ACs resume after returning from a system call, and are initiated on a TC via a system call. Starting and resuming a process on an AC is simple: the process performs a system call on the TC, the TC saves the process context, and passes a pointer to it, along with a function to call, via the ICC structure. We show the runac function, used in the kernel, in Fig. 16.7.

```
rc = runac(core, acret_from_syscall, tlbflush_if_needed, args);
```

Fig. 16.7 TC code to run a function on an AC

```
void acsyscall(void)
{
    Proc *p = current;

    DBG("acsyscall: cpu%d\n", machno);

    _pmcupdate();
    p->actime1 = fastticks(nil);
    icc->rc = ICCSYSCALL;
    cr2 = cr2get(); // in case of page fault
    fpuprocsave(p);
    mfence();
    icc->fn = nil;
    ready(p); // so it will run on the TC
    /*
     * Subtleties:
     * fn is nil, so acsched will block on fn.
     * acshed will check its call stack and also
     * call a different function.
     * we never return here.
     * the process will resume on the TC since we called ready(p).
     */
    acsched();
}
```

Fig. 16.8 AC system call handling code

The runac function runs a function on a core, with arguments. The function in this case is acret_from_syscall(): system call return code for an AC. The tlbflush_if_needed parameter, if set, indicates that a TLB flush is needed.

The acsysret function is a simple C wrapper for 12 lines of assembly code that provides the standard Plan 9 system call return. While the use of the ICC looks a like a Remote Procedure Call (RPC), we can use shared memory to make it a simpler: the function is indicated by function pointer, not an integer as in RPC; parameters are passed directly; and the function on the AC can return more than just an integer, but pass more complex return values using the note pointer in the ICC.

When a process on an AC needs to do a system call, it performs a standard system call trap: the sequence is no different on an AC than a TC. We show the AC system call code in Fig. 16.8.

For purposes of this discussion, key parts of this function are the assignment of nil to icc->fn, and the mfence() which ensures that change is pushed to memory. Finally, the process is marked ready. This enables the process to run on the TC. Note, again, that we are able to call TC kernel functions directly because memory is shared. We do not need to send a message to the TC asking it to mark the process ready; we just call the function. The ICC is used to sequence interactions between TC and AC, but is not needed to provide TC functions to the AC.

The other item of interest is the call to acsched. As the comment indicates, call nesting might become an issue in the AC kernel with this call, but because the most likely next operation is a return to user mode, which resets the kernel stack, the stack does not continue to grow, since the kernel stack pointer is reset when the system call exits.

16.4.4 Bigger and Bigger Pages

The basic page size of NIX is 2 MiB. This implementation derived in part from our Blue Gene port, in which we moved to 1 MiB pages. In NIX, again driven by our HPC needs, we adopted a novel model for the process address space: all heap above 1 GiB is backed by 1 GiB pages. This nonuniform heap model was ideal for HPC workloads, which were characterized by a few small programs and one very large computation.

NIX applications are in most cases four 2 MiB pages: code, data, heap, and stack. There is almost always just one large application on a machine, these being single-application systems, and even on the then-large systems with 256 GiB of memory, a large application only needed 767 PTEs: 512 for the 2 MiB pages for the first GiB and 255 for the rest. If we use Address Space Identifiers (ASIDs), TLBs on current processors can easily hold all the TLB entries for all processes on NIX without eviction. Small applications have a three level, not four-level page table and large applications, for most of the address space, we have only a two-level page table due to the use of 1 GiB pages. In contrast, on a system with 4,096 byte pages, a 256 GiB app would need 67,108,864 PTEs, requiring a very large TLB.

Finally, for processes on an AC, we added the option to pre-page the process image on an *exec*. Plan 9, as most Unixes, does not pre-page any part of a new process image; even the first instruction causes a page fault. NIX allowed us to not only pre-page memory when the process started, but also to mark a process such that any heap allocated would also be pre-paged. Pre-paging eliminated almost all page faults. For general use, this could increase memory pressure, but in HPC, it is a good practice.

For reasons of space, we will not discuss the implementation further. The code is available at https://github.com/rminnich/nix-os.

16.5 Discussion

Researchers from Sandia National Laboratories, the Laboratorio de Sistemas at Universidad Rey Juan Carlos of Madrid, Bell Labs, and Vita Nuova Inc. created NIX from the Plan 9 "9k" Blue Gene kernel in 4 weeks in May 2011. We put much more work into getting the design right than into actual coding, which is a hallmark of Plan 9 from its earliest days at Bell Labs. The result was a very simple model which worked almost immediately. The two key ideas were continuing to use shared memory, which made it easy for the AC kernel to use TC kernel functionality as needed; and making AC user code start and exit look like a system call. Sharing memory made the AC kernel easy to write, and the AC user mode startup model made it easy to shift user code back and forth from AC to TC.

What was a bit surprising was how smoothly the system worked. Note that our model was not, as in other systems, writing a server-to-server user code requests. Instead, the user code served its own requests, by transitioning back to running on the TC each time it did a system call. Further, the user code could gain even more control using the /proc ctlmodifies the stateinterface, by moving back to the TC at the end of the computation, for example. It was very easy for a process to align its compute phases with running on a TC or an AC.

Adding notations to the shell to allow selection of ACs for parts of a pipeline proved to be a powerful idea. The same composition provided by pipes could be used to compose a pipeline of mixed compute and I/O tasks.

In terms of our HPC goals, the changes were very successful. We used the FTQ (Sottile and Minnich 2004) benchmark to measure OS noise on the ACs. We do not plot it here because there's nothing to show: there was no noise at all. Even on the Blue Gene systems, there was always a small amount of noise over a long enough period. On the ACs, there was absolutely no noise. There were several key components to removing the noise, which are given as follows:

- Dedicated, non-preemptable cores,
- Running a different kernel on those cores that did not participate in normal OS housekeeping tasks,
- Disable all interrupts, even the APIC timer interrupt, and
- Nonuniform heap, i.e., 2 MiB pages for heap up to the 1 GiB boundary, and then 1 GiB pages above that. On processors that have reasonable TLB implementations,[6] this results in zero TLB reloads for large applications.

16.5.1 Lessons Learned

Despite its meeting the goals we initially set for it, NIX did not succeed. Because some of the reasons apply to other kernels, we thought we would mention them.

The main reason NIX failed was that the expectations for HPC systems changed dramatically between 2005, when we started the "Plan 9 for HPC project", and 2012, when the NIX project ended. In a nutshell, NIX was not Linux, and Linux is what people assume they will have on HPC systems. There are many facets of this change as given below:

- *C dialect* NIX, as does Plan 9, has its own compiler toolchain, dating to 1995 when gcc was much less prevalent than today. Most applications today require "GCC" compatibility, not just "C99" or "C11" compatibility.[7] This situation has improved

---

[6]i.e. not Opterons with 4 TLB entries for 2 MiB pages.

[7]Some projects such as coreboot even require gnu11 compatibility, not c11!

recently due to the wider use of CLANG, but even today much software will not compile correctly unless gcc is used.

- *mediocre tool chain* Even were all tools to compile, the toolchain is a classic C compiler implementation and does very little optimization. Many libraries for HPC count on the optimization options of the toolchain.

- *missing system calls* Plan 9 is delightfully simple, but many system calls people expect from Linux do not exist. There are now almost 500 system calls in Linux and it seems none of them are dispensable. Some piece of software, somewhere, will fail because an obscure system call is missing.

- *Linux*/proc and /sys The Linux ABI is far more than just its system calls. There are hundreds of files in /proc and /sys, and many programs use them. It is not easy to port Linux code to non-Linux environments, if they make extensive use of these files. Further, libraries also make use of these files and their use changes constantly.

- *no* mmap Plan 9 has never had *mmap*, and *mmap* is critical for facilities like shared libraries. Shared libraries are used in many runtimes for computational steering; in these cases, static linking is not an option.

- *poor TCP performance* NIX uses Plan 9's TCP stack and that stack is old and has not kept up with changes; the world has passed it by.

- *slow drivers* NIX drivers, based on Plan 9 drivers, are compact, easy to read and debug—and not nearly as performant as the vendor drivers provided in Linux.

- *chipset support* NIX did not have ACPI, DMI, MSI, and modern power management support—in this case, because there were not enough people active in Plan 9 to bring these post-2002 features in. Further, and this issue impacts many open-source non-Linux kernels, chipset support is evolving more quickly than it used to, and in many cases can only be provided by a vendor. Realistically, CPU vendors only target Windows and Linux. This makes the task of non-Linux kernels that much harder.

- *GPUs are ACs* Possibly the biggest change we did not foresee was that application-only cores would come into existence—as GPU cores, not main processor cores. These cores are incompatible with the main CPUs and use a DMA model for getting arguments and results. It is not practical to implement NIX across the CPU/GPU boundary. We made the wrong assumptions about the direction architectures were taking.

NIX was a technical success for statically linked, pre-paged binaries running on a homogeneous instruction set architecture typical of HPC in 2005. By 2012, for the most part, that mode of usage had vanished; HPC systems run Linux and users expect all Linux capabilities to be available; what we thought of as ACs are not specialized CPU cores but, rather, are GPUs. NIX is an OS for HPC systems that no longer exist.

Acknowledgements Jim McKie, of Bell Labs, provided support for HPC development on Plan 9 from 2005 to 2011, and kept us on track over the last year as we made NIX work. Francisco J. Ballesteros, Gorka Guardiola, and Enrique Soriano hosted me for the month of May 2011 at the Laboratorio de Sistemas and each contributed key ideas that made NIX successful; in particular, if memory serves, Francisco created the Inter-Core Calling structures and conventions. Charles Forsyth of Vita Nuova provided the port of the Plan 9 toolchain to 64-bit x86 in 2005 (in 6 weeks!) and was very active in the NIX work, pushing hard to make use of shared memory and take advantage of what it provided. Eric Van Hensbergen, then of IBM, worked closely with us from 2005 to 2011 to make the Blue Gene port of Plan 9 possible; this work was the foundation of NIX.

References

Forsyth, C., McKie, J., Minnich, R., & Hensbergen, E. V. (2010). Night of the Lepus: A Plan 9 perspective on Blue Gene's interconnects.

Hoare, C. A. R. (1978). Communicating sequential processes. *Communications of the ACM, 21*(8), 666–677.

Sottile, M., Minnich, R. (2004). *Analysis of microbenchmarks for performance tuning of clusters.* In IEEE international conference on cluster computing.

Minnich, R., & Mckie, J. (2009). Experiences porting the Plan 9 research operating system to the IBM Blue Gene supercomputers. *Computer Science - Research and Development, 23(3–4), 117–124, June 2009.*

Padlipsky, M. A. (1985). *The Elements of Networking Style: And Other Essays and Animadversions on the Art of Intercomputer Networking.* Upper Saddle River, NJ, USA: Prentice-Hall Inc.

Pike, R., Presotto, D. L., Dorward, S., Flandrena, B., Thompson, K., Trickey, H., et al. (1995). Plan 9 from Bell Labs. *Computing Systems, 8*(2), 221–254.

Chapter 17
IHK/McKernel

Balazs Gerofi, Masamichi Takagi and Yutaka Ishikawa

Abstract IHK/McKernel is a lightweight multi-kernel operating system that is designed for extreme-scale HPC systems. The basic idea of IHK/McKernel is to run Linux and a lightweight kernel (LWK) side by side on each compute node to provide both LWK scalability and full Linux compatibility. IHK/McKernel is one of the first multi-kernels that has been evaluated at large scale and that has demonstrated the advantages of the multi-kernel approach. This chapter describes the architecture of IHK/McKernel, provides insights into some of its unique features, and describes its ability to outperform Linux through experiments. We also discuss our experiences and lessons learned so far.

17.1 Project Overview and Motivation

The IHK/McKernel project (IHK stands for Interface for Heterogeneous Kernels) started in early 2012 at the University of Tokyo with the aim of providing a lightweight multi-kernel-based operating system for many-core coprocessors where computational CPU cores had limited cache and memory resources (Shimosawa 2011). After the initial implementation, McKernel has been extended to stand-alone many-core CPUs, and at the time of writing this chapter, it remains under active development. The McKernel project is currently being led by RIKEN Center for Computational Science, and is developed in collaboration with Hitachi and Fujitsu.

Similarly to other lightweight multi-kernel projects, IHK/McKernel'sbasic motivation is three-fold.

B. Gerofi (✉) · M. Takagi · Y. Ishikawa
RIKEN Center for Computational Science, Kobe, Japan
e-mail: bgerofi@riken.jp

M. Takagi
e-mail: masamichi.takagi@riken.jp

Y. Ishikawa
e-mail: yutaka.ishikawa@riken.jp

© Springer Nature Singapore Pte Ltd. 2019
B. Gerofi et al. (eds.), *Operating Systems for Supercomputers and High-Performance Computing*, High-Performance Computing Series,
https://doi.org/10.1007/978-981-13-6624-6_17

- First and foremost, the system needs to provide a scalable execution environment for large-scale parallel applications (i.e., HPC simulations).
- Second, the kernel needs to retain full Linux compatibility, which is essential for supporting tools, debuggers, and libraries that rely on the Linux/POSIX APIs.
- Third, the kernel must be able to rapidly adapt to system software needs for emerging hardware features, such as new memory technologies, the increasing importance of power awareness, and heterogeneous processors.

In a similar vein, the easy adaptivity of a lightweight kernel code base also can significantly contribute to establishing a fertile ground for rapid experimentation with exotic kernel features that would be highly intrusive to implement and maintain in Linux.

Although a converged system software infrastructure for supporting both traditional HPC workloads and emerging Big data analytics, as well as machine learning type of workloads is highly desired (BDEC Committee 2017), in the realm of lightweight multi-kernels, this does not necessitate all workloads be run on the LWK co-kernel. The reconfigurable, dynamic fashion of IHK (as discussed below) enables runtime specialization of the system software by deploying application-specific OS kernels on a subset of node resources.

While McKernel is still under active development, we have already demonstrated some of the strengths of the multi-kernel approach (Gerofi et al. 2013, 2014, 2016, 2018), which are discussed in detail below. The most important upcoming milestones of the project are the scheduled deployment McKernel on the Oakforest-PACS supercomputer (Joint Center for Advanced HPC (JCAHPC) 2018), as well as on the Post-K machine, the successor of the K Computer (RIKEN Advanced Institute for Computational Science 2018).

17.2 Hardware Background

Before discussing the architecture of the IHK/ McKernel software stack, we provide a brief overview of the specific hardware platforms McKernel that has been developed and deployed on.

As mentioned above, at the beginning of the project, we focused on targeting many-core coprocessors. Specifically, we used the Intel® Xeon Phi® Knights Corner chip for early development and evaluation. The host machine for the KNC was an Intel Xeon CPU E5-2670, with 64 Gigabytes of RAM. The *Knights Corner* Xeon Phi 5110P card was connected to the host machine via PCI Express bus. The KNC provides 8 GB of RAM and a single chip with 60 1 GHz x86 cores, each processor core supporting a multi-threading depth of four. The chip includes coherent L1 and L2 caches and the inter-processor network is a bidirectional ring (Jeffers and Reinders 2013). KNC has a separate physical memory space from the host CPU, but it provides DMA engines specifically for data movement.

Our current test environment is primarily the Intel® Xeon Phi™ 7250 *Knights Landing* (KNL) processor. As of today, all of our large-scale experiments were performed on Oakforest-PACS (OFP), a Fujitsu built, 25 peta-flops supercomputer installed at JCAHPC organized by The University of Tsukuba and The University of Tokyo (Joint Center for Advanced HPC (JCAHPC) 2018). OFP is comprised of 8000 compute nodes that are interconnected by Intel's Omni-Path network. Each node is equipped with the abovementioned KNL processor, which consists of 68 CPU cores, with four hardware threads per core. The processor provides 16 GB of integrated, high-bandwidth, multi-channel DRAM (MCDRAM), which is accompanied by 96 GB of DDR4 RAM. For most experiments, we configure the KNL processor in SNC-4 flat mode, i.e., MCDRAM and DDR4 RAM are addressable at different physical memory locations and both are split into four NUMA domains. On each compute node, the operating system sees 272 logical CPUs organized around eight NUMA domains. At the time of writing, this chapter, the software environment on OFP was as follows. Compute nodes run XPPSL 1.4.1 with Linux kernel version 3.10.0-327.22.2. XPPSL is a CentOS-based distribution with a number of Intel provided kernel-level enhancements specifically targeting the KNL processor. We used Intel MPI 2018 Beta Build 20170209 that offers a few unreleased improvements for parallel job spawning.

We emphasize that both the KNC and the KNL processors provide multiple memory types in compute nodes which makes them an excellent testbed for exploring operating system techniques to support these memories. We also note that IHK/McKernel currently supports Cavium ThunderX (64 bit ARM) (Cavium 2014) and Fujitsu FX100 (SPARC-V9) (Yoshida et al. 2015) architectures as well. The ports have been developed by Fujitsu in preparation for the Post-K machine.

17.3   Architecture

An architectural overview of IHK/McKernel is shown in Fig. 17.1. There are two main components of the software stack, a low-level software infrastructure, called Interface for Heterogeneous Kernels (IHK) (Shimosawa et al. 2014) and a lightweight co-kernel called McKernel.

17.3.1   Interface for Heterogeneous Kernels (IHK)

The Interface for Heterogeneous Kernels provides capabilities for partitioning resources in many-core environments (e.g., CPU cores and physical memory) and it enables management of lightweight kernels. IHK is capable of allocating and releasing host resources dynamically and no reboot of the host machine is required when altering configuration. Specifically, IHK reserves CPU cores from Linux using the CPU hot-unplug feature (i.e., offlining) while it simply allocates memory invoking

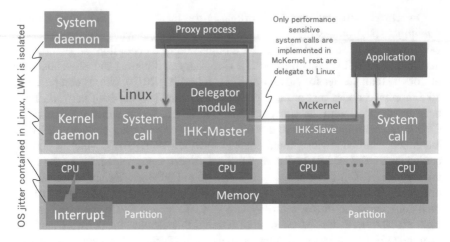

Fig. 17.1 Overview of the IHK/McKernel architecture and the system call forwarding mechanism

Linux kernel allocation routines. The latest version of IHK is implemented as a collection of Linux kernel modules without any modifications to the Linux kernel itself. This enables straightforward deployment of the multi-kernel stack on a wide range of Linux distributions. Besides resource and LWK management, IHK also facilitates an Inter-kernel Communication (IKC) layer, which is used for implementing system call delegation.

IHK is organized in a modular structure. A core IHK driver provides interfaces for registering IHK drivers. For example, there used to be a driver for the Xeon Phi KNC module, which was a PCI Express attached coprocessor. The main IHK driver module currently is the so-called SMP driver which supports managing many-core CPUs on which cores see the entire physical memory in a cache coherent fashion.

17.3.2 McKernel

McKernel is a lightweight co-kernel developed on top of IHK. It is designed explicitly for high-performance computing workloads, but it retains a Linux compatible Application Binary Interface (ABI) so that it can execute unmodified Linux binaries. There is no need for recompiling applications or for any McKernel specific libraries. McKernel implements only a small set of performance-sensitive system calls and the rest of the OS services are delegated to Linux. Specifically, McKernel provides its own memory management, it supports processes and multi-threading, it has a simple round-robin cooperative (tick-less) scheduler, and it implements standard POSIX signaling. It also implements inter-process memory mappings and it offers interfaces for accessing hardware performance counters.

For each OS process executed on McKernel there exists a process in Linux, which we call the *proxy-process*. The proxy process' main role is to assist system call off-loading. Essentially, it provides the execution context on behalf of the application so that off-loaded system calls can be invoked in Linux. For more information on system call off-loading, refer to Gerofi et al. (2013). The proxy process also provides means for Linux to maintain various state information that would have to be otherwise kept track of in the co-kernel. McKernel, for instance, has no notion of file descriptors, but it simply returns the number it receives from the proxy process during the execution of an *open* system call. The actual set of open files (i.e., file descriptor table, file positions, etc.) are managed by the Linux kernel. Note that the proxy process is multi-threaded, which enables simultaneous system call off-loads from multi-threaded McKernel processes.

17.3.3   Unified Address Space

To motivate the need for unified address space, we begin with a more detailed description of the system call off-loading mechanism illustrated in Fig. 17.2. During system call delegation, McKernel marshalls the system call number along with its arguments and sends a message to Linux via a dedicated IKC channel. The corresponding proxy process running on Linux is by default waiting for system call requests through an *ioctl* call into IHK'ssystem call delegator kernel module. The delegator kernel module's IKC interrupt handler wakes up the proxy process, which returns to user space and simply invokes the requested system call. Once it obtains the return value, it instructs the delegator module to send the result back to McKernel, which subsequently passes the value to user space.

Notice, however, that certain system call arguments may be merely pointers (e.g., the buffer argument of a *read* system call) and the actual operation takes place on the contents of the referred memory. Thus, the main problem is how the proxy process on Linux can resolve virtual addresses in arguments so that it can access the memory of the application running on McKernel.

The unified address space model in IHK/McKernel ensures that off-loaded system calls can seamlessly resolve arguments even in case of pointers. This mechanism is depicted in Fig. 17.2 and it is implemented as follows. First, the proxy process is compiled as a position-independent binary, which enables McKernel to map the code and data segments specific to the proxy process to an address range which is explicitly excluded from the LWK user space. The red box on the right side of the figure demonstrates the excluded region. Second, the entire valid virtual address range of McKernel'sapplication user space is covered by a special mapping in the proxy process for which we use a pseudofile mapping in Linux. This mapping is indicated by the green box on the left side of the figure.

Note, that the proxy process does not need to fill in any virtual-to-physical mappings at the time of creating the pseudomapping and it remains empty unless an address is referenced. Every time an unmapped address is accessed, however, the

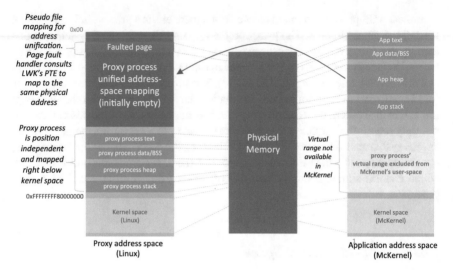

Fig. 17.2 Overview of the *unified address space* between the application and its corresponding proxy process

page fault handler of the pseudomapping consults the page tables corresponding to the application on the LWK, and maps it to the exact same physical page. Such mappings are demonstrated in the figure by the small boxes on the left labeled as *faulted page*. This mechanism ensures that the proxy process, while executing system calls, has access to the same memory content as the application. Needless to say, Linux's page table entries in the pseudomapping have to be synchronized with McKernel when the application calls *munmap* or modifies certain mappings.

17.3.4 Device Driver Transparency

Applications running on Unix-based operating systems normally interact with devices either through I/O system calls (e.g., *read*, *write*, *ioctl*, etc.) on dedicated device files or by mapping device memory directly into user space.

We have already mentioned that McKernel does not implement I/O calls, but instead, it forwards them to Linux. Thus, with the help of unified address space, applications running on McKernel can transparently interact with devices through I/O system calls. What is more challenging in a hybrid kernel setting, however, is to provide support for memory-mapped device files. We have carefully designed IHK and McKernel in a way so that devices can be memory mapped without any modification to existing driver code.

We summarize the main steps of mapping device files in McKernel as follows. The application invokes the *mmap* system call on a device file and McKernel forwards the request to the delegator IHK component in Linux. The kernel module memory maps the device file into the proxy process' address space and creates a tracking object that will be used to serve future page faults. Linux replies to McKernel so that it can also allocate its own virtual memory range in the address space of the application. Note that in the proxy process (on the Linux side), the entire valid user space of the actual application is covered by the unified address space's pseudomapping and thus the two mappings result in different virtual addresses.

What is important, however, is that although the virtual memory ranges in Linux and in McKernel are different, the proxy process on Linux will never access its mapping, because the proxy process never runs actual application code. Rather, the following steps occur. The application accesses an address in the mapping and causes a page fault. McKernel'spage fault handler knows that the device mapping requires special attention and it requests the IHK module on Linux to resolve the physical address based on the tracking object and the offset in the mapping. Linux replies the request and McKernel fills in the missing page table entry.

Modern high-performance networks (such as InfiniBand 2016) device mappings are usually established in application initialization phase and the actual interaction with the device is comprised of mostly regular `load`/`store` instructions carried out entirely in user space. For more details, on device driver support refer to Gerofi et al. (2016).

17.3.5   Support for Linux Pseudofile Systems

We mentioned earlier that compliance with the Linux pseudofile systems, e.g., `/proc` and `/sys`, is essential for supporting tools, debuggers, and libraries that rely on pseudofiles to obtain kernel information. McKernel provides a unique solution to this problem.

Because interaction with file systems is performed through the proxy process, McKernel provides a specialized view of `/proc` and `/sys` by overlapping McKernel-specific files with contents that correspond to LWK internals. We utilize the Linux overlay file system for implementing this feature, however, certain modifications were required to support interaction with McKernel. For example, the Linux overlay file system does not allow write operations to a file in the stacked file system to be executed in the underlying file system, but a copy of the original file is made first, which is referred to as *copy-up*. In case of McKernel, a special Linux kernel module, called `mcoverlayfs`, has been developed with modifications to the original Linux overlay file system that allows *write* system calls to avoid *copy-up* and operate on the original underlying file. This is required for operations which update kernel settings through pseudofiles.

Figure 17.3 shows the architecture of `mcoverlayfs`. As seen, certain files (e.g., `/proc/meminfo`) are overlapped with McKernel-specific content so that when they are accessed from the application running on the LWK (i.e., through the proxy process) the content reflects McKernel-specific information. Note the overlap occurs only in the proxy process as it uses a privatized mount namespace, a technique

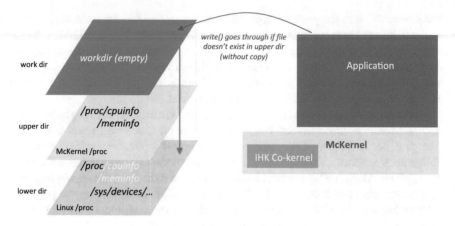

Fig. 17.3 Overview of the mcoverlayfs architecture

similar to the file system versioning mechanism of Docker's container engine (Merkel 2014). For more information on the original overlay file system, see the Linux kernel documentation (Brown 2018).

17.3.6 Hierarchical Memory Management

One of the early features of McKernel we demonstrated on the KNC platform was a hierarchical memory management scheme where the operating system moved memory transparently between the KNC's on-board Graphics Double Data Rate (GDDR) memory and the host machine's DRAM (Gerofi et al. 2013, 2014). The goal was to explore what the implications of many-core CPUs would be for operating system-level memory management in a multi-layer memory system. An overview of the various data movement scenarios we considered is shown in Fig. 17.4.

The leftmost figure represents the conventional setup in heterogeneous compute platforms where computation is off-loaded to the coprocessor and data movement is performed entirely by the user. The middle figure extends this architecture to an OS driver approach where memory is moved back and forth transparently by the system software. Finally, the figure on the right shows this model applied to stand-alone many-core systems (e.g., the KNL chip) with multiple levels of the memory hierarchy.

Our primary goal in using the KNC card was to investigate how a single address space can be efficiently maintained in a configuration, where the operating system keeps track of the physical memory, manages the mapping from virtual-to-physical addresses, and moves data between the card and the host in an application transparent fashion. While OS-level data movement may sound analogous to swapping in traditional operating systems, the scenario of many-core coprocessor-based mem-

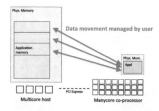

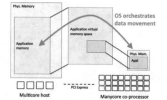

(a) Manual data movement between the host and many-core co-processor. *(Offload model.)*

(b) OS driven data movement between the host and many-core co-processor. *(Unified model.)*

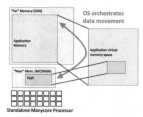

(c) OS driven data movement on standalone many-core CPUs with multiple levels of memory hierarchy. *(Unified model.)*

Fig. 17.4 Overview of data movement scenarios on systems with multiple layers of hierarchical memory

ory management is considerably different than regular disk-based swapping on a multi-core CPU. First, data movement between the coprocessor's RAM and the host memory, which takes place through the PCI Express bus, is *significantly faster* than accessing a disk in the host. This makes the relative cost of data movement during page fault handling *much lower* than in a disk-based setup. Second, the large number of CPU cores on the coprocessor renders the cost of remote TLB invalidations using regular page tables (i.e., shared by all cores) much higher than in a multi-core CPU. In the traditional OS process model, all CPU cores in an address space refer to the same set of page tables and TLB invalidation is done by means of looping through each CPU core and sending an Inter-processor Interrupt (IPI). Indeed, one of our main findings was that the TLB invalidation IPI loop becomes extremely expensive when frequent page faults occurred simultaneously on a large number of CPU cores (Gerofi et al. 2013).

However, we also found that in many HPC applications, the computation area (the memory area on which computation takes place) is divided among CPU cores and only a relatively small part of the memory is utilized for communication. Consequently, CPU cores do not actually access the entire computation area and when an address mapping is modified, most of the CPU cores are not affected. Nevertheless, the information of which cores' TLB have to be invalidated is not available due to

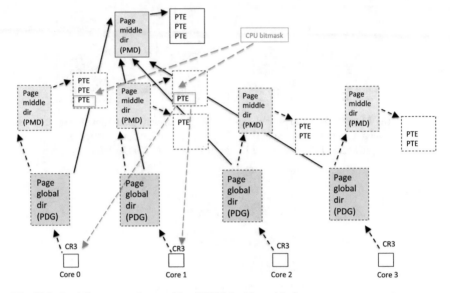

Fig. 17.5 Partially separated page tables (PSPT) for hierarchical memory management

the centralized bookkeeping of address translations in the address-space-wide page tables.

In order to overcome this problem, we have proposed per-core *partially separated page tables (PSPT)*, shown in Fig. 17.5. In PSPT, each core has its own last level page table, i.e., Page Global Directory (PGD). Kernel-space and regular user-space mappings point to the same Page Middle Directories (PMD), and thus use the same PTEs to define the address space (regular boxes in the top of Fig. 17.5). However, for the computation area per-core private page tables are used (denoted by dashed boxes in Fig. 17.5). There are multiple benefits of such arrangement. First, each CPU core sets up PTEs exclusively for addresses that it actually accesses. Second, when a virtual-to-physical mapping is changed, it can be precisely determined which cores' TLB might be affected, because only the ones which have a valid PTE for the particular address may have cached a translation. Consider the red dashed lines in Fig. 17.5, PTE invalidation in case of regular page tables require sending an IPI for each core, while PSPT invalidates the TLB only on $Core_0$ and $Core_1$. Third, synchronization (particularly, holding the proper locks for page table modifications) is performed only between affected cores, eliminating coarse-grained, address space wide locks that are often utilized in traditional operating system kernels (Clements et al. 2012).

In addition to PSPT, we proposed, implemented, and evaluated a specific page replacement policy, which exploits the auxiliary knowledge of the number of mapping CPU cores of each memory page. Note that such information cannot be obtained from regular page tables due to their centralized bookkeeping of address mappings. The basic idea was that during page reclamation, the OS would prioritize pages which were mapped by only a small number of CPU cores and thus further reduce the TLB invalidation cost of remapping the corresponding virtual address. For more information on this page replacement policy refer to Gerofi et al. (2014).

The multi-kernel architecture enabled us to experiment with new ideas and to provide an implementation in a short period of time, which were crucial for both PSPT and the proposed page replacement policy. Implementing per-thread page tables in the Linux kernel would be a significantly more labor-intensive undertaking.

17.4 Evaluation

This section provides performance evaluation on the IHK/McKernel multi-kernel operating system.

17.4.1 Hierarchical Memory Management

The first measurements we provide evaluate hierarchical memory management. Specifically, they demonstrate the usage of partially separated page tables as well as the proposed core-map Count-based Page Replacement Policy (CMCP) (Gerofi et al. 2014).

Although in our original study, we covered a wider range of applications, due to space limitations we only include two applications from the NAS Parallel Benchmarks (Bailey et al. 1991) in this chapter, namely, Lower-Upper symmetric Gauss–Seidel (LU) and Block Tridiagonal (BT). With respect to memory usage, we used the small configuration, i.e., the B class of NPB benchmarks. In order to move the computation data into the PSPT memory region, we interface a C block with the Fortran code which explicitly memory maps allocations to the area covered by the separated subtree of page tables. In all experiments, we pinned application threads to separate CPU cores, because we dedicated some of the hyperthreads to the page usage statistics collection mechanism for LRU. Regarding page replacement policies, we compared our proposal against an LRU approximation, which implements the same algorithm employed by the Linux kernel (Mauerer 2010).

Results of our experiments are shown in Fig. 17.6. For each benchmark, we ran five configurations. First, using regular page tables and providing sufficient physical memory so that data movement does not occur. This is indicated by the legend no data movement. We limit physical memory so that FIFO replacement using PSPT achieves approximately half of the performance of the no data movement configuration. This translates to physical memory limitation of 64% for BT, 66% for LU. We measured the performance of FIFO replacement for both regular and partially separated page tables, indicated by regular PT + FIFO and PSPT + FIFO, respectively. Additionally, we compare the performance of page replacement

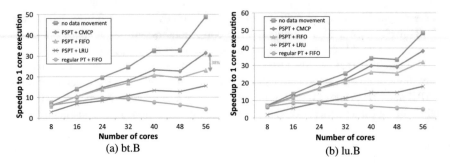

Fig. 17.6 Performance measurements of NAS Parallel benchmarks comparing regular page tables and PSPT using various page replacement policies

policies by evaluating the effect of LRU, denoted by `PSPT + LRU`, and core-map count-based replacement, indicated by `PSPT + CMCP`.

There is nothing wrong with regular page tables in case no data movement (and thus no address remapping) is performed by the OS. However, when frequent page faults occur concurrently on several cores, regular page tables hardly scale up to 24 cores, resulting in completely unacceptable performance. In fact, there is slow down in most cases when more than 24 cores are utilized.

On the other hand, partially separated page tables provide relative speedups (i.e., scalability) similar to the no data movement configuration. Surprisingly, we found that LRU yields lower performance than FIFO. Nevertheless, the key observation with regards to page replacement policies is the superior performance of the core-map count-based replacement policy, which consistently outperforms FIFO, yielding 38 and 25% better results when running on 56 CPU cores for BT (Fig. 17.6a), LU (Fig. 17.6b), respectively. For more information on detailed analysis of page faults and remote TLB invalidations, as well as on further investigation regarding the behavior, see our previous work (Gerofi et al. 2014).

17.4.2   Scalability

Recently, we have demonstrated that lightweight multi-kernels can outperform Linux on various HPC mini-applications when evaluated on up to 2,048 Intel Xeon Phi nodes interconnected by Intel's Omni-Path network (Gerofi et al. 2018). In this chapter, we provide measurements using the following three applications:

AMG2013, from the CORAL benchmark suite, is a parallel algebraic multigrid solver for linear systems arising from problems on unstructured grids. The code is written in ISO standard C (Henson and Yang 2002).

MiniFE, also from CORAL, is a proxy application for unstructured implicit finite element codes. It is similar to HPCCG (Dongarra et al. 2015) but provides a much more complete vertical covering of the steps in this class of applications.

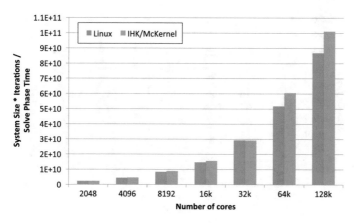

Fig. 17.7 Scaling results of AMG2013 (CORAL benchmarks)

Like HPCCG, MiniFE is intended to be the best approximation to an unstructured implicit finite element or finite volume application, but in 8,000 lines of code or fewer (Heroux et al. 2009).

CCS-QCD, from the The University of Hiroshima, benchmarks the performance of a linear equation solver with a large sparse coefficient matrix appearing in lattice Quantum Chromodynamics (QCD) simulations explaining the nature of protons and neutrons in terms of elementary particles called quarks and gluons. It solves the equation for the O(a)-improved Wilson–Dirac quarks using the BiCGStab algorithm (Ishikawa et al. 2017).

Figure 17.7 shows the results we obtained for the AMG2013 mini-application. The X-axis represents the number of CPU cores, where we used 64 cores per node, i.e., we scaled the benchmark up to 2,048 nodes. Although McKernel yields only a modest 12% improvement over Linux, the performance gain increases with the scale and thus we anticipate further improvements once we can go over 2,048 nodes.

Figure 17.8 shows the evaluation of CCS-QCD. We observed up to 38% improvement over Linux for this benchmark. CCS-QCD utilizes a large amount of memory, and while Linux cannot manage efficiently the large number of NUMA nodes of the KNL chip in SNC-4 mode, McKernel has been developed to support multiple types of memory, and can maximally utilize the on package high-bandwidth memory of the chip. For more explanation on the particulars of these results, see our previous work (Gerofi et al. 2018).

Our final benchmark, miniFE, shown in Fig. 17.9, from CORAL (which we ran in strong scaled configuration), behaved rather unexpectedly. On Linux, once reaching over 512 nodes, the performance degraded rapidly. McKernel, however, continued to scale further achieving a 3.5X speed up compared to Linux on 1,024 nodes. Due to the limited availability of large-scale dedicated resources, we were unable to pinpoint the issue with Linux, but we believe that it has likely to do with memory management or that miniFE spends a lot of time in MPI_Allreduce(), which strongly favors a jitterless environment.

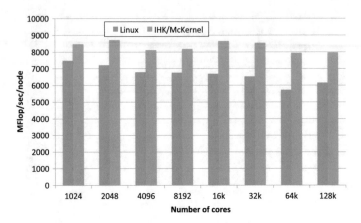

Fig. 17.8 Scaling results of CCS-QCD (University of Hiroshima)

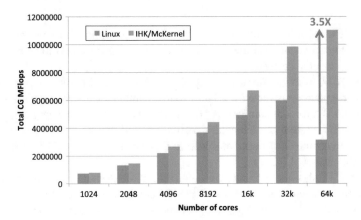

Fig. 17.9 Scaling results of miniFE (CORAL benchmarks)

17.5 Lessons Learned

In its sixth year of active development, the IHK/McKernel project has from many perspectives lived up to expectations. Most importantly, large-scale evaluations show notable performance improvements over Linux. In addition, the ease of experimentation with unconventional kernel features enabled by McKernel'ssmall code base has also proven extremely beneficial. IHK's dynamic nature of LWK management lets us rapidly explore novel OS ideas that would be otherwise highly intrusive to implement in Linux.

On the negative side, developing an operating system kernel is a major undertaking and requires years to smooth out all the details. For example, the *ptrace* implementation has been a long-standing burden, as well as providing the right content in /proc and /sys pseudofile systems. The Linux kernel community worked decades on making sure these things work and re-implementing them (even in a lightweight co-kernel) is time-consuming and of no research interest.

Deployment of the multi-kernel stack on the Oakforest-PACS machine for general availability is in progress at the time of writing this chapter. We faced several issues along the way, e.g., instability of the parallel file system when CPU cores are dynamically off-lined and re-onlined or the Linux kernel failing in IHK's memory reservation routines, etc. A large number of problems have been already ironed out, but unexpected issues keep arising. Nevertheless, the team is looking forward to feedback from future users.

Acknowledgements This work has been partially funded by MEXT's program for the Development and Improvement of Next Generation Ultra High-Speed Computer Systems under its subsidies for operating the Specific Advanced Large Research Facilities in Japan.

We acknowledge Tomoki Shirasawa, Gou Nakamura, and Ken Sato from Hitachi for their McKernel development efforts. We thank Prof. Taisuke Boku from The University of Tsukuba and Prof. Nakajima Kengo from The University of Tokyo for their support to let us access the Oakforest-PACS supercomputer. We also thank the Intel *mOS* team for all the invaluable discussions on design considerations of multi-kernel operating systems and for providing us with information on the configuration of mini-applications we used for evaluation. Finally, we acknowledge Takahiro Ogura and Toshiro Saiki from Fujitsu for their relentless support regarding the operation of the OFP machine.

References

Bailey, D., Barszcz, E., Barton, J., Browning, D., Carter, R., Dagum, L., et al. (1991). The nas parallel benchmarks. *The International Journal of High Performance Computing Applications, 5*(3), 63–73.

BDEC Committee, (2017). The BDEC "Pathways to convergence" report. http://www.exascale.org/bdec/.

Brown, N. (2018). Overlay filesystem documentation. https://www.kernel.org/doc/Documentation/filesystems/overlayfs.txt.

Cavium, (2014). ThunderX_CP family of workload optimized compute processors.

Clements, A. T., Kaashoek, M. F., & Zeldovich, N. (2012). Scalable address spaces using RCU balanced trees. In *Proceedings of the Seventeenth International Conference on Architectural Support for Programming Languages and Operating Systems, ASPLOS '12.*

Dongarra, J., Heroux, M. A., & Luszczek, P. (2015). HPCG benchmark: A new metric for ranking high performance computing systems. Technical Report UT-EECS-15-736, University of Tennessee, Electrical Engineering and Computer Science Department.

Gerofi, B., Riesen, R., Takagi, M., Boku, T., Ishikawa, Y., & Wisniewski, R. W. (2018). Performance and scalability of lightweight multi-kernel based operating systems. In *2018 IEEE International Parallel and Distributed Processing Symposium (IPDPS).*

Gerofi, B., Shimada, A., Hori, A., & Ishikawa, Y. (2013). Partially separated page tables for efficient operating system assisted hierarchical memory management on heterogeneous architectures. In *13th International Symposium on Cluster, Cloud and Grid Computing (CCGrid).*

Gerofi, B., Shimada, A., Hori, A., Masamichi, T., & Ishikawa, Y. (2014). CMCP: A novel page replacement policy for system level hierarchical memory management on many-cores. In *Proceedings of the 23rd International Symposium on High-performance Parallel and Distributed Computing, HPDC* (pp. 73–84). New York, NY, USA: ACM.

Gerofi, B., Takagi, M., Hori, A., Nakamura, G., Shirasawa, T., & Ishikawa, Y. (2016). On the scalability, performance isolation and device driver transparency of the IHK/McKernel hybrid lightweight kernel. In *2016 IEEE International Parallel and Distributed Processing Symposium (IPDPS)* (pp. 1041–1050).

Henson, V. E., & Yang, U. M. (2002). BoomerAMG: A parallel algebraic multigrid solver and preconditioner. *Applied Numerical Mathematics, 41*, 155–177.

Heroux, M. A., Doerfler, D. W., Crozier, P. S., Willenbring, J. M., Edwards, H. C., Williams, A., et al. (2009). Improving performance via Mini-applications. Technical Report SAND2009-5574, Sandia National Laboratories.

InfiniBand Trade Association. (2016). InfiniBand Architecture Specification, Release 1.3.1.

Ishikawa, K.-I., Kuramashi, Y., Ukawa, A., & Boku, T. (2017). CCS QCD application. https://github.com/fiber-miniapp/ccs-qcd.

Jeffers, J., & Reinders, J. (2013). *Intel Xeon Phi coprocessor high performance programming.* Burlington: Morgan Kaufmann.

Joint Center for Advanced HPC (JCAHPC) (2018). Basic specification of Oakforest-PACS. http://jcahpc.jp/files/OFP-basic.pdf.

Mauerer, W. (2010). *Professional Linux kernel architecture* (1st ed.). Birmingham: Wrox Press.

Merkel, D. (2014). Docker: Lightweight Linux containers for consistent development and deployment. *Linux Journal, 2014*(239).

RIKEN Advanced Institute for Computational Science (2018). K computer. http://www.aics.riken.jp/en/k-computer/about/.

Shimosawa, T. (2011). Operating system organization for manycore systems. http://www.ipsj.or.jp/magazine/hakase/2011/OS01.html.

Shimosawa, T., Gerofi, B., Takagi, M., Nakamura, G., Shirasawa, T., Saeki, Y. (2014). Interface for heterogeneous Kernels: A framework to enable hybrid OS designs targeting high performance computing on manycore architectures. In *21th International Conference on High Performance Computing, HiPC.*

Yoshida, T., Hondou, M., Tabata, T., Kan, R., Kiyota, N., Kojima, H., et al. (2015). Sparc64 XIfx: Fujitsu's next-generation processor for high-performance computing. *IEEE Micro, 35*(2), 6–14.

Chapter 18
mOS for HPC

Rolf Riesen and Robert W. Wisniewski

Abstract This chapter describes the design and implementation of the mOS multi-kernel project at Intel Corp. The multi-Operating System (mOS) for High-Performance Computing (HPC) combines a Linux and a lightweight kernel (LWK) to provide the required Linux functionality, and the scalability and performance of an LWK. In this chapter, we explain the thought process that led to the current design of mOS. We highlight the difficulties of running two kernels on the compute nodes of a supercomputer, while maintaining Linux compatibility, and tracking recent Linux kernel developments. And, we show how analyzing these sometimes conflicting goals helped us make design and implementation decisions.

18.1 Introduction

Research and practical experiments have shown that Lightweight Kernels (LWKs) scale and perform well on past High-Performance Computing (HPC) machines. These are characteristics which are even more important on tomorrow's extreme-scale systems. In recent years, Linux has become ubiquitous in HPC, including high-end systems, and it has become clear that Linux compatibility is important for managing HPC systems, writing applications for them, and using common tools to debug, tune, and measure performance. Therefore, combining LWK performance with Linux compatibility seems like a good approach for providing an Operating System (OS) for HPC and extreme-scale machines. Although the concept is simple,

Intel and the Intel logo are trademarks of Intel Corporation in the U.S. and/or other countries. Linux is the registered trademark of Linus Torvalds in the U.S. and other countries.
*Other names and brands may be claimed as the property of others.

R. Riesen (✉)
Intel Corporation, Hillsboro, OR, USA
e-mail: rolf.riesen@intel.com

R. W. Wisniewski
Intel Corporation, New York City, NY, USA
e-mail: robert.w.wisniewski@intel.com

© Springer Nature Singapore Pte Ltd. 2019
B. Gerofi et al. (eds.), *Operating Systems for Supercomputers and High Performance Computing*, High-Performance Computing Series,
https://doi.org/10.1007/978-981-13-6624-6_18

307

designing and implementing the idea is a challenge that has more than one solution as witnessed by the other multi-kernel projects in this part of the book. There are many trade-offs to be made, and each has consequences that affects performance, maintainability, and Linux compatibility.

The Multi-Operating System (*mOS*) (Wisniewski et al. 2014)) project at Intel Corp. has been influenced by the SUNMOS/Puma (Riesen et al. 2009) line of LWK from Sandia National Laboratories and the University of New Mexico, IBM's Compute Node Kernel (CNK) (Giampapa et al. 2010) and FusedOS (Park et al. 2012), and by the Interface for Heterogeneous Kernels IHK/McKernel (Shimosawa et al. 2014) project at RIKEN.

The goal of the *mOS* project at Intel is to combine Linux and an LWK into a single compute node OS. Both kernels run at the same time, each doing what it does best. The project started in 2013 with a small team that began generating and evaluating different architectural approaches and embarked on an initial prototype implementation. *mOS* is under active development, open source (Intel 2018), and targeted to run on extreme-scale systems.

18.2   The Architecture of mOS

The idea of running the Linux kernel on one or a few cores of a many-core CPU and an LWK on the remaining cores is alluring. It provides a high level of Linux compatibility and partitions a single node into a service and a compute partition. Such a partitioning is not unlike how Massively Parallel Processors (MPP) of the 1990s were configured. The partitioning has the effect of isolating the two kernels, letting each do what it does best, and providing applications a specific set of resources that they can use without interference.

Accomplishing concurrent execution of two kernels, while preserving the desired performance qualities and functionality features, presents many challenges and there are multiple ways to design such an implementation.

18.2.1   Design Space

mOS and LWKs in general, are targeted at the high end of HPC, often referred to as capability computing. This is in contrast to Linux, which has a much broader spectrum of application areas. Figure 18.1 illustrates this graphically. Linux spans the spectrum from mobile phones to supercomputers. However, the same design that gives it that versatility, also limits its ability to provide maximum performance for a particular slice of the spectrum, such as capability-class HPC.

The Linux kernel is a fast moving and quickly evolving code base. This presents two challenges to a project like *mOS* . It must be quick and straightforward to couple the *mOS* LWK with the latest Linux kernel version to leverage all the features in

Fig. 18.1   Usage targets for mOS

Fig. 18.2   The design space
for mOS

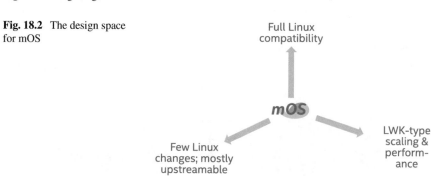

Linux that the *mOS* LWK is not providing. And, the combined kernel must provide benefits that Linux alone does not.

The tension resulting from these challenges is illustrated in Fig. 18.2. Linux compatibility with recent kernel versions must be retained. At the same time, we cannot give up the main reason for a multi-kernel's existence: Provide the LWK benefits of performance and scalability. But, there is a third requirement or limiter: The effort to couple the LWK with a new version of the Linux kernel must be kept small. These three constraints define the design space for a multi-kernel like *mOS* (Gerofi et al. 2015).

Linux compatibility extends beyond the system call interface . The `/proc` and `/sys` pseudo file systems provide additional ways to interact with the Linux kernel. Runtime systems and high-performance libraries depend on these pseudo file systems to learn about the installed hardware and architecture of the node, and use them to control how the Linux kernel behaves, i.e., setting policies. For a multi-kernel to be compatible with Linux, it needs to provide these pseudo files, including the information and control they provide.

Traditionally, LWKs have provided a limited amount of functionality in order to deliver the highest performance and scalability on high-end HPC systems. Unfortunately, this has meant that functions and features that application developers have come to rely on in Linux may not be available when running on an LWK.

Figure 18.3 illustrates this with a gray line pointing down. Code running in the LWK domain has high scalability and good performance, but only limited Linux compatibility. A given functionality is either provided by the LWK, or, with a traditional LWK, applications cannot utilize that capability at all.

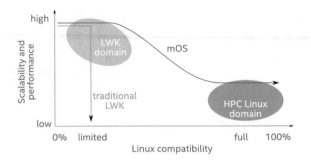

Fig. 18.3 Traditional LWK and mOS compatibility with Linux

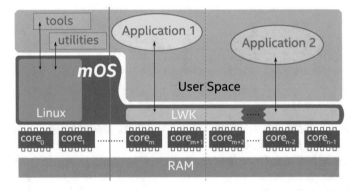

Fig. 18.4 Conceptual view of mOS

mOS provides an alternative that removes the sharp drop of functionality beyond the LWK domain. All Linux functionality is available to application running on *mOS*. The blue line spanning the graph from left to right in Fig. 18.3 illustrates this. However, as we move toward the right-hand side of the graph, we are giving up some of the performance and scalability available in the LWK domain.

This is not the same as graceful degradation under load. The move along the blue line happens when the application is being designed and when it runs and makes use of certain Linux features. Graceful degradation is a Full-Weight Kernel (FWK) characteristic that LWKs try to avoid as it leads to unpredictable behavior, something shown to be detrimental at scale. See Fig. 18.5 for an example.

The goal is for the LWK to service OS calls that are HPC performance critical with other requests being handled by Linux. The application programmer chooses which system calls to use and thus determines the trade-off between performance and generality.

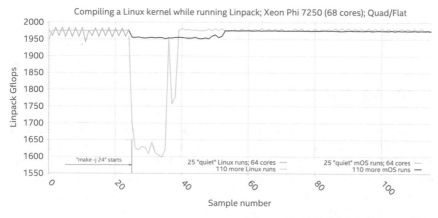

Performance data subject to Optimization Notice on page 344.

Fig. 18.5 Linux and mOS LWK behavior under load

18.2.2   mOS Overview

Figure 18.4 shows a conceptual overview of *mOS*. Each compute node is partitioned into two parts: The cores and memory that are managed by Linux, and the cores and memory that are managed by the LWK. The majority of processes run in one or the other partition. For the most part, it is not our intent to allow processes to span the partition boundary shown as a red line in Fig. 18.4. Utility threads that run in the same address space as an application, but are spawned by the runtime system, e.g., monitors or progress engines are one possible exception.

Note, though, that *mOS* itself straddles the partition line. *mOS* consists of a Linux kernel in one partition and an LWK running in the other partition. We modified the Linux kernel to enable the symbiosis with the LWK, but a regular Linux process in the Linux partition will not be aware of that.

The *mOS* LWK is different from traditional LWKs in that it has even less functionality. We were able to accomplish a lighter LWK because of the resident Linux kernel in the same memory coherence domain. As an example of such an optimization, there is no code to boot the node or initialize devices. Most of the Linux functionalities, like the `init` process or other daemons, are not run on the LWK cores.

Application processes in the LWK partition are isolated from each other the same way Linux protects individual processes from each other. The dashed vertical red line in Fig. 18.4 represents that.

Although not usually done on a large parallel system, it is possible to login to a node running *mOS*. The shell executes on the Linux side. It is not possible to login to the LWK side; there is no login daemon running in the LWK partition.

Tasks such as launching an LWK process or attaching a debugger are done from the Linux side. A parallel debugging tool, for example, would have a server on the Linux side of *mOS* nodes. This implies that a tool on the Linux side must be able to interact with LWK processes in the other partitions. System calls like *prctl* and *ptrace* commonly used for that purpose, work in *mOS* across the red boundary.

18.2.3 Lightweight Kernels

We have mentioned an LWK several times and indicated that the ones used in multi-kernels can be simpler than the original ones in the early 1990s. A precise definition of an LWK is surprisingly difficult (Riesen et al. 2015). In part, this is due to that several classes of OS kernels could be considered "lightweight". Another reason is that there is not a large base of LWKs from which to generalize. Further, there is a lack of common terminology and features because LWKs were often designed for a particular system. Finally, the LWK deployed in multi-kernels like mOS and IHK/McKernel (Shimosawa et al. 2014) are significantly different from traditional LWKs.

Traditional LWKs provide resource management functions for processes, memory, and the high-bandwidth network interface. Sometimes there is a hardware abstraction layer, and there is code to handle signals, interrupts, and machine checks and exceptions.

What is different from a full-weight kernel is that there is no file system, the system call interface is greatly reduced, and process and memory management are simplified. The scheduler deals with one or at most a handful of processes, and it is often non-preemptive. "LWKs are designed and streamlined for the high end of HPC ...These systems have extreme scales and levels of parallelism." (Riesen et al. 2015)

LWKs have different design goals from FWKs. The former is targeted for specific use, emphasizes efficiency over functionality, and maximizes the amount of resources, e.g., CPU cycles and physical memory space, available to applications. In the context of multi-kernels, these attributes have to be achieved while providing the full set of features a traditional kernel supplies.

Behavior under load is different for LWKs than it is for FWKs. The latter are designed to gracefully degrade as load increases. LWKs are often designed to exhibit no degradation until the load exceeds the capacity of the underlying hardware, and then often have precipitous performance fall off. This is not the desired behavior in a desktop system or a server environment.

Not having to degrade gracefully allows an LWK to exhibit more consistent, deterministic performance. This is necessary for tightly coupled applications to achieve high scalability.

Figure 18.5 provides an example. On a 68-core Intel® Xeon Phi™ processor 7250, we use four cores to compile a Linux kernel while the remaining 64 cores run Linpack. The length of the graph, the *x*-axis, shows 135 Linpack runs using the node booted into Linux, and another 135 runs using *mOS* with Linpack running in the LWK partition. For the first 25 runs under both OSs, the node is "quiet", i.e., only Linpack is running.

Just before the 26th Linpack run, we start a parallel compile of a Linux kernel. Under *mOS*, the kernel compile happens on the four cores that run the Linux kernel, while Linpack runs on the 64 cores of the LWK partition. In the all-Linux scenario, we let Linux decide where to place the compile and Linpack runs.

With both Linux and *mOS*, there is some degradation due to the compilation. This is because the underlying hardware is shared. While *mOS* isolates memory and cores between Linux and the LWK, there are still some resources, including memory bandwidth, that have to be shared within the Xeon Phi chip.

However, the plot shows that the intrusion from the second job on the same node affects the Linpack performance on the LWK much less. This is one of the desired behaviors of an LWK in a multi-kernel and can be useful in workflows that run machine learning or analytics code on the Linux side and a scientific simulation on the LWK.

There have been efforts to use Linux containers to achieve resource isolation suitable for HPC. The Argo researchers have shown positive results with a container approach for some types of workloads (see Chap. 12). However, as containers are built on top of Linux, they are still susceptible to interference from the OS. A multi-kernel, on the other hand, is able to isolate resources down to the hardware.

Performance isolation is an important goal in other multi-kernel architectures as well (Ouyang et al. 2015; Kocoloski and Lange 2014).

18.2.4   Partitioning

Achieving LWK design goals is accomplished by simplifying process and memory management, and by omitting functionality. Space sharing of compute nodes is one of these simplifying measures. The compute nodes of the past are now individual cores that can be allocated in bulk to applications or to another OS that provides services that an LWK does not implement.

The partitioned supercomputers of the past have shrunk into a single chip. Function shipping between a compute node and a service node can now happen more efficiently between cores that run different OS kernels. The supercomputer partitioning concept is a fundamental principle in *mOS* where resource management is split into three phases.

Partitioning between Linux and the LWK, and between *mOS* processes is a fundamental principle of *mOS*. It is important for the isolation we seek between Linux and the LWK, it is used to maintain Non-Uniform Memory Access (NUMA) separation, and is needed to "hold" resources on a node for later process starts.

Creating these partitions is a three-step process, which is as follows:

1. *Designation* of resources to the LWK happens at boot time or between jobs when the node is idle.
2. *Reservation* of a subset of designated resources happens at process launch time.
3. *Allocation* of reserved resources happens at runtime.

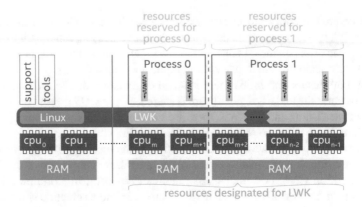

Fig. 18.6 mOS partitioning and space sharing

Resources to the left and right of the vertical red line in Fig. 18.4 are managed by Linux and the *mOS* LWK, respectively. The red line represents the separation between the Linux and the LWK partition. We call determining where that red line is placed on a node **resource designation**. In the first version of *mOS*, *designation* had to be done at boot time. The goal was to isolate CPUs and memory early during the boot, allowing only the *mOS* LWK to manage them. Today's *mOS* is more dynamic and allows moving that partition barrier even after boot to accommodate shifting workload needs.

The second phase in *mOS* resource management is called **resource reservation**. It occurs at process launch time, when the launch utility, yod, creates a sub-partition from the already *designated* LWK resources. The typical example is when multiple Message Passing Interface (MPI) ranks share a single compute node. Each of the ranks gets a portion of the designated resources. Figure 18.6 illustrates this.

During the lifetime of a process, a reservation remains static. The process cannot request more CPUs or allocate memory beyond the reserved amount. On the other hand, the resources reserved for that process are guaranteed to remain reserved throughout its lifetime.

The third phase, **resource allocation**, happens while the application is running. System calls like *mmap* and *sched_getaffinity* allocate memory and CPU resources from the pool that has been reserved for the calling process.

With each step, new partition walls are created as shown in Fig. 18.7. This partition model lends itself to space sharing, a concept that has been exploited by previous-generation LWKs and is a good match for the ever-increasing number of cores and hardware threads in modern CPUs.

There are several important advantages to dealing with resources as described. The resource management model is easy to understand for OS and runtime developers as well as users. It is simple to implement and get right. It is highly predictable and a key ingredient in implementing the repeatability and determinism requirements of

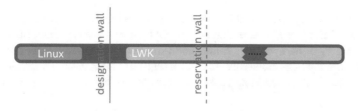

Fig. 18.7 Resource designation and reservation create partition walls

mOS. A priori knowledge of the resources within a partition enables simpler page and CPU management, and makes using large pages easier.

There are disadvantages as well to handling resource management in this manner. Some applications need more flexibility and cannot function in such an environment. Unlike an LWK though, in *mOS* those applications have access to the Linux kernel. Another possible disadvantage is that any form of partitioning can lead to fragmentation. However, the above advantages also make it easier for runtime systems to do a better job at using the available resources and avoid fragmentation.

18.2.5   LWK Coupling with an FWK

A multi-kernel LWK can only exist if there is an FWK nearby that provides Portable Operating System Interface for Unix (POSIX) compatibility, file I/O, and other features that are not part of the LWK design.

Function shipping on previous supercomputers had to pay the overhead of communicating with another node. With the advent of many-core systems, multi-kernels or co-kernels, where both the LWK and the FWK run on the same node, have become possible. More important than reducing function shipping overhead, however, is that combining two kernels on the same node facilitates greater Linux compatibility (Ali et al. 2009; Ouyang et al. 2015; Brightwell et al. 2013; Akkan et al. 2013; Otstott et al. 2014).

Several current projects are exploring how to best couple multiple kernels. They include Kitten/Palacios (Lange et al. 2010), FusedOS (Park et al. 2012), IHK/McKernel (Shimosawa et al. 2014; Gerofi et al. 2016), Fast Fault-tolerant Micro-Kernel (FFMK) (Weinhold et al. 2016), and *mOS* (Wisniewski et al. 2014). These projects differ in how they provide Linux functionality while achieving LWK performance and scalability, demonstrating that there are multiple possible solutions, and that consensus on what is best has not been formed yet.

Because a full-featured kernel is now available on the same node, and interacting with it is a local operation, the *mOS* LWK is in many ways simpler than its predecessors. For example, the *mOS* LWK has almost no direct dependency on the hardware it runs on. We let Linux boot and initialize devices, and the *mOS* LWK then uses Linux kernel functions and macros for further configurations.

Consider setting up page tables. The Linux kernel does not have a clearly defined and isolated Hardware Abstraction Layer (HAL). But, because Linux runs on such a wide variety of hardware, its source code structure and the low-level functions it provides to setup page tables, access control registers, shoot down Translation Look-aside Buffer (TLBs), send interrupts, etc. form an implicit HAL that our LWK can use.

Relying on Linux for most of the functionality an OS kernel must provide, simplifies the LWK. However, there is one piece that previous-generation LWK did not have: A way for the two kernels on a node to interact. There are different ways of achieving this. One is a proxy model, used by IHK/McKernel, where for each LWK process there also exists a user-space process on the Linux side. That proxy makes the Linux system calls when instructed by the LWK, and transfers the results back to the LWK process. Another approach, which is used by *mOS*, is letting the LWK call directly into the Linux kernel. These two approaches are contrasted in (Gerofi et al. 2015).

To summarize, multi-kernel LWKs like the one in *mOS*

- target a specific set of machines and application types,
- rely on an FWK on the same node,
- do not change their behavior under load (i.e., no graceful degradation),
- are as deterministic as possible, and
- consist of components and functionality that are simplified as compared to a Linux kernel.

18.3   The Design of mOS

The vision for *mOS* provided by Robert W. Wisniewski was clear: Place Linux and an LWK together onto a many-core compute node. Have the LWK implement the performance- and scale-critical system calls and have Linux provide the remaining functionality, thereby achieving the high performance and scalability of LWKs while providing compatibility with Linux.

Going from vision to idea, to design, to implementation, including assembling a team to do it, took almost two years. There were several design options that we considered within our design space from Sect. 18.2.1. From early in the project, we had a productive collaboration with the team at the Institute of Physical and Chemical Research (RIKEN) in Japan, which was working on the IHK/McKernel (Shimosawa et al. 2014). They had a prototype running and we learned a lot from its design and the people working on IHK/McKernel.

In this section, we will describe the key steps from the original vision to the current *mOS* implementation. As part of doing this, we explain some of the key differences to IHK/McKernel to illustrate the trade-offs in multi-kernels.

18.3.1   *From Vision to Design*

The original development plan evolved and became more refined as we started to think about how we would implement it. The following sections describe this process.

18.3.1.1   First Steps Toward a Design

The vision for *mOS* came out of the observed need for Linux compatibility for high-end HPC, and the observation that extreme-scale systems would benefit from a specialized OS, an ExaOS, that could quickly be adapted to efficiently use new supercomputing hardware, scale well, and perform at the expected level. This leads to Fig. 18.8a.

LWKs have proven themselves in extreme-scale systems and seemed a logical choice for the role of the ExaOS in the diagram below. Few applications interact with the OS kernel directly. Rather, it is libraries, such as libc, that trap into the kernel. Therefore, if the new OS had the ability to support the libc API, or even better, its Application Binary Interface (ABI), and had an LWK for the performance critical aspects, then we would have a much better OS foundation. This is expressed in Fig. 18.8b. At this point, we needed to decide how to run the two kernels simultaneously on a compute node. Since *mOS* is targeting many-core architectures, we simply run Linux on some of those cores and the LWK on the others. This is shown in Fig. 18.8c.

The idea is that HPC applications would run on the cores controlled by the LWK, which led to some more refinements of the idea. The vertical red line between the cores is meant to symbolize the partitioning of cores to either OS. Because the rectangle representing the application is no longer straddling the two OS kernels, we need a way to forward service requests to Linux. Without being specific yet, the horizontal line between the two kernels represents that interaction.

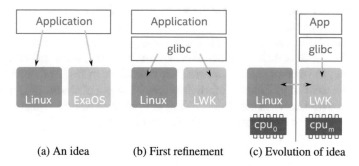

     (a) An idea   (b) First refinement   (c) Evolution of idea

Fig. 18.8 The evolution of an idea

Fig. 18.9 Dividing the work

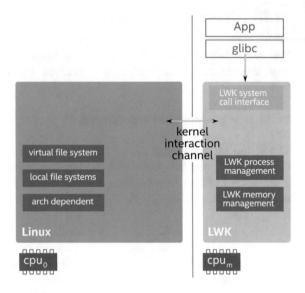

18.3.1.2   Dividing the Work

The original idea in Fig. 18.8a was to divide the work between the two OSs and let each do what it does best. From past experiences, we knew that we wanted the LWK to handle memory and process management. Obviously, we need Linux to handle the compatibility part. Figure 18.9 expands Fig. 18.8c and shows how we want the work to be divided among the two OSs.

Past LWKs did not internally support a file system. File I/O capability was either handled by user-space libraries or off-loaded to I/O nodes. In *mOS*, we expect Linux to handle local files, such as a RAM disk for example. High-speed parallel I/O is, as in the past, off-loaded to external nodes.

Since the LWK shares the node with Linux, we can leverage Linux to boot the node and manage devices, as well as interact with the rest of the machine. This excludes the high-performance fabric, which should deliver data directly into LWK space, but includes Reliability, Availability, and Serviceability (RAS) and login functionality.

We decided, due to their importance on performance, that system calls for process management and memory management should be handled by the LWK, with all other system calls handled by Linux. Unfortunately, as we began implementing, it became clear the division is not that simple. We had not considered some issues that had a major impact on the design and implementation of *mOS*.

18.3.1.3   A More Complete Picture Emerges

Up to this point, we had not considered what the Linux side would look like. We knew what we wanted the *application view* to be, and what it meant to make system

Fig. 18.10 Application and tools view of the system

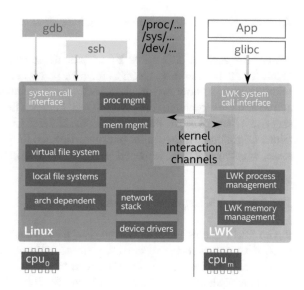

calls on the LWK side. But, in order for *mOS* to be a fully functional OS, tools such as debuggers and performance monitors, need to work with LWK processes.

These tools run in the Linux partition but need to be able to monitor and control aspects of the LWK processes and memory. Many Linux tools do this through the /proc and /sys pseudo file systems and system calls like *ptrace*. These tools make system calls to access the pseudo file system from the Linux partition. We call this the *tools view* and Fig. 18.10 illustrates it.

Note that the /proc and /sys pseudo file systems are also visible to regular Linux processes. HPC processes in the LWK partition need to be able to access them as well. Pseudo file system information about LWK processes and resources is provided on the Linux side. Control commands like pkill, *ptrace*, and *prctl* originate on the Linux side, but affect processes on the LWK side. Therefore, the kernel interaction channels in Fig. 18.10 need to be asynchronous and bidirectional.

18.3.1.4   Kernel Interactions

The interface between the two OSs needs to be asynchronous. If a tool like gdb makes a request on the Linux side using the *ptrace* system call, the LWK side has to provide the requested information or take actions, e.g., stopping an LWK process. Most of these types of interactions, e.g., status requests, need to happen without interrupting the LWK, because that would introduce OS noise. Next, we address what capabilities these kernel interaction channels, as shown in Fig. 18.10, need to have.

18.3.2 Kernel Interaction Requirements

We use the abstract concept of kernel interaction channels to enumerate requirements for the two kernels in *mOS* to interact. In this section, we describe the needed
functionality, not how it is implemented. These channels connect the two kernels
and enable the crossing of the partition wall between the two OSs. We consider two
scenarios: Sect. 18.3.2.1: Requests from the LWK to Linux and Sect. 18.3.2.2: Operations originating in the Linux partition. In Sect. 18.3.2.3, we discuss file-backed
mmap, which needs to be managed jointly by the two kernels.

18.3.2.1 LWK Requests to Linux

Figure 18.11 shows the control and data flow when an LWK application makes
a request via a system call the LWK does not implement. The flow starts when
an application makes a library call which traps into the LWK①. Then, the LWK
determines it should be forwarded to Linux ②. For I/O calls such as *read* or *write* ,
which fit this pattern of channel usage, there is some data movement in or out of
LWK memory ③. When the request is done, a return code must be passed back to
the LWK application ④ and ⑤.

This scenario is not all that difficult to implement, but it identifies three channel
requirements as given below:

Req 1:   Requests need to be served by an actor on the Linux side
Req 2:   Requests must go through the Linux system call interface
Req 3:   Linux needs a way to direct data to and from LWK controlled memory

Fig. 18.11 LWK requests to
Linux

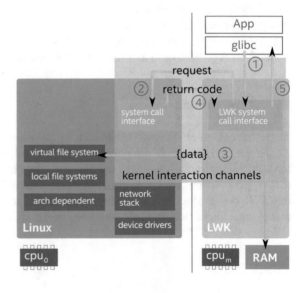

Fig. 18.12 Tools like gdb interacting with the LWK

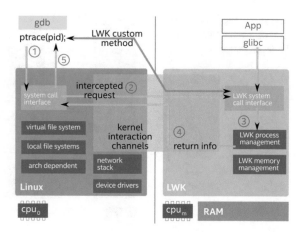

For Requirement Req 1, some kind of actor on the Linux side must be waiting for and handling system call requests from all the LWK processes on the node. This could be an interrupt handler or a user-level process running on the Linux core.

Requirement Req 2 exists because we need Linux to decode and handle I/O requests like *read*. The HPC application on the LWK side may request data from a local RAM disk, the pseudo file system, or an external device.

Since the two OSs run in a shared-memory environment, requirement Req 3 would seem straightforward to satisfy. However, LWK applications use virtual addresses to identify buffers. I/O system calls on the Linux side also operate on virtual addresses. Unless there is a mechanism to make these virtual addresses identical (pointing to the same physical address) or translate one into another, data cannot be simply streamed from the Linux kernel into an LWK application buffer.

18.3.2.2   Requests Originating on the Linux Side

The tools views discussion in Sect. 18.3.1.3 states that requests and operations may originate on the Linux side, but require information or action from the LWK side. Figure 18.12 shows an example of gdb interacting with an LWK process.

Ptrace: gdb uses *ptrace* to inspect and set the registers and memory locations of a process, as well as stopping, continuing, and single stepping it. These are all operations that need to work with processes running on the LWK.

When designing *mOS*, we considered two ways to implement system calls like *ptrace*: Intercept the *ptrace* call from gdb, or provide a custom LWK access method. The latter, of course, would require that tools like gdb are ported to *mOS* which is not desirable. As described later, in the end we found another solution. The important aspect is that this thinking led to requirement Req 4:

Req 4:   *ptrace* has to work, or a custom *mOS* interface is required for tools

Fig. 18.13 The command top displaying LWK and Linux processes

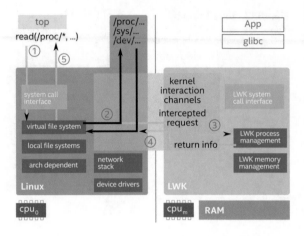

In Fig. 18.12, the intercept or redirection of *ptrace* has to happen in the Linux system call interface ①. If it is determined that the *ptrace* is for an LWK process, it is forwarded to the LWK②. The *ptrace* call is satisfied by the LWK③, and a return code or data is sent back to the caller ④ and ⑤.

Although less likely, *ptrace* calls may originate in the LWK partition as well. The LWK may have code to handle that, or we can use the principle in Sect. 18.3.2.1 to forward the request to Linux and then use the same path as a request originating on the Linux side.

Pseudo file systems: Implicit in Fig. 18.12 is that gdb needs to know the Process Identifier (PID) of the process to debug. Therefore, LWK processes need to be at least partially visible under Linux. Tools like ps and top provide process and memory information by interrogating the /proc pseudo file system. Figure 18.13 illustrates this.

For top to do its work, it traps into the Linux kernel and performs file operations on /proc . The kernel interaction channels need to provide a mechanism to intercept these file system operations in Linux. Since top also collects information about Linux processes, the channel has to be able to filter what needs to be handled by the LWK and what needs to be processed by the Linux kernel.

As shown in Fig. 18.13 that intercept needs to happen in the virtual file system layer ②. The LWK process and memory management components need to provide the necessary information for these requests ③ when data about LWK processes or resources is requested.

Req 5:   /proc and /sys need to provide access to LWK processes

Signal handling: The kernel interaction channels need to provide a mechanism to forward signals from the Linux partition to LWK processes. This is needed for commands like kill and pkill. Intercepting signals needs to happen inside the Linux kernel, since all signals have to be forwarded, and not all signals can be intercepted at the user level.

Req 6:   Signal propagation across OS boundary

Launch an LWK process: Because the Linux kernel handles file I/O and knows how to decode various binary formats, e.g., Executable and Linkable Format (ELF), and how to enable dynamic libraries, the launch of an LWK process involves the Linux kernel. This is an example of functionality we do not need to put into the LWK since we can rely on Linux to provide it.

Req 7:   Launch an LWK process

In *mOS*, we use the yod utility in the Linux partition to launch processes into the LWK partition. The name goes back to the beginning of the 1990s when SUNMOS introduced a launch command by that name; see Chap. 3. The *mOS* yod is a process launcher, not an MPI job launcher. It performs resource reservations among the LWK designated resources and uses Linux functions to load and create a process. *mOS* is binary compatible with Linux and supports, through Linux, dynamically linked libraries.

Booting the LWK: We mentioned earlier that we want to use as much existing Linux functionality as possible. Linux already knows how to bring up a CPU and we can think of enabling the LWK on a CPU core as another requirement for our abstract interaction channels.

Req 8:   Boot of LWK and setup of kernel interaction channels

18.3.2.3   Interoperability

At the beginning of this section, we started out with the assumption that I/O functions are separated from memory management. The former is to be handled by the Linux side, while the latter is done by the LWK. A file-backed *mmap* request involves both I/O and memory management. Therefore, the kernel interaction channels have to provide the necessary support.

Req 9:   File-backed *mmap* support

We now have derived a set of nine requirements for our multi-kernel. The kernel interaction channels we have used to do that are an abstract device to help guide our design process. We will see later that the *mOS* implementation does not rely on explicit communication or interaction channels between the two kernels. On the other hand, the IHK portion of the IHK/McKernel project (Chap. 17) does implement something that is similar to the abstraction we have described in this section.

18.3.3   *System Call Control Flow*

Assuming , we have some form of kernel interaction channels as described in the previous section, we describe in this section how they would be used to ship system

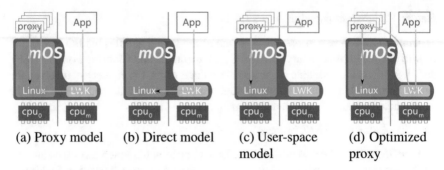

(a) Proxy model   (b) Direct model   (c) User-space   (d) Optimized
                                              model   proxy

Fig. 18.14 Four ways to interact with the Linux side

calls that the LWK does not handle, from the LWK side to the Linux side. There are several ways to accomplish that. Figure 18.14 shows four of them graphically.

Requirement Req 1 requires that there is an entity on the Linux side that acts on behalf of the LWK process. In three of the models shown in Fig. 18.14, the actor is a proxy process. These are Linux user-level processes that represent the LWK process on the Linux side. When an LWK issues a *read* request, it gets forwarded to its proxy which makes the *read* request to the Linux kernel.

The kernel code of a system call has to be executed inside a process context. That context keeps track of open file descriptors, process status, access permissions, etc. In the models that employ a proxy, the proxy process context serves that purpose. There has to be one proxy process on the Linux side for each process on the LWK side. This is necessary because the kernel relies on state stored with each process.

In the direct model in Fig. 18.14b, the actor is the Linux kernel itself. Essentially, the LWK sends the request directly to the Linux kernel which then executes the appropriate system call. That model requires that a context is created on the fly or the context of an LWK process is shared between Linux and the LWK. We provide more detail on the proxy and direct model below.

18.3.4   The Proxy Model

In this model, Fig. 18.14a, an LWK application traps into the LWK when it makes a system call. If the LWK determines that the call should be handled by Linux, the LWK sets up the necessary information for Linux and uses an Inter-Processor Interrupt (IPI) or similar mechanism to request service from Linux. Linux then uses an up-call into the appropriate proxy process to execute the call. This model requires the installation of an interrupt handler in Linux for the IPI, or a polling thread, that can interact with the LWK and make up-calls into a user process.

The proxy processes should have the same address map as the corresponding LWK processes. That means that a virtual address in a proxy points to the same physical memory location as the same virtual address in the LWK process. For a *read*

Fig. 18.15 Transitions in
the basic proxy model

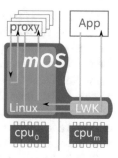

Fig. 18.16 Transitions in
the direct model

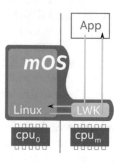

call from a proxy, the Linux kernel will stream data into the buffer that is seen by
the LWK process. No memory-to-memory copy is necessary.

Figure 18.15 shows the control flow in more detail. The LWK process traps into the
LWK and the LWK forwards the request to the Linux side. Later, the proxy process
wakes up, examines the request and performs a system call into Linux. When the
system call finishes, the proxy process traps into the Linux kernel one more time
to send the result and control back to the LWK process. The Linux kernel informs
the LWK that the request has been completed, and the LWK unblocks the LWK
application and returns control to it. A total of three round trips into kernel space are
needed for each system call an LWK process makes.

This model makes fulfilling some requirements, e.g., requirements Req 1 and
Req 2, simple, but it has difficulties with some of the others, for example, require-
ment Req 4. Making tools and *ptrace* work on the Linux side would be daunting.
IHK/McKernel, which employs a proxy model, runs tools in the LWK partition.

18.3.5   The Direct Model

This is the only variation that does not require a proxy process on the Linux side.
See Fig. 18.14b for an illustration. This model is appealing because it has fewer user
space to kernel transitions as Fig. 18.16 shows.

We previously mentioned that for system calls to work, they have to be executed in a process context. For example, in order to open a file, the kernel has to verify that the process has the appropriate privileges. Knowledge about the open file, its current file pointer, for instance, has to be stored with the process that made the request.

Adding that bookkeeping to Linux would be intrusive. Another way is to share process context between the LWK and Linux. Process context, the state of a process, is stored in a data structure called Process Control Block (PCB). In Linux that structure is named a task structure. If both kernel agree to use the same representation of that structure and can share it, it is possible for the direct model to work.

This is the model we have chosen for *mOS* and is one of the key distinguishing features from IHK/McKernel. Although it seemingly has less overhead than the proxy model, it turns out that is not the case when we measured system call overhead (Gerofi et al. 2015). This is due to the task migration implementation we have chosen for *mOS* (see Sect. 18.4.1).

Although system calls that are handled by Linux are costly in both models, we do not believe this will have a significant impact on application performance. The expectation is that HPC applications do not make system calls in their performance critical inner loops, or that these calls are handled quickly by the LWK.

The user-space model in Fig. 18.14c and the optimized proxy model in Fig. 18.14d are variations we have not implemented or explored in depth. The user-space model would probably require a modified libc or shim layer.

18.4   Implementation of mOS

In designing *mOS*, we viewed the kernel interaction channels in the previous section as an abstract device to help us make decisions. In the actual implementation of *mOS* , we went down a different path to fulfill the requirements in Sect. 18.3.2.

In *mOS*, the LWK is embedded inside the Linux kernel by compiling it into the same kernel binary. If we looked at the kernel text segment of a running *mOS* system, we would see the drawing in Fig. 18.17a. Most of the data is Linux kernel code, but there are small amounts of *mOS* and the LWK in the executable.

The different pieces of code are executed on different cores. Figure 18.17b shows that cores that we have designated as Linux cores, run the Linux kernel. To applications and tools running on these cores almost everything looks like a normal Linux system. Cores that we have designated as LWK cores, run the LWK code and are not available to standard Linux processes. In Fig. 18.17b, there is a little bit of Linux code on the *mOS* side of the executable on the LWK core. This symbolizes that the *mOS* LWK does run some Linux code. For example, the Linux kernel has macros to read CPU status registers and timers which the LWK uses.

Because the LWK is compiled into Linux, it runs in the same address space and can use the same data structures. For example, we augmented the Linux task struct, which is used to hold a process' state, to include LWK-specific fields. Both kernels use the same data structure, but Linux ignores the LWK-specific fields. The Linux

Fig. 18.17 View of Linux
and LWK code

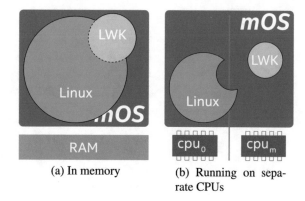

(a) In memory

(b) Running on separate CPUs

kernel system call *getpid* is simple. It dereferences a pointer into the task struct of the currently running process and returns the contents of the field `pid`. That code works for both the LWK and Linux and is an example where the *mOS* LWK simply calls Linux code.

Intel and vendors, in general, make sure that Linux runs on the latest CPUs. When we embed the *mOS* LWK into the latest Linux kernel, we automatically get access to the latest bug fixes and features available in the new hardware.

The *mOS* project uses the Linux kernel source tree and `git`. When we decide to move *mOS* to a newer Linux kernel, we re-base our code. Depending on the Linux changes, there may be subtleties involved and thus the process requires close inspection for changes in the kernel interfaces we are using. However, most upgrades so far were done in a day or two (with additional time for testing and performance impact evaluation).

Embedding the *mOS* LWK into the Linux kernel solves the three conflicting corners of the design triangle in Sect. 18.2.1. It is relatively easy to track the Linux kernel, *mOS* is very Linux compatible, and the compute cores run an LWK. In the sections below, we provide more detail on the implementation.

18.4.1   System Call Forwarding

To the Linux kernel, an LWK task (process) looks like any other task. When it makes a system call that we have decided Linux should handle, *mOS* migrates the task to one of the cores designated for Linux system call handling and moves it into a high-priority queue. The destination core executes the system call and afterward migrates the task back to the LWK core where it originated. This works because the two kernels share process state and memory. It is one of the fundamental differences between a multi-kernel and earlier LWK systems where remote calls had to be packed into a message and sent to another node.

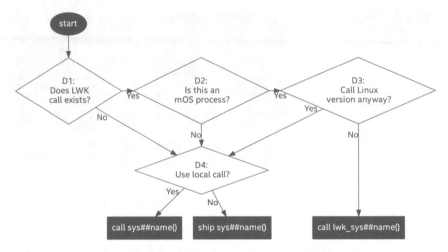

Fig. 18.18 System call decision flowchart

This allows *mOS*'s decision of where to handle a system call to be flexible. The
flow chart in Fig. 18.18 shows the possibilities. If the LWK has an implementation
for a specific system call, it can execute it. If it is only partially implemented and
the calling arguments require Linux services, it can still be forwarded to Linux. For
example, an *mmap* is a system call that the *mOS* LWK handles, except when it is a
file-backed *mmap*. In the latter case, it gets shipped to Linux.

Because the LWK is embedded inside the Linux kernel, there are two methods
by which Linux can handle a given call. The task can be migrated to a Linux core,
or the *mOS* LWK can call into Linux locally. In other words, the LWK is executing
Linux code on the LWK core where the system call originated.

In *mOS*, it is possible to always execute systems calls by running Linux code
on the LWK core. However, we only do this for debugging and testing purposes
because some Linux system calls have unwanted (from an LWK perspective) side
effects. The *open* call, for example, sets a timer to flush buffers a few seconds after
the open succeeded. This introduces noise into the application. The timer interrupt
occurs on the core that handled the *open* system call, so it is better to do that in the
Linux partition.

18.4.2 Resource Management

In Sect. 18.2.4, we discussed resource partitioning and the *designation, reservation,*
and *allocation* strategy *mOS* employs. For the yod process launcher to reserve some
or all of the resources that have been designated to the LWK and are still available,
it coordinates with the kernel portion of *mOS* that keeps track of that information.
Figure 18.19 shows that we use pseudo files to do that and the different parts of the

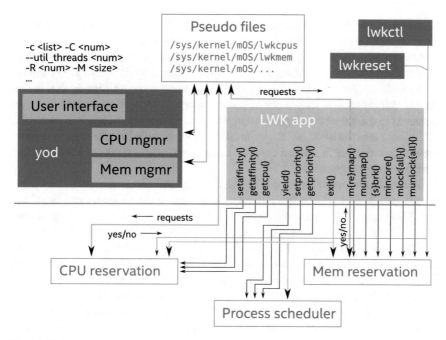

Fig. 18.19 User space and kernel interactions in mOS

LWK that are involved. The same figure also shows how other user-space utilities and applications interact with the LWK. In the latter case, it is mostly through Linux standard system calls.

When yod has been able to make the requested reservations, it marks itself as an LWK process, migrates into the LWK partition, and starts executing the application. This differs from other job launchers that stay behind and become a proxy process for the application.

Both the LWK and yod are aware of the NUMA properties of a compute node and make reservation decisions using that knowledge. There are several command line options that can be used to provide information to yod to express the desired configuration. Note that once a reservation is made, it remains fixed for the duration of the process' life. In particular, if the number of MPI ranks is a multiple of the NUMA domains, yod will nicely align the two.

18.4.2.1   Task Scheduling and Management

mOS, like other LWKs, has a simple, non-preemptive task scheduler. It has as goals low noise, deterministic scheduling decisions, and strict CPU affinity. But, task management in *mOS* is more involved than that. This is due to the need to integrate with Linux as well as other requirements. Task management in *mOS* includes special treatment of utility threads, system call shipping , and it must inter-operate with the Linux scheduler and existing Linux debug and performance tools.

Some runtime systems and a few HPC applications spawn utility threads in addition to the threads that perform the main computational work. These utility threads range from once-a-second monitors to heavy-polling progress threads that ensure data is quickly moved in and out of process space. These utility threads are asynchronous to the computation and can impact performance because they add noise. In *mOS*, there are heuristics and an Application Programming Interface (API) to move these utility threads to unused cores or Linux cores where their presence does not interfere with computation.

The *mOS* task manager is also NUMA aware and places newly created tasks, absent specific instructions from user space, in a topologically aware manner. Command line options to yod can be used to indicate layout preferences. Applications retain the ability to move threads to other CPUs within its reservation domain.

One of the more complex pieces of the LWK scheduler is the integration with the Linux scheduler. In the Linux partition, the *mOS* scheduler is integrated as a new Linux scheduler class with the highest priority. When an LWK task is migrated to a Linux CPU for system call execution, it is dispatched into the *mOS* scheduling class.

On an LWK core, the Linux scheduling class hierarchy no longer exists. The only run queue is the *mOS* queue. It has priority scheduling, but is non-preemptive. Linux can and does enqueue kernel tasks on LWK designated CPUs. This is necessary for cross-CPU locking mechanisms (RCU) and the migration task that allows *mOS* to ship system calls to the Linux side. Since LWK and Linux CPUs cooperate and share memory, locking is sometimes necessary. Access to the LWK scheduling queue is strictly gated. Only LWK processes can run, and a few select, well-known, previously identified Linux kernel tasks. Any other task is flagged and prevented from running on an LWK CPU. This is one of the key methodologies used to achieve *mOS*'s low noise.

Figure 18.20 shows a Linux kernel running the Performance and architecture laboratory System Noise Activity Program (PSNAP) (NERSC 2013) benchmark on the 68 cores of an Intel® Xeon Phi™ processor 7250. There is one MPI rank per core. Each rank repeatedly does 1,000 μs of "work", i.e., no-op that do not access memory. Ideally, each loop iteration on each core would take exactly 1,000 μs.

The plot shows a histogram for each core (MPI rank). The vertical z-axis is logarithmic and counts the number of samples when it took a specific amount of time to execute the 1,000 μs worth of work. If all loop executions on all cores took the minimum amount of time, there would be a green wall at the right side of the plot.

Outliers, those instances that took about 3% or more time, are shown in red. A standard HPC Linux configuration as shown in Fig. 18.20 has on some cores loop instances that took almost twice as long as the planned work. Since the benchmark does not access memory or make system calls inside its loop, these variations are caused by the CPU core doing work other than running the benchmark, e.g., interrupts, other scheduled work, and Linux administrative overhead.

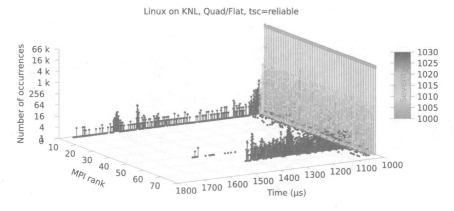

Performance data subject to Optimization Notice on page 344.

Fig. 18.20 Linux running the PSNAP benchmark

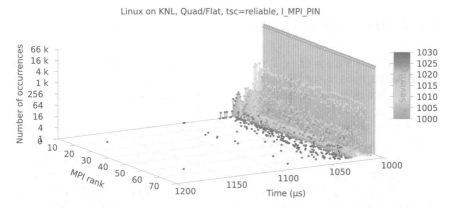

Performance data subject to Optimization Notice on page 344.

Fig. 18.21 Linux running the PSNAP benchmark using the Intel `I_MPI_PIN()` option

Linux is infinitely configurable. There are always multiple ways to tune it for a specific workload. Figure 18.21 shows an example where we used the Intel MPI `I_-MPI_PIN()` option. The noise profile has improved considerably and we changed the scale of the *x*-axis.

However, it is far from optimal as Fig. 18.22 demonstrates. That plot shows the much more deterministic behavior of *mOS*. The `I_MPI_PIN()` is not necessary in this case. *mOS* attempts to always do the "right thing" for HPC applications without long trial and error experiments on what configurations or usage patterns might work best on a specific node architecture.

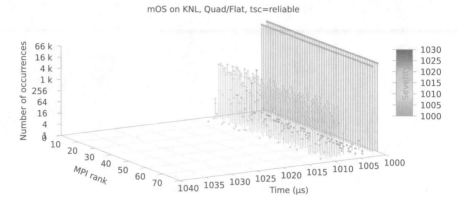

Performance data subject to Optimization Notice on page 344.

Fig. 18.22 mOS running the PSNAP benchmark

18.4.3 Memory Management

Up to the current version of *mOS*, virtual address space management has been left to Linux. At the moment, the LWK only manages physical memory, but we have plans to change that in the future. Letting Linux allocate and manage the virtual address space is easy in *mOS* and has many advantages. While the *mOS* LWK reserves and allocates physical memory, we use Linux Virtual Memory Area (VMA) kernel structures to represent the LWK physical memory regions.

This is possible because the LWK is compiled into the Linux kernel and has the advantage that Linux functions and processes can easily access LWK memory when needed. There is only one virtual address space for a given process and it is the same no matter which partition that process runs in. System calls executed on behalf of a process on the Linux side see the same memory as when that process is back on the LWK side running as part of the application.

Memory management in *mOS* is NUMA aware and tries to allocate contiguous, large pages (2 MB or 1 GB) whenever it is possible and makes sense. The process text segment and main stack reside on the Linux side. Memory for that is allocated early when Linux instantiates the process. We are planning to move the main stack into LWK memory.

Thread stacks, the heap, and *mmap* memory are in LWK space and managed by *mOS*. The heap grows in 2 MB increments and we do not release memory when it shrinks. For most HPC applications, the heap does not shrink, memory is allocated once at the beginning, and large pages are a huge benefit.

While these characteristics have been known to be beneficial from LWK learnings, there is more work to do. Determinism, allocating the exact same physical memory pages each time an application runs in a given configuration is a key contributor, along with non-preemptive scheduling, to ensure low run-to-run variation.

18.5   Status

mOS is open source and an early version is available on GitHub (Intel 2018). It is under active development at Intel and has run on up to 2,048 Xeon Phi nodes.

Acknowledgements This project is a direct result of the work by the current mOS team John Attinella, Sharath Bhat, Jai Dayal, David van Dresser, Tom Musta, Rolf Riesen, Lance Shuler, Andrew Tauferner, and Robert W. Wisniewski, but has been influenced and shaped by many people. Conversations, feedback, advice, and review of our work helped make mOS what it is today. People who provided guidance include Michael Blocksome, Todd Inglett, Pardo Keppel, Jim Dinan, Keith Underwood, Joe Robichaux, Ulf Hannebutte, Thomas Spelce, and Philippe Thierry.
We had many interactions with the IHK/McKernel team and greatly benefited from being able to use early prototypes of IHK/McKernel. We thank, Yutaka Ishikawa, Balazs Gerofi, and Masamichi Takagi.
Evan Powers, Steven T. Hampson, and Kurt Alstrup worked on the first prototype of mOS. Kurt created the first scheduler and greatly reduced noise. Ravi Murty was very much involved in early mOS architecture discussions and helped to create an initial list of requirements.
We thank Andi Kleen and Ramakrishna (Rama) Karedla for their help and suggestions with BIOS settings and Linux boot command options, and Andi for help understanding how Linux works.
James Cownie had the idea to collect progress threads on a single logical CPU by making it the default for all newly created threads which do not specifically request a CPU. Eric Barton and Jeff Hammond participated in thread scheduling and placement discussions and provided insight into the needs of MPI, SHMEM, and high-performance I/O.
Ralph Castain helped refine the Linux-side requirements.
A large number of supercomputing OS experts helped refine the characteristics and definition of an LWK. We thank Ron Brightwell, Kurt Ferreira, Kamil Iskra, Larry Kaplan, Mike Lang, Jack Lange, David Lombard, Arthur B. (Barney) Maccabe, Yoonho Park, and Kevin Pedretti.
Michael H. O'Hara managed the implementation team for the first year and helped organize getting the first prototype off the ground. Mike Julier took over and continued to drive the implementation team toward v0.1 of mOS.
We have been working closely with Balazs Gerofi and thank him for much valuable input and helping us understand IHK/McKernel better.
Optimization Notice Software and workloads used in performance tests may have been optimized for performance only on Intel microprocessors. Performance tests, such as SYSmark and MobileMark, are measured using specific computer systems, components, software, operations, and functions. Any change to any of those factors may cause the results to vary. You should consult other information and performance tests to assist you in fully evaluating your contemplated purchases, including the performance of that product when combined with other products. For more complete information visit http://www.intel.com/performance. *Other names and brands may be claimed as the property of others.

References

Akkan, H., Ionkov, L., & Lang, M. (2013). Transparently consistent asynchronous shared memory. In *Proceedings of the 3rd International Workshop on Runtime and Operating Systems for Supercomputers, ROSS '13*. New York, NY, USA: ACM.
Ali, N., Carns, P., Iskra, K., Kimpe, D., Lang, S., Latham, R., et al. (2009). Scalable I/O forwarding framework for high-performance computing systems. In *IEEE International Conference on Cluster Computing and Workshops, 2009. CLUSTER '09*. (pp. 1–10).

Brightwell, R., Oldfield, R., Maccabe, A. B., & Bernholdt, D. E. (2013). Hobbes: Composition and virtualization as the foundations of an extreme-scale OS/R. In *Proceedings of the 3rd International Workshop on Runtime and Operating Systems for Supercomputers, ROSS '13* (pp. 2:1–2:8).

Gerofi, B., Takagi, M., Ishikawa, Y., Riesen, R., Powers, E., & Wisniewski, R. W. (2015). Exploring the design space of combining Linux with lightweight kernels for extreme scale computing. In *Proceedings of the 5th International Workshop on Runtime and Operating Systems for Supercomputers, ROSS '15*. New York, NY, USA: ACM.

Gerofi, B., Takagi, M., Hori, A., Nakamura, G., Shirasawa, T., & Ishikawa, Y. (2016). On the scalability, performance isolation and device driver transparency of the IHK/McKernel hybrid lightweight kernel. In *2016 IEEE International Parallel and Distributed Processing Symposium (IPDPS)* (pp. 1041–1050).

Giampapa, M., Gooding, T., Inglett, T., & Wisniewski, R. (2010). Experiences with a lightweight supercomputer kernel: Lessons learned from Blue Gene's CNK. In *2010 International Conference for High Performance Computing, Networking, Storage and Analysis (SC)*.

Intel (2018). mOS for HPC. https://github.com/intel/mOS/wiki.

Kocoloski, B. & Lange, J. (2014). HPMMAP: Lightweight memory management for commodity operating systems. In *Proceedings of the 2014 IEEE 28th International Parallel and Distributed Processing Symposium, IPDPS '14* (pp. 649–658). Washington, DC, USA: IEEE Computer Society.

Lange, J., Pedretti, K., Hudson, T., Dinda, P., Cui, Z., Xia, L., et al. (2010). Palacios and Kitten: New high performance operating systems for scalable virtualized and native supercomputing. In *IEEE International Symposium on Parallel Distributed Processing (IPDPS)*.

NERSC (2013). PAL system noise activity program (PSNAP). https://www.nersc.gov/users/computational-systems/cori/nersc-8-procurement/trinity-nersc-8-rfp/nersc-8-trinity-benchmarks/psnap/.

Otstott, D., Evans, N., Ionkov, L., Zhao, M., & Lang, M. (2014). Enabling composite applications through an asynchronous shared memory interface. In *2014 IEEE International Conference on Big Data, Big Data 2014, Washington, DC, USA, October 27–30, 2014* (pp. 219–224).

Ouyang, J., Kocoloski, B., Lange, J., & Pedretti, K. (2015). Achieving performance isolation with lighweight co-kernels. In *Proceeding of the 24th International ACM Symposium on High Performance Distributed Computing (HPDC)*.

Park, Y., Van Hensbergen, E., Hillenbrand, M., Inglett, T., Rosenburg, B., Ryu, K. D., & Wisniewski, R. (2012). FusedOS: Fusing LWK performance with FWK functionality in a heterogeneous environment. In *2012 IEEE 24th International Symposium on Computer Architecture and High Performance Computing (SBAC-PAD)* (pp. 211–218).

Riesen, R., Brightwell, R., Bridges, P. G., Hudson, T., Maccabe, A. B., Widener, P. M., et al. (2009). Designing and implementing lightweight kernels for capability computing. *Concurrency and Computation: Practice and Experience, 21*(6), 793–817.

Riesen, R., Maccabe, A. B., Gerofi, B., Lombard, D. N., Lange, J. J., & Pedretti, K., et al. (2015). *What is a lightweight kernel? In Proceedings of the 5th International Workshop on Runtime and Operating Systems for Supercomputers, ROSS '15*. New York, NY, USA: ACM.

Shimosawa, T., Gerofi, B., Takagi, M., Nakamura, G., Shirasawa, T., Saeki, Y., et al. (2014). Interface for heterogeneous kernels: A framework to enable hybrid OS designs targeting high performance computing on manycore architectures. In *21th International Conference on High Performance Computing, HiPC*.

Weinhold, C., Lackorzynski, A., Bierbaum, J., Küttler, M., Planeta, M., Härtig, H., et al. (2016). FFMK: A fast and fault-tolerant microkernel-based system for exascale computing. In H.-J. Bungartz, P. Neumann & W. E. Nagel (Eds.) *Software for exascale computing - SPPEXA 2013–2015* (pp. 405–426). Cham: Springer International Publishing.

Wisniewski, R. W., Inglett, T., Keppel, P., Murty, R., & Riesen, R. (2014). mOS: An architecture for extreme-scale operating systems. In *Proceedings of the 4th International Workshop on Runtime and Operating Systems for Supercomputers, ROSS '14* (pp. 2:1–2:8). New York, NY, USA: ACM.

Chapter 19
FFMK: An HPC OS Based on the L4Re Microkernel

Carsten Weinhold, Adam Lackorzynski and Hermann Härtig

Abstract The German research project FFMK aims to build a new HPC operating system platform that addresses hardware and software challenges posed by future exascale systems. These challenges include massively increased parallelism (e.g., nodes and cores), overcoming performance variability, and most likely higher failure rates due to significantly increased component counts. We also expect more complex applications and the need to manage system resources in a more dynamic way than on contemporary HPC platforms, which assign resources to applications statically. The project combines and adapts existing system-software building blocks that have already matured and proven themselves in other areas. At the lowest level, the architecture is based on a microkernel to provide an extremely lightweight and fast execution environment that leaves as many resources as possible to applications. An instance of the microkernel controls each compute node, but it is complemented by a virtualized Linux kernel that provides device drivers, compatibility with existing HPC infrastructure, and rich support for programming models and HPC runtimes such as MPI. Above the level of individual nodes, the system architecture includes distributed performance and health monitoring services as well as fault-tolerant information dissemination algorithms that enable failure handling and dynamic load management. In this chapter, we will give an overview of the overall architecture of the FFMK operating system platform. However, the focus will be on the microkernel and how it integrates with Linux to form a multi-kernel operating system architecture.

C. Weinhold (✉) · A. Lackorzynski · H. Härtig
TU Dresden, Department of Computer Science, 01062 Dresden, Germany
e-mail: carsten.weinhold@tu-dresden.de

A. Lackorzynski
e-mail: adam.lackorzynski@tu-dresden.de

H. Härtig
e-mail: hermann.haertig@tu-dresden.de

© Springer Nature Singapore Pte Ltd. 2019
B. Gerofi et al. (eds.), *Operating Systems for Supercomputers
and High Performance Computing*, High-Performance Computing Series,
https://doi.org/10.1007/978-981-13-6624-6_19

335

19.1 Introduction

In the HPC community, the operating system (OS) is often considered to be in the way of applications. But what is meant by "the OS" and how exactly it disturbs applications is not always well articulated. In the following, we revisit the benefits brought by re-architecting the OS kernel for HPC systems. We then make the case that the role of the OS must expand in order to address challenges posed by upcoming exascale systems.

Noise-sensitive Applications One concern that has already been discussed in Chap. 13 is that the OS may adversely affect the performance of applications by briefly interrupting their execution in order to perform housekeeping tasks or schedule background activities. This problem is called "OS noise" and it particularly hurts applications based on the bulk-synchronous programming (BSP) model. These applications are characterized by alternating computation and communication phases that must both be perfectly synchronized across all participating threads in order to achieve maximum performance. If few (or just one) of the compute threads are delayed, all other threads have to wait longer for input from the stragglers, thereby wasting CPU time. Other types of applications such as stencil codes suffer from similar performance degradation, if computation times are not perfectly balanced.

Avoiding OS Noise Multi-kernel OS architectures are a way to address the OS noise problem by running compute threads of HPC applications on top of a lightweight kernel (LWK). The LWK minimizes execution-time jitter, because it does not preempt compute threads like Linux would do in order to schedule background tasks or system daemons. Instead, these activities are performed by a traditional kernel such as Linux, which runs on just a few of the cores in each node. Usually, one or two such service cores are enough for cluster management daemons, to monitor node health, and similar tasks. Additionally, as the LWK cannot fully replace a traditional complex kernel, it also offloads certain system calls to Linux that are typically not critical for application performance.

Re-Architecting the OS for HPC The multi-kernel approach gives HPC applications the best of both worlds: the LWK ensures low noise and high performance, whereas Linux offers convenience, familiar APIs, a rich feature set, and compatibility with huge amounts of legacy infrastructure. But in addition to that, the approach also demonstrates how crucial it is to make a clear distinction between different parts of the system software and not just regard it as "the OS" that may cause trouble. The multi-kernel architecture is based on the realization that commodity OS kernels such as Linux require adaptations in order to optimize them for HPC applications. But compatibility with the constantly evolving Linux kernel is essential, too. This need for compatibility is at odds with HPC-specific modifications, as it requires significant and continuous engineering effort. Running an LWK next to Linux is a way to avoid performance problems of the general-purpose kernel by replacing parts of it with a specialized implementation. However, the multi-kernel approach is maintainable and, by extension sustainable, only if the functionality being replaced is minimal.

Therefore, we argue that the LWK itself and the hooks into the Linux kernel should be as simple and as small as possible.

A Microkernel as a Universal LWK LWKs primarily target highly tuned and well-balanced BSP-style applications, because they are helped most by eliminating OS noise. However, this class of applications represents only a part of the very diverse landscape of HPC software packages. Given that the system-software community for HPC is fairly small and its resources limited, the development and maintenance effort for an LWK has to pay off also for other classes of HPC applications. Based on extensive, decade-long experience with multi-kernel OS architectures in the area of real-time, security, and fault-tolerant systems, we believe that multi-kernel architectures are not just a sweet spot for noise-sensitive HPC codes:

- To address real-time requirements, we isolated timing-sensitive cores of applications to let them run on an L4 microkernel (Liedtke 1995), which is capable of guaranteeing much lower response times than a commodity OS such as Linux. Low latency is also essential to high performance in HPC workloads (Härtig et al. 2006).
- The approach of separating a software system into a small critical part and a more complex noncritical part has also proven highly effective to improve security and fault-tolerance properties of a system. In both usage scenarios, an L4 microkernel was at the core of small trusted computing bases (Singaravelu et al. 2006; Weinhold and Härtig 2008, 2011) (i.e., all software that needs to be trusted to enforce security requirements) and a fault-tolerant OS architecture (Döbel and Härtig 2014; Döbel et al. 2012).

As we shall explain in more detail in Sect. 19.3.2, we are confident that strict splitting of responsibility between critical and uncritical functionality can be used to optimize performance/latency-sensitive workloads in HPC as well. Furthermore, we argue that this approach, especially when using a truly minimal and maintainable microkernel, is well-suited to address some of the challenges along the way to exascale systems. We lay out the reasons in the following:

- **Composite Applications**: Some big HPC programs are like cloud applications in the sense that they consist of multiple programs that work in concert to solve a more complex problem (i.e., composite applications consisting of multiple programs). For performance reasons, it is not desirable (or even practical) to write intermediate results to a parallel file system just to be read back by the next processing stage of the application. Instead, data must be processed, analyzed, or visualized in situ, with individual parts of composite applications running concurrently. Thus, different processes with diverse resource demands compete for resources such as caches, memory, cores, and communication bandwidth. Yet, it is difficult or even impossible for developers and administrators to assign resources a priori for optimal performance. The system software, including OS and runtimes, are in a much better position to manage and dynamically adapt resource assignment.

We think flexible and low-latency mechanisms for quickly switching between competing threads can best be implemented in an LWK with minimal cache footprint. An L4 microkernel is a readily available instantiation of such an LWK, because the performance of context switching operations was one of the primary optimizations goals.

- **Heterogeneous Cores**: Past and current hardware architectures already embrace the idea of dedicated service cores, which are set aside to run nonperformance but essential parts of a multi-kernel OS. For example, on IBM Blue Gene systems, the multi-kernel OS does not "waste" CPU cores by setting them aside for background and management tasks of the OS but runs those tasks on dedicated service cores. The current No. 1 system in the TOP500 list of supercomputers, China's Sunway TaihuLight system (Fu et al. 2016), has a heterogeneous core architecture with big cores capable of running an OS and kernel and many small compute cores optimized for computation.

- **Performance Variability**: Today, many HPC systems are built from standard, commercial-of-the-shelf (COTS) hardware to achieve high performance at an acceptable price point. However, COTS hardware, especially CPUs, are designed not only for high performance, but also to achieve the best performance at high power efficiency. While those techniques help to improve average performance of a processor and especially its single-thread performance, they also result in performance variability. For example, Intel CPUs supporting "Turbo Boost" continuously monitor themselves and adapt voltages and clock frequencies to stay within a certain thermal envelope, but at the cost of stable and predictable performance; run times for the same workload may vary over time, as well as across CPUs with the same specification, due to minor chip-level differences caused by the manufacturing process. Because those mechanisms are built into the processor itself, the software has only very limited control.

  Given the limitations for total power consumption at many HPC centers and cost constraints, it is likely that at least some future exascale systems will suffer from hardware performance variability. It seems counterintuitive to run a low-noise multi-kernel OS on such hardware, however, the LWK will still avoid the often significant (Lackorzynski et al. 2016b) jitter caused by the OS and management services. Moderate oversubscription of cores may help reduce imbalances even further. This measure requires fast context switching and low wake-up latency; an L4 microkernel is well-suited for handling many application threads on oversubscribed cores, even if simultaneous multi-threading (SMT) cannot be used.

- **Fault Tolerance**: Assuming failure rates increase because the entire system consists of more components, the management plane of the OS will need to reassign resources to applications. Multi-kernels do not reduce the overall failure rate, but a microkernel has much less internal state than a commodity kernel like Linux. Such a small kernel is more likely to survive transient faults, allowing a node to recover much faster by micro-rebooting Linux within a few seconds instead of power-cycling the entire node, which often takes on the order of minutes before the kernel even starts booting.

Arguably, the OS is in the best position to address the challenges described above and it may no longer be a viable option that every application takes care of them on their own. Therefore, the overarching goal of our research is to build an OS architecture on top of an L4 microkernel that is capable of monitoring resource utilization, coordination of multiple cooperating parts of composite applications, and to control and adjust resource assignment. It shall free application developers from the burden of managing a dynamic system. We will describe our approach in the following sections.

19.2   Architecture

In this section, we give an overview of the complete architecture of the HPC OS platform that we designed in the research project "FFMK: A Fast and Fault-tolerant Mikrokernel-based Operating System for Exascale Computing." This project has been funded by the German Research Foundation[1] from 2013 through 2018 as part of the German Priority Program 1648 "Software for Exascale Computing." We will discuss the components of the FFMK OS platform and present research results demonstrating the feasibility of some of its key building blocks; a more detailed discussion of this description including all building blocks can be found in a separate publication (Weinhold et al. 2016). The focus of this chapter is on the evolution of the underlying foundation, namely the node OS based on the L4 microkernel and L4Linux. The in-depth discussion of these components and how they integrate with HPC runtimes starts in Sect. 19.3.

19.2.1   Microkernel-based Node OS

From decade-long experience, we know that developing, stabilizing, and maintaining an OS kernel is hard, often complicated, and it involves huge effort and dedication. In addition to the kernel, any practical OS platform also requires additional components such as convenience frameworks and tool support. Thus, contrary to other HPC OS projects, the FFMK project does not aim to develop a new LWK from scratch, but instead, we build upon a proven microkernel-based OS platform: the L4Re Operating System Framework (Lackorzynski and Warg 2009). L4Re is an open-source but commercially supported system that is used in various industry sectors for highly diverse use cases. It has proven itself in practice and it provides a stable basis for a flexible OS layer that can be specialized for particular use cases and application needs.

   As shown in Fig. 19.1, our L4 microkernel is in control of each node right from the moment the node boots up. Initially, it owns all memory and it remains in control

---

[1]Deutsche Forschungsgemeinschaft (DFG).

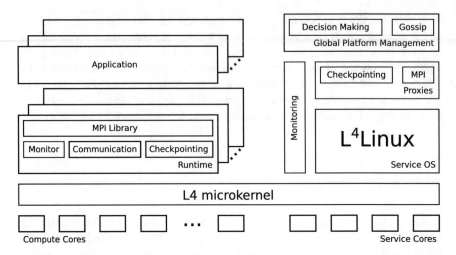

Fig. 19.1 L4Re-based node OS architecture. This figure has originally been published in Weinhold et al. (2016)

of every activity on any core during the entire runtime. A set of user-level services is launched right after boot that provides higher level OS functionality. As the microkernel supports virtualization, we run Linux (Härtig et al. 1997) on top of it as a service OS for HPC infrastructure and a provider of all Linux APIs and functionality that HPC applications require. The virtualized Linux is binary compatible to a native Linux kernel, but it is assigned only a subset of the node's resources, especially cores, to perform tasks that are not critical to application performance (e.g., system initialization, health monitoring, and controlling application life cycles).

19.2.2 Dynamic Platform Management

Since the HPC systems we have today already suffer from performance variability, we assume that exascale machines that must operate at a much higher performance-per-watt ratio will exhibit similar problems. Additionally, we expect that failures will occur more frequently in these systems due to drastically increased component counts.

Dynamic Platform Management Given this increased dynamism in the system, we assume that it will no longer be practical to assign resources statically to applications. This leads to the requirement that the system platform must support dynamic load and health monitoring. Decisions based on observed performance (or anticipated failures) must be done at the following three levels: (1) on each node, (2) among multiple nodes per application partition, and (3) based on a global view of the whole system.

In line with researchers behind other HPC system-software projects such as Argo (Beckman et al. 2019), we propose to increase parallelism within each node such that node-local schedulers can take care of level (1). However, this measure cannot help with load balancing across node boundaries, nor is it capable of compensating for whole-node failures. Thus, to handle dynamism at levels (2) and (3), we propose to use fault-tolerant gossip algorithms in combination with distributed decision-making. Gossip algorithms enable management daemons running on each node to build up a distributed bulletin board that provides information on the status of all nodes. This information includes available parallelism on each node, its load in terms of compute cycles, cache utilization, or memory usage, as well as the health status of the node (e.g., anticipated component failures based on hardware monitoring, which nodes became nonresponsive, etc.). Possible actions based on the (distributed) decision-making is proactive migration of processes away from failing nodes or migration of processes from overloaded or overheating nodes.

Randomized Gossip The FFMK OS platform uses a randomized gossip algorithm to disseminate per-node information among all nodes, thereby updating local copies of a distributed bulletin board on each of the participating nodes. In its basic form, the gossip algorithm is executed by a daemon on each node. It sends periodically a message with the latest information about the local node as well as other nodes it heard about previously to the daemon of another, randomly selected node. Thus, on average, each node sends and receives one message in each round of communication of the algorithm. On each node, information received from other nodes is merged into the local copy of the distributed bulletin board (newer records only, older information is discarded). Thus, each node learns about the state of all other nodes overtime and keeps it up to date for as long as the algorithm continues to run.

The work of Barak et al. (2015) has shown that gossip algorithms are resilient against node failures and that gossip scales to exascale systems. However, it may be necessary to limit the number of nodes that gossip with each other by splitting the system into sets of nodes called *colonies*. The size of a colony should be in the order of a thousand nodes so as to ensure that recent information is disseminated fast (see Fig. 19.2 for age distributions for different colony sizes). To obtain a complete view across the whole system, Barak et al. propose to add a second layer of so-called master nodes above all colonies. These master nodes gossip with a few nodes in each of the colonies in order to collect information from them and to send coarse-grained information about the whole system back into the colony layer. Thus, decentralized decision-making across colony boundaries is possible to perform load balancing, but with less detailed information than within colonies.

Quality of Information and Overhead The study also showed that the implementation of the gossip algorithm on a real supercomputer, a Blue Gene/Q system, behaves as predicted by simulations and a formal model (Barak et al. 2015). Furthermore, we evaluated overhead that the gossip algorithm has on HPC applications running in parallel on the same system (Levy et al. 2014). Figure 19.3 shows performance measurements of two different applications, while the gossip algorithm sends 1 kilobyte messages between nodes at various message rates. When the inter-

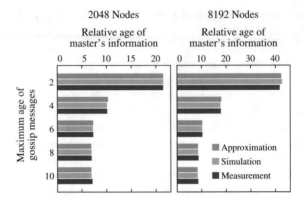

Fig. 19.2 Average age of the master's information using different age thresholds for gossip message entries (sending only newest information). The age is given relative to the interval of gossip messages; Approximations, simulations, and measurements on Blue Gene/Q match very well. This figure has originally been published in Levy et al. (2014)

Fig. 19.3 Runtime overhead of gossip on two benchmark applications on 8,192 Blue Gene/Q nodes when varying the interval of gossip messages. The inner red part indicates the MPI portion. This figure has originally been published in Levy et al. (2014)

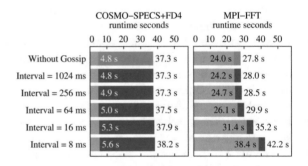

val between messages is 256 ms or higher, we observe no noticeable overhead, but the communication-intensive MPI-FFT benchmark suffers slightly from higher message rates.

We conclude from these experiments that the inherently fault-tolerant gossip algorithm is a solid foundation for building a distributed and failure-resilient management plane. More details on how to build a complete OS platform on top of it can be found in a separate publications (Weinhold et al. 2016). The remainder of this chapter focuses on the multi-kernel node OS.

19.3   History and Timeline

In this section, we discuss the design and implementation of our multi-kernel OS architecture for HPC workloads. We first give an overview of what an L4 microkernel is, how to build a complete OS on top of it, and how to support legacy OSs like Linux in order to achieve broad compatibility with existing infrastructure. Then we describe our initial attempt to adapt this platform for HPC workloads. The lessons we learned while building this first prototype led to a new architecture and design, which we describe in the third part of this section.

19.3.1 The L4Re Microkernel and L^4Linux

The name "L4" designates a whole family tree of microkernels that started in 1993. Our node OS is based on the L4Re microkernel (Lackorzynski and Warg 2009) system, which has been developed at TU Dresden in Germany. It is complemented by L^4Linux running on top of it to achieve binary compatibility with Linux applications. This microkernel, the surrounding ecosystem, and L^4Linux have an open-source history that goes back more than two decades. Additional commercial support is available since 2013, which is also the year when the FFMK project started to investigate how L4 can be used in HPC.

L4 Microkernel The core principle of L4 (Liedtke 1995) is that the kernel should provide only the minimal amount of functionality that is necessary to build a complete OS on top of it. Thus, an L4 microkernel is not intended to be a minimized Unix, but instead, it provides only a few basic abstractions: address spaces, threads, and inter-process communication (IPC). For performance reasons, a thread scheduler is also implemented within the kernel. However, other OS functionality such as device drivers, memory management, or file systems are provided by system services running as user-level programs on top of the microkernel.

Applications and User-level Services Applications communicate with each other and with system services by exchanging IPC messages. These IPC messages can not only carry ordinary data, but they may also transfer access rights for resources. Being able to map memory pages via IPC allows any two programs to establish shared memory between their address spaces. Furthermore, because it is possible to revoke memory mappings at any time, this feature enables user-level services to implement arbitrary memory-management policies. In much the same way an L4 program can pass a *capability* referencing a resource to another application or service, thereby granting the receiver the permission to access that resource. A capability can refer to a kernel object such as a `Thread` or a `Task`, representing an independent flow of execution or an address space, respectively. But they may also point to an `Ipc_gate`, which is a communication endpoint through which any user-space program can offer an arbitrary service to whomever possesses the corresponding capability.

I/O Device Support An important feature of the L4Re microkernel is that it maps hardware interrupts to IPC messages. A thread running in user space can receive interrupts by waiting for messages from an `Irq` kernel object. In conjunction with the possibility to map I/O memory regions of hardware devices directly into user address spaces, it is possible to implement device drivers outside the microkernel.

Virtualization In general, virtualization is the ability to securely run other software on a system by providing the necessary environment this software expects. For operating systems, this means that the virtualization system needs to provide the CPU, memory, and platform interfaces the guest operating system expects and is able to handle. Thus, the virtualization system must provide memory virtualization, trap-and-emulate capabilities as well as virtual hardware devices. Using hardware features supporting virtualization, such as Intel's VT-x, is needed for achieving best performance.

In the L4Re system, duties for virtualization are split between the microkernel and user-level components. While the microkernel, acting as a hypervisor, handles all the privileged functionality such as running vCPUs, user-level components provide the virtual platform for the guest, by, for example, arranging hardware device pass-through, device emulation, and memory allocation. The L4Re microkernel is a fully functional hypervisor capable of hosting virtual machines running unmodified guest operating systems. It employs hardware-assisted virtualization on the instruction set architectures that support it, including x86, ARM, and MIPS.

Virtualized Linux However, faithful virtualization is not the only way to run a legacy OS on top of the L4Re microkernel. L^4Linux is a paravirtualized Linux kernel that has been adapted to run on the interfaces provided by L4Re as a user-level program instead of running in the privileged mode of the CPU. Still, it is binary compatible with standard Linux programs. The adaption means that the Linux kernel runs as a multi-threaded user-level program that controls its Linux processes that are running in other L4 tasks (i.e., other address spaces). Linux programs on L^4Linux experience the same protection as on native Linux; they cannot read or write the Linux kernel's memory and they are protected from each other like processes on native Linux. L^4Linux is kept up to date with every major mainline Linux version. Updating L^4Linux takes about a day.

For execution, L^4Linux employs vCPUs, a mechanism provided by the microkernel that allows for an asynchronous execution model where a vCPU migrates between executing code in the L^4Linux kernel as well as in Linux processes. Threads of user processes are thus multiplexed on a single vCPU. For any event that needs to be handled by the Linux kernel, such as system calls and page faults by processes, or external interrupts by devices, the vCPU switches to the L^4Linux kernel to handle them.

The number of vCPUs assigned to L^4Linux and their pinning to physical CPU cores determines how much hardware parallelism an L^4Linux-based virtual machine can use; all other cores are exclusively under control of the L4Re microkernel. Thus, when we think of our L4-based OS and L^4Linux as a multi-kernel architecture for HPC workloads, the allocation of vCPUs to the paravirtualized kernel is how we divide resources between the LWK and Linux.

19.3.2 Initial Architecture: Native Ports to L4Re

The fundamental design decision to be made in a multi-kernel architecture is how to divide the responsibilities between the two kernels and how applications will execute on such an architecture. These decisions are driven by the optimization goal to be achieved. In previous work (Döbel and Härtig 2014; Döbel et al. 2012; Härtig et al. 2006; Singaravelu et al. 2006; Weinhold and Härtig 2008, 2011), where we researched system architectures to improve real-time and security properties, we found that there is often a comparatively small part of the software stack that is critical to meeting the respective goal (e.g., finish work under strict timing constraints or protect confidential data). However, the majority of the code base is not critical to achieve the real-time or security goal and, if isolated from the small part, need only be relied upon for overall functional requirements. We now want to apply the same approach to HPC.

L4Re Native Execution Model In HPC, the optimization goals are application performance and latency. As HPC codes are monolithic, compute-mostly programs, we decided to treat the entire application as a "critical" component that must therefore run directly on the L4Re microkernel. It provides application processes a noise-free execution environment, because they run on cores that are not available to L^4Linux (i.e., no L^4Linux vCPUs are assigned to cores that run application code).

POSIX and Fortran Compatibility Since L4Re is not compatible with Linux (or any Unix-like system) at the system call level, the applications and any library they depend on have to be cross-compiled for our OS platform. A port of μClibc (Andersen 2010), an embedded C library originally developed for Linux, provides important POSIX APIs on L4Re; it also enables C++ support via up-to-date ports of the GNU C++ standard library. To support legacy HPC applications, we ported the runtime library of the GNU Fortran compiler to L4Re, thereby enabling support for this still common HPC coding language. With support for C, C++, Fortran, and POSIX in place, we were able to compile existing codes such as HPL (LINPACK), CP2K (The CP2K Developers Group 2019) and an MPI benchmark suite (Reussner et al. 2002) for our microkernel platform without further modification. This includes most of their dependencies such as numerics libraries (BLAS, fftw3, etc.).

Requirements of HPC Infrastructure However, the most important dependency to get HPC codes to run on any platform is support for the Message Passing Interface (MPI). Applications link directly against the MPI runtime, but this library has complex dependencies of its own. First, implementations such as MVAPICH 2 (mvapichweb 2019) or Open MPI (Graham et al. 2005) use TCP/IP network sockets provided by the OS kernel for communication between MPI ranks on the compute nodes and an MPI process manager running on a separate machine. Second, the primary function of MPI is to abstract from the HPC interconnect, which in turn is accessible only through a device driver provided by the OS. Unfortunately, L4Re does not natively support TCP/IP-based networking, nor does it provide drivers for HPC interconnects such as InfiniBand. L^4Linux, on the other hand, inherits mature implementations of both network stacks from the mainline Linux kernel from which it is derived. These subsystems must be made accessible to the MPI library in order to get a working L4Re-based build of an MPI library.

We found it impractical to port all this infrastructure directly to the L4Re microkernel. The only realistic approach is to embrace the multi-kernel idea and forward network-related API calls from L4Re-based MPI applications to L⁴Linux. This approach maximizes compatibility as device drivers and the highly complex IP stack implementation remain in their natural environment (i.e., the Linux kernel).

Anatomy of the LinuxInfiniBand Stack On native Linux, as it is running on many contemporary HPC systems, the InfiniBand driver stack consists of two parts: a Linux kernel module and two libraries, which implement a device-specific user-space driver and the generic *verbs* interface. For current Mellanox InfiniBand cards, these libraries are libmlx5 and libibverbs, respectively. The kernel part of the driver initializes the InfiniBand host channel adapter (HCA). It also maps I/O registers of the HCA into the process running the user-space driver, which can therefore perform certain HCA operations directly. This architecture completely avoids the overhead associated with system calls for those operations that are most critical to performance (e.g., sending and receiving messages). System calls into the Linux kernel module are necessary only for infrequent operations such as registering memory buffers with the HCA or to create queue pairs. The two user-space libraries request these operations to be performed through *ioctl* and *read/write* calls on character devices in the /dev/infiniband directory; they are the interface for the in-kernel InfiniBand driver.

InfiniBand Device Driver and Socket Forwarding The division of work between the kernel-mode driver and its user-space counterpart is an excellent fit for our multi-kernel architecture. It works similar to how IHK/McKernel (Gerofi et al. 2016b) forwards access to the InfiniBand subsystem, meaning we also do function shipping from L4Re-based applications to the L⁴Linux kernel. We ported libmlx5 and libibverbs to L4Re such that they can be linked into an L4Re program together with the MPI library. These programs run as MPI ranks on compute cores exclusively controlled by the L4Re microkernel. For each of the MPI ranks, we create a proxy process running on L⁴Linux. The purpose of this proxy is to perform *ioctl*, *read*, and *write* calls on behalf of the L4Re program, which is linked against the InfiniBand user-space libraries but cannot access the character devices directly. We forward requests from the L4Re side to the proxy on the L⁴Linux side by means of a VFS interposition library, which looks for *open* calls on any files in /dev/infiniband. The interposition library then forwards the *open* call and any operation on the resulting file descriptor to the proxy process on L⁴Linux. This forwarding is accomplished by an "L4Re IPC device driver" in L⁴Linux, which establishes a shared-memory area between an L4Re program with the interposition library and its proxy process on L⁴Linux.

The implementation of the InfiniBand proxy builds on a generic mechanism for forwarding (shared memory and two-way signaling), but it still requires specialized code to handle the particular types of operations on the InfiniBand device nodes. For example, the proxy must establish in its own address space a shadow mapping of each memory buffer that the InfiniBand user-space driver wants to register with the HCA. Since its own memory layout differs from the L4Re task's address space, it must inspect all *ioctl* requests and translate virtual-memory addresses of buffers. This code must be changed whenever the contract between the in-kernel and user-space parts of the InfiniBand stack changes, or another type of HPC interconnect, e.g., Cray networks or Intel Omni-Path, has to be supported.

The proxy and interposition library also take care of forwarding socket operations, which the MPI library performs in order to communicate with the MPI process manager. This API requires proxy code to marshal and unmarshal all arguments and results of the fairly complex BSD socket API.

Critique: Engineering Effort and Maintainability We developed the architecture described in the preceding paragraphs into a working prototype capable of running MPI programs (based on MVAPICH 2) on a multi-node cluster with Mellanox Infini-Band HCAs. We tested it with an MPI benchmark suite (Reussner et al. 2002), small proxy codes, and real-world HPC packages such as CP2K (The CP2K Developers Group 2019) and COSMO-SPECS+FD4 (Lieber et al. 2012). However, we found that the engineering effort to develop and maintain forwarding proxies was much greater than anticipated. We identified several dependencies with non-negligible maintenance overhead; we discuss them in more detail in Sect. 19.5.

To improve maintainability, we revisited our design options and took a different approach to building a multi-kernel OS for HPC. We present this second iteration of our architecture in the following subsection.

19.3.3   Revised Architecture: Decoupled Execution

We identified HPC applications as the key software component that is critical to reaching performance and latency targets. Hence, in our initial architecture, we decided on an execution model where each application runs as a native L4Re application. However, due to the complexity of real-world applications and their numerous dependencies, a lot of Linux functionality and APIs that L4Re does not provide had to be made available outside L^4Linux via proxy processes. To avoid the significant engineering and maintenance costs of the proxies, we must remove them from the picture. Consequently, since all HPC codes are developed for Linux and require so many of its APIs, we must find a way to let them stay Linux programs *and* have them execute on the noise-free L4Re microkernel.

L^4Linux Process Model To achieve these two contradictory goals, we exploit the unique integration of L^4Linux and the L4Re microkernel. L^4Linux manages the address spaces of Linux user processes through `Task` objects provided by the L4Re microkernel. Thus, every Linux process and the contents of its address space are known to the microkernel. Furthermore, L^4Linux multiplexes all user-level threads executing in such an address space onto its vCPUs. Thus, the L4Re microkernel is

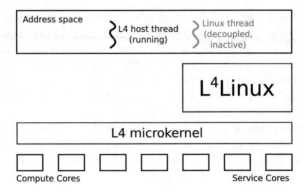

Fig. 19.4 Schematic view of the decoupling mechanism. The L4Re microkernel runs on every core of the system, while the virtualized L^{4}Linux runs on a subset of those cores only. All normal Linux applications are thus restricted to those cores. Decoupling pulls off threads and runs them on cores not available to L^{4}Linux. This figure has originally been published in Weinhold et al. (2016)

involved in every context switch of any Linux user thread. In particular, it is responsible for forwarding any exceptions raised by a Linux program to the L^{4}Linux kernel. Exceptions occur when a thread makes a system call, when a page fault occurs during its execution, or when a hardware device signals an interrupt. L^{4}Linux receives these exceptions at a previously registered vCPU entry point, to which the microkernel switches the control flow when it migrates the vCPU from the Task of the faulting Linux user program to the address space of the virtualized Linux kernel.

Decoupling Thread Execution from L^{4}Linux This interaction between the L4Re microkernel and L^{4}Linux allows us to conveniently implement a new mechanism we call *decoupling*. The purpose of decoupling is to separate execution of a thread in a Linux process from the vCPU it is normally running on. To this end, we create a separate, native L4Re host thread that runs in the same L4 Task (i.e., address space) as the Linux process, but not under control of L^{4}Linux (Fig. 19.4). The Linux user code running in the L4Re thread will raise exceptions just as if it were executed by a vCPU, except that the microkernel forwards each of them to L^{4}Linux as an *exception IPC message*. A message of this type carries a thread's register state and fault information as its payload, and is delivered by the microkernel to an exception handler. We configure L^{4}Linux to be the exception handler of the "decoupled" Linux user threads.

One Mechanism for the Best of Both Worlds The net gain of the decoupling mechanism is that we can combine noise-free execution on our LWK (i.e., the L4Re microkernel) with the rich execution environment of Linux, including all its APIs and the HPC infrastructure built for it. Furthermore, we now have a *single* mechanism for forwarding any system call and all exceptions, instead of many specialized proxies that are difficult to maintain. Thus, applications are built for Linux and start running as Linux processes, but we pull their threads of out of Linux's scheduling regime so they can run on dedicated cores without being disturbed by L^{4}Linux. Effectively, decoupled threads run directly on the microkernel. However, they can use all services provided by L^4Linux, which will continue to handle Linux system calls and resolve page faults.

Since the InfiniBand driver in the L^4Linux kernel maps the I/O registers of the HCA into the address space of each MPI rank, the high performance and minimal latency of the user-space part of the driver is not impaired; a decoupled thread can program performance-critical operations just like it would on native Linux.

Implementation Details A challenge to overcome is that the Linux kernel must be informed that it should not schedule or otherwise manipulate a thread while it is decoupled. As the execution model of the Linux kernel is synchronous with regard to switching control flow between threads running in kernel and user mode, either the L^4Linux kernel will run or the user thread. However, when we decouple a thread, we want both activities—the decoupled thread (i.e., the native L4Re thread on its own core) *and* the L^4Linux vCPUs—to continue running. The L^4Linux kernel should continue scheduling other work. To prevent L^4Linux from scheduling a decoupled thread on a vCPU, we set the respective Linux thread context to *uninterruptible* state; the Linux scheduler will then believe this thread is blocked.

Any exception that is caused by a decoupled thread is sent via exception IPC to the L^4Linux kernel, thus, there is effectively a second entry point for incoming exceptions that L^4Linux must ultimately handle on one of its vCPUs. However, when L^4Linux receives an exception IPC, another context within Linux may be running on a vCPU already. So, L^4Linux stores the exception state in the Linux context of the decoupled thread and uses a *wakeup* call to reactivate the thread in Linux. As it is ready now, this thread will eventually be picked up by the Linux scheduler. Once the exception has been handled, the thread's Linux context will go into *uninterruptible* state again and execution continues on the L4Re host thread on a different core.

In the following, we describe further details of our implementation:

- **Signal Handling**: Since a decoupled thread is blocked in *uninterruptible* state in the L^4Linux kernel, our mechanism interferes with the way how signals such as SIGKILL are handled. Usually, a Linux thread is delivered a signal when it is in the kernel or enters it. A thread running in user mode will enter the Linux kernel when an asynchronous event forces a kernel entry, like when a timer interrupt occurs. However, a decoupled thread will not enter the Linux kernel if such an event is to be handled by Linux; the decoupled thread continues to execute independently in its own L4Re thread. To ensure timely delivery of signals, the L^4Linux kernel periodically scans all decoupled threads and those that have signals pending are forced to enter the L^4Linux kernel so the signals are processed as required.
- **Memory**: By default, all the memory that a decoupled thread touches belongs to the Linux process the thread is running in. Therefore, the L^4Linux kernel manages this memory in the same way as for a non-decoupled process. As a result, Linux is allowed to perform page replacement as it sees fit, which might negatively impact performance by causing unexpected page faults even though all threads are decoupled. However, paging can be avoided by using the *mlock* and *mlockall* system call. It is also recommended to use large pages to minimize TLB pressure.

An application can obtain memory that is not managed by L⁴Linux; we will explain how to do so on p. 351.

- **Floating Point Unit**: The L4Re microkernel helps with multiplexing the state of the floating point unit (FPU) for the various threads of execution that L⁴Linux puts on a vCPU. Thus, each Linux thread has its own FPU state, but only one at a time is active on each vCPU. However, decoupled Linux threads are independent L4Re threads running in parallel to whatever L⁴Linux schedules on its vCPUs. When a decoupled thread raises an exception, its FPU state must be transferred to the L⁴Linux exception handler, which has to update the saved FPU state of the suspended Linux thread context. The exception IPC mechanism in L4Re supports automatic FPU state transfer (in CPU registers) to the handler, but this is safe only if the handler does not currently use the FPU itself; otherwise, FPU state of the handler will be overwritten. Unfortunately, the exception handler of the L⁴Linux kernel runs on a vCPU, which may therefore have active FPU state of its own, depending on what activity was scheduled on it at the time when the exception occurred in the decoupled thread. To avoid this problem, we extended the microkernel such that it allows to retrieve the FPU state of another thread explicitly, such that L⁴Linux does not have to use the potentially unsafe implicit transfer. An explicit way of restoring the FPU state of a decoupled thread upon reactivation is not needed, because automatic transfer when replying to the exception IPC happens when the Linux context of the decoupled thread is active and the correct FPU state is already present in CPU registers.

- **User Interface**: Instead of adding a new system call to L⁴Linux, we implemented a /sys FS-based interface to initiate and control the decoupling of threads. This method allows users and administrators to easily enable decoupling for a specific process without having to modify the application to make it use the system call. The decoupling state is retained even after starting a new program binary with the *execve* system call. Thus, users and administrators can write wrapper scripts like the following to transparently start a process in decoupled state:

```
#! /bin/sh
SYSFS_PATH=/sys/kernel/L4/detach
echo $$ > $SYSFS_PATH/detach
echo $HOST_CORE_ID > $SYSFS_PATH/$$/cpu
exec "$@"
```

As shown, the /sys fs interface also allows users to specify the host CPU on which the decoupled thread shall run. Note that, if an application creates additional threads, they will remain under L⁴Linux' control. However, it is possible to inject a library at load time using the LD_PRELOAD mechanism to wrap or overwrite scheduling-related functions, including *pthread_create* and *sched_setaffinity*, such that they use the /sys FS interface for transparent decoupling support.

19.3.4 Hybrid Applications: L4Re System Calls in Linux Programs

Decoupled threads are not limited to executing user-mode instructions and making Linux system calls, but they can also interact with the L4Re microkernel and services running outside L⁴Linux. In the following, we outline possible use cases.

Decoupled Interrupts A decoupled thread can perform native L4 system calls and use the API of the L4Re microkernel. This is, for example, useful for implementing control loops that do work periodically, or for receiving messages from `Irq` kernel objects through which the microkernel delivers device interrupts. With the possibility to deliver hardware interrupts directly to a decoupled thread, our architecture enables Linux applications to bypass the interrupt handling code in the Linux kernel, thereby reducing interrupt response latency (Lackorzynski et al. 2017).

To attach to an `Irq` and receive interrupt messages from it, the decoupled thread needs a *capability* that gives it access to this kernel object. As L⁴Linux is in control of the `Task` object that represents the address space in which the decoupled thread executes, it is in the position to map the required capabilities to the user-space program. We developed an additional L⁴Linux-specific `/sys` FS interface that allows a Linux program to request that `Irq` capabilities be mapped into its address space.

Special Memory Pools Additionally, decoupled threads can communicate with arbitrary L4Re services via IPC, as long as they possess the capabilities to do so. Thus, a decoupled thread can receive page mappings from an L4Re service in order to share memory with it, but it must take care where in its virtual address space these pages appear. As the L⁴Linux kernel is not aware of these mappings, the applications should block the target region of its address space using the *mmap* call.

19.4 Experimental Results

The decoupling mechanism is the core feature of our multi-kernel OS architecture. In this section, we evaluate how effective it is at reducing execution-time jitter, i.e., OS noise. Our measurements are based on the fixed-work quantum (FWQ) (Lawrence Livermore National Laboratory 2019) benchmark. This benchmark repeatedly measures the time required to perform a fixed amount of work. On a perfectly noise-free system, each iteration of the work loop will always take the same time. Increases in execution time are caused by other activities in the system, including but not limited to "OS noise".

Baseline Various studies (Seelam et al. 2010; Hoefler et al. 2010) have already investigated root causes and performance impact of OS noise. To establish a baseline for evaluating our own L4Re-based multi-kernel OS, we first ran the FWQ benchmark on an HPC production system with the vendor-provided OS to show the behavior of such a system. This system, which is installed at the Center for Information

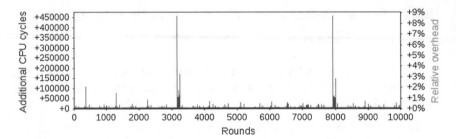

Fig. 19.5 OS noise on a Taurus node with Linux-based vendor OS. This figure has originally been published in Lackorzynski et al. (2016b)

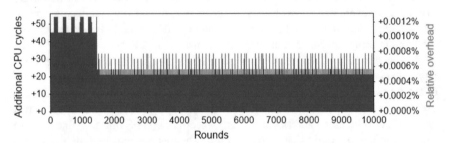

Fig. 19.6 Minimal OS noise remaining in decoupled execution; L⁴Linux running on same socket. This figure has originally been published in Lackorzynski et al. (2016b)

Services and High-Performance Computing (ZIH) at TU Dresden, Germany, is an FDR InfiniBand cluster. Each node has two Xeon® E5-2680v3 processors with 12 cores each and 64 GiB memory. The OS is based on RHEL 6.4 with a heavily modified Linux kernel 2.6.32.

Figure 19.5 shows results from a single-threaded run of the FWQ on this system. The benchmark executed its work loop 10,000 times within approximately 10 s. We determined the minimum execution time (i.e., without any interruption) for the fixed amount of work using the `rdtsc` instruction. The Y axis in the diagram visualizes, for each iteration of the work loop, by how many additional CPU cycles the benchmark has been delayed relative to this baseline. We observed that OS noise with the vendor-provided OS can increase the time to completion for the fixed work quantum by up to 450,000 cycles or 200 μs, which translates to about 8.7%.

Decoupled Thread Execution In contrast, a prototype version of our multi-kernel OS, based on the L4Re microkernel and L⁴Linux, reduced noise dramatically when running FWQ decoupled from the virtualized Linux kernel on a dedicated core. With our OS, the noise amounts to about 50 CPU cycles when using a core in the same socket as the service cores allocated to L⁴Linux (Fig. 19.6), or or as little as 4 cycles when the benchmark runs on the second socket of the node (Fig. 19.7). Note that these initial measurements of decoupling performance had to be done on a test machine in our lab (a dual-socket Intel Xeon® X5650 system), because bare metal access to nodes of the Taurus cluster was not possible at the time.

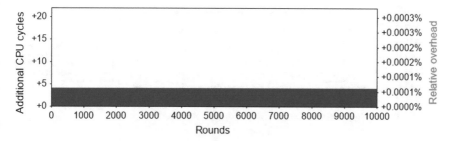

Fig. 19.7 Minimal OS noise remaining in decoupled execution; L⁴Linux running on different socket. This figure has originally been published in Lackorzynski et al. (2016b)

We later had the opportunity to run our own L4Re-based OS on 50 Taurus nodes that were equipped with two Xeon® E5-2690 processors with 8 cores per socket; these CPUs operate at a higher clock rate than the 12-core E5-2680 v3 processors we used in our initial OS noise experiment described at the beginning of this section.

Parallel FWQ Benchmark To benchmark the decoupling mechanism in an HPC configuration, we extended the FWQ benchmark into an MPI program that executes 10,000 iterations of the work loop in each participating MPI rank. This modified version, called *MPI-FWQ* has two modes of operation:

1. In *StartSync* mode, MPI-FWQ uses a single barrier across all ranks before starting the work. It simulates an embarrassingly parallel (EP) application.
2. In *StepSync* mode, MPI-FWQ waits on a barrier after each iteration of the work loop. This mode simulates an application that alternates between computation and global synchronization among the ranks; this pattern is common for the bulk-synchronous programming (BSP) model.

For all experiments with decoupling enabled, we allocated one core to L⁴Linux, while the remaining 15 cores ran MPI-FWQ under control of the L4Re microkernel. We compare these runs against a "standard" configuration of L⁴Linux, where the virtualized Linux kernel had access to 16 vCPUs pinned to all available cores, but only 15 of them ran the benchmark. Thus, MPI-FWQ threads were scheduled by the Linux kernel scheduler like in the HPC OS provided by the system vendor.

Decoupled Execution with StartSync: Figure 19.8 shows the results for several MPI-FWQ runs in *StartSync* mode; the X axis indicates the total number of cores used in the respective experiment. The two graphs labeled with "Min" show that decoupled execution reduces run time of the benchmark slightly below the minimum completion time observed for the "standard" L⁴Linux configuration on any of the cores involved. The graphs labeled with "Max" show that decoupling reduces the noise compared to running MPI-FWQ in L⁴Linux. However, we observed a "slow core" phenomenon where even with decoupling enabled, some cores would temporarily slow down before returning to higher speed in later experiments (see graph labeled L4Linux-DC-Max). But still our mechanism improves throughput by approximately 1 percent.

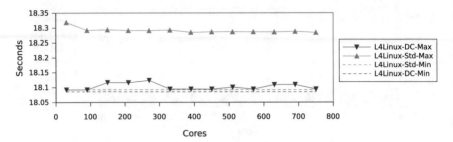

Fig. 19.8 EP-style MPI-FWQ (*StartSync* mode) on L⁴Linux (Std) and with decoupled thread execution (DC) on Taurus. This figure has originally been published in Lackorzynski et al. (2016b)

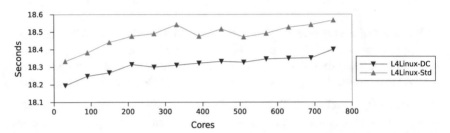

Fig. 19.9 BSP-style MPI-FWQ (*StepSync* mode) on L⁴Linux (Std) and with decoupled thread execution (DC) on Taurus. This figure has originally been published in Lackorzynski et al. (2016b)

Decoupled Execution with StepSync: Figure 19.9 visualizes the run time *StepSync* mode runs of MPI-FWQ. For standard L⁴Linux and L⁴Linux with decoupled execution the values are extremely close so that we only show the "Min" values. As the graphs show, the decoupled execution is always faster.

More information on the decoupling mechanism, use cases, and evaluations results can be found in separate publications (Lackorzynski et al. 2016a, b, 2017). Based on all our experiments, we can conclude that the decoupling mechanism is able to reduce the OS noise experienced by applications and thus reduce their run time.

19.5 Lessons Learned

We initially thought that porting HPC codes to L4Re was the best approach to provide them with a noise-free execution environment. However, even though the process of recompiling was straightforward, it involved significant manual work as the build systems for both applications and the HPC support packages (e.g., SCALAPACK) had to be completely rewritten for L4Re. Furthermore, it turned out that the engineering effort to develop and maintain forwarding proxies was much greater than anticipated and could not always be done in a generic way. For example, we started work on a forwarding proxy for Xtreemfs (XtreemFS 2019), a parallel file system, but eventually stopped because it could not become a generic component that would also work for other HPC file storage solutions such as Lustre or the General Parallel File System (GPFS). Also, there is often a tight interaction between MPI and cluster management systems such as SLURM. Integration of these services would become unavoidable eventually, requiring even more specialized proxying code.

Coming from a real-time and security background, this outcome was not what we hoped for. The main reason for the described maintainability problem was that we set out run monolithic and highly complex applications on L4Re. They depend on many more Linux subsystems than the use cases we studied in the context of real-time and security systems. In this previous research, we could identify and isolate the specific parts of a program that were critical to meeting real-time requirements or security properties; but they were fairly simple and had few dependencies other than the main program they were isolated from. Thus, in hindsight, the approach of running MPI-based HPC applications as native L4Re programs proved possible, but at greater engineering cost than originally anticipated. The lesson we learned was that huge, complex codes with lots of dependencies on Linux and existing HPC infrastructure should remain Linux programs, while kernel-level mechanisms such as decoupled threads are used to minimize specific sources of performance overheads (e.g., execution-time jitter and scheduling overhead).

19.6 Conclusions

Major improvements to supercomputer architectures have always required adaptation of applications, runtime environments, and the low-level system software. With regard to future exascale machines, the HPC community must adapt the operating system layer again to help applications cope with more nodes, higher core counts, and support to maintain reliability. Commodity OSs such as Linux are not a good enough fit for HPC workloads, because they are too generic, heavy-weight, and they often take away precious CPU cycles from applications that demand well-balanced and interrupt-free execution.

However, there is an equally strong consensus that the feature set, tool support, and compatibility of Linux is essential even for supercomputers. Multi-kernel architectures that combine Linux with a lightweight kernel are an excellent compromise. However, just because an HPC-optimized kernel is "lightweight" does not mean that it is easy to develop one from scratch. We think reusing an existing noise-free kernel is the better way and we believe that the mature L4Re microkernel is well-suited to support HPC workloads. Together with the paravirtualized L⁴Linux, which tightly integrates with L4Re, it gains binary compatibility down to the level of the Linux system call API. Thus, our system can support any HPC runtime that works on Linux, not just MPI.

Our decoupling mechanism, which allows threads of a Linux process to execute noise-free on the microkernel, is an elegant way to combine the best of both kernels and maximizes reuse of legacy infrastructure. However, even though both the L4Re microkernel and L⁴Linux already existed when we started the project, we had to learn the lesson that a Linux-first execution model is ultimately a better approach than trying to make Linux APIs available to an application that has been ported to become a native L4Re program. In hindsight, bridging the two kernels by decoupling just the execution of threads would have had the potential to free up scarce developer resources much earlier.

Acknowledgements We would like to thank the German priority program 1648 "Software for Exascale Computing" for supporting the project FFMK (FFMK 2019), the ESF-funded project microHPC (microHPC 2019), and the cluster of excellence "Center for Advancing Electronics Dresden" (cfaed). We also acknowledge the Julich Supercomputing Centre, the Gauss Centre for Supercomputing, and the John von Neumann Institute for Computing for providing compute time on the JUQUEEN and JURECA supercomputers. We would also like to deeply thank TU Dresden's ZIH for allowing us bare metal access to nodes of their Taurus system, as well as all our fellow researchers in the FFMK project for their advise, contributions, and friendly collaboration.

References

Andersen, E. (2010). μClibc. https://uclibc.org.

Barak, A., Drezner, Z., Levy, E., Lieber, M., & Shiloh, A. (2015). Resilient gossip algorithms for collecting online management information in exascale clusters. *Concurrency and Computation: Practice and Experience, 27*(17), 4797–4818.

Beckman, P. et al. (2015). Argo: An exascale operating system. http://www.argo-osr.org/. Accessed 20 Nov 2015.

Döbel, B., & Härtig, H. (2014). Can we put concurrency back into redundant multithreading? *Proceedings of the 14th International Conference on Embedded Software, EMSOFT 2014* (pp. 19:1–19:10). USA: ACM.

Döbel, B., Härtig, H., & Engel, M. (2012). Operating system support for redundant multithreading. *Proceedings of the Tenth ACM International Conference on Embedded Software EMSOFT 2012* (pp. 83–92). USA: ACM.

FFMK. FFMK Project Website. https://ffmk.tudos.org. Accessed 01 Feb 2018.

Fu, H., Liao, J., Yang, J., Wang, L., Song, Z., Huang, X., et al. (2016). The Sunway TaihuLight supercomputer: system and applications. *Science China Information Sciences, 59*(7), 072001.

Gerofi, B., Takagi, M., Hori, A., Nakamura, G., Shirasawa, T., & Ishikawa, Y. (2016). On the scalability, performance isolation and device driver transparency of the IHK/McKernel hybrid lightweight kernel. *2016 IEEE International Parallel and Distributed Processing Symposium (IPDPS)* (pp. 1041–1050).

Graham, R. L., Woodall, T. S., & Squyres, J. M. (2005). Open MPI: A flexible high performance MPI. *Proceedings, 6th Annual International Conference on Parallel Processing and Applied Mathematics*. Poland: Poznan.

Härtig, H., & Roitzsch, M. (2006). Ten Years of Research on L4-Based Real-Time. *Proceedings of the Eighth Real-Time Linux Workshop*. China: Lanzhou.

Härtig, H., Hohmuth, M., Liedtke, J., Schönberg, S., & Wolter, J. (1997). The performance of μ-kernel-based systems. *SOSP 1997: Proceedings of the sixteenth ACM symposium on Operating systems principles* (pp. 66–77). USA: ACM Press.

Hoefler, T., Schneider, T., & Lumsdaine, A. (2010). Characterizing the influence of system noise on large-scale applications by simulation. *Proceedings of the 2010 ACM/IEEE International Conference for High Performance Computing, Networking, Storage and Analysis, SC 2010*. USA: IEEE Computer Society.

Lackorzynski, A., & Warg, A. (2009). Taming subsystems: capabilities as universal resource access control in L4. *IIES 2009: Proceedings of the Second Workshop on Isolation and Integration in Embedded Systems* (pp. 25–30). USA: ACM.

Lackorzynski, A., Weinhold, C., & Härtig, H. (2016a). Combining predictable execution with full-featured commodity systems. *Proceedings of OSPERT2016, the 12th Annual Workshop on Operating Systems Platforms for Embedded Real-Time Applications OSPERT 2016* (pp. 31–36).

Lackorzynski, A., Weinhold, C., & Härtig, H. (2016b). Decoupled: Low-effort noise-free execution on commodity system. *Proceedings of the 6th International Workshop on Runtime and Operating Systems for Supercomputers ROSS 2016*. USA: ACM.

Lackorzynski, A., Weinhold, C., & Härtig, H. (2017). Predictable low-latency interrupt response with general-purpose systems. *Proceedings of OSPERT2017, the 13th Annual Workshop on Operating Systems Platforms for Embedded Real-Time Applications OSPERT 2017* (pp. 19–24).

Lawrence Livermore National Laboratory. The FTQ/FWQ Benchmark.

Levy, E., Barak, A., Shiloh, A., Lieber, M., Weinhold, C., & Härtig, H. (2014). Overhead of a decentralized gossip algorithm on the performance of HPC applications. *Proceedings of the ROSS 2014* (pp. 10:1–10:7). New York: ACM.

Lieber, M., Grützun, V., Wolke, R., Müller, M. S., & Nagel, W. E. (2012). Highly scalable dynamic load balancing in the atmospheric modeling system COSMO-SPECS+FD4. *Proceedings of the PARA 2010* (Vol. 7133, pp. 131–141). Berlin: Springer.

Liedtke, J. (1995). On micro-kernel construction. *SOSP 1995: Proceedings of the fifteenth ACM symposium on Operating systems principles* (pp. 237–250). USA: ACM Press.

microHPC. microHPC Project Website. https://microhpc.tudos.org. Accessed 01 Feb 2018.

mvapichweb. MVAPICH: MPI over InfiniBand. http://mvapich.cse.ohio-state.edu/. Accessed 29 Jan 2017.

Reussner, R., Sanders, P., & Larsson Träff, J. (2002). SKaMPI: a comprehensive benchmark for public benchmarking of MPI (pp. 10:55–10:65).

Seelam, S., Fong, L., Tantawi, A., Lewars, J., Divirgilio, J., & Gildea, K. (2010). Extreme scale computing: Modeling the impact of system noise in multicore clustered systems. *2010 IEEE International Symposium on Parallel Distributed Processing (IPDPS)*.

Singaravelu, L., Pu, C., Härtig, H., & Helmuth, C. (2006). Reducing TCB complexity for security-sensitive applications: three case studies. *Proceedings of the 1st ACM SIGOPS/EuroSys European Conference on Computer Systems 2006, EuroSys 2006* (pp. 161–174). USA: ACM.

The CP2K Developers Group. Open source molecular dynamics. http://www.cp2k.org/. Accessed 20 Nov 2015.

Weinhold, C. & Härtig, H. (2011). jVPFS: adding robustness to a secure stacked file system with untrusted local storage components. *Proceedings of the 2011 USENIX Conference on USENIX Annual Technical Conference, USENIXATC 2011*, (p. 32). USA: USENIX Association.

Weinhold, C., & Härtig, H. (2008). VPFS: building a virtual private file system with a small trusted computing base. *Proceedings of the 3rd ACM SIGOPS/EuroSys European Conference on Computer Systems 2008, Eurosys 2008* (pp. 81–93). USA: ACM.

Weinhold, C., Lackorzynski, A., Bierbaum, J., Küttler, M., Planeta, M., Härtig, H., et al. (2016). Ffmk: A fast and fault-tolerant microkernel-based system for exascale computing. *Software for Exascale Computing—SPPEXA 2013–2015* (Vol. 113, pp. 405–426).

XtreemFS. XtreemFS - a cloud file system. http://www.xtreemfs.org. Accessed 16 May 2018.

Chapter 20
HermitCore

Stefan Lankes, Simon Pickartz and Jens Breibart

Abstract The complexity of future supercomputers will increase on their path to exascale systems and beyond. System software has to adapt to this complexity to simplify the development of scalable applications. A small, scalable, adaptable, and highly tuned kernel would be best suitable for high-performance computing if common programming interfaces (e.g., MPI, OpenMP) were still supported. Similar characteristics are likewise important in the cloud computing domain. Here, small environments are desirable as well since the applications mostly run in virtual machines which may influence each other, i.e., the activity of a virtual machine on a neighboring core may decrease the performance due to issues such as cache contamination—which is commonly referred to as the noisy neighbor problem. In addition, small environments reduce the attack vector which is an important aspect for cloud providers. In this chapter, we present the operating system HermitCore, combining two different kernel designs for high performance and cloud computing. HermitCore is a multi-kernel providing the scalability of a lightweight kernel and the flexibility of a full-weight kernel. HermitCore can also be run as a unikernel. These are specialized, single-address-space machine images constructed using library operating systems. This approach supports the removal of obsolete code and allows the compiler to perform link-time optimizations of the whole software stack including the library operating system itself. We show that HermitCore promises excellent performance and propose a novel checkpoint/restart technique for unikernels.

S. Lankes (✉) · S. Pickartz
Institute for Automation of Complex Power Systems, RWTH Aachen University,
Aachen, Germany
e-mail: slankes@eonerc.rwth-aachen.de

S. Pickartz
e-mail: spickartz@eonerc.rwth-aachen.de

J. Breibart
Bosch Chassis System Control, Stuttgart, Germany
e-mail: jens.breibart@de.bosch.com

© Springer Nature Singapore Pte Ltd. 2019
B. Gerofi et al. (eds.), *Operating Systems for Supercomputers
and High Performance Computing*, High-Performance Computing Series,
https://doi.org/10.1007/978-981-13-6624-6_20

20.1 Introduction

Currently, data centers as well as computing centers employ a software stack which is nearly 40 years old, possessing a huge amount of legacy code. The High-Performance Computing (HPC) community commonly uses Linux which is designed for a broad range of systems (e.g., routers, smartphones, servers, etc.). With the goal to reduce overhead and system noise, specialized Linux versions are developed (e.g., ZeptoOS in Chap. 10) by removing unneeded features from the upstream sources. However, the maintenance of the resulting code basis is rather difficult, i.e., with an increasing gap between the Vanilla and optimized version, new kernel features are difficult to merge between these versions.

The cloud community has similar demands to reduce kernel features. Here, the applications run mostly within Virtual Machines (VMs) and virtual I/O devices are handled by legacy code, e.g., disk elevator algorithms—which are used to increase I/O throughput—are only suitable for real hard disks. In addition, the systems possess at least two resource managers (the host and the guest kernel), which imposes overhead and potentially results in performance degradation. Unikernels are a feasible solution to this problem. These are specialized, single-address-space machine images, constructed using library Operating Systems (OSs). First, this approach supports the removal of obsolete code, and reduces the attack surface. This is an important characteristics for the cloud community since it increases system security. Second, unikernels are interesting from a performance perspective, especially for the HPC community: the compiler is able to perform link-time optimizations of the whole software stack, including the library OS. In addition, the absence of system calls—which are replaced by common function calls—improves the performance of the system software. These features promise excellent performance behavior.

The HPC community has a strong interest in checkpointing their applications because the increasing complexity of the hardware also increases the probability of node failures. Checkpoint/Restart (C/R) mechanisms allow for backward recovery upon failure by restarting the process from an intermediate state. This prevents significant data losses and the resuming of the affected application from the beginning. Although the virtual instances in cloud computing are commonly stateless, similar techniques are still of interest. C/R mechanisms build the basis for migration, i.e., the transfer of the process state during runtime, supporting workload consolidations, and facilitating maintenance. Each community uses different approaches for checkpointing. The cloud community commonly employs VMs where a checkpoint comprises the whole system image. In contrast, checkpoints of HPC jobs are usually created at the application level and do not store whole system images. However, this approach entails the problem of residual dependencies (Milojičić et al. 2000) if the application is resumed on a different host system.

In this chapter, we present the lightweight OS kernel HermitCore[1] (Lankes et al. 2016, 2017) which spans both worlds. It can be used as traditional unikernel within a VM, but also provides multi-kernel features, as it is able to run the same image

---

[1]http://www.hermitcore.org.

bare-metal, side by side with a Linux instance. Moreover, we present a novel technique to create small checkpoints without additional hardware support or kernel extensions.

20.2 Related Work

Chapter 13 in this book provides an overview of different multi-kernel approaches and their history. Consequently, this section summarizes only the history of unikernels and their advantages for HPC. Unikernels (or library OSs) are specialized, single-address-space architectures that are tailored to the needs of a particular application. In doing so, they target minimal overhead in the application's execution. These kernels are built by compiling high-level languages directly into specialized machine images. Thereby, system calls are replaced by common function calls, which promise faster handling of resource requests. For these reasons, unikernels are not only attractive for cloud computing but also an interesting alternative for the HPC community. Unikernels are able to run directly on a hypervisor or bare-metal hardware. They provide a smaller footprint compared to traditional OS kernels and have higher prospects to optimize the applications. Consequently, F. Manco, et al. were able to show in Manco et al. (2017) that unikernels provide better scalability in comparison to common container technologies.

Currently, unikernels are mostly used in the area of cloud computing, and are not designed with HPC in mind. This results in various disadvantages. For example, MirageOS (Madhavapeddy et al. 2013) is designed for the high-level language OCaml which is hardly used in HPC. The first version of *IncludeOS* (Bratterud et al. 2015) do not support multicore-processor systems which are indispensable for HPC workloads. Recently, IncludeOS was extended to support symmetric multi-processor (SMP) systems (Morshedi and Haugerud 2017). However, the support of OpenMP or similar runtimes is missing, which is important to support current HPC applications. *Rumprun* kernels (Kantee 2012) are partially virtualized and rely on a hypervisor to provide a thread abstraction. Consequently, none of these approaches is able to support both communities.

20.3 Design of HermitCore

HermitCore supports two operating modes: (1) the OS kernel can be executed bare-metal, side by side with a Linux kernel. The reduced OS complexity—compared to traditional Full-Weight Kernels (FWKs) such as Linux—enhances the application performance of HPC workloads due to reduced OS noise. (2) HermitCore's stand-alone mode supports its execution without a Linux instance running alongside. This is suitable for cloud computing environments, i.e., on top of a hypervisor this provides more predictable execution times than a traditional OS. It is important to note that the same binary can be used for both operating modes without the need to recompile the application.

One of the major motivations for the development of HermitCore is the improvement of programmability as well as scalability of HPC systems. Additionally, it supports novel service models such as virtual clusters (Zhang et al. 2016; Breitbart et al. 2017). These can be started, stopped, and migrated within real clusters transparently to the applications running inside. Furthermore, unikernels ease the creation of checkpoints since the application, including all dependencies, is encapsulated within an isolated environment. This improves the resiliency of current and future HPC systems without application-level support. For the same reason, load balancing is facilitated since virtual machines provide means for migrations across the cluster (Pickartz et al. 2016).

The HermitCore kernel is implemented as a library OS. Therefore, all system calls are translated into common function calls, reducing overhead compared to traditional OSs and promising better runtime behavior in HPC and real-time environments. This design requires that the initialization routines of the library OS have to be located at predictable addresses and are accessible at boot time of the HermitCore application. To simplify the boot process, the kernel is stored in a special section and located at the beginning of the application.

The small 64-bit kernel of HermitCore provides basic OS functionality, e.g., memory management and priority-based round-robin scheduling. Currently, it supports mainly the Intel 64 Architecture and comes with support for SMT, SSE4, AVX 2, and AVX 512. However, a prototype of aarch64 support is available on GitHub. Although no more than a single process is executed at a time, HermitCore still provides a scheduler. Thus, HermitCore provides oversubscription: more threads than available cores. This is important for features of managed programming languages, e.g., garbage collection, or performance monitoring tools. Currently, the scheduler does not support load balancing since explicit thread placement is favored over automatic strategies in HPC. The scheduling overhead is reduced to a minimum by the employment of a dynamic timer, i.e., the kernel does not interrupt computation threads which run exclusively on certain cores, and does not use any timers. As the evaluation results show, we are therefore able to reduce system noise introduced by the OS kernel (see Sect. 20.5.2).

20.3.1   Toolchain

HermitCore applications can be built using a cross toolchain which is based on the *GNU binutils* and the *GNU Compiler Collection*. Therefore, HermitCore supports all programming languages which are supported by gcc. The support for HermitCore in the original GNU toolchain requires only minimal modifications of the upstream sources. Only the targets for HermitCore, *x86_64-hermit* and *aarch64-hermit*, had to be integrated into the cross-configure script of binutils and gcc. Runtime was ported to

HermitCore by removing all methods related to process creation and inter-processor communication.

HermitCore applications are not restricted to the GNU toolchain. Other C/C++ compilers (e.g., Intel's C compiler) can be used instead of our cross-compiler suite. In this case, the respective compiler has to use the header files of HermitCore instead of the Linux headers. The resulting object files have to be converted to HermitCore objects as the compilers generate Linux objects by default. Therefore, we provide an adapted version of `elfedit` as part of HermitCore's toolchain.

20.3.2 Multi-Kernel Mode

In multi-kernel mode, one HermitCore instance is executed per NUMA node. This approach supports HermitCore's main design principle, namely, the improvement of the programmability and scalability of HPC systems. Each HermitCore instance is solely responsible for the local resources of its NUMA node, e.g., the memory and the CPU cores (see Fig. 20.1), which hides the hardware complexity by presenting the application developer a traditional UMA architecture. In general, one MPI rank is mapped to one NUMA domain. Inter-kernel communication among the HermitCore instances is realized by means of a virtual IP device based on the lightweight IP stack $LwIP^2$ or by the message-passing library iRCCE (Clauss et al. 2013, 2015).

iRCCE is an extension of the communication library RCCE (Mattson and van der Wijngaart 2010; Mattson et al. 2010), which was originally designed as customized message-passing interface for the Single-Chip Cloud Computer (SCC) (Matsson 2010). This lightweight message-passing environment, that is, in turn based on a simple one-sided communication mechanism (RCCE_put / RCCE_get) offers two sided but blocking (often also referred to as synchronous) point-to-point communication functions (RCCE_send / RCCE_recv) as well as a set of collective communication operations (RCCE_barrier, RCCE_bcast, RCCE_reduce, ...). However, the lack of non-blocking point-to-point communication capabilities within the current RCCE library was the motivation to extend RCCE by such asynchronous message-passing functions (iRCCE_isend / iRCCE_irecv). Furthermore, iRCCE improves the performance of basic RCCE functions, as, for example, the blocking send and receive operations, added wildcard features to receive messages from any source and any length and supports also x86-based processors beside the SCC. iRCCE is an important component of HermitCore because it is used as communication layer for our own MPI implementation SCC-MPICH (Clauss et al. 2011). It is comparable with a traditional shared memory mechanisms used by MPI implementations on NUMA systems, but with a more portable and easy to use interface to create shared segments between HermitCore nodes but also between HermitCore and Linux nodes. Consequently, SCC-MPICH is able to run on top of both operating

---

[2]http://savannah.nongnu.org/projects/lwip/.

Fig. 20.1 A NUMA system with one satellite kernel per NUMA node (from Lankes et al. (2016))

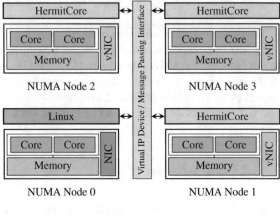

Fig. 20.2 The software stack of HermitCore in a multi-kernel setup (from Lankes et al. (2016))

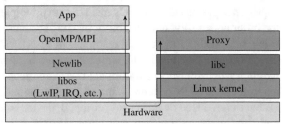

systems, where the Linux nodes can be used for pre- (reading the input data from an I/O device) and post-processing (visualization of the results).

To facilitate the usability of HermitCore in multi-kernel environments, a special loader is registered with the Linux instance that is capable of starting HermitCore applications. Therefore, it uses a slightly modified *executable link format* (ELF). This identifies HermitCore applications by a magic number in the binary's header. Furthermore, the loader launches a proxy (see Fig. 20.2) that enables communication between the HermitCore application and the outside world. In doing so, standard logging mechanisms and available tools for pre- and post-processing are supported.

The application itself is booted on an exclusive set of cores which is provided by the Linux kernel. Therefore, HermitCore leverages the Linux' hot-plugging feature facilitating the registration/unregistration of cores from the Linux kernel at runtime. In doing so, the Linux kernel relinquishes its control over the respective cores for the course of the application, i.e., this approach avoids system noise generated by kernel threads in standard Linux environments. Missing functionality, e.g., the access to a network file system can be provided by the Linux instance running alongside. Therefore, according to remote procedure calls (RPCs) are posted via the IP connection to the proxy which, in turn, requests the Linux kernel to perform the respective operation. Although most system calls like memory allocation and network access are directly handled by HermitCore, this mechanism offers backward compatibility at the expense of a reduced peak performance.

The presented approach only requires minor modifications to the Linux upstream sources. A device driver realizes the IP connection between HermitCore and Linux, and the boot process requires support within Linux for the initialization of the cores. However, until now these modifications did not cause any issues when merging with current upstream kernel sources.

20.3.3   Hypervisor Mode

For cloud environments, the proxy is able to boot HermitCore directly within a VM without the need for a Linux kernel running alongside. Common hypervisors expose a complex, general-purpose virtual hardware abstraction and initialize all virtual devices at boot time. This even includes devices that are not required by the guest.

Therefore, specialized hypervisors providing a hardware abstraction that is tailored to the demands of a particular guest may significantly improve the boot times of the unikernel. In this context, Dan Williams and Ricardo Koller present a hypervisor prototype (Williams and Koller 2016) for the unikernel Solo5,[3] which is the base layer of MirageOS (Madhavapeddy et al. 2013). Based on this approach, we created a hypervisor called *uhyve*.[4] Uhyve uses the kernel virtual machine (KVM) API (Triplett 2015) which is part of the Linux kernel and the interface to realize a hardware-accelerated hypervisor. During the initialization, the hypervisor—which, in turn, is a regular Linux process—allocates a memory buffer that serves as guest physical memory, i.e., the start address of this buffer is the physical address $0x0$ of the guest.

HermitCore's address space is contiguously mapped into the address space of the hypervisor. Consequently, guest physical addresses are easily converted to the corresponding virtual address in the hypervisor's address space by adding an offset to the guest address. Therefore, sharing memory between uhyve and HermitCore is straightforward. This mechanism is used extensively to forward file-system system calls made by HermitCore to the host without additional data copies. After initialization, uhyve creates a thread for each virtual CPU and registers them to KVM. In contrast to Solo5, uhyve supports machine specific registers, enables the usage of more than 4 GiB of guest memory, and supports multiprocessor systems. These are crucial characteristics for deployment in HPC environments.

Missing functionality is provided in a similar way to the multi-kernel setup. HermitCore can simply pass the corresponding requests to uhyve by means of hypercalls. Uhyve is then able to execute them via the Linux host.

---

[3]https://github.com/Solo5/solo5.
[4]Uhyve is an acronym for *Unikernel Hypervisor*.

20.4   New Checkpointing Techniques for a Unikernel

C/R mechanisms are especially important for HPC where long application execution times that exceed the Mean Time Between Failures (MTBF) are common. There are two different approaches for checkpointing: *user-level* checkpointing, which requires application support and *system-level* checkpointing, which works without modification of the application code. The latter approach is most interesting for legacy codes. However, it may result in larger checkpoints than actually required due to the lack of information, e.g., in virtualized environments the hypervisor is not aware of the memory regions that are required for the seamless restart of the respective application. In this section, we present a novel technique that enables the reduction of this overhead by leveraging the fact that HermitCore is a unikernel. For the sake of simplicity, we ignore the handling of I/O devices here. This is planned for future work and can be solved by a wrapper tracking device access.

In a traditional FWK such as Linux, each process possesses its own address space, and hence its own set of page tables. When switching to a new process, the address of the first-level page table has to be registered with the CPU. Therefore, a checkpoint mechanism would have to traverse each virtual address space of *all* processes running within the guest. Since this approach can be quite costly, the whole guest physical address space is commonly included in the checkpoint image. In contrast, the checkpointing of a unikernel can be realized much more simply. As this is a single-address-space OS, there is only one first-level page table and its location is well known by the hypervisor. This is because a valid page table is required at boot time before the kernel switches into 64-bit mode, e.g., in HermitCore it corresponds to the second page of the application image. Four-level page tables are comparable to a tree with 512 children at every node and a depth that is limited to four. The creation of a minimal checkpoint of a unikernel image can hence be done by traversing every leaf and checking if it points to a valid page, respectively. This approach works without host kernel interactions. This is because the page tree is mapped into the address space of the hypervisor which can directly access the corresponding memory regions.

Incremental checkpoints are supported by evaluating the *DIRTY* flags of the guest page tables. They are reset by the hypervisor during the traversal of the page tables and will be automatically set by the memory management unit (MMU) upon further page modifications by the process running within the unikernel. On an x86 CPU, this approach does not interfere with the guest's execution, since HermitCore does not use these flags.

Future generations of HPC systems are likely to pose a mixture of traditional DRAM, high-bandwidth memory, and also nonvolatile memory. With a memory hierarchy like that, the volatile state of the system has to be saved as checkpoints in nonvolatile memory
paginationxspace. To reduce overhead and to reach peak bandwidth between volatile and nonvolatile memories, the creation of checkpoints has to be parallelized. This requirement can be easily met by our checkpointing approach because it is completely

realized in the user space of the hypervisor. Therefore, common parallelization methods can be applied. Saving of the memory content to the hard disk or to nonvolatile memory
paginationxspaceis the most costly operation in the described mechanism.

20.5 Performance Evaluation

All benchmarks were performed on a two-socket NUMA system with 10 physical cores, exposing 20 cores in total. These are Intel Haswell CPUs (E5-2650 v3) clocked at 2.3 GHz, equipped with 64 GiB DDR4 RAM and 25 MB L3 cache. Processor features like SpeedStep Technology and TurboMode are deactivated to avoid side effects. We used an adapted 4.2.5 Linux kernel on a Fedora 23 (Workstation Edition) installation and compiled the benchmarks using gcc version 5 with enabled optimizations, AVX 2, and FMA support.[5]

Benchmarks, which ran on the unmodified Fedora system, were compiled with gcc (Red Hat 5.3.1-2), which is part of the Fedora's software distribution, while benchmarks on the HermitCore kernel used gcc 5.3.0. For HermitCore applications, we also added the compiler flag -mno-red-zone to avoid using a red zone for stack pointer optimizations. However, within a kernel the red zone is not supported because the protection of the stack during interrupt handling requires a valid stack pointer.

A couple of benchmarks are based on MPI. These test ran on an unmodified Fedora system with ParaStation MPI (Clauss et al. 2016). On HermitCore, we used an adapted version of SCC-MPICH (Clauss et al. 2011), which was originally designed for the Single-Chip Computer (SCC) and based on the communication layer iRCCE (Clauss et al. 2013, 2015). Like ParaStation MPI, SCC-MPICH is based on MPICH and has been extended to support other x86 processors besides the SCC.

For an estimation of OS noise, we performed additional measurements using the Linux kernel's *isolcpu*[6] feature. This allows for excluding, i.e., isolating, a set of cores from the balancing and scheduling algorithms for user tasks, which promises lower OS noise. To use these cores, they have to be specified explicitly via CPU *sched_setaffinity* system calls.

20.5.1 Operating System Micro-Benchmarks

First, we evaluated the overhead of a system call and the cost of a rescheduling operation. After a cache warm-up, the benchmark invokes the system calls *getpid* and *sched_yield* 10,000 times. The *getpid* system call does almost no work and very closely reflects the total overhead of a system call. The system call *sched_yield* checks

---

[5]The compiler flags -O3 -march=native -mtune=native are used.

[6]https://www.kernel.org/doc/Documentation/kernel-parameters.txt.

Table 20.1 Results of basic
system services in CPU cycles

System activity	HermitCore	Linux
getpid	14	143
sched_yield	97	370
write	3,520	1,079
`malloc()`	3,715	6,575
First write access to a page	2,018	4,007

if another task is ready to run and switches to it. In our case, the system is idle and consequently the system call returns immediately after checking the ready queues. Table 20.1 summarizes the cost of these system calls as average number of CPU cycles for Linux and HermitCore. The overhead of HermitCore is clearly smaller because in a library OS the system calls are mapped to common functions. Furthermore, the difference between *getpid* and *sched_yield* on HermitCore is smaller, which proves the low overhead of HermitCore's scheduler.

In HermitCore, system calls like *write*, *read*, *close*, and *open* are delegated via the IP interface to the Linux kernel. We compare the performance of such system calls via a write operation to the standard error output file descriptor. The benchmark writes, after a cache warm-up, a single byte 10,000 times to the device. Table 20.1 shows that the *write* system call requires more time on HermitCore compared to Linux. The difference includes the communication cost between HermitCore and Linux via the virtual IP interface. In the future, we want to use iRCCE to transfer such kind of system calls to Linux, which promise a lower overhead in comparison to an IP interface.

Finally, we evaluated memory allocation and initialization performance. In both, OSs `malloc()` reserves a space on the heap. The first access to the allocated memory region triggers a page fault and the page-fault handler maps a page frame to the virtual address space. The benchmark allocates 1,024 arrays with an array size of 1 MiB. Afterward, the benchmark writes one byte into each allocated page. By writing such a small amount of data, the first write access is dominated by page-fault handling. Both, memory allocation and page-fault handling are clearly faster in HermitCore than in Linux (see Table 20.1). For this benchmark, support of huge pages is disabled in both systems to increase the number of page faults to achieve more meaningful results.

20.5.2 Hourglass Benchmark

To measure OS noise, we used the *Hourglass* benchmark (Regehr 2002). It was introduced to analyze the time slices assigned by the OS to multiple processes. In this work, we used it to determine the *gaps* in execution time caused mainly by the OS. The benchmark continuously reads the time stamp counter of the processor. Other than some blocked system services, the benchmark runs exclusively on the

Table 20.2 Results of the *Hourglass* benchmark in CPU cycles

OS	Gaps	
	Avg	Max
Linux	69	31,068
Linux (isolcpu)	69	51,840
HermitCore (w/ LwIP)	68	12,688
HermitCore (w/o LwIP)	68	376

system and is bound to a specific core. Consequently, if a larger gap between two read operations occurs, the OS kernel has stolen some time from the user application to maintain the system (e.g., scheduling or interrupt handling).

Table 20.2 shows the maximum and average gap size in CPU cycles for Linux and HermitCore in different configurations, while Table 20.3 presents a histogram for gaps larger than 1,000 cycles. The results were obtained from one benchmark run per configuration, and in each run the time stamp counter was read $3 \cdot 10^9$ times. The maximum values vary slightly with the point in time when the benchmark was executed. The average cycle count for reading the time stamp counter is constant over all configurations with around 70 cycles. When executed in Linux compared to HermitCore, the maximum observed gap is more than doubles. The isolation feature of the Linux kernel has only a limited effect because kernel threads are still scheduled on the isolated cores. Only user-level threads have to be explicitly assigned via `taskset` to the isolated core. In HermitCore, the maximum gap can be further reduced by two orders of magnitude, by running the benchmark on a core not executing the LwIP thread. In this case, the gap is lower than 1,000 cycles and consequently not noticeable in Fig. 20.3d. However, one LwIP thread is needed to maintain the IP connection between Linux und HermitCore. The results indicate that traditional FWK such as Linux tends to exhibit more system noise which might have an effect on the performance of HPC applications. This benchmark does not reveal any performance gains using the isolation feature, as it was run on an idle system in all cases.

20.5.3 Inter-Kernel Communication Benchmark

For the analysis of key figures assessing the communication performance of communication among multiple HermitCore instances, we used benchmarks from the iRCCE communication library. For the assessment of the point-to-point bandwidth, we used the *PingPong* benchmark which performs a blocking message exchange for ascending message sizes.

Our current version of iRCCE (Clauss et al. 2013, 2015) is a direct port from the 32-bit platform SCC (Mattson et al. 2010) to our test system and still lacks tuning for current state-of-the-art HPC systems. Figure 20.4 shows the communication throughput between two NUMA nodes. We compare the iRCCE results to a

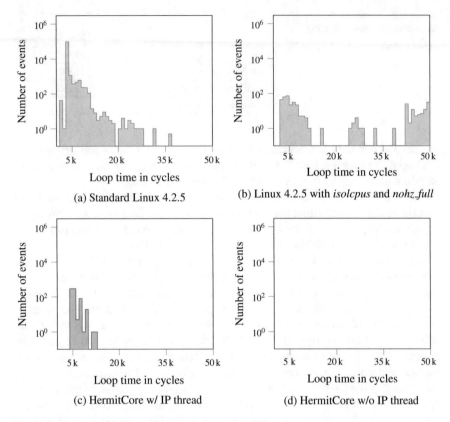

(a) Standard Linux 4.2.5

(b) Linux 4.2.5 with *isolcpus* and *nohz_full*

(c) HermitCore w/ IP thread

(d) HermitCore w/o IP thread

Fig. 20.3 *Hourglass* histogram for gaps larger than 1,000 cycles

Fig. 20.4 Throughput
Results of the Inter-Kernel
Communication Layer

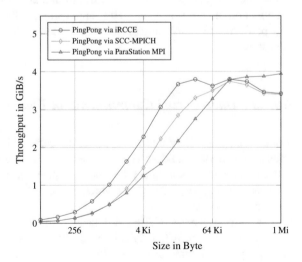

Fig. 20.5 Overhead of
OpenMP synchronization
directives

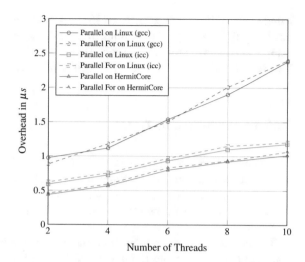

similar benchmark (Clauss and Pickartz 2015) that was run using ParaStation MPI (Clauss et al. 2016) on Linux. On HermitCore, we used SCC-MPICH (Clauss et al. 2011) as the message passing interface between two NUMA nodes. These are very promising results and even without tuning such as detecting the ideal shared segment size,[7] iRCCE and SCC-MPICH reach nearly the same peak performance as the highly optimized ParaStation MPI implementation. In contrast to MPI, iRCCE is a lightweight communication library, which explains the higher bandwidth for smaller messages and proves the excellent behavior of iRCCE.

20.5.4 OpenMP Micro-Benchmarks

From the EPCC OpenMP micro-benchmark suite (version 3.1) (Bull et al. 2012), we used the benchmarks *PARALLEL* and *PARALLEL FOR* for an evaluation of the OpenMP runtime performance. The first benchmark determines the overhead for the creation of parallel regions while the second benchmark evaluates the overhead of a parallel for loop.

In Linux, the benchmarks were bound to a NUMA node and used the number of cores in this NUMA node as the maximum number of threads. In HermitCore, the benchmarks were started on an isle, which is per default bound to a NUMA node and its cores. Besides the flag `-outer-repetitions 1000`, which is used to increase the computation time, the benchmark was used with the default configuration.

Figure 20.5 shows the overhead with respect to the number of threads. On Linux, we tested GNU's and Intel's C compilers and their OpenMP runtimes. The figures show that Intel's runtime has lower overhead than GNU's runtime. The overhead of

---

[7]Per default, we used 64 KiB as the shared segment size.

using OpenMP is clearly smaller on HermitCore than on Linux, although we used *gcc* but with Intel's OpenMP runtime to compile these benchmarks for HermitCore. The performance improvements are due to the use of a unikernel in combination with the use of Intel's OpenMP runtime instead of *libgomp*.

20.5.5 Instantiation Times

Cloud applications are typically stateless. If the load for a certain service increases, additional services will be automatically started to distribute the load between the services. A typical use case is a web service, which runs within a container. Docker is often used to build a cloneable image, which contains the service and all required libraries.

To compare a common container technology with HermitCore, we build a Docker container based on Ubuntu 18.04 with a simple web service, which is written in Go and responses all http requests with a simple static website. By HermitCore's Go support, the same application can be used as unikernel on top of our lightweight hypervisor *uhyve*.

To evaluate the performance, we start up to 200 instances of the web service within a Docker container or as HermitCore unikernel and measure the boot time. As test platform, we use a similar setup like our previous evaluations. However, we used a 4.15.8 Linux kernel on a Fedora 28 (Workstation Edition) and Docker 18.03.1-ce.

Figure 20.6 shows the boot time of the web services including the initialization time of the network. HermitCore on top of *uhyve* outperforms Docker and is able to start 200 virtual machines in less than a second. Docker uses a daemon to handle all container images. This centralized approach decreases the performance in comparison with HermitCore.

Fig. 20.6 HermitCore boot times versus Docker containers

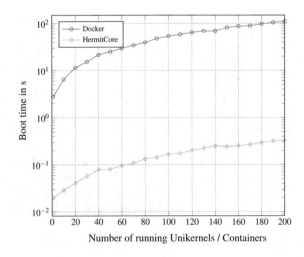

20.6 Conclusion and Outlook

In this chapter, we presented the unikernel HermitCore. By combining the unikernel approach with multi-kernel features, HermitCore supports a wide range of application areas. In HPC, it can be deployed in multi-kernel setups for an optimization of the applications' performance. In this case, the HermitCore application is executed bare-metal, profiting from reduced system noise enabled by the unikernel design. In cloud environments, the unikernel can be executed stand-alone on top of a hypervisor. In addition to support for QEMU, HermitCore is shipped with uhyve, a hypervisor that is tailored to the demands of unikernels. Besides the performance-related aspects, namely, low system noise and good scalability, the design of HermitCore facilitates an extremely simple and efficient implementation of checkpointing techniques.

By adhering to the most prevalent POSIX interfaces and HPC standards, e.g., OpenMP and Pthreads, HermitCore is very adaptable to the needs of various applications and runtimes. This facilitates the porting and tuning of complex software such as the Go runtime system in a short time frame. The smooth integration of uhyve into a desktop system allows software developers to use their workstations to test and to develop their applications. Afterward, they can be run on HPC systems without further modifications while reaching peak performance.

HermitCore has been designed with focus on the Intel 64 Architecture. The emerging *aarch64* architecture is already supported in a prototypic state. Furthermore, we have early experience with the integration ofInfiniBand support, enabling the use of HermitCore at a larger scale. The presented checkpoint technique will be improved and extended to support the multi-kernel mode as well.

Acknowledgements This research and development was supported by the Federal Ministry of Education and Research (BMBF) under Grant 01IH16010C (Project ENVELOPE).

References

Bratterud, A., Walla, A., Haugerud, H., Engelstad, P.E., & Begnum, K. (2015). IncludeOS: A resource efficient unikernel for cloud services. *Proceedings of the 2015 IEEE 7th International Conference on Cloud Computing Technology and Science (CloudCom)*.

Breitbart, J., Pickartz, S., Weidendorfer, J., Lankes, S., & Monti, A. (2017). Dynamic co-scheduling driven by main memory bandwidth utilization. *2017 IEEE International Conference on Cluster Computing (CLUSTER 2017)*. Accepted for Publication.

Bull, J.M., Reid, F., & McDonnell, N. (2012). A microbenchmark suite for OpenMP tasks. *Proceedings of the 8th International Conference on OpenMP in a Heterogeneous World, IWOMP 2012* (pp. 271–274). Heidelberg: Springer.

Clauss, C., & Pickartz, S. (2015). A collection of MPI benchmarks. https://doi.org/10.5281/zenodo. 50723.

Clauss, C., Lankes, S., Reble, P., & Bemmerl, T. (2011). Recent advances and future prospects in iRCCE and SCC-MPICH. *Proceedings of the 3rd Symposium of the Many-core Applications Research Community (MARC)*. Germany: KIT Scientific Publishing. Poster Abstract.

Clauss, C., Lankes, S., Reble, P., Galowicz, J., Pickartz, S., & Bemmerl, T. (2013). iRCCE: A non-blocking communication extension to the rcce communication library for the intel single-chip cloud computer—version 2.0 iRCCE FLAIR. Technical report, Chair for Operating Systems, RWTH Aachen University. Users' Guide and API Manual.

Clauss, C., Moschny, T., et al. (2016). Dynamic process management with allocation-internal co-scheduling towards interactive supercomputing. *Proceedings of 1st Workshop Co-Scheduling of HPC Applicat.*

Clauss, C., Lankes, S., Reble, P., & Bemmerl, T. (2015). New system software for parallel programming models on the Intel SCC many-core processor. *Concurrency and Computation: Practice and Experience, 27*(9), 2235–2259.

Kantee, A. (2012). Flexible Operating System Internals – The Design and Implementation of the Anykernel and Rump Kernels. Ph.D. thesis, Department of Computer Science and Engineering, Aalto University, Aalto, Finland.

Lankes, S., Pickartz, S., & Breitbart, J. (2016). HermitCore: A unikernel for extreme scale computing. *Proceedings of the 6th International Workshop on Runtime and Operating Systems for Supercomputers, ROSS 2016* (pp. 4:1–4:8). USA: ACM.

Lankes, S., Pickartz, S., & Breitbart, J. (2017). A low noise unikernel for extrem-scale systems (pp. 73–84). Cham: Springer International Publishing.

Madhavapeddy, A., Mortier, R., Rotsos, C., Scott, D., Singh, B., Gazagnaire, T., Smith, S., Hand, S., & Crowcroft, J. (2013). Unikernels: Library operating systems for the cloud. *Proceedings of the Eighteenth International Conference on Architectural Support for Programming Languages and Operating Systems, ASPLOS 2013* (pp. 461–472). USA: ACM.

Manco, F., Lupu, C., Schmidt, F., Mendes, J., Kuenzer, S., Sati, S., et al. (2017). My VM is Lighter (and Safer) than your Container. USA: ACM.

Matsson, T. (2010). The future of many core computing—a tale of two processors. Accessed 06 Nov 2015.

Mattson, T. & van der Wijngaart, R. (2010). RCCE: a Small Library for Many-Core Communication. Intel Corporation. Software 1.0-release.

Mattson, T.G., van der Wijngaart, R.F., Riepen, M., Lehnig, T., Brett, P., Haas, W., et al. (2010). The 48-core SCC processor: the programmer's view. *2010 International Conference for High Performance Computing Networking Storage and Analysis (SC)* (pp. 1–11).

Milojičić, D.S., Douglis, F., Paindaveine, Y., Wheeler, R., & Zhou, S. (2000). Process migration. *ACM Computing Surveys (CSUR).*

Morshedi, M., & Haugerud, H. (2017). Making the case for highly efficient multicore enabled unikernels with IncludeOS. *CLOUD COMPUTING 2017.*

Pickartz, S., Lankes, S., Monti, A., Clauss, C., & Breitbart, J. (2016). Application migration in HPC—a driver of the exascale era? *2016 International Conference on High Performance Computing Simulation (HPCS)* (pp. 318–325).

Regehr, J. (2002). Inferring scheduling behavior with hourglass. *Proceedings of the USENIX Annual Technical Conference, FREENIX Track* (pp. 143–156). USA.

Triplett, J. (2015). Using the KVM API. Accessed 25 Nov 2017.

Williams, D. & Koller, R. (2016). Unikernel monitors: Extending minimalism outside of the box. *8th USENIX Workshop on Hot Topics in Cloud Computing (HotCloud 16).* USENIX Association: USA.

Zhang, J., Lu, X., Chakraborty, S., & Panda, D. K. D. (2016). *Slurm-V: Extending Slurm for Building Efficient HPC Cloud with SR-IOV and IVShmem* (pp. 349–362). Springer: International Publishing.

Bibliography

App, 2017. (2017). appc: App container specification and tooling. https://github.com/appc/spec.

Accetta, M. J., Baron, R. V., Bolosky, W. J., Golub, D. B., Rashid, R. F., Tevanian, A., et al. (1986). Mach: A new kernel foundation for UNIX development. In *Proceedings of the USENIX Summer Conference*.

Ahn, D. H., Garlick, J., Grondona, M., Lipari, D., Springmeyer, B., & Schulz, M. (2014). Flux: A next-generation resource management framework for large HPC centers. In *43rd International Conference on Parallel Processing Workshops (ICCPW), 2014* (pp. 9–17). IEEE.

Ajima, Y., Inoue, T., Hiramoto, S., Takagi, Y., & Shimizu, T. (2012). The Tofu interconnect. *IEEE Micro, 32*(1), 21–31.

Akkan, H., Ionkov, L., & Lang, M. (2013). Transparently consistent asynchronous shared memory. In *Proceedings of the 3rd International Workshop on Runtime and Operating Systems for Supercomputers, ROSS '13*. New York, NY, USA: ACM.

Alam, S., Barrett, R., Bast, M., Fahey, M. R., Kuehn, J., McCurdy, C., et al. (2008). Early evaluation of IBM BlueGene/P. In *Proceedings of the 2008 ACM/IEEE Conference on Supercomputing, SC '08* (pp. 23:1–23:12). Piscataway, NJ, USA: IEEE Press.

Ali, N., Carns, P., Iskra, K., Kimpe, D., Lang, S., Latham, R., et al. (2009). Scalable I/O forwarding framework for high-performance computing systems. In *IEEE International Conference on Cluster Computing and Workshops, 2009. CLUSTER '09* (pp. 1–10).

Alverson, B., Froese, E., Kaplan, L., & Roweth, D. (2012). Cray Inc., white paper WP-Aries01-1112. Technical report, Cray Inc.

Alverson, G. A., Kahan, S., Korry, R., McCann, C., & Smith, B. J. (1995). Scheduling on the Tera MTA. In *Proceedings of the Workshop on Job Scheduling Strategies for Parallel Processing, IPPS '95* (pp. 19–44). London, UK: Springer.

Alverson, R., Callahan, D., Cummings, D., Koblenz, B., Porterfield, A., & Smith, B. (1990). The Tera computer system. In *Proceedings of the 4th International Conference on Supercomputing, ICS '90* (pp. 1–6). New York, NY, USA: ACM.

Andersen, E. (2010). μClibc. https://uclibc.org.

Anderson, T. E., Culler, D. E., & Patterson, D. A. (1995). The berkeley networks of workstations (NOW) project. In *Proceedings of the 40th IEEE Computer Society International Conference, COMPCON '95* (p. 322). Washington, DC, USA: IEEE Computer Society.

Arcangeli, A. (2010). Transparent hugepage support. In *KVM forum*. https://www.linux-kvm.org/images/9/9e/2010-forum-thp.pdf.

Hori, A. (2009). *PMX Specification –DRAFT–*. Allinea Software.

Bailey, D., Barszcz, E., Barton, J., Browning, D., Carter, R., Dagum, L., et al. (1991). The nas parallel benchmarks. *International Journal of High Performance Computing Applications, 5*(3), 63–73.

© Springer Nature Singapore Pte Ltd. 2019   375
B. Gerofi et al. (eds.), *Operating Systems for Supercomputers
and High Performance Computing*, High-Performance Computing Series,
https://doi.org/10.1007/978-981-13-6624-6

Balan, R., & Gollhardt, K. (1992). A scalable implementation of virtual memory HAT layer for shared memory multiprocessor machines. In *Proceedings of USENIX Summer 1992 Technical Conference*.

Barach, D. R., Wells, R., Uban, T., & Gibson, J. (1990). Highly parallel virtual memory management on the TC2000. In *Proceedings of the 1990 International Conference on Parallel Processin, ICPP '90* (pp. 549–550).

Barak, A., Drezner, Z., Levy, E., Lieber, M., & Shiloh, A. (2015). Resilient gossip algorithms for collecting online management information in exascale clusters. *Concurrency and Computation: Practice and Experience, 27*(17), 4797–4818.

Baskett, F., Howard, J. H., & Montague, J. T. (1977). Task communication in DEMOS. In *Proceedings of the Sixth ACM Symposium on Operating Systems Principles, SOSP '77* (pp. 23–31). New York, NY, USA: ACM.

Bautista-Gomez, L., Gainaru, A., Perarnau, S., Tiwari, D., Gupta, S., Cappello, F., et al. (2016). Reducing waste in large scale systems through introspective analysis. In *IEEE International Parallel and Distributed Processing Symposium (IPDPS)*.

BDEC Committee, (2017). The BDEC "Pathways to convergence" report. http://www.exascale. org/bdec/.

Beckman, P. et al. (2015). Argo: An exascale operating system. http://www.argo-osr.org/. Retrieved November 20, 2015.

Beckman, P., Iskra, K., Yoshii, K., & Coghlan, S. (2006a). The influence of operating systems on the performance of collective operations at extreme scale. In *IEEE International Conference on Cluster Computing*. Cluster.

Beckman, P., Iskra, K., Yoshii, K., & Coghlan, S. (2006b). Operating system issues for petascale systems. *ACM SIGOPS Operating Systems Review, 40*(2), 29–33.

Beckman, P., Iskra, K., Yoshii, K., Coghlan, S., & Nataraj, A. (2008). Benchmarking the effects of operating system interference on extreme-scale parallel machines. *Cluster Computing, 11*(1), 3–16.

Beeler, M. (1990). Inside the TC2000 computer.

Beserra, D., Moreno, E. D., Endo, P. T., Barreto, J., Sadok, D., & Fernandes, S. (2015). Performance analysis of LXC for HPC environments. In *International Conference on Complex, Intelligent, and Software Intensive Systems (CISIS)*.

Black, D. L., Tevanian, A., Jr., Golub, D. B., & Young, M. W. (1991). Locking and reference counting in the Mach kernel. In *In Proceedings of the 1991 ICPP, Volume II, Software* (pp. 167–173). CRC Press.

Blumofe, R. D., Joerg, C. F., Kuszmaul, B. C., Leiserson, C. E., Randall, K. H., & Zhou, Y. (1995). Cilk: An efficient multithreaded runtime system. In *Proceedings of the Fifth ACM SIGPLAN Symposium on Principles and Practice of Parallel Programming, PPOPP '95* (pp. 207–216). New York, NY, USA: ACM.

Boden, N. J., Cohen, D., Felderman, R. E., Kulawik, A. E., Seitz, C. L., Seizovic, J. N., et al. (1995). Myrinet: A gigabit-per-second local area network. *IEEE Micro, 15*(1), 29–36.

Boehme, D., Gamblin, T., Beckingsale, D., Bremer, P.-T., Gimenez, A., LeGendre, M., et al. (2016). Caliper: Performance introspection for HPC software stacks. In *Proceedings of the 29th ACM/IEEE International Conference for High Performance Computing, Networking, Storage and Analysis, (SC)*.

Boku, T., Itakura, K., Nakamura, H., & Nakazawa, K. (1997). CP-PACS: A massively parallel processor for large scale scientific calculations. In *Proceedings of ACM 11th International Conference on Supercomputing* (pp 108–115). Vienna, Austria.

Bolen, J., Davis, A., Dazey, B., Gupta, S., Henry, G., Robboy, D., et al. (1995). Massively parallel distributed computing. In *Proceedings of the Intel Supercomputer Users' Group. 1995 Annual North America Users' Conference*.

Bratterud, A., Walla, A., Haugerud, H., Engelstad, P.E., & Begnum, K. (2015). IncludeOS: A resource efficient unikernel for cloud services. In *Proceedings of the 2015 IEEE 7th International Conference on Cloud Computing Technology and Science (CloudCom)*.

Breitbart, J., Pickartz, S., Weidendorfer, J., Lankes, S., & Monti, A. (2017). Dynamic co-scheduling driven by main memory bandwidth utilization. In *2017 IEEE International Conference on Cluster Computing (CLUSTER 2017)*. Accepted for Publication.

Brightwell, R., Fisk, L. A., Greenberg, D. S., Hudson, T., Levenhagen, M., Maccabe, A. B., et al. (2000). Massively parallel computing using commodity components. *Parallel Computing, 26*(2–3), 243–266.

Brightwell, R., Hudson, T., & Pedretti, K. (2008). SMARTMAP: Operating system support for efficient data sharing among processes on a multi-core processor. In *Proceedings of the International Conference for High Performance Computing, Networking, Storage, and Analysis (SC'08)*.

Brightwell, R., Hudson, T., Riesen, R., & Maccabe, A. B. (1999). The Portals 3.0 message passing interface. Technical report SAND99-2959, Sandia National Laboratories.

Brightwell, R., Maccabe, A. B., & Riesen, R. (2002). Design and implementation of MPI on Portals 3.0. In D. Kranzlmüller, P. Kacsuk, J. Dongarra & J. Volkert (Eds.), *Recent Advances in Parallel Virtual Machine and Message Passing Interface: 9th European PVM/MPI Users' Group Meeting, Linz, Austria, September 29–October 2, 2002. Proceedings*. Lecture notes in computer science (Vol. 2474, pp. 331–340). Springer.

Brightwell, R., Maccabe, A. B., & Riesen, R. (2003a). Design, implementation, and performance of MPI on Portals 3.0. *The International Journal of High Performance Computing Applications, 17*(1), 7–20.

Brightwell, R., Oldfield, R., Maccabe, A. B., & Bernholdt, D. E. (2013). Hobbes: Composition and virtualization as the foundations of an extreme-scale OS/R. In *Proceedings of the 3rd International Workshop on Runtime and Operating Systems for Supercomputers, ROSS '13* (pp. 2:1–2:8).

Brightwell, R., Riesen, R., Underwood, K., Bridges, P. G., Maccabe, A. B., & Hudson, T. (2003b). A performance comparison of Linux and a lightweight kernel. In *IEEE International Conference on Cluster Computing* (pp. 251–258). Cluster.

Brooks, E. (1990). Attack of the killer micros. In *Talk at. Supercomputing'91*.

Brooks, E. D., Gorda, B. C., Warren, K. H., & Welcome, T. S. (1991). BBN TC2000 architecture and programming models. In *Compcon Spring '91. Digest of papers* (pp. 46–50).

Brown, N. (2018). Overlay filesystem documentation. https://www.kernel.org/doc/Documentation/filesystems/overlayfs.txt.

Brugger, G., & Streletz. (2001). Network livermore time sharing system (NLTSS). http://www.computer-history.info/Page4.dir/pages/LTSS.NLTSS.dir/pages/NLTSS.pdf.

Bull, J. M., Reid, F., & McDonnell, N. (2012). A microbenchmark suite for OpenMP tasks. In *Proceedings of the 8th International Conference on OpenMP in a Heterogeneous World, IWOMP'12* (pp. 271–274). Berlin, Heidelberg: Springer.

Buntinas, D., Mercier, G., & Gropp, W. (2006). Design and evaluation of Nemesis, a scalable, low-latency, message-passing communication subsystem. In *Sixth IEEE International Symposium on Cluster Computing and the Grid, 2006. CCGRID 06* (Vol. 1, pp. 10–530).

Butcher, H. R. (2004). LOFAR: First of a new generation of radio telescopes. *Proceedings SPIE, 5489*, 537–544.

Cappello, F., Richard, O., & Etiemble, D. (2001). Understanding performance of SMP clusters running MPI programs. *Future Generation Computer Systems, 17*(6), 711–720. I: PaCT. II: HPC applications.

Carns, P. H., Ligon, W. B, I. I. I., Ross, R. B., & Thakur, R. (2000). PVFS: A parallel file system for Linux clusters. In *4th Annual Linux Showcase and Conference* (pp. 317–327). Atlanta.

Cavium. (2014). ThunderX_CP family of workload optimized compute processors.

Clauss, C., Lankes, S., Reble, P., & Bemmerl, T. (2011). Recent advances and future prospects in iRCCE and SCC-MPICH. In *Proceedings of the 3rd Symposium of the Many-core Applications Research Community (MARC)*. Ettlingen, Germany: KIT Scientific Publishing. Poster Abstract.

Clauss, C., Lankes, S., Reble, P., & Bemmerl, T. (2015). New system software for parallel programming models on the Intel SCC many-core processor. *Concurrency and Computation: Practice and Experience, 27*(9), 2235–2259.

Clauss, C., Lankes, S., Reble, P., Galowicz, J., Pickartz, S., & Bemmerl, T. (2013). iRCCE: A non-blocking communication extension to the RCCE communication library for the intel single-chip cloud computer – version 2.0 iRCCE FLAIR. Technical report, Chair for operating systems, RWTH Aachen University. Users' Guide and API Manual.

Clauss, C., Moschny, T., et al. (2016). Dynamic process management with allocation-internal co-scheduling towards interactive supercomputing. In *Proceedings of the 1th Workshop Co-Scheduling of HPC Application*.

Clauss, C., & Pickartz, S. (2015). *A collection of MPI benchmarks*. https://doi.org/10.5281/zenodo.50723.

Clements, A. T., Kaashoek, M. F., & Zeldovich, N. (2012). Scalable address spaces using RCU balanced trees. In *Proceedings of the Seventeenth International Conference on Architectural Support for Programming Languages and Operating Systems, ASPLOS '12*.

Cluster File Systems Incorporated. (2002). Lustre: A scalable, high-performance file system. Technical report.

Crowther, W., Goodhue, J., Gurwitz, R., Rettberg, R., & Thomas, R. (1985). The Butterfly parallel processor. *IEEE Computer Architecture Newsletter*, 18–45.

Dayal, J., Bratcher, D., Eisenhauer, G., Schwan, K., Wolf, M., Zhang, X., et al. (2014). Flexpath: Type-based publish/subscribe system for large-scale science analytics. In *Proceedings of the 14th IEEE/ACM International Symposium on Cluster, Cloud and Grid Computing, (CCGrid)*.

Döbel, B., & Härtig, H. (2014). Can we put concurrency back into redundant multithreading? In *Proceedings of the 14th International Conference on Embedded Software, EMSOFT '14* (pp. 19:1–19:10). New York, NY, USA: ACM.

Döbel, B., Härtig, H., & Engel, M. (2012). Operating system support for redundant multithreading. In *Proceedings of the Tenth ACM International Conference on Embedded Software, EMSOFT '12* (pp. 83–92). New York, NY, USA: ACM.

Dongarra, J., Beckman, P., et al. (2011). The international exascale software project roadmap. *International Journal of High Performance Computing*.

Dongarra, J., Heroux, M. A., & Luszczek, P. (2015). HPCG benchmark: A new metric for ranking high performance computing systems. Technical report UT-EECS-15-736, University of Tennessee, Electrical Engineering and Computer Science Department.

Dreher, M., & Raffin, B. (2014). A flexible framework for asynchronous in situ and in transit analytics for scientific simulations. In *IEEE/ACM International Symposium on Cluster, Cloud and Grid Computing (CLUSTER)*.

Edmond, W., Bumenthal, S., Echenique, A., Storch, S., & Calderwood, T. (1986). The Butterfly satellite IMP for the wideband packet satellite network. In *ACM SIGCOMM Computer Communication Review* (Vol. 16, pp. 194–203). ACM.

Ellsworth, D., Patki, T., Perarnau, S., Seo, S., Amer, A., Zounmevo, J., et al. (2016). Systemwide power management with Argo. In *High-Performance, Power-Aware Computing (HPPAC)*.

Espasa, R., Valero, M., & Smith, J. E. (1997). Out-of-order vector architecture. In *Proceedings of the 30th Annual ACM/IEEE International Symposium on Microarchitecture (MICRO 30)*.

Ferreira, K. B., Bridges, P., & Brightwell, R. (2008). Characterizing application sensitivity to OS interference using kernel-level noise injection. In *Proceedings of the 2008 ACM/IEEE Conference on Supercomputing, SC '08* (pp. 19:1–19:12). Piscataway, NJ, USA: IEEE Press.

FFMK. FFMK Project Website. https://ffmk.tudos.org. Retrieved February 01, 2018.

Forsyth, C., McKie, J., Minnich, R., & Hensbergen, E. V. Night of the Lepus: A Plan 9 perspective on Blue Gene's interconnects.

Fu, H., Liao, J., Yang, J., Wang, L., Song, Z., Huang, X., et al. (2016). The Sunway TaihuLight supercomputer: System and applications. *Science China Information Sciences*, *59*(7), 072001.

Fujii, H., Yasuda, Y., Akashi, H., Inagami, Y., Koga, M., Ishihara, O., et al. (1997). Architecture and performance of the Hitachi SR2201 massively parallel processor system. In *Proceedings of IEEE 11th International Symposium on Parallel Processing (IPPS97)* (pp. 233–241).

Gara, A., et al. (2005). Overview of the Blue Gene/L system architecture. *IBM Journal of Research and Development*, *49*(2/3), 189–500.

Geist, A., Beguelin, A., Dongarra, J., Jiang, W., Manchek, R., & Sunderam, V. (1994). *PVM: parallel virtual machine: A users' guide and tutorial for networked parallel computing*. Cambridge, MA, USA: MIT Press.

Gerofi, B., Ishikawa, Y., Riesen, R., Wisniewski, R. W., Park, Y., & Rosenburg, B. (2016a). A multi-kernel survey for high-performance computing. In *Proceedings of the 6th International Workshop on Runtime and Operating Systems for Supercomputers, ROSS '16* (pp. 5:1–5:8). New York, NY, USA: ACM.

Gerofi, B., Riesen, R., Takagi, M., Boku, T., Ishikawa, Y., & Wisniewski, R. W. (2018). Performance and scalability of lightweight multi-kernel based operating systems. In *2018 IEEE International Parallel and Distributed Processing Symposium (IPDPS)*.

Gerofi, B., Shimada, A., Hori, A., & Ishikawa, Y. (2013). Partially separated page tables for efficient operating system assisted hierarchical memory management on heterogeneous architectures. In *13th International Symposium on Cluster, Cloud and Grid Computing (CCGrid)*.

Gerofi, B., Shimada, A., Hori, A., Masamichi, T., & Ishikawa, Y. (2014). CMCP: A novel page replacement policy for system level hierarchical memory management on many-cores. In *Proceedings of the 23rd International Symposium on High-Performance Parallel and Distributed Computing, HPDC* (pp. 73–84). New York, NY, USA: ACM.

Gerofi, B., Takagi, M., Hori, A., Nakamura, G., Shirasawa, T., & Ishikawa, Y. (2016b). On the scalability, performance isolation and device driver transparency of the IHK/McKernel hybrid lightweight kernel. In *2016 IEEE International Parallel and Distributed Processing Symposium (IPDPS)* (pp. 1041–1050).

Gerofi, B., Takagi, M., Ishikawa, Y., Riesen, R., Powers, E., & Wisniewski, R. W. (2015). Exploring the design space of combining Linux with lightweight kernels for extreme scale computing. In *Proceedings of the 5th International Workshop on Runtime and Operating Systems for Supercomputers, ROSS '15*. New York, NY, USA: ACM.

Giampapa, M., Gooding, T., Inglett, T., & Wisniewski, R. (2010). Experiences with a lightweight supercomputer kernel: Lessons learned from Blue Gene's CNK. In *International Conference for High Performance Computing, Networking, Storage and Analysis (SC), 2010*.

Gioiosa, R., Petrini, F., Davis, K., & Lebaillif-Delamare, F. (2004). Analysis of system overhead on parallel computers. In *IEEE International Symposium on Signal Processing and Information Technology (ISSPIT)*.

Glosli, J. N., Richards, D. F., Caspersen, K. J., Rudd, R. E., Gunnels, J. A., & Streitz, F. H. (2007). Extending stability beyond CPU millennium: A micron-scale atomistic simulation of Kelvin-Helmholtz instability. In *Proceedings of the 2007 ACM/IEEE Conference on Supercomputing, SC '07* (pp. 58:1–58:11). New York, NY, USA: ACM.

Goodale, T., Allen, G., Lanfermann, G., Massó, J., Radke, T., Seidel, E., et al. (2003). The Cactus framework and toolkit: Design and applications. In *Vector and Parallel Processing – VECPAR'2002, 5th International Conference*. Lecture notes in computer science. Berlin. Springer.

Graham, R. L., Woodall, T. S., & Squyres, J. M. (2005). Open MPI: A flexible high performance MPI. In *Proceedings, 6th Annual International Conference on Parallel Processing and Applied Mathematics*. Poznan, Poland.

Gropp, W., Huss-Lederman, S., Lumsdaine, A., Lusk, E., Nitzberg, B., Saphir, W., et al. (1998). *MPI - The Complete Reference: Volume 2, The MPI-2 Extensions*. Cambridge, MA, USA: MIT Press.

Gschwind, M. (2012). Blue Gene/Q: Design for sustained multi-petaflop computing. In *Proceedings of the 26th ACM International Conference on Supercomputing* (pp. 245–246). ACM.

Hale, K., & Dinda, P. (2015). A case for transforming parallel runtimes into operating system kernels. In *Proceedings of the 24th International ACM Symposium on High Performance Parallel and Distributed Computing, (HPDC)*.

Hale, K., Hetland, C., & Dinda, P. (2016). Automatic hybridization of runtime systems. In *Proceedings of the 25th International ACM Symposium on High Performance Parallel and Distributed Computing, (HPDC)*.

Hammond, S., Mudalige, G., Smith, J. A., Davis, J. A., Jarvis, S., Holt, J., et al. (2010). To upgrade or not to upgrade? Catamount versus Cray Linux environment. In *2010 IEEE International Symposium on Parallel Distributed Processing, Workshops and Phd Forum (IPDPSW)*.

Hansen, P. B. (1970). The nucleus of a multiprogramming system. *Communications of the ACM*, *13*(4), 238–250.

Harada, H., Ishikawa, Y., Hori, A., Tezuka, H., Sumimoto, S., & Takahashi, T. (2000). Dynamic home node reallocation on software distributed shared memory. In *HPC Asia 2000*.

Hargrove, W. W., Hoffman, F. M., & Sterling, T. (2001). The do-it-yourself supercomputer, *265*(2), 72–79.

Haring, R., Ohmacht, M., Fox, T., Gschwind, M., Satterfield, D., Sugavanam, K., et al. (2012). The IBM Blue Gene/Q compute chip. *IEEE Micro*, *32*(2), 48–60.

Henson, V. E., & Yang, U. M. (2002a). BoomerAMG: A parallel algebraic multigrid solver and preconditioner. https://codesign.llnl.gov/amg2013.php.

Henson, V. E., & Yang, U. M. (2002b). BoomerAMG: A parallel algebraic multigrid solver and preconditioner. *Applied Numerical Mathematics*, *41*, 155–177.

Heroux, M. A., Doerfler, D. W., Crozier, P. S., Willenbring, J. M., Edwards, H. C., Williams, A., et al. (2009). Improving performance via Mini-applications. Technical report SAND2009-5574, Sandia National Laboratories.

Hicks, A., Lumens, C., Cantrell, D., & Johnson, L. (2005). *Slackware Linux essentials*. Brentwood, CA: Slackware Linux Inc.

Hiroko, T., Emiko, M., Atsuhisa, O., Koji, S., Satoshi, S., & Toshiyuki, K. (2008). Outline of the SUPER-UX, operating system for the SX-9. http://www.nec.com/en/global/techrep/journal/g08/n04/pdf/080410.pdf.

Hoare, C. A. R. (1978). Communicating sequential processes. *Communications of the ACM*, *21*(8), 666–677.

Hoefler, T., Schneider, T., & Lumsdaine, A. (2010). Characterizing the influence of system noise on large-scale applications by simulation. In *Proceedings of the 2010 ACM/IEEE International Conference for High Performance Computing, Networking, Storage and Analysis, SC '10*. Washington, DC, USA: IEEE Computer Society.

Hori, A., & (2001). SCore: An integrated cluster system software package for high performance cluster computing. In *2001 IEEE International Conference on Cluster Computing (CLUSTER), 8–11 October 2001*. CA, USA: Newport Beach.

Hori, A., Tezuka, H., & Ishikawa, Y. (1997). Global state detection using network preemption. In *JSSPP* (pp 262–276).

Hori, A., Tezuka, H., & Ishikawa, Y. (1998). Highly efficient gang scheduling implementation. In *Proceedings of the 1998 ACM/IEEE Conference on Supercomputing (CDROM), Supercomputing '98* (pp. 1–14). Washington, DC, USA: IEEE Computer Society.

Hori, K. (1997). Supercomputer SX-4 multinode system. *NEC Research and Development*, *38*(4), 461–473.

Howe, C. D. (1988). An overview of the Butterfly GP1000: A large-scale parallel Unix computer. In *Proceedings of the Third International Conference on Supercomputing, ICS '88*.

Härtig, H., & Roitzsch, M. (2006). Ten years of research on L4-based real-time. In *Proceedings of the Eighth Real-Time Linux Workshop*, Lanzhou, China.

Härtig, H., Hohmuth, M., Liedtke, J., Schönberg, S., & Wolter, J. (1997). The performance of μ-kernel-based systems. In *SOSP '97: Proceedings of the Sixteenth ACM Symposium on Operating Systems Principles* (pp. 66–77). New York, NY, USA. ACM Press.

IBM Blue Gene Team. (2008). Overview of the IBM Blue Gene/P project. *IBM Journal of Research and Development*, *52*(1/2), 199–220.

IEEE. (2013). IEEE Standard test access port and boundary-scan architecture. *IEEE Std*, *1149*, 1.

InfiniBand Trade Association. (2016). InfiniBand Architecture Specification. Release 1.3.1.

Intel. Running average power limit – RAPL. https://01.org/blogs/2014/running-average-power-limit---rapl.

Intel (2018). mOS for HPC. https://github.com/intel/mOS/wiki.

Intel Corporation. IMB: Intel MPI Benchmarks. https://software.intel.com/en-us/articles/intel-mpi-benchmarks.

Intel Corporation (2009). *Intel® 64 and IA-32 Architectures Software Developer's Manual.*

International Business Machines Corporation. IBM Power Systems Software - AIX: Overview. https://www.ibm.com/power/operating-systems/aix.

Ishikawa, K.-I., Kuramashi, Y., Ukawa, A., & Boku, T. (2017). CCS QCD application. https://github.com/fiber-miniapp/ccs-qcd.

Ishikawa, Y. (1996). MPC++ approach to parallel computing environment. *SIGAPP - Applied Computing Review, 4*(1), 15–18.

Ishikawa, Y., Hori, A., Tezuka, H., Sumimoto, S., Takahashi, T., & Harada, H. (1999). Parallel C++ programming system on cluster of heterogeneous computers. *Heterogeneous Computing Workshop*, 73–82.

Iskra, K., Romein, J. W., Yoshii, K., & Beckman, P. (2008). ZOID: I/O-forwarding infrastructure for petascale architectures. *13th ACM SIGPLAN Symposium on Principles and Practice of Parallel Programming, PPoPP* (pp. 153–162). UT: Salt Lake City.

Jacobsen, D. M., & Canon, R. S. (2015). Contain this, unleashing Docker for HPC. *Proceedings of the Cray User Group.*

JAMSTEC (2017). Earth Simulator. https://www.jamstec.go.jp/es/en/index.html.

Jeffers, J., & Reinders, J. (2013). *Intel Xeon phi coprocessor high performance programming.* Burlington: Morgan Kaufmann.

Jiang, M., Van Essen, B., Harrison, C., & Gokhale, M. (2014). Multi-threaded streamline tracing for data-intensive architectures. In *IEEE Symposium on Large Data Analysis and Visualization (LDAV).*

Jin, H. W., Sur, S., Chai, L., & Panda, D. K. (2005). LiMIC: support for high-performance MPI intra-node communication on Linux cluster. In *2005 International Conference on Parallel Processing (ICPP'05)* (pp. 184–191).

Joint Center for Advanced HPC (JCAHPC) (2018). Basic specification of Oakforest-PACS. http://jcahpc.jp/files/OFP-basic.pdf.

Jones, P. W., Worley, P. H., Yoshida, Y., White, J. B, I. I. I., & Levesque, J. (2005). Practical performance portability in the Parallel Ocean Program (POP). *Concurrency and Computation: Practice and Experience, 17*(10), 1317–1327.

Jones, T., Dawson, S., Neely, R., Tuel, W., Brenner, L., Fier, J., et al. (2003). Improving the scalability of parallel jobs by adding parallel awareness to the operating system. In *ACM/IEEE Conference on Supercomputing, SC*, Phoenix, AZ.

Kantee, A. (2012). Flexible operating system internals – the design and implementation of the any kernel and rump kernels. PhD thesis, Department of Computer Science and Engineering, Aalto University, Aalto, Finland.

Kaplan, L. (2007). Cray CNL. In *FastOS PI Meeting and Workshop.*

Kaplan, L. S. (1991). A flexible interleaved memory design for generalized low conflict memory access. In *The Sixth Distributed Memory Computing Conference, 1991. Proceedings* (pp. 637–644).

Karo, M., Lagerstrom, R., Kohnke, M., & Albing, C. (2006). The application level placement scheduler. In *Proceedings of the Cray User Group Meeting.*

Kelly, S., Dyke, J. V., & Vaughan, C. (2008). Catamount N-Way (CNW): An implementation of the Catamount light weight kernel supporting N-cores version 2.0. Technical report, Sandia National Laboratories.

Kelly, S. M., & Brightwell, R. (2005). Software architecture of the light weight kernel, Catamount. In *47th Cray User Group Conference*, CUG, Albuquerque, NM.

Kerbyson, D. J., & Jones, P. W. (2005). A performance model of the Parallel Ocean Program. *International Journal of High Performance Computing Applications, 19*(3), 261–276.

Kernel.org (2004). Linux control groups. https://www.kernel.org/doc/Documentation/cgroup-v1/cgroups.txt.

Kitai, K., Isobe, T., Tanaka, Y., Tamaki, Y., Fukagawa, M., Tanaka, T., et al. (1993). Parallel processing architecture for the Hitachi S-3800 shared-memory vector multiprocessor. In *ICS'93 Proceedings of the 7th International Conference on Supercomputing*.

Kocoloski, B., & Lange, J. (2014). HPMMAP: Lightweight memory management for commodity operating systems. In *Proceedings of the 2014 IEEE 28th International Parallel and Distributed Processing Symposium, IPDPS '14* (pp. 649–658), Washington, DC, USA: IEEE Computer Society.

Kocoloski, B., & Lange, J. (2015). XEMEM: Efficient shared memory for composed applications on multi-OS/R exascale systems. In *Proceedings of the 24th International ACM Symposium on High Performance Parallel and Distributed Computing, (HPDC)*.

Kocoloski, B., Lange, J., Abbasi, H., Bernholdt, D., Jones, T., Dayal, J., et al. (2015). System-level support for composition of application. In *Proceedings of te 5th International Workshop on Runtime and Operating Systems for Supercomputers, (ROSS)*.

Kondo, M., Hayashida, T., Imai, M., Nakamura, H., Nanya, T., & Hori, A. (2003). Evaluation of checkpointing mechanism on score cluster system. *IEICE Transactions on Information and Systems, 86*(12), 2553–2562.

Krieger, O., Auslander, M., Rosenburg, B., Wisniewski, R. W., Xenidis, J., Silva, D. D., et al. (2006). K42: Building a real operating system. In *Proceedings of EuroSys'2006* (pp. 133–145). ACM SIGOPS.

Krone, M., Stone, J. E., Ertl, T., & Schulten, K. (2012). Fast visualization of Gaussian density surfaces for molecular dynamics and particle system trajectories. In *EuroVis Short Papers*.

Kumar, S., Dozsa, G., Almasi, G., Heidelberger, P., Chen, D., Giampapa, M. E., et al. (2008). The deep computing messaging framework: Generalized scalable message passing on the Blue Gene/P supercomputer. In *22nd Annual International Conference on Supercomputing, ICS* (pp. 94–103).

Kumar, S., Mamidala, A., Faraj, D., Smith, B., Blocksome, M., Cernohous, B., et al. (2012). PAMI: A parallel active message interface for the Blue Gene/Q supercomputer. In *2012 IEEE 26th International Parallel Distributed Processing Symposium (IPDPS)* (pp. 763–773).

Kumon, K., Kimura, T., Hotta, K., & Hoshiya, T. (2004). RIKEN super combined cluster (RSCC) system. Technical report 2, Fujitsu.

Laboratory, C. D. G. L. A. N. (1982). *CTSS Overview*. Los Alamos National Laboratory, la-5525-m (Vol. 7).

Lackorzynski, A., & Warg, A. (2009). Taming subsystems: Capabilities as universal resource access control in L4. In *IIES '09: Proceedings of the Second Workshop on Isolation and Integration in Embedded Systems* (pp. 25–30). New York, NY, USA: ACM.

Lackorzynski, A., Weinhold, C., & Härtig, H. (2016a). Combining predictable execution with full-featured commodity systems. In *Proceedings of OSPERT2016, the 12th Annual Workshop on Operating Systems Platforms for Embedded Real-Time Applications, OSPERT 2016* (pp. 31–36).

Lackorzynski, A., Weinhold, C., & Härtig, H. (2016b). Decoupled: Low-effort noise-free execution on commodity system. In *Proceedings of the 6th International Workshop on Runtime and Operating Systems for Supercomputers, ROSS '16*. New York, NY, USA: ACM.

Lackorzynski, A., Weinhold, C., & Härtig, H. (2017). Predictable low-latency interrupt response with general-purpose systems. In *Proceedings of OSPERT2017, the 13th Annual Workshop on Operating Systems Platforms for Embedded Real-Time Applications, OSPERT 2017* (pp. 19–24).

Lange, J., Pedretti, K., Hudson, T., Dinda, P., Cui, Z., Xia, L., Bridges, P., Levenhagen, M., Brightwell, R., Gocke, A., & Jaconette, S. (2010). Palacios and Kitten: New high performance operating systems for scalable virtualized and native supercomputing. In *Proceedings of the 24th IEEE International Parallel and Distributed Processing Symposium, (IPDPS)*.

Lange, J. R., Pedretti, K., Dinda, P., Bridges, P. G., Bae, C., Soltero, P., et al. (2011). Minimal-overhead virtualization of a large scale supercomputer. In *Proceedings of the 7th ACM SIGPLAN/SIGOPS International Conference on Virtual Execution Environments (VEE)*.

Lankes, S., Pickartz, S., & Breitbart, J. (2016). HermitCore: A unikernel for extreme scale computing. In *Proceedings of the 6th International Workshop on Runtime and Operating Systems for Supercomputers, ROSS '16* (pp. 4:1–4:8). New York, NY, USA: ACM.

Lankes, S., Pickartz, S., & Breitbart, J. (2017). *A low noise unikernel for extrem-scale systems* (pp. 73–84). Cham: Springer International Publishing.

Lawrence Livermore National Lab (2017). UMT: Unstructured Mesh Transport. https://asc.llnl.gov/CORAL-benchmarks/Summaries/UMT2013_Summary_v1.2.pdf.

Lawrence Livermore National Laboratory. The FTQ/FWQ Benchmark.

Lawrence Livermore National Laboratory (2001). SPhot: Single Physics Photon Transport. https://asc.llnl.gov/sequoia/benchmarks/SPhot_summary_v1.0.pdf.

Lawrence Livermore National Laboratory (2003a). IRS: Implicit Radiation Solver. https://asc.llnl.gov/sequoia/benchmarks/IRS_summary_v1.0.pdf.

Lawrence Livermore National Laboratory (2003b). The Phloem benchmark. https://asc.llnl.gov/sequoia/benchmarks/PhloemMPIBenchmarks_summary_v1.0.pdf.

LeBlanc, T. J., Scott, M. L., & Brown, C. M. (1988). Large-scale parallel programming: Experience with BBN Butterfly parallel processor. In *Proceedings of the ACM/SIGPLAN Conference on Parallel Programming: Experience with Applications, Languages and Systems, PPEALS '88* (pp. 161–172). New York, NY, USA: ACM.

Leiserson, C. E., Abuhamdeh, Z. S., Douglas, D. C., Feynman, C. R., Ganmukhi, M. N., Hill, J. V., et al. (1996). The network architecture of the connection machine CM-5. *Journal of Parallel and Distributed Computing, 33*(2), 145–158.

Levy, E., Barak, A., Shiloh, A., Lieber, M., Weinhold, C., & Härtig, H. (2014). Overhead of a decentralized gossip algorithm on the performance of HPC applications. In *Proceedings of the ROSS '14* (pp. 10:1–10:7). ACM.

Lieber, M., Grützun, V., Wolke, R., Müller, M. S., & Nagel, W. E. (2012). Highly scalable dynamic load balancing in the atmospheric modeling system COSMO-SPECS+FD4. In *Proceedings of the PARA 2010*. LNCS (Vol. 7133, pp. 131–141). Springer.

Liedtke, J. (1995). On micro-kernel construction. In *SOSP '95: Proceedings of the Fifteenth ACM Symposium on Operating Systems Principles* (pp. 237–250). New York, NY, USA: ACM Press.

Liu, R., Klues, K., Bird, S., Hofmeyr, S., Asanovic, K., & Kubiarowicz, J. (2009). Tessellation: Space-time partitioning in a manycore client OS. In *Proceeding of the 1st USENIX Conference on Hot Topics in Parallelism, (HotPar)*.

Lofstead, J., Zheng, F., Klasky, S., & Schwan, K. (2009). Adaptable, metadata rich IO methods for portable high performance IO. In *Proceedings of the 23rd IEEE International Parallel and Distributed Processing Symposium, (IPDPS)*.

Maccabe, A. B., McCurley, K. S., Riesen, R., & Wheat, S. R. (1994). SUNMOS for the Intel Paragon: A brief user's guide. In *Proceedings of the Intel Supercomputer Users' Group. 1994 Annual North America Users' Conference* (pp. 245–251).

Maccabe, A. B., Riesen, R., & van Dresser, D. W. (1996). Dynamic processor modes in Puma. *Bulletin of the Technical Committee on Operating Systems and Application Environments (TCOS), 8*(2), 4–12.

Maccabe, A. B., & Wheat, S. R. (1993). Message passing in PUMA. Technical report SAND93-0935, Sandia National Laboratories.

Madhavapeddy, A., Mortier, R., Rotsos, C., Scott, D., Singh, B., Gazagnaire, T., Smith, S., Hand, S., & Crowcroft, J. (2013). Unikernels: Library operating systems for the cloud. In *Proceedings of the Eighteenth International Conference on Architectural Support for Programming Languages and Operating Systems, ASPLOS '13* (pp. 461–472). New York, NY, USA: ACM.

Manco, F., Lupu, C., Schmidt, F., Mendes, J., Kuenzer, S., Sati, S., et al. (2017). *My VM is lighter (and safer) than your container*. New York, USA: ACM.

Markoff, J. (1991). The attack of the 'killer micros'. *The New York Times*.

Maruyama, T., Yoshida, T., Kan, R., Yamazaki, I., Yamamura, S., Takahashi, N., et al. (2010). Sparc64 VIIIfx: A new-generation octocore processor for petascale computing. *IEEE Micro, 30*(2), 30–40.

Matsson, T. (2010). The future of many core computing – a tale of two processors. Retrieved November 11, 2015.

Mattson, T., & van der Wijngaart, R. (2010). *RCCE: a Small Library for Many-Core Communication*. Intel Corporation. Software 1.0-release.

Mattson, T. G., van der Wijngaart, R. F., Riepen, M., Lehnig, T., Brett, P., Haas, W., et al. (2010). The 48-core SCC processor: the programmer's view. In *2010 International Conference for High Performance Computing, Networking, Storage and Analysis (SC)* (pp. 1–11).

Mauerer, W. (2010). *Professional Linux Kernel Architecture* (1st ed.). Birmingham: Wrox Press.

McBryan, O. A. (1994). An overview of message passing environments. *Parallel Computing, 20*(4):417–444. Message Passing Interfaces.

Merkel, D. (2014). Docker: Lightweight Linux containers for consistent development and deployment. *Linux Journal, 2014*(239).

Meuer, H., Strohmaier, E., Dongarra, J., & Simon, H. (2005). Top500 supercomputer sites. www.top500.org.

microHPC. microHPC Project Website. https://microhpc.tudos.org. Retrieved February 01, 2018.

Milojičić, D. S., Douglis, F., Paindaveine, Y., Wheeler, R., & Zhou, S. (2000). Process migration. *ACM Computing Surveys (CSUR)*.

Minnich, R. G., & Mckie, J. (2009). Experiences porting the Plan 9 research operating system to the IBM Blue Gene supercomputers. *Computer Science - Research and Development, 23*(3), 117–124.

Morari, A., Gioiosa, R., Wisniewski, R., Cazorla, F., & Valero, M. (2011). A quantitative analysis of OS nøise. In *Parallel Distributed Processing Symposium (IPDPS), 2011 IEEE International* (pp. 852–863).

Morari, A., Gioiosa, R., Wisniewski, R., Rosenburg, B., Inglett, T., & Valero, M. (2012). Evaluating the impact of TLB misses on future HPC systems. In *Parallel Distributed Processing Symposium (IPDPS), 2012 IEEE 26th International* (pp. 1010–1021).

Moreira, J. E., et al. (2005). Blue Gene/L programming and operating environment. *IBM Journal of Research and Development, 49*(2/3), 367–376.

Moreira, J. E. et al. (2006). Designing a highly-scalable operating system: The Blue Gene/L story. In *ACM/IEEE Conference on Supercomputing*, SC, Tampa, FL.

Morshedi, M., & Haugerud, H. (2017). Making the case for highly efficient multicore enabled unikernels with IncludeOS. *Cloud Computing 2017*.

Morton, D. (2015). IBM mainframe operating systems: Timeline and brief explanation for the IBM System/360 and beyond.

mvapichweb. MVAPICH: MPI over InfiniBand. http://mvapich.cse.ohio-state.edu/. Retrieved January 29, 2017.

Nataraj, A., Morris, A., Malony, A., Sottile, M., & Beckman, P. (2007). The ghost in the machine: Observing the effects of kernel operation on parallel application performance. In *ACM/IEEE Conference on Supercomputing*, SC.

NEC Corporation (2017). SX-Aurora TSUBASA. http://jpn.nec.com/hpc/sxauroratsubasa/index.html.

NEC Corporation (2018). SX-Aurora TSUBASA. http://www.nec.com/en/global/solutions/hpc/sx/index.html.

Nek5000 (2008). NEK5000: A fast and scalable high-order solver for computational fluid dynamics. https://nek5000.mcs.anl.gov/.

NERSC (2013a). MIMD Lattice Computation (MILC). http://www.nersc.gov/users/computational-systems/cori/nersc-8-procurement/trinity-nersc-8-rfp/nersc-8-trinity-benchmarks/milc.

NERSC (2013b). PAL system noise activity program (PSNAP). https://www.nersc.gov/users/computational-systems/cori/nersc-8-procurement/trinity-nersc-8-rfp/nersc-8-trinity-benchmarks/psnap/.

Next Generation Technical Computing Unit, Fujitsu Limited (2014). White paper, FUJITSU Supercomputer PRIMEHPC FX100 evolution to the next generation, 2014. https://www.fujitsu.com/global/Images/primehpc-fx100-hard-en.pdfl.

Nieplocha, J., & Carpenter, B. (1999). ARMCI: A portable remote memory copy library for distributed array libraries and compiler run-time systems. In *International Parallel Processing Symposium (IPPS)* (pp. 533–546). Berlin: Springer.

Nishioka, T., Hori, A., & Ishikawa, Y. (2000). Consistent checkpointing for high performance clusters. *CLUSTER* (pp. 367–368).

Noriyuki, A., Yasuhiro, K., Masaki, S., & Takahito, Y. (2008). Hardware technology of the SX-9 (2) - internode switch. http://www.nec.com/en/global/techrep/journal/g08/n04/pdf/080404.pdf.

Nugent, S. F. (1988). The iPSC/2 direct-connect communications technology. In *Proceedings of the Third Conference on Hypercube Concurrent Computers and Applications: Architecture, Software, Computer Systems, and General Issues - Volume 1*, C3P (pp. 51–60). New York, NY, USA. ACM.

O'Carroll, F., Tezuka, H., Hori, A., & Ishikawa, Y. (1998). The design and implementation of zero copy MPI using commodity hardware with a high performance network. In *International Conference on Supercomputing* (pp. 243–250).

Oral, S., Wang, F., D. Dillow, R. M., Shipman, G., Maxwell, D., Henseler, D., et al. (2010). Reducing application runtime variability on Jaguar XT5. In *Proceedings of Cray User Group*.

Otstott, D., Evans, N., Ionkov, L., Zhao, M., & Lang, M. (2014). Enabling composite applications through an asynchronous shared memory interface. In *2014 IEEE International Conference on Big Data, Big Data 2014, Washington, DC, USA, October 27–30, 2014* (pp. 219–224).

Ouyang, J., Kocoloski, B., Lange, J., & Pedretti, K. (2015). Achieving performance isolation with lightweight co-kernels. In *Proc. 24th International ACM Symposium on High Performance Parallel and Distributed Computing, (HPDC)*.

Padlipsky, M. A. (1985). *The elements of networking style: And other essays and animadversions on the art of intercomputer networking*. Upper Saddle River, NJ, USA: Prentice-Hall Inc.

Pakin, S., Karamcheti, V., & Chien, A. A. (1997). Fast messages: Efficient, portable communication for workstation clusters and MPPs. *IEEE Parallel and Distributed Technology, 5*, 60–73.

Palmer, J. F. (1988). The NCUBE family of high-performance parallel computer systems. In *Proceedings of the Third Conference on Hypercube Concurrent Computers and Applications: Architecture, Software, Computer Systems, and General Issues - Volume 1*, C3P (pp. 847–851). New York, NY, USA: ACM.

Park, Y., Van Hensbergen, E., Hillenbrand, M., Inglett, T., Rosenburg, B., Ryu, K. D., et al. (2012). FusedOS: Fusing LWK performance with FWK functionality in a heterogeneous environment. In *2012 IEEE 24th International Symposium on Computer Architecture and High Performance Computing (SBAC-PAD)* (pp. 211–218).

Partridge, C., & Blumenthal, S. (2006). Data networking at BBN. *IEEE Annals of the History of Computing, 28*(1), 56–71.

Perarnau, S., Thakur, R., Iskra, K., Raffenetti, K., Cappello, F., Gupta, R., et al. (2015). Distributed monitoring and management of exascale systems in the Argo project. In *IFIP International Conference on Distributed Applications and Interoperable Systems (DAIS), Short Paper*.

Perarnau, S., Zounmevo, J. A., Dreher, M., Essen, B. C. V., Gioiosa, R., Iskra, K., et al. (2017). Argo NodeOS: Toward unified resource management for exascale. In *IEEE International Parallel and Distributed Processing Symposium (IPDPS)*.

Peters, A., King, A., Budnik, T., McCarthy, P., Michaud, P., Mundy, M., et al. (2008). Asynchronous task dispatch for high throughput computing for the eServer IBM Blue Gene® supercomputer. In *IEEE International Symposium on Parallel and Distributed Processing IPDPS*.

Petitet, A., & Cleary, A. (2008). HPL: A portable implementation of the high-performance linpack benchmark for distributed-memory computers. http://www.netlib.org/benchmark/hpl/.

Petrini, F., Kerbyson, D. J., & Pakin, S. (2003). The case of the missing supercomputer performance: Achieving optimal performance on the 8,192 processors of ASCI Q. In *Proceedings of the 2003 ACM/IEEE conference on Supercomputing, SC '03*. New York, NY, USA: ACM.

Pickartz, S., Lankes, S., Monti, A., Clauss, C., & Breitbart, J. (2016). Application migration in HPC – a driver of the exascale era? In *2016 International Conference on High Performance Computing Simulation (HPCS)* (pp. 318–325).

Pierce, P. (1988). The NX/2 operating system. In *Proceedings of the Third Conference on Hypercube Concurrent Computers and Applications: Architecture, Software, Computer Systems, and General Issues - Volume 1*, C3P (pp. 384–390). New York, NY, USA: ACM.

Pierce, P. (1994). The nx message passing interface. *Parallel Computing, 20*(4):463–480. Message Passing Interfaces.

Pike, R., Presotto, D. L., Dorward, S., Flandrena, B., Thompson, K., Trickey, H., et al. (1995). Plan 9 from Bell labs. *Computing Systems, 8*(2), 221–254.

Plimpton, S. (1995). Fast parallel algorithms for short-range molecular dynamics. *Journal of Computational Physics, 117*(1), 1–19.

Pronk, S., Pall, S., Schulz, R., Larsson, P., et al. (2013). GROMACS 4.5: A high-throughput and highly parallel open source molecular simulation toolkit. *Bioinformatics*.

Raicu, I., Foster, I. T., & Zhao, Y. (2008a). Many-task computing for grids and supercomputers. In *Workshop on Many-Task Computing on Grids and Supercomputers, MTAGS*.

Raicu, I., Zhang, Z., Wilde, M., Foster, I., Beckman, P., Iskra, K., et al. (2008b). Toward loosely coupled programming on petascale systems. In *ACM/IEEE Conference on Supercomputing, SC*.

Raicu, I., Zhao, Y., Dumitrescu, C., Foster, I., & Wilde, M. (2007). Falkon: A fast and light-weight task execution framework. In *ACM/IEEE Conference on Supercomputing, SC*.

Raymond, E. S. (2001). *The Cathedral and the Bazaar: Musings on Linux and Open Source by an Accidental Revolutionary*. Newton: O'Reilly Media.

Regehr, J. (2002). Inferring scheduling behavior with hourglass. In *Proceedings of the USENIX Annual Technical Conference, FREENIX Track* (pp. 143–156). Monterey, CA, USA.

Rettberg, R., Wyman, C., Hunt, D., Hoffman, M., Carvey, P., Hyde, B., et al. (1979). Development of a voice funnel system: Design report. Technical report, Bolt Beranek and Newman Inc. Cambridge, MA.

Reussner, R., Sanders, P., & Larsson Träff, J. (2002). SKaMPI: a comprehensive benchmark for public benchmarking of MPI. *10*, 55–65.

Rhoden, B., Klues, K., Zhu, D., & Brewer, E. (2011). Improving per-node efficiency in the datacenter with new OS abstractions. In *Proceedings of the 2nd ACM Symposium on Cloud Computing, (SOCC)*.

Riesen, R., Brightwell, R., Bridges, P. G., Hudson, T., Maccabe, A. B., Widener, P. M., et al. (2009). Designing and implementing lightweight kernels for capability computing. *Concurrency and Computation: Practice and Experience, 21*(6), 793–817.

Riesen, R., Brightwell, R., Fisk, L. A., Hudson, T., Otto, J., & Maccabe, A. B. (1999). Cplant. In *Proceedings of the Second Extreme Linux Workshop at the 1999 USENIX Annual Technical Conference*. California: Monterey.

Riesen, R., Brightwell, R., & Maccabe, A. B. (1998). Differences between distributed and parallel systems. Technical report SAND98-2221, Sandia National Laboratories.

Riesen, R., & Maccabe, A. B. (2011). Single system image. In D. A. Padua (Ed.), *Encyclopedia of parallel computing* (pp. 1820–1827). US: Springer.

Riesen, R., Maccabe, A. B., Gerofi, B., Lombard, D. N., Lange, J. J., Pedretti, K., et al. (2015). What is a lightweight kernel? In *Proceedings of the 5th International Workshop on Runtime and Operating Systems for Supercomputers, ROSS '15*. New York, NY, USA: ACM.

Riesen, R., Maccabe, A. B., & Wheat, S. R. (1994). Active messages versus explicit message passing under SUNMOS. In *Proceedings of the Intel Supercomputer Users' Group. 1994 Annual North America Users' Conference* (pp. 297–303).

RIKEN Advanced Institute for Computational Science (2018). K computer. http://www.aics.riken. jp/en/k-computer/about/.

Ritsko, J. J., Ames, I., Raider, S. I., & Robinson, J. H., (Eds.). (2005). Blue gene (Vol. 49). IBM Journal of Research and Development, IBM Corporation: Riverton.

Rogado, J. (1992). A strawman proposal for the cluster project. Technical report, OSF Research Institute.

Romein, J. W., Broekema, P. C., Mol, J. D., & van Nieuwpoort, R. V. (2010). The LOFAR correlator: Implementation and performance analysis. In *15th ACM SIGPLAN Symposium on Principles and Practice of Parallel Programming, PPoPP* (pp. 169–178).

Romein, J. W., Broekema, P. C., van Meijeren, E., van der Schaaf, K., & Zwart, W. H. (2006). Astronomical real-time streaming signal processing on a Blue Gene/L supercomputer. *ACM Symposium on Parallel Algorithms and Architectures, SPAA* (pp. 59–66). Cambridge, MA.

Rosner, R., Calder, A., Dursi, J., Fryxell, B., Lamb, D. Q., Niemeyer, J. C., et al. (2000). Flash code: Studying astrophysical thermonuclear flashes. *Computing in Science Engineering, 2*(2), 33–41.

Rostedt, S. (2009). Finding origins of latencies using ftrace. In *Real Time Linux Workshop (RTLWS)*.

Roy, P., Noveck, D., & Netterwala, D. (1993). The file system architecture of OSF/1 AD Version 2. Technical report, OSF Research Institute, Cambridge, MA.

Saini, S., & Simon, H. (1994). Applications performance under OSF/1 AD and SUNMOS on Intel Paragon XP/S-15. In *Supercomputing '94, Proceedings* (pp. 580–589).

Saini, S., Talcott, D., Thakur, R., Rabenseifner, P. A. R., & Ciotti, R. (2007). Parallel i/o performance characterization of Columbia and NEC SX-8 Superclusters. In *IEEE International Parallel and Distributed Processing Symposium (IPDPS)*.

Sakagami, H., Murai, H., Seo, Y., & Yokokawa, M. (2002). 14.9 TFlops three-dimensional fluid simulation for fusion science with HPF on the Earth Simulator. In *Proceedings of the 2002 ACM/IEEE Conference on Supercomputing, SC '02* (pp. 1–14). IEEE Computer Society Press.

Sakai, K., Sumimoto, S., & Kurokawa, M. (2012). High-performance and highly reliable file system for the K computer. *Fujitsu Scientific and Technical Journal, 48*, 302–309.

Sato, M., Harada, H., Hasegawa, A., & Ishikawa, Y. (2001). Cluster-enabled OpenMP: An OpenMP compiler for the SCASH software distributed shared memory system. *Scientific Programming, 9*(2, 3), 123–130.

Seelam, S., Fong, L., Tantawi, A., Lewars, J., Divirgilio, J., & Gildea, K. (2010). Extreme scale computing: Modeling the impact of system noise in multicore clustered systems. In *2010 IEEE International Symposium on Parallel Distributed Processing (IPDPS)*.

Seo, S., Amer, A., & Balaji, P. (2018). BOLT is OpenMP over lightweight threads. http://www.bolt-omp.org/.

Seo, S., Amer, A., Balaji, P., Bordage, C., Bosilca, G., Brooks, A., et al. (2017). Argobots: A lightweight low-level threading and tasking framework. *IEEE Transactions on Parallel and Distributed Systems*, PP(99):1–1.

Sheltzer, A., Hinden, R., & Haverty, J. (1983). The DARPA internet: Interconnecting heterogeneous computer networks with gateways. *Computer, 16*, 38–48.

Shimizu, M., Ogasawara, K., Funyu, M., & Yonezawa, A. (March 2008). Remote process management for the heterogeneous system (in Japanese). *Transactions of ACS, 49*(No. SIG2 (ACS21)), 10–19.

Shimizu, M., Tobe, K., Hitomi, Y., Ukai, T., Sanpei, H., Iida, T., & Fujita, F. (May 2006). An implementation of single system functionality in the cluster environment (in Japanese). In *Proceedings of the 4th IPSJ Symposium on Advanced Computing Systems and Infrastructures (SACSIS 2006)* (Vol. 2006, No. 5, pp. 289–296).

Shimizu, M., Ukai, T., Sanpei, H., Iida, T., & Fujita, F. (September 2005). HSFS: Hitachi striping file system for super technical server SR11000 (in Japanese). In *Forum on Information Technology (FIT2005) Letters*.

Shimizu, M., & Yonezawa, A. (May 2010). Remote process execution and remote file I/O for heterogeneous processors in cluster systems. In *Proceedings of 2010 10th IEEE/ACM International Conference on Cluster, Cloud and Grid Computing (CCGrid)* (pp. 145–154), Melbourne, VIC.

Shimosawa, T. (2011). Operating system organization for manycore systems. http://www.ipsj.or.jp/magazine/hakase/2011/OS01.html.

Shimosawa, T., Gerofi, B., Takagi, M., Nakamura, G., Shirasawa, T., Saeki, Y., et al. (2014). Interface for heterogeneous kernels: A framework to enable hybrid OS designs targeting high performance computing on manycore architectures. In *21th International Conference on High Performance Computing, HiPC*.

Shingu, S., Takahara, H., Fuchigami, H., Yamada, M., Tsuda, Y., Ohfuchi, W., et al. (2002). A 26.58 TFlops global atmospheric simulation with the spectral transform method on the earth simulator. In *Proceedings of the 2002 ACM/IEEE Conference on Supercomputing, SC '02* (pp. 1–19). IEEE Computer Society Press.

Shinichi, H., Mitsuo, Y., & Shigemune, K. (2003). The development of the earth simulator. *IEICE TRANSACTIONS in Information and Systems, E86-D*(10), 1947–1954.

Shmueli, E., Almási, G., Brunheroto, J., Castaños, J., Dózsa, G., Kumar, S., et al. (2008). Evaluating the effect of replacing CNK with Linux on the compute-nodes of Blue Gene/L. In *22nd ACM International Conference on Supercomputing, ICS* (pp. 165–174), Kos, Greece.

Singaravelu, L., Pu, C., Härtig, H., & Helmuth, C. (2006). Reducing TCB complexity for security-sensitive applications: Three case studies. In *Proceedings of the 1st ACM SIGOPS/EuroSys European Conference on Computer Systems 2006, EuroSys '06* (pp. 161–174). New York, NY, USA: ACM.

Slattery, S., Wilson, P. P., & Pawlowski, R. (2013). The data transfer kit: A geomteric rendezvous-based tool for multiphysics data transfer. In *Proceedings of the International Conference on Mathematics and Computational Methods Applied to Nuclear Science & Engineering, (M&C)*.

Smith, J. E., & Pleszkun, A. R. (1985). Implementation of precise interrupts in pipelined processors. In *Proceedings of the 12th Annual International Symposium on Computer Architecture (ISCA '85)*.

Snir, M., Otto, S., Huss-Lederman, S., Walker, D., & Dongarra, J. (1998). *MPI-the complete reference, Volume 1: The MPI core* (2nd. (Rev.) ed.). Cambridge, MA, USA: MIT Press.

Sterling, T. L., Savarese, D., Becker, D. J., Dorband, J. E., Ranawake, U. A., & Packer, C. V. (1995). Beowulf: A parallel workstation for scientific computation. In P. Banerjee (Ed.), *Proceedings of the 1995 International Conference on Parallel Processing* (pp. 11–14). CRC Press.

Strohmaier, E., Dongarra, J. J., Meuer, H. W., & Simon, H. D. (1999). The marketplace for high-performance computers. *Parallel Computing, 25*(13–14), 1517–1544.

Sumimoto, S., Naruse, A., Kumon, K., Hosoe, K., & Shimizu, T. (2004). PM/InfiniBand-FJ: A high performance communication facility using InfiniBand for large scale PC clusters. In *Proceedings of the Seventh International Conference on High Performance Computing and Grid in Asia Pacific Region, 2004* (pp. 104–113).

Sumimoto, S., Tezuka, H., Hori, A., Harada, H., Takahashi, T., & Ishikawa, Y. (1999). The design and evaluation of high performance communication using a Gigabit Ethernet. In: *International Conference on Supercomputing* (pp. 260–267).

Sumimoto, S., Tezuka, H., Hori, A., Harada, H., Takahashi, T., & Ishikawa, Y. (2000a). GigaE PM: A high performance communication facility using a Gigabit Ethernet. *New Generation Computing, 18*(2), 177–186.

Sumimoto, S., Tezuka, H., Hori, A., Harada, H., Takahashi, T., & Ishikawa, Y. (2000b). High performance communication using a commodity network for cluster systems. In *HPDC* (pp. 139–146).

Sunderam, V. S. (1990). PVM: A framework for parallel distributed computing. *Concurrency: Practice and Experience, 2*(4), 315–339.

Takahashi, T., O'Carroll, F., Tezuka, H., Hori, A., Sumimoto, S., Harada, H., et al. (1999). Implementation and evaluation of MPI on an SMP cluster. In *IPPS/SPDP Workshops* (pp. 1178–1192).

Takahashi, T., Sumimoto, S., Hori, A., Harada, H., & Ishikawa, Y. (2000). PM2: A high performance communication middleware for heterogeneous network environments. In *SC*.

Tamaki, Y., Sukegawa, N., Ito, M., Tanaka, Y., Fukagawa, M., Sumimoto, T., & Ioki, N. (1999). Node architecture and performance evaluation of the Hitachi super technical server SR8000. In *Proceedings of 12th International Conference on Parallel and Distributed Computing Systems* (pp. 487–493).

Tanenbaum, A. S., & van Renesse, R. (1985). Distributed operating systems. *ACM Computing Surveys, 17*(4), 419–470.

Tang, W., Lan, Z., Desai, N., & Buettner, D. (2009). Fault-aware, utility-based job scheduling on Blue Gene/P systems. In *IEEE International Conference on Cluster Computing and Workshops, Cluster*.

Tezuka, H., Hori, A.,& Ishikawa, Y. (1997). PM: A high performance communication library for multi-user parallel environments. In *Usenix'97*.

Tezuka, H., O'Carroll, F., Hori, A., & Ishikawa, Y. (1998). Pin-down Cache: A virtual memory management technique for zero-copy communication. In *Proceedings of the 12th International Parallel Processing Symposium on International Parallel Processing Symposium, IPPS '98* (p. 308). Washington, DC, USA: IEEE Computer Society.

The CP2K Developers Group. Open source molecular dynamics. http://www.cp2k.org/. Retrieved November 20, 2015.

The Open Group Consortium. Open Software Foundation. http://www.opengroup.org/.

Torvalds, L. (2001). *Just for fun: The story of an accidental revolutionary*. New York, NY: Harper Business.

Tournier, J.-C., Bridges, P. G., Maccabe, A. B., Widener, P. M., Abudayyeh, Z., Brightwell, R., et al. (2006). Towards a framework for dedicated operating systems development in high-end computing. *Operating Systems Review: Special Issue on System Software for High-End Computing Systems, 40*(2), 16–21.

Triplett, J. (2015). *Using the KVM API*. Retrieved November 25, 2017.

UNI. (1995). *UNICOS MCPF-2580394*. Cray Research.

Unknown. (1996). Folklore: An innovative approach to a user interface. *Cryptolog - The Journal of Technical Health, XXI, I*(4), 11–16.

v. Eicken, T., Culler, D. E., Goldstein, S. C., & Schauser, K. E. (1992). Active messages: A mechanism for integrated communication and computation. In *Proceedings the 19th Annual International Symposium on Computer Architecture* (pp. 256–266).

Van Essen, B., Hsieh, H., Ames, S., Pearce, R., & Gokhale, M. (2015). DI-MMAP: A scalable memory map runtime for out-of-core data-intensive applications. *Cluster Computing*.

Various. (1955–1989). *Control Data Corporation records. Product literature*. Charles Babbage Institute Archives, University of Minnesota.

von Eicken, T., Basu, A., Buch, V., & Vogels, W. (1995). U-Net: a user-level network interface for parallel and distributed computing. *SIGOPS Operating Systems Review, 29*, 40–53.

Wallace, D. (2007). Compute node Linux: Overview, progress to date and roadmap. In *Proceedings of the Cray User Group (CUG)*.

Warren, M. S., Becker, D. J., Goda, M. P., Salmon, J. K., & Sterling, T. (1997a). Parallel supercomputing with commodity components. In *International Conference on Parallel and Distributed Processing Techniques and Applications*.

Warren, M. S., Salmon, J. K., Becker, D. J., Goda, M. P., Sterling, T., & Winckelmans, W. (1997b). Pentium pro inside: I. A treecode at 430 Gigaflops on ASCI Red, II. price/performance of $50/Mflop on Loki and Hyglac. In *Supercomputing, ACM/IEEE 1997 Conference* (pp. 61–61).

Weinhold, C., & Härtig, H. (2008). VPFS: Building a virtual private file system with a small trusted computing base. In *Proceedings of the 3rd ACM SIGOPS/EuroSys European Conference on Computer Systems 2008, Eurosys '08* (pp. 81–93). New York, NY, USA. ACM.

Weinhold, C., & Härtig, H. (2011). jVPFS: Adding robustness to a secure stacked file system with untrusted local storage components. In *Proceedings of the 2011 USENIX Conference on USENIX Annual Technical Conference, USENIXATC'11* (pp. 32–32). Berkeley, CA, USA: USENIX Association.

Weinhold, C., Lackorzynski, A., Bierbaum, J., Küttler, M., Planeta, M., Härtig, H., et al. (2016). FFMK: A fast and fault-tolerant microkernel-based system for exascale computing. In *Software for Exascale Computing - SPPEXA 2013-2015* (Vol. 113, pp. 405–426).

Wheat, S. R., Maccabe, A. B., Riesen, R., van Dresser, D. W., & Stallcup, T. M. (1994). PUMA: An operating system for massively parallel systems. *Scientific Programming, 3*, 275–288.

Wheeler, K. B., Murphy, R. C., & Thain, D. (2008). Qthreads: An API for programming with millions of lightweight threads. In *2008 IEEE International Symposium on Parallel and Distributed Processing* (pp. 1–8).

WhiteDB. (2017). Whitedb. http://whitedb.org.

Williams, D., & Koller, R. (2016). Unikernel monitors: Extending minimalism outside of the box. In *8th USENIX Workshop on Hot Topics in Cloud Computing (HotCloud 16)*. Denver, CO, USA: USENIX Association.

Wisniewski, R. W., Inglett, T., Keppel, P., Murty, R., & Riesen, R. (2014). mOS: An architecture for extreme-scale operating systems. In *Proceedings of the 4th International Workshop on Runtime and Operating Systems for Supercomputers, ROSS '14* (pp. 2:1–2:8). New York, NY, USA: ACM.

Womble, D., Greenberg, D., Wheat, S., & Riesen, R. (1993a). Beyond core: Making parallel computer I/O practical. In *DAGS'93 Proceedings* (pp. 56–63).

Womble, D. E., Greenberg, D. S., Riesen, R. E., & Wheat, S. R. (1993b). Out of core, out of mind: Practical parallel I/O. In *Proceedings of the Scalable Libraries Conference* (pp. 10–16). Mississippi State University.

Woodacre, M., Robb, D., Roe, D., & Feind, K. (2003). The SGI Altix 3000 global shared-memory architecture. Technical report, Silicon Graphics International Corporation.

Wulf, W., Cohen, E., Corwin, W., Jones, A., Levin, R., Pierson, C., et al. (1974). HYDRA: The kernel of a multiprocessor operating system. *Communications of the ACM, 17*(6), 337–345.

Xavier, M. G., Neves, M. V., Rossi, F. D., Ferreto, T. C., Lange, T., & De Rose, C. A. F. (2013). Performance evaluation of container-based virtualization for high performance computing environments. In *Euromicro International Conference on Parallel, Distributed and Network-Based Processing (PDP)*.

XtreemFS. XtreemFS - a cloud file system. http://www.xtreemfs.org. Retrieved May 16, 2018.

Yanagawa, T., & Suehiro, K. (2004). Software system of the earth simulator. *Parallel Computing, 30*(12), 1315–1327. The Earth Simulator.

Yoshida, T., Hondou, M., Tabata, T., Kan, R., Kiyota, N., Kojima, H., et al. (2015). Sparc64 XIfx: Fujitsu's next-generation processor for high-performance computing. *IEEE Micro, 35*(2), 6–14.

Yoshii, K., Iskra, K., Naik, H., Beckman, P., & Broekema, P. (2009). Characterizing the performance of "Big Memory" on Blue Gene Linux. In *2nd International Workshop on Parallel Programming Models and Systems Software for High-End Computing, P2S2* (pp. 65–72).

Yoshii, K., Iskra, K., Naik, H., Beckman, P., & Broekema, P. C. (2011a). Performance and scalability evaluation of "Big Memory" on Blue Gene Linux. *International Journal of High Performance Computing Applications, 25*(2), 148–160.

Yoshii, K., Naik, H., Yu, C., & Beckman, P. (2011b). Extending and benchmarking the "Big Memory" implementation on Blue Gene/P Linux. In *1st International Workshop on Runtime and Operating Systems for Supercomputers, ROSS* (pp. 65–72).

Zajcew, R., Roy, P., Black, D., Peak, C., Guedes, P., Kemp, B., et al. (January 1993). An OSF/1 Unix for massively parallel multicomputers. In *Proceedings of the Winter 1993 USENIX Conference* (pp. 449–468).

ZeptoOS. (2005). ZeptoOS: Small Linux for big computers. http://www.mcs.anl.gov/research/projects/zeptoos/.

Zhang, J., Lu, X., Chakraborty, S., & Panda, D. K. D. (2016). *Slurm-V: Extending Slurm for Building Efficient HPC Cloud with SR-IOV and IVShmem* (pp. 349–362). Berlin: Springer International Publishing.

Zhao, Y., Hategan, M., Clifford, B., Foster, I., von Laszewski, G., Nefedova, V., et al. (2007). Swift: Fast, reliable, loosely coupled parallel computation. In *IEEE Congress on Services* (pp. 199–206).

Zheng, F., Yu, H., Hantas, C., Wolf, M., Eisenhauer, G., Schwan, K., et al. (2013). GoldRush: Resource efficient in situ scientific data analytics using fine-grained interference aware execution. In *Proceedings of the 26th ACM/IEEE International Conference for High Performance Computing, Networking, Storage and Analysis, (SC)*.

Zounmevo, J., Perarnau, S., Iskra, K., Yoshii, K., Giososa, R., Essen, B. V., et al. (2015). A container-based approach to OS specialization for exascale computing. In *Proceedings of the 1st Workshop on Containers, (WoC)*.

Index

© Springer Nature Singapore Pte Ltd. 2019
B. Gerofi et al. (eds.), *Operating Systems for Supercomputers and High Performance Computing*, High-Performance Computing Series,
https://doi.org/10.1007/978-981-13-6624-6

Printed in the United States
By Bookmasters